BY FOFI G.

A/Aa

« A/Aa »
a

its [possessive]

aá

him, her, it [object]

it; that place, time, reason, fact
·Du táayi gukshitú áwé tléiñw áa akaawahaa. She planted berries in the corner of her garden.
·Áa agaýtool'oon yé yinaadé yaa gagú! Walk toward the place we will hunt!

á

[puts focus on preceding phrase]

aa

one, one of [object]
·Yées aa a kádi awliyéý. He made a new spear head.
·Tlél ushik'éiyi aa yoo ý'atánk áwé tsá a.aýji nooch . She always only hears the bad talk.

áa

lake
·Áa kaadé ýaatéen teet. I see waves on the lake.
·Yagéi a kaayí wé áa tlein. The size of that big lake is immense.

aaá

yes

áadaa

spear (for fish and seal)
·Yées aa áadaa aawa.oo. He bought a new spear.
·Áadaa du jeet awsitán. She gave him a spear.

aaçáa

then, around, after, for
·Náakw s'é áa yéi kñwa.oo aý keey aaçáa tsá wéi kashóok' gwéil. I
will put medicine on my knee first, then the heating pad.
·Daýadooshú yagiyee shunaaxéex aaçáa daak wusitani yé. It has
been raining for seven days.

áak'w

little lake; pond
·Áak'wde aawa.aat. People walked to the pond.
·Wé áak'w déint áwé át woogoot wé sheech dzísk'u tlein. The big cow
moose was walking around in the vicinity of the pond.

Áak'w

Auke Bay
·Áak'wde yaa nañúý. He is driving to Auke Bay.
·Áak'wx' uwaýéi wé shaawát. That woman camped at Auke Bay.

Áak'w Ñwáan

people of Auke Bay, southern Lynn Canal, Juneau area,
and northern Admiralty Island
·Áak'w Ñwáaný has sitee. They are Auke Bay people.
·Áak'w Ñwáan has al'eiý. The Auke Bay people are dancing.

,

Dictionary of Tlingit

áa ñuyadujee yé
du áali

correctional facility

his/her grandparent

aan

town; village; settlement; inhabited or owned land
·Daañw aan sáwé? Which town is that?
·Ñ'alkátsk yáxwch'ich yaý yawsiýáa haa aaní kaadáý. The sea otter has devoured the yellowneck clams on our land.

aan

with it
·Aan adul'eiý aýáa kañach'áak'wt áyá áa ýat jikawduwañaa. I have been commissioned to carve a dance paddle.
·Aan áwé shóot aýwdi.ák wé kayeiýtáçu. I built a fire with the wood shavings.

aandaat kanahík

monkey
aandaat kanahígi (T), aandaat kanaheek (At), aandaat keneheek (C)
·Wé at yátx'i aandaat kanahík has awsiteen. The children saw the monkey.
·Wé aandaat kanahík wéiý yaa nashíx. The monkey is running along there.

aandaayaagú

rowboat
·Tláakw aýáa du aandaayaagú. He is rowing his rowboat quickly.
·Aý éek' du aandaayaagú áwé. That is my brother's rowboat.

aan galañú

flood
aan galñú
·Aan galañú dei kanaý yaawadáa. The flood went over the road.
·Ch'áakw aan galañú yaa kandutlákw. A flood from long ago is being researched.

Aangóon

Angoon
·Yaa Aangóont áyá la.áa haa hídi Aanx'aagi Hít yóo duwasáakw.
Our clan house standing in Angoon is called Aanx'aagi Hít.
·Wé yaakw tlein Aangóonx' tleiyéi yéi wootee. The big boat stopped in
Angoon.

áanjís

orange
·Áanjís akawdi.oo. She bought herself oranges.
·At yátx'i áanjís has du tuwáa sigóo. Children like oranges.

áanjís kahéeni

orange juice
·Áanjís kahéeni ñaa ée yak'éi. Orange juice is good for people.
·Héen áanjís kahéeni ýoot akawsixáa. He poured water in with the
orange juice.

aankadushxit át

camera
·Tsaa geení aankadushxit át teen akawshixít. She took a picture of the
seal tail flippers with a camera.

,

,

A/Aa

aankanáagu

large-leaved avens (Geum macrophyllum) or possibly
arnica species-- Arnica species, especially A. amplexicaulus, A. latifolia, A.
gracilis
Warning: arnica increases body temperature when taken
internally, externally it acts as an antiseptic
·Aankanáagu ayawsiháa. She gathered large leafed avens.
·Aankanáagu tín sh wudzineiý. She healed herself with medicine from the
land.

aankayéýaa

plane for scraping wood
·Aankayéýaa tín akaawayéý. He planed it with a plane.
·Wé ñáa aý éesh jeedáý aankayéýaa aawahées'. The man borrowed a
plane from my Dad.

Áankich

Anchorage

·Áankich yóo duwasáakw Lingít ý'éináý Anchorage. Anchorage is called Áankich in Tlingit.
·Shayadihéin Áankichx' ñuwa.oowu Lingít. There are a lot of Tlingit people living in Anchorage.

aan kwéiyi

flag
·Du hídi kináak áwé át wulis'ees wé aan kwéiyi. The flag is blowing around above his house.
·Anóoshi aan kwéiyi áwé át wududziyíñ wé s'ísaa yaakw ýuká. They raised a Russian flag on the deck of that sailboat.

aan kwéiyi tugáas'i

flagpole
·Tlaçanís aan kwéiyi tugáas'iý has awliyéý. They made a flagpole out of a sapling.

aanñáawu

rich man; man of wealth; chief
·Káa tlein yíkt át yawduwaýaa wé aanñáawu. The rich person is being driven around in a limosine.
·Dáýnáý aanñáax'u wé atyátx'i jeeyís has at wooshee. Two chiefs sang for the children.

Aanñáawu

God, Lord
·Johnch héent ayaawatée haa Aanñáawu. John baptised our lord.

aan s'aatí

mayor
·Lingít shaawát áwé haa aan s'aatí. Our mayor is a Tlingit woman.
·Yées aan s'aatí has du jee yéi yatee. They have a new mayor.

aantñeení

townspeople; crowd or large group of people
·Dei káx' yéi jinéiyi ý'eis has at gawdzi.ée wé aantñeení. The townspeople cooked food for the people working on the road.
·Wé aantñeení woosh ji.een gán has aawaxásh. The townspeople cut wood together.

aan ý'ayee

in a town, on the streets of a town
·Aan ý'ayeedé (ha)s woo.aat du káani teen. She and her sister-in-law

,

Dictionary of Tlingit

went downtown.
·Aan ý'ayeex' awduwal'eiý. People danced in the streets of town.

aanyádi

high class person, aristocrat
aanyédi (C)
·Aanyádi áwé wé shaatk'. The young girl is an aristocrat
·Aanyátx'i áwé wéide iyatéen. Those are high class people you see there.

aan yaduxas' át

razor
aan yatxas' át
·Tlagu aan yaduxas' át aawat'ei. He found an old-time razor.
·Aan yaduxas' át du jeewú wé ñáa shaan. The old man has a razor.

aas

tree (esp. conifer)
·Aaý xásh wé aas x'áni! Cut the outer limbs of the tree off!
·Yóo tliyaa aasdéi ksaxát wéi kaxées' aý at shí ñóok gúgu yís! Attach
the wire to that tree over there for my radio antenna!

aasdaaçáadli

bracket fungus
·Aasdaaçáadli ayatéen. She sees the tree fungus.
·Aasdaaçáadli aaý aawas'úw. He chopped off the tree fungus.

aasdaak'óoý'u

tree pitch
·Aasdaak'óoý'u náakw sákw yéi awsinei. She gathered tree pitch for
medicine.
·Náakwý awliyéý aasdaak'óoý'u. She made medicine out of pitch.

aasdaax'ées'i

tumor in a tree, with branches growing from it
·Aasdaax'ées'i tléil aas ée uk'é. A tree tumor is not good for the tree.
·Aasdaax'ées'i yakoogé ayatéen. He sees lots of tree tumors.

aasgutú

forest; timbered area
aasgatú (T), aasgetú (C)
·Kalaçéi nooch aasgutú yeist ñuwuhaayí. The forest is brilliant when fall

comes.
·Aasgutóot wugoodí, dzísk'w ý'us.eetí awsiteen. He saw moose tracks when he was walking in the woods.

aas jiseiyí

the shelter of a tree
aas seiyí (At)
·Aas seiyí áa wdlisáa. He rested in the shelter of the tree.
·Wé aas seiyít wujixíx séew tóodáý. She ran to the shelter of the tree to get out of the rain.

aas yádi

sapling
asyádi

aashát

steelhead trout
·Aashát tlein awdzit'eiý. She hooked a big steelhead trout.
·A káý akçwast'éiý aashát yaa yanahéini. He will fish for steelhead trout when they run upriver.

,

,

A/Aa

du aat

his/her paternal aunt
·Yak'éiyi ý'ayeit áwé du jeewú aý aat. My paternal aunt has nice dishes.
·Wé hoon s'aatí een yóo ý'ali.átk aý aat. My paternal aunt is talking with the storekeeper.

aatlein

much, lots of, really
·Aatlein dáxw aawa.ín. She picked lots of lowbush cranberries.
·Aatlein shaaý kanéegwál' yéi ýwsinei. I made a lot of gray currant berry sauce.

Áa Tlein

Atlin
·Áa Tlein káa kawduwayél'. It is calm on Atlin Lake.

Áa Tlein Ñwáan

people of Atlin

·Áa Tlein Ñwáan áwé yáax' haat has uwa.át. Atlin Lake people came here.
·Áa Tlein Ñwáan áwé has aawal'eiý. The Atlin people danced.

áa yaý

turning over

ách at dusýa át

fork
ách at yadusýa át
The variant listed here contains the ya- prefix and is the form used by one of the fluent speakers consulted for this project.
·Haandé wé ách at dusýa át! Hand me the fork!
·Ách at dusýa át tlein aawa.oo. She bought a big fork.

ach kooshý'íl'aa yeit

sled (for recreational sledding)
ech koolý'íl'aa yeit (C)

adátx'i

children
atyátx'i, atyétx'i (T), adétx'i (T), edétx'i (C)
·Wéi Sheet'kaadáý adátx'i at gutóox' áwé has du ée at dultóow. The kids from Sitka are taught out in the wilderness.

adawóotl

war; trouble; rush, hurry
·Adawóotl yáý at woonei du aaníx'. There was trouble in her town.
·Wé éil' héen diyáanaý.á adawóotl yáý áa at yatee. There is a war going on across the ocean.

Aganáa!

Oh no!; Yikes!

ágé

[focus + interrogative]

áhé

this/that (over here), the other [focus]

akahéiýi

farmer
·Wé akahéiýi jeedáý k'únts' has aawa.oo. They bought potatoes from the

farmer.

·Wasóos wé akahéiýi jee shayadihéin. The farmer has lots of cows.

,

Dictionary of Tlingit

akoolýéitl'

fear
akoolýéetl' (AnAT), ekoolýéitl' (C)

ákyá

this (right here) [interrogative]

ákyú

that (distant), yonder [interrogative]

ák.hé

this/that (over here), the other [interrogative]

ák.wé

that (at hand) [interrogative]
·Héen táatý ák.wé du.een wéi kantáñw? Is the lupine picked from the water?
·Ch'as héen ák.wé a kaadéi yóo yadudzixéik yá kat'ákýi? Is water all that was put on these dried berries?

aldaawáa
alñáa

checkers; games played using string in the hands
gambling; game of chance

al'eiý

dance
·Aý al'eiý k'oodás'i ch'áagu kawóot áwé a daawú á. There are old beads on my dance shirt.

al'óon

hunt
·Al'óon wugoodí uýganñáas' du çaltóode ayaawa.oo. When he was going hunting, he put matches in his pocket.
·Wé al'óon tlél wáa sá wootee. The hunt went alright.

al'óoni

hunter
·Al'óoni wé wanadóo ítý kei nagút. The hunter is following the sheep that

is going uphill.

·Éil' héeni diyáanaý.á áa yéi yatee wé al'óoni. The hunter lives across the ocean.

Anáaski

Alaska

anahoo

rutabaga; turnip
·Anahoo s'ín teen wudustaayí yak'éi. Turnip boiled with carrots is good.
·Anahoo has akanahéijin. They used to plant turnips.

Ana.óot

Aleut
·Ana.óot ñu.oo haa ýánt has uwa.át. Aleut people came to see us.
·Ana.óot ýoox' uwawát wé ñáa. That man grew up among the Aleut people.

ánk'w

person who cries easily
·Ñúnáý ánk'w áwé wé shaatk'átsk'u. The young girl is a real crybaby.
·Ánk'w áwé kéi has anaswát wéit lingítch. Those people are raising a crybaby.

Anóoshi

Russian
·Yáa aý éesh yinaanáý ñu.aa áyá Anóoshiý wusitee, Héený Ñuwala.aadíý wusitee. My father's side was Russian, he was a baptizer.

,

,

A/Aa

·Anóoshi aan kwéiyi áwé át wududziyíñ wé s'ísaa yaakw ýuká. They raised a Russian flag on the deck of that sailboat.

Anóoshi aaní

Russia
·Anóoshi Aanídáý áyá yaa San Fransiscot has wuligás'. They had moved to San Fransisco from Russia.
·Ch'a yóo Anóoshi Aaníx' yaa German shaawát áyá du ýánx' yéi wootee. While in Russia he was with a German woman.

asgutuyiksháa

spider

asçeiwú

seine fisherman; seine boat
·Yaakw ña çeiwú asçeiwú jishagóoný sitee. A boat and a net are a seine fisherman's tools.
·Asçeiwú s'aatíý sitee aý wóo. My father-in-law is a master seiner.

ast'eiýí

fisherman (troller)

asx'aan sháach'i
ashalýóot'i

green bird (sparrow or finch)

sport fisherman

át

thing
·At géit wudzigít wé ñáa átx'i aawutáawu. He went against the law when he stole the man's belongings.
·L át yáý ñoonook. He doesn't act normal.

átk' aheen

faith
étk' eheen (C), átx' aheen (T)

átk' aheení

believer
étk' eheení (C), átx' aheení (T)

atk'átsk'u

child
·Yá atk'átsk'u li.oos ch'ak'yéis' yáý. This child is as playful as a young eagle.
·Ch'a tlákw áwé yéi nateech aý ýúý, ch'u atk'átsk'uý sateeyídáý.
My husband is like this often, and has been even since he was a child.

át ñukawu.aaçú

director, planner; commander
át at kawu.aaçú, ét et kawu.aaçú (C), ét ñukawu.aaçú (C)

atxaayí

centipede
·Héen kát jinaskwanchi át áwé wé atxaayí. The centipede swims on top of the water.
·Lushik'éiyi át ákwé atxaayí? Is the centipede poisonous?

atx'aan hídi

smokehouse
etx'aan hídi (C)
·Aý atx'aan hídi tleidooshú ñaa ý'oos ña daax'ooný sitee. My smoke house is six feet by four feet.
·Jikañáas' káý ashayaawatée wé çaat atx'aan hídi yeex'. She hung the sockeye salmon on the stick in the smokehouse.

,

Dictionary of Tlingit

atýá

food, a meal
·Costcodáý aawa.óow atýá. He bought food from Costco.
·Cháanwaan atýaayíçaa awóo! Order some Chinese food!

atýa át

moth
·Atýa átch áwé uwaýáa aý kinaak.ádi. A moth ate my coat.
·Atýa át náagu a ýoo yan yéi ksané! Put some moth balls among it!

atýá daakahídi

restaurant; tavern
·Atýá daakahídix' gishoo taayí ña k'wát' awdziçáaý. She ordered bacon and eggs at the restaurant.
·Tle a tuwán áwé atýá daakahídi áa wdudliyéý. They built a restaurant next to it.

atýá jishagóon

kitchen utensil

atyátx'i

children
atyétx'i (T), adétx'i (T), edétx'i (C), adátx'i
·Sgóonwaan atyátx'i has shayadihéin Yaakwdáatx'. There are a lot of school children in Yakutat.
·Dáýnáý aannáax'u wé atyátx'i jeeyís has at wooshee. Two chiefs sang for the children.

atyátx'i latíni

babysitter
·Keil atyátx'i latíniý naýsatee yá xáanaa. Let Keil be the babysitter this evening.
·Atoosçeiwú atyátx'i latíni ýáný has çañéech aý yátx'i. When we are gillnetting my children stay with a babysitter.

átl'áni
Atskanée!

slime (inside clamshell)
Yikes!; Scary!

áwé

that (at hand) [focus]
·Ch'as a gooshí áwé duteen nooch kéet. All that can be seen of a killerwhale is the dorsal fin.
·Tl'aadéin áwé át tán wé ñóok. The box is sitting sideways.

áx' ñaa ée at dultóow yé

school
·Áx' ñaa ée at dultóow yé áa yéi ýat guçwatée seiçán. I will be in school tomorrow.

aý

my [possessive]
·Giyañw Ñwáaný sitee aý ýooní, Russell. My friend Russell is Alutiq.
·Wáançaneensx' yanaý kei shak'íý'ch aý yoo ý'atángi. Sometimes my words get hung up.

aýáa

paddle
·Daax'oon yatee aý aýáayi yaakw yíx'. There are four paddles in my skiff.
·Aan adul'eiý aýáa kañach'áak'wt áyá áa ýat jikawduwañaa. I have been commissioned to carve a dance paddle.

,

,

áyá

A/Aa

this (right here) [focus]
·Ñúnáý k'eeljáa yéi ayaguýdatée ách áyá haa yaagú dáñde tusaýút'x'. It's going to get stormy so we are dragging our boats up.
·L'ook kaháagu áyá yak'éi kanat'á kanéegwál' sákw. Coho salmon eggs are good for blueberry sauce.

ayaheeyáa
ayáý
áyú

curlew
thus, that's how

that (distant), yonder [focus]

,

« Ch »
-ch

because of; by means of
Indicates agent of transitive verb with definite object.
·Jiduñéi at wuskóowuý sateeyéech. He is paid because he is a
knowledgeable person.
·Sheendé! Táach ikçwasháa. Get up! You're going to oversleep. (Lit: Sleep
will marry you.)

CHAA
• akawlicháa | aklachéiý | aklachéiý
s/he strained it | s/he is straining it | s/he strains it (regularly).
O-ka-S-l-chaa~ (ø act)
for S to strain, filter, drain off O
·Akawsitaayi tléiñw kaçádaa tóonáý akawlicháa. He strained the
boiled berries through cheesecloth.
CHAAK
• akaawachák | akacháak | akacháký
s/he packed it | s/he's packing it | s/he packs it (regularly).
O-ka-S-ø-cháak~ (ø act)
for S to pile, stack away neatly, pack O (food, clothing, firewood, etc.)
·Cháash a kaadéi kawtuwachák wé wutuwa.uni dzísk'w. We packed
branches on the moose that we shot.
·A k'óol'de kaychák! You all pack it in the stern!

du chaan

his/her mother-in-law

CHAAN
• wulichán | lichán | kei lachánch
he/she/it stank | he/she/it stinks | he/she/it stinks (regularly).
O-l-chán (ga state)
for O to stink, have unpleasant odor, smell bad; for O to smell strongly
·Wé ýéel' wuls'eexí lichán. When the slime rots it stinks.

Cháanwaan

Chinese
·Cháanwaanch áwé wuliyéý yá ýáat daakahídi. The Chinese built this
cannery.
·Cháanwaan atýaayíçaa awóo! Order some Chinese food!

cháas'

pink salmon; humpy, humpback salmon
·Cháas' yak'éi s'eiñý sateeyí. Pink salmon is good smoked.

·A wanáax' yakoojél wé cháas'! Put the Humpback salmon separate from them!

,

,

Ch

cháash

bough, branch with needles on it, especially of spruce
·Cháash a kaadéi kawtuwachák wé wutuwa.uni dzísk'w. We packed branches on the moose that we shot.
·K'idéin kachák wé cháash! Pack the branches well!

cháatl

halibut
·Cháatl tíx'i yaa (ha)s a shuká nañúý. They're setting halibut gear.
·Tséek éen has awsi.ée wé cháatl. They barbecued the halibut.

cháatl ast'eiýí

halibut fisherman

cháaý

horned grebe or red-necked grebe
·Cháaý héen táade awjit'ákw. The grebe dove into the water.

cháayoo

tea
·Wé shaatk' gúx'aa kát cháayoo aý jeet awsi.ín. The young girl gave me tea in a cup.
·Gúx'aa kat'óott kaawadáa wé cháayoo. The cup is filled part way up with tea.

chál

platform cache; house cache; shed
chíl
·É! Shahíký haa cháli çaatáa yéi daatooneiyí. Check it out! When we are out trapping, our storehouse is full.
·Wé héen ý'ayaaý chál wutuliyéý. We built a storehouse on the edge of the river.

cheech

porpoise
·Daýyeekaadéi cheech áwé yaa éil' kaadéi ýwsiteen. I have seen two

kinds of porpoise in this ocean.
·Chichuwaa cheech yáý kaaxát. Dolphins look like porpoise.

chéý'i (C)

shade, shadow(s) cast by landforms, etc.
chíý'i (T), chéeý'i (At), chéeý'aa (At), chéiý'aa (C)
·Wé aas chéý'i tayeet áwé tooñéen. We are sitting in the shade of the tree.
·Awdlisín chéý'i tóox'. He is hiding in the shadows.

chichuyaa

shark (porpoise-like)
chichuwaa
·Chichuwaa cheech yáý kaaxát. Dolphins look like porpoise.

chíl xook

fish air-dried in cold weather and allowed to freeze
chál xook
·Ñúnáý yasixúkk chíl xook. That salmon smoked after freezing dries very
easily.
·Yéi ýa.áýjin yáa chíl xook Jilñáatx' áwé yéi daadunéiyin. I used to
hear of smoked salmon being prepared on the Chilkat.

chookán

grass
chookén (C), chookwán (T)

,

Dictionary of Tlingit

Chookaneidí

Chookaneidí; a clan of the Eagle moiety whose principal
crests are the Porpoise and Brown Bear

CHOON
• awlichún | --- | alchúný
s/he injured it | --- | s/he injures it (regularly).
O-S-l-choon~ (ø event)
for S to wound, injure, bruise O
·Du goosh awlichún. He hurt his thumb.
·Du ñatlyá awlichún. He hurt his side.
• wudichún | --- | dachúný
he/she/it is injured | --- | s/he gets injured (regularly).
O-d-choon~ (ø event)
for O to be wounded, injured, bruised; for O to be hurt (emotionally)
The most common use of this verb is in the perfective form.
Note that it can also refer to a mental state, as in: ñúnáý haa
wdichún "we're really hurting (emotionally)" (after the loss of a
family member, e.g.).
·Ñaa dzísk'w gwéinli wudichún. The hoof of the bull moose is injured.

chooneit

arrow
·Chooneitý áwé dulyéiý wé ch'áal'. Willow is made into arrows.
·Téix' gwáa wégé átý dulyeiýín chooneit sákw. Little stones must have
been used to make arrows.

CHOOX
• akaawachúx | akachóox | akachóoxý
s/he kneaded it | s/he kneads it; s/he is kneading it | s/he kneads it (regularly).
O-ka-S-ø-choox~ (ø act)
for S to knead, press, pat O with palm of hand

chudéi

tomcod
·A eeýí geiý yá chudéi dus.eeyí. There is a lot of oil in the tom cod when it's
cooked.
·Chudéi áwé a ñ'anooýú áwu. Tom cod have a beard.

,

,

Ch'

« Ch' »
ch'a

the very, just
·Ch'a áa yan awli.át wé gán láý'i. He just left the wet outer part of firewood there.
·Yáa ñutaanx' aadé ñugaýtootéen ixkée ch'a çaaýtusatéen wé sháa.
This summer we are going to travel down south just to see the girls.

ch'a aadóo sá

anyone, anybody; whoever

ch'a aa sá

ch'a aan

although, even though, however, nonetheless, yet
·Wusi.áax'w du yoo ý'atángi, ch'a aan áwé du ý'éide ñuwdudzi.aaý.
His words were biting, yet people listened to him.

ch'a aa sá

anyone, anybody; whoever
ch'a aadóo sá

ch'áagu

old
·Aý al'eiý k'oodás'i ch'áagu kawóot áwé a daawú á. There are old beads on my dance shirt.
·Dei ch'áagu at sheeyí ñúnáý du tuwáa sagóo nuch. S/he always likes old time songs.

ch'áakw

long ago; back then; in the old days
ch'ákw
·Ch'áakw ý'eint'áax'aa shaawát ý'é yéi ndu.eich. Long ago women would wear a labret.
·Tléi ch'áakw ýá wé aatý kéi haa wsidáñ. It was a long time ago that we migrated from there.

ch'áak'

bald eagle
·Ch'áak' naaý ýat sitee. I am of the eagle moiety.
·Ch'áak' lú yóo katán. A bald eagle's beak is curved.

ch'áak' loowú

dark yellow; eagle's beak

·Ch'áak' loowú yáý néegwál' ýwaa.oo. I bought some dark yellow paint.
·Ch'áak' loowú yáý néegwál' teen ýwaanéegwál' kaýach'áagu
kootéeyaa. I painted my totem carving with dark yellow paint.

CH'AAK'W
• akaawach'ák'w | akach'áak'w | akach'ák'wý
s/he carved it | s/he is carving it | s/he carves it (regularly).
O-ka-S-ø-ch'áak'w~ (ø act)
for S to carve O (usually smaller, detailed work) using a knife
·Xíxch' a yáax' kaýwaach'ák'w. I carved a frog on it's face.

,

Ch'

Dictionary of Tlingit

·At xáshdi téel sákw áwé kanágaa akaawach'ák'w aý jeeyís. He
carved a form for making moccasins for me.

ch'áal'

willow
·Chooneitý áwé dulyéiý wé ch'áal'. Willow is made into arrows.
·Du jináñ daak wulihásh wé ch'áal'. The willow drifted out away from
him.

du ch'áatwu

his/her skin (surface)

CH'ÁCH'Ý
• --- | kadlich'ách'ý | ----- | it's spotted | ---.
ka-d-l-ch'ách'ý (state)
for a natural object (wood, rock, etc.) to be spotted
This verb only occurs in the imperfective.

ch'a daa sá

anything; whatever

ch'a goot'á sá

anywhere, anyplace; wherever
ch'a goot'é sá (C)

ch'a gwátgeen sá

any time (in the future); whenever (in the future)

ch'a çéçaa

in vain; for nothing; without success
·Ch'a çéçaa ýaýooý. I call him (but he won't come).
·Ch'a çéçaa aaý kei dahánch. He tries to stand up from there (but is unable
to).

ch'a çóot

different, other
·Ch'a çóot ñáa at óowu, tléil áý ooshee. You don't touch another person's
possessions.
·Hú ñu.aa áýá ch'a çóot yéide yan kawdiýáa aý tláa, du éeshch áýá
du yát saa uwatí Shaaxeidi Tláa. But with my mother it happened
differently, because her father named her Shaaxeidi Tláa.

Ch'a keetáanáý!
ch'a koogéiyi
ch'ákw

Cool it!; Calm down!
however, any which way

long ago; back then; in the old days
ch'áakw

ch'a k'ikát

at least, once in a while
ch'a k'át, ch'a k'eekát (AtT)
·Ch'a k'ikát du jeeyís at na.oo! At least buy him something!
·Tsaa Éiý' kaadáý áwé yawtuwadlaañ ch'a k'ikát wé kaneilts'ákw.
We finally managed to get some swamp currants from Seal Slough.

ch'ak'yéis'

immature eagle
·Ch'akyéis' áwé yéi has kaaxát atýá çaa. Young eagles are after food.

,

,

Ch'

·Yá atk'átsk'u li.oos ch'ak'yéis' yáý. This child is as playful as a young
eagle.

ch'a ldakát át

everything

ch'a ldakát ñáa

everyone, everybody

ch'a ldakát yé

everywhere

ldakát yé

ch'as

only, just
·Ch'as a gooshí áwé duteen nooch kéet. All that can be seen of a
killerwhale is the dorsal fin.

·Ch'as k'éets'an áyá yáaçaa wootee. There's nothing but false azalea around here.

ch'a tlákw

always, all the time, constantly
·Ch'a tlákw áwé yéi nateech aý ýúý, ch'u atk'átsk'uý sateeyídáý.
My husband is like this often, and has been even since he was a child.

ch'a yák'w

suddenly, immediately, right away
ch'a yáak'w, ch'a yóok'

ch'a yéi

ordinary, usual

ch'a yóok'

suddenly, immediately, right away
ch'a yák'w, ch'a yáak'w

ch'éen

ribbon
·Ý'aan ch'éen i shaýaawú káx' kei kçwak'éi. A red ribbon in your hair would be good.
·Wooch çunayáadei ch'éen i dlaak' jeewú. Your sister has different kinds of ribbons.

ch'eet

auklet or murrelet
·Ch'eet sheishóoý áwé akaawach'ák'w. She carved a murrelet rattle.

ch'éetçaa

skate (ocean creature related to the shark and the ray)
·Ch'éetçaa kéi awdzit'éý. He pulled up a skate.

ch'eeý'

thimbleberry
ch'eiý'
·Ñuk'éet' gaýtoo.áat ch'eeý'çaa. We are going to pick thimbleberries.
·Ch'eeý' yagéi yóo dei yaaý. There are plenty of thimbleberries along the road.

du ch'éeý'i

his/her first finger

CH'EIÝ'W
• awlich'éý'w | yaa analch'éý'w | alch'éý'wý
s/he got it dirty | s/he's getting it dirty | s/he gets it dirty (regularly).
O-S-l-ch'éiý'w~ (ø event)
for S to dirty, soil O (esp. clothing or person)

,

Ch'

• wulich'éý'w | yaa nalch'éý'w | --he/she/it is dirty | he/she/it is getting dirty | ---.
O-l-ch'éiý'w~ (ø event)
for O to be dirty
·I jín wulich'éý'w. Your hands are dirty.
·Ñúnáý wulich'éý'w yoo ý'atánk áwé átý ilayéiý. You are using very
dirty language.

ch'éiý'w

dirt, dust
·K'idéin aaý na.óos' ch'éiý'w! Wash the dirt off good!
·A yaadéi gé ch'éiý'w iyatéen? Do you see dirt on the face of it?

ch'iyáash

sea otter hunting canoe with an angular prow for breaking the
waves
·Nas'gadooshú ch'iyáash kaýwaach'ák'w hun yayís. I carved eight sea
otter hunting canoes to sell.

ch'u

still, even
ch'oo
·Ch'a tlákw áwé yéi nateech aý ýúý, ch'u atk'átsk'uý sateeyídáý.
My husband is like this often, and has been even since he was a child.
·Ý'aan yakawlikís'. Wé kél't' ñu.aa, ch'u uwat'áa. The fire has gone out
but the ashes are still warm.

ch'u déiý

both

ch'u shóogu

the same
·Ch'u shóogu aan wududliyeýi túñl' áwé a kaýyee wéi ANB hall.
Those are the original young spruce they used to build the ceiling of the ANB hall.

ch'u tlei
ch'u tleiý

when, while
forever

,

,

D

« D »
a daa

around it; about it; concerning it
·Wé x'akaskéin daax' áwé yéi jiné. She is working on the unfinished basket.
·I tuñ'atáali i daaý yei jeekanaxíx. Your pants are falling down.
1

DAA

• anaý yaawadáa | anaý yaa nadéin | --it flowed through it | it is flowing through it | ---.
P-náý ya-ø-daa~ (ø motion)
for water, the tide to flow through P; for water, the tide to flood P
·Aan galañú dei kanaý yaawadáa. The flood went over the road.
• át kaawadáa | --- | --the (water) level rose to there | --- | ---.
P-t~ ka-ø-daa~ (ø motion)
for water to flow, rise to P
·Gúx'aa kat'óott kaawadáa wé cháayoo. The cup is filled part way up
with tea.
• át uwadáa | aadé yaa nadéin | áý daa
it flowed to it | it's flowing to it | it flows to it (regularly).
P-t~ ø-daa~ (ø motion)
for water to flow to P
·Ý'ahéeni du ý'éit uwadáa. He is drooling.
• áý kaawadaa | áý kanaadaa | --it flowed along it | it's flowing along it | ---.
P-ý ka-ø-daa~ (na motion)
for water, blood to flow, run along P
·Du tl'átgi dagiygé áwé héenák'w áý kanaadaa. A small stream flows in
the middle of her land.
·Çíl' yáý kanaadaa wé héen. The water is flowing down the face of the rock
cliff.
• daañ uwadáa | daañ nadéin | --the tide is in | the tide is coming in | ---.
daañ ø-daa~ (ø motion)
for the tide to rise, come in
·Daañ uwadáa. The tide is in.
• kaawadaa | --- | --it flowed; it's flowing | --- | ---.
ka-ø-daa~ (na motion)
for water, blood to flow; for a nose to run
·Du ý'ahéeni kaawadaa. His saliva is flowing.
• kei uwadáa | kei nadéin | --the water level rose | the water level is rising | ---.

,

kei ø-daa~ (ø motion)
for water level, tide to rise
·Haat kei wudaayí tléil uýsatínch. He has not seen the tide rise yet.
2

DAA

• du

ý'éiý woodaa | du ý'éiý yaa nadéin | du ý'éiý yoo
yadéik

s/he got used to (the flavor, pronunciation of) it | s/he is getting used to (the
flavor, pronunciation of) it | s/he gets used to (the flavor, pronunciation of) it
(regularly).
N ý'éiý ø-daa~ (na event)
for N to become used to, accustomed to it (of manner of speech or flavor of food)
·Aý ý'éiý woodaa. I got used to (the pronunciation, flavor of) it.

dáa

weasel

du daadleeyí

his/her flesh

dáadzi

firestone; iron pyrite

dáaçi

out of the water onto the beach, shore

daak

out to sea; out into the open; (falling) down
·Watsíx áa káa daak has awlikél' wé çooch. The wolves chased the
caribou out onto the lake.
·Has du yáa daak uwagút wé xóots tlein kanat'á has a.éeni. While
they were picking blueberries, the brown bear came face to face with them.

a daaká

around the outside surface of it
·K'idéin layéý yá ñ'anáaýán wé gishoo daaká yís! Build this fence well
around those pigs!

du daakanóox'u

his/her grandparent (term of respect)
·Aangóondáý áwé aý káani du daakanóox'u. My sister-in-law's ancestors are from Angoon.

du daakashú

his/her fate

daakeit

container for it
·Wé náakw daakeidí áyá. This is a container for that medicine.
·Kóox daakeit káa yéi du.úýx'. Rice is put into a container.

daañ

up in the woods; inland; back (away from the open, away from the water's edge, inside)
·Daañ uwadáa. The tide is in.
2

DAAÑ

• kei wsidáñ | --- | --s/he migrated | --- | ---.
kei O-s-daañ~ (ø motion)
for O to move household (permanently), migrate

,

,

D

·Tléi ch'áakw ýá wé aatý kéi haa wsidáñ. It was a long time ago that we migrated from there.

daañw.aa sá

which (one); some (certain one)
·Daañw aan sáwé? Which town is that?
·Tléil ýwasakú daañw.aa ýáat sá a ñ'anooýú ñusteeyí. I don't know which fish have beards.

DAAL
• woodál | yadál | kei dálch
it got heavy | it's heavy | it gets heavy (regularly).
O-ø-dál (ga state)
for O to be heavy (usually of inanimate things); (fig.) to be weighty, important (of abstracts)

·Yadál wé tináa. The copper shield is heavy.
·A kat'óott shalatl'ít', tlél kei kçwadál! Fill it halfway, then it won't be heavy!

a daaleilí

its wrinkled, baggy skin, hide

a dáali

its rumen, main stomach (of ruminant)
·Dzísk'u tl'óoçu ña a dáali aý ý'é yak'éi. I like to eat moose liver and its tripe.
·Watsíx dáali agawdzi.ée. She cooked caribou tripe for herself.

DAAL'
• akawlidál' | akladáal' | akladál'ý
s/he typed it | s/he is typing it | s/he types it (regularly).
O-ka-S-l-dáal'~ (Ø act)
for S to type O

dáanaa

silver

dáanaa

money, coin, dollar
·Aý dáanayi a wanáa yéi aa na.oo! Put my money separate from the others!
·Du jintáax' yéi yatee du dáanayi. His money is in his grip.

dáanaa kat'éeý'i
dáanaa s'aatí

rich man

dáanaa shoowú
dáanaa t'éeý'i

silversmith

half dollar; fifty cents
silversmith

DAAS'
• awdlidás' | --- | aldás'ý
s/he snared it | --- | s/he snares it (regularly).
O-S-d-l-dáas'~ (ø event)

,

Dictionary of Tlingit

for S to snare O
·Çáý awdlidás'. She snared a rabbit.

dáas'aa

snare

du daashagóon

his/her body parts
du daashegóon

a daat

(telling) about it
·Yáa a daat x'úx' yáý áwé a daax' yéi jiýwaanei. I worked on it
according to the book.
·Tlél kei guýlats'áa i daat sh kalneek. Gossip about you is not going to
smell good.

daaw

seaweed, kelp on which herring spawn

daax'oon

four
·Aý atx'aan hídi tleidooshú ñaa ý'oos ña daax'ooný sitee. My smoke
house is six feet by four feet.
·Daax'oon ñaa ý'oos a kaayí wé nadáakw. That table measures four feet.

daax'oondahéen

four times
daax'oondehéen (C)

daax'oonínáý

four (people)
This is used for counting people only.
·Daax'oonínáý ñáa shaa shakéede al'óon has woo.aat. Four men went
up on the mountain hunting.

dáaý

canoe under construction

a daaý yaa dulsheech át

a daayí
at daayí

banister; railing

its bark
birch
et daayí (C)

at daayí ñákw
du daa.eit ý'áak
du daa.it

birch bark basket
his/her joints

his/her/its body

daa.ittunéekw

arthritis
daa.ittunóok (T)

du daa.itwéis'i

his/her gland

a dachóon

straight towards it; directly towards it
·Dzísk'w awusteení tle a dachóon kéi uwagút. When he saw the moose
he turned to walk straight towards it.

'

'

D

du dachýán

his/her grandchild
·Çuwakaan at xáshdi téel aý dachýánk' jeeyís aý tuwáa sigóo. I
would like deer skin moccasins for my grandchild.
·Teiñweidí dachýán áyá ýát. I am a grandchild of the Teikweidí.

dágáa

indeed, for sure
sdágáa

dagatgiyáa

hummingbird
degwatgeeyáa (C), dagwatgiyáa (AtT)
·Dagwatgiyáa lú yayát' ña yéi kwlisáa. A hummingbird's beak is long and
skinny.

a dagiygé

middle of it
a dagikyé, a dagiyigé
·Wé áak'w ñúnáý a dagiygé áwé watsíx át hán. A caribou is standing
right in the middle of the pond.
·Du tl'átgi dagiygé áwé héenák'w áý kanaadaa. A small stream flows in
the middle of her land.

daça-

[pluralizer]
daý-, dañThe distributive prefix "daça-" attaches to the verb and
indicates plurality of the referent, and refers only to inanimate or
recessive animate participants, while the pluralizer "has" refers to
animate (non-recessive) participants. The distributive prefix is
only used to refer to the absolutive argument (the subject of an
intransitive verb or the object of a transitive or objective verb).
·Yú sgóon tl'átgi tlein, a góonnáý daýyanaagóo wé káa. The cars are
traveling on the isthmus of the big school yard.
·Çunakadeit daat tlaagú daýñudzitee. There are legends about sea
monsters.

daçanñú

afterlife, "happy hunting ground"
·Daçanñúde woogoot. He left us (died).

daçasaa
dahooní

squid
dañsaa
salesman; clerk; storekeeper

dákde át

thing heading offshore, esp. wind
·Dákde át xóon áwé ayawditee. An offshore east wind is blowing.

dákdesak'aak

mackerel
dákdesax'aak

dákwtasi

cracklings of rendered fat, grease unfit for consumption
·Dákwtasi átý dulyéiý táay yíx'. Rendered fat is used in the garden.

dáñde

toward the inland, interior; up to the woods; back (away from the

open)

,

D

Dictionary of Tlingit

dáñdei
·Dáñde ñákw aawayaa i léelk'w. Your grandmother died. (Lit: Your grandmother took her basket into the woods).
·Ñúnáý k'eeljáa yéi ayaguýdatée ách áyá haa yaagú dáñde tusaýút'x'. It's going to get stormy so we are dragging our boats up.

dañéis'

sewing
·Ýalak'ách' ýaawú dañéis' teen átý dulyéiý. Porcupine quills are used in sewing.
·Du jiyeex' yan awli.át du dañéis'i. She placed her sewing nearby for her.

dañká

up in the woods; inland; back (away from the open, away from the water's edge, inside); inland; interior
·Dañká yoo aawa.át. People walked into the interior.
·Tléil yá dañkáx' yéi utí wé çanook. Here in the Inland we don't have any petrels.

Dañl'aweidí

Dakl'aweidí, locally called "Killer Whale"; a clan of the Eagle moiety whose principal crest is the Killer Whale

daleiyí

lake trout
·Tléil a ñ'anooýú ñoostí daleiyí. Lake trout do not have beards.

at danáayi
daneit

drunk; drunkard
large box for storing grease, oil

daséikw

life; breath
·Yées daséikwçaa woogoot. He went to get fresh air.

dáxw

lowbush cranberry, bog cranberry
·Aatlein dáxw aawa.ín. She picked lots of lowbush cranberries.
·Sháchgi káa ka.éiý dáxw. Lowbush cranberries grow in the meadow.

-dáý

from, out of; since
-tý
Note that when -dáý attaches to a noun ending in a vowel,
-dáý optionally loses its vowel, becoming -tý. For example, either
of the following are acceptable for "from around the house": wé hít
daadáý / wé hít daatý. These nouns and relational nouns have
alternate forms when combined with -dáý:
á "it, there"+ dáý = aadáý / aaý "from it; from there"
a ká "surface" + -dáý = a kaadáý / a kaaý "from its surface"
a yá "its face" + -dáý = a yaadáý / a yaaý "from its face"
a tú "its inside" + -dáý = a tóodáý / a tóoý "from its inside"
·Aý éek' si.áat'i héen goondáý ayáayin. My brother used to pack cold
water from a spring.
·Ñunáagu jeedáý jika.át yéi aya.óo. He is wearing a wrist guard from the
doctor.

daýáchx'i

tugboat
·Daýáchx'i yaakw tlénx' át has anaýáchch.. Tugboats tow large vessels.

,

,

daýadooshóonáý

D

seven (people)

daýadooshú

seven
·Daýadooshú kaay yéi kunaaléi wé aan, héen sháakdáý. The town is
seven miles from the head of the river.
·Daýadooshú yagiyee shunaaxéex aaçáa daak wusitani yé. It has
been raining for seven days.

daýdahéen

twice, two times
déiý dahéen
·Daýdahéen yan yaawagás'. He fell on his face twice.

dáýçaa

two at a time, two by two
·Dáýçaa a yíkde has woo.aat wé yaakw. They boarded the boat two by
two.

dáýçaanáý

two (people) at a time
·Dáýçaanáý yaa has anal'éý. They're dancing two by two.

dáýnáý

two (people)
This is used for counting people only.
·Dáýnáý naa sháadi náñx'i wé at yátx'i has du jeeyís has at
wooshee. Two chiefs sang for the children.
·Dáýnáý ñáa ya.áak áwé. It's wide enough for two people.

daýyeekaadé

two different kinds, types; two different ways, directions
daýyeekaadéi
·Daýyeekaadéi cheech áwé yaa éil' kaadéi ýwsiteen. I have seen two
kinds of porpoise in this ocean.

a dayéen

facing it
·Wé shaa dayéen áayáý uwahán. He turned around to face the mountain.
·Aý dayéen hán xóon niyaa. He is standing facing me, shielding me from
the North Wind.

de

already, (by) now
dei
·S'eek de has du ñoowú tóode has woo.aat. Black bears have already
gone into their dens.
·Dei át has woo.aat wéi yées kéidladi. The young seagulls are already
walking around.

deegáa

dipnet (for eulachon)
·Yawóol yá deegáa. This 'dipnet has holes in it.

DEES
• awdlidées | --- | yei aldéesch
the moon is shining | --- | the moon shines (regularly).
a-d-l-dées~ (ça event)
for the moon to shine

,

Dictionary of Tlingit

·Wé kaçít tóoý yaa ntoo.ádi awdlidées. As we walked along in the darkness, the moon shined bright.

DEEX'

• aý'eiwadíx' | --- | aý'adíx'ý

s/he corked it up | --- | s/he corks it up (regularly).

O-ý'e-S-ø-déex'~ (ø event)

for S to cork up O (bottle); for S to shut, cover mouth of O

·Ñ'ateil tóodei yanasxá k'idéin ý'adíx'! Pour it in the jug and cork it up!

dei

path, trail; road, street

·Dei káx' yéi jinéiyi ý'eis has at gawdzi.ée wé aantñeení. The townspeople cooked food for the people working on the road.

·Téil dei yaaýt la.át. Scraps of pitchwood are lying along the road.

déi

now, this time

·Tlél déi ýwateen aý kawóot ka.íshaa. I can't see my needle anymore.

·S'íx' ýoot ilt'ách déi! Wash up the dishes now! (Lit: Slap (up) the dishes now).

Déi áwé!

Stop it!; That's enough!

-dé(i) ~ -de(i)

to, toward; until; in the manner of

The tone on the postposition -dei is the opposite of that on the final syllable of the noun which it attaches to. This postposition can be pronounced long or short (-dei or -de), depending on speaker dialect.

Some nouns and relational nouns undergo changes in vowel length and/or tone when combined with -dé(i):

á "it, there" + -dé(i) = aadé(i) "toward it; toward there"

a ká "its surface" + -dé(i) = a kaadé(i) "toward (the surface of) it"

a yá "its face" + -dé(i) = a yaadé(i) "toward (the face of) it"

a tú "its inside" + -dé(i) = a tóode(i) "toward (the inside of) it"

·Çítçaa ayaýsaháa yóode woogoot. She went over there to gather spruce needles.

·Dleeyçáa áwé aadéi aawa.aat. People went there for meat.

Deikeenaa

Haida

·Deikeenaa ña Ts'ootsxán áa shayadihéin Kichýáan. There are a lot of Haida and Tsimshian people in Ketchikan.

·Deikeenaa tóode haa kdlixwás'. Our roots stem from the Haida

déili

shelter (from wind or weather), harbor
·Déili áa has shawdziyaa. They anchored in a harbor.
·Çeey tá déilit awsiñúý du yaagú. She drove her boat to the head of the bay.

a déin

(in) the area of it or around it, (in) its vicinity
·Wé áak'w déint áwé át woogoot wé sheech dzísk'u tlein. The big cow moose was walking around in the vicinity of the pond.
·Wé shaa a déinde áa yaa nagút. He is walking in the direction of the mountain.

,

,

D

a déinde aa

the rest of it
·A déinde aa du naa.ádi aaý awli.aat. She picked up the rest of her clothes.
·A déinde aa wé gán yaý ayakawlixút'. He chopped up the rest of the wood.

Deisleen

Teslin
·Deisleenx' keijín has yatee ñaa sháade náñx'i. In Teslin there are five leaders.
·Deisleen jáaji k'idéin wududzikóo. Teslin snowshoes are well-known.

Deisleen Ñwáan

Teslin Lake people

Deisheetaan

Deisheetaan, locally called "Beaver"; a clan of the Raven
moiety whose principal crest is the Beaver
·S'igeidí Deisheetaan ñaa at oohéini áwé. The Beaver is the property of the Deisheetaan Clan.

Deishú

Haines

·Ts'ak'áawásh Deishúdáý has aawa.oo. They bought dried fish strips from Haines.
·Deishúx' awsiteen wé çanook. She saw a petrel in Haines.

déiý

two
·Déiý ýáat haa jeex' ajeewanáñ. He left two salmon for us.
·Tlei déiý ñ'ateil yáý áwé wutusineiý shákw kahéeni. We just saved two gallons of the strawberry juice.

dei yaaý

side of the path, trail, road, street
·Ch'eeý' yagéi yóo dei yaaý. There are plenty of thimbleberries along the road.

dei yík

on the path, trail, road; bed of the path, trail, road

digitgiyáa

hummingbird
·Aý tl'eiñ káa wjiñaañ digitgiyáa. A hummingbird landed on my finger.

Dikáanñáawu

God
Dikée aanñáawu

Dikée aanñáawu

God
Dikáanñáawu
·Dikée aanñáawu du éek' atuwaheen. We believe in God.
·Dikée aanñáawu du yéet ítý na.aadí has du een sh káa ý'awdigáx'. Jesus prayed with his disciples.

dís

month
·Yées dís áwé haadé yaa nagút. A new month is coming.

dís

moon
·Wé dís kagáni káax' yéi jiné. He works by moonlight.

,

D

Dictionary of Tlingit

dís wooýéiyi

calendar

dís ý'usyee

moonbeam
·Dís ý'usyee kawdli.ít'ch wé dleit káý. Moonbeams are sparkling on the snow.

du díý'

his/her back
·Du díý' néekw nooch. His back always hurts.

diyáanaý.á

area across, on the other side (especially of body of water)
·Wé éil' héen diyáanaý.á adawóotl yáý áa at yatee. There is a war going on across the ocean.
·Yóo diyáanaý.aadáý áwé haat yaýwaaýáa wéi kax'ás'ti haa hídi sákw. I hauled the lumber from across the other side for our house.

Diyée aanñáawu

Satan
·Diyée aanñáawu jeet wudzigít. He fell into satan's hands.

Doó!

See how you are!; Look what you did!

a doogú

its skin (of animal); hide
·Ý'alitseen wé ýalt'ooch' naaças'éi doogú. The skin of a black fox is expensive.
·Téil yéi aya.óo at doogú aklas'éñýi yís. She is using dry wood for smoking that hide.

du dook

his/her skin, complexion
·Du dook yak'éi. Her complexion is good.

dóol

sandhill crane

du doonyaa

under or inside his/her clothes; next to his/her skin

doonyaaý k'oodás'

undershirt
·Du doonyaaý k'oodás'i áý çaashóo. His undershirt is hanging out.

doonyaaýl'aak

petticoat; slip
·Doonyaaýl'aak yéi aya.óo. She's wearing a slip.

dóosh

cat
·Wé dóosh kadaçááý. The cat is crying.
·Wé dóosh jín dleit kaaý kínde alshát. The cat is holding its paw up off the snow.

dóosh yádi

kitten
·Dóosh yádi een áwé ash koolyát wé atk'átsk'u. The boy is playing with a kitten.

DOOX'
• akaawadúx' | akadóox' | akadúx'ý
s/he tied it | s/he's tying it | s/he ties it (regularly).
O-ka-S-ø-dóox'~ (ø act)

,

,

D

for S to tie O in a knot
·Du téel ý'adzaasí akaawadúx'. She tied her shoelaces.

du

his/her [possessive]
·Du keidlí du jináñ ñut wujixeex. His dog ran away from him.
·Wé ñáa du jishagóoni ñut kaawasóos. The man's tools are lost.

dúñ

cottonwood
·Dúñ een dulyéiý seet yaakw. The canoe is made out of cottonwood.

dúñ

canoe made of cottonwood

dúñl'

young spruce or hemlock

dús'

soot
·Dús' áa yagéi wé ý'aan eetí. There's soot where the fire was.

dúsh

tadpole; polliwog

,

Dictionary of Tlingit

« Dl »
du dlaak'

his sister
·Wooch çunayáadei ch'éen i dlaak' jeewú. Your sister has different kinds
of ribbons.
·Aý dlaak' tín Xunaadé ñugaýtootéen kanat'á ñuk'éet' yís. We are
going to travel to Hoonah to pick blueberries with my sister.

DLAAÑ
• ayaawadlaañ | --- | yoo ayaadláñk
s/he won it | --- | s/he wins it (regularly).
O-ya-S-ø-dlaañ~ (na event)
for S to win, gain, get, obtain, acquire O; for S to succeed, accomplish O; for S to
defeat, beat O
The prohibitive forms "Don't win it!" require context in order
to make sense. An example would be this statement, said jokingly:
Líl yoo yeedláñgiñ - yakñwadláañ! "Don't win it - I'm going to win
it!"
·Xákw ká ayaawadlaañ. He made it to the sand bar.
·Tsaa Éiý' kaadáý áwé yawtuwadlaañ ch'a k'ikát wé kaneilts'ákw.
We finally managed to get some swamp currants from Seal Slough.
DLAAN
• woodlaan | çaadlaan | yei dlánch
it became deep | it's deep | it gets deep (regularly).
ø-dlaan~ (ça state)
for water to be deep; for snow to be piled thickly
This verb is one of a very small set of dimensional verbs
with extensional imperfective forms (Leer, 1991). It is
distinguished by an imperfective form which requires the çaconjugation prefix.
·Kaldaaçéináý yaa gaýtooñóoý, tlél çwadlaan yá éiý' yík. We will
travel along slowly, it's not deep in this slough.
• yan kaawadlán | yánde yaa kanadlán | --it's piled up | it's beginning to pile up | ---.
yan~ ka-ø-dlaan~ (ø motion)
for grain-like objects, pine needles, snow to be deep, thick, pile up
• yéi kaawadláan | yéi kçwaadláan | --it got that deep | it's that deep | ---.
yéi ka-u-ø-dláan (ça state)
for a body of water to be so deep
·Tleiñáa waat yéi kçwaadláan. It's twenty fathoms deep.

,

,

Dl

DLAAÝ'W
• yaý woodláaý'w | --- | yaý kei dláý'wch

it got stuck on the beach | --- | it gets stuck on the beach (regularly).
yaý ø-dláaý'w~ (ga event)
for a boat, sea mammal to get stuck (on beach), be beached
·Wé yáay yaý woodláaý'w. The whale is stuck on the beach.
·Yaý kei kçwadláaý'w wé yaakw. The boat will get stuck on the beach.

dlagwáa

fish spear; harpoon for spearing salmon

dlágwaa

peavy
·Yées aa dlágwaa áwé. That is a new peavey.
·Dlágwaa tín yéi jiné. He is working with a peavey.

dleey

meat, flesh
·Wé çuwakaan dleeyí at ý'aýéedli k'idéin aaý xásh, téiý sákw! Cut
the trimming off the deer meat well for the broth!
·Wé dleey yat'éex'. The meat is tough.

dleit

snow
·Dís ý'usyee kawdli.ít'ch wé dleit káý. Moonbeams are sparkling on the
snow.
·Héen sákw wé dleitdáý kalóoýjaa tayeex' yan tán! Set that below the
snow drip for our water!

dleit

white
·Wé çáý dleit yáý ýasitee. The rabbit is white.
·Gúñl' dleit yáý daçaatee. Swans are white.

dleit çéedi
dleit kakétsk

snowstorm, snow shower
dry snow

dleit ñáa

White, European, Caucasian (man or person)
·Dleit ñáach áwé awliyéý wé ý'éi shadagutýi lítaa. The white man
invented the pocket knife.

dleit ñaadí

snowslide; snow avalanche

dleit tléiçu

snowberry

DLÉNÝAA
• akaawadlénýaa | akoodlénýaa | yoo akayadlénýaa
he/she/it tempted him/her | he/she/it is tempting him/her | he/she/it tempts him/her
(regularly).
O-ka-u-S-ø-dlénýaa (na act)
for S to tempt, try out, test O
·Dáanaa tín has akoodlénýaa. They tempted him with money.
·Wáa yateeyi aa shaax'wsáani sá ash koodlénýaa? What kind of girls
does he find tempting?

,

Dz

Dictionary of Tlingit

« Dz »
dzaas

babiche, string, leather thonging
·Du jáaji a dzaasí yei nasháash. The thongs of his snowshoes are wearing thin.
·Dzaas áwé yéi akçwa.oo çeeçách' akawusneiyí. She will use string when she crochets a hammock.

dzánti

flounder
·Cháatl yátx'i oowayáa dzánti. Flounders look like little halibut.
·Dzánti áwé cháatl x̱ín x̱udligéi. Flounders are smaller than halibut.

Dzántik'i Héeni

Juneau; Gold Creek (in Juneau)
·Dzántik'i Héenix' áwé x̱at x̱oowdzitee. I was born in Juneau.
·K'idéin has jidux̱éi katíx̱'aa s'aatí Dzántik'i Héenix'. Jailers are paid well in Juneau.

DZEE
• wulidzée | lidzée | kei ladzéech
it was difficult | it's difficult | it gets difficult (regularly).
O-l-dzée (ga state)
for O to be difficult, frustrating
·Yaaw x̱ídlaa yéi wdu.oowú, tlél uldzée nooch. Using a herring rake is not difficult.
·Lidzée kayaaní a kaadéi kawuls'éesi wé laañ'ásk. It's frustrating when leaves are blown onto the black seaweed.

dzéex'w

baby clams

dzeit

ladder; stairs
·Dzeit áý kei wlishóo. The ladder extends up there.

dzeit

dock, pier

dzeit shuyee

at the landing of a dock

·Dzeit shuyeet uwañúý wé yaakw. The boat motored to the landing.

dzísk'w

moose
·Dzísk'u çádzi yaa anayéin. He is packing a moose hindquarter.
·Kat'íshaa JoAnne Fabricsdáý ýwaa.oo dzísk'u doogú yís. I bought a leather needle from JoAnne Fabrics for (sewing) moose hide.

dzísk'w (AtT)

owl; great horned owl

dziyáagin

after a while; later on
·Ch'a tle dziyáaginx' tsá çunéi gaýtoo.áat. Pretty soon we're going to start walking.

,

,

dziyáak

Dz

just now; a while ago, earlier
·Dziyáak áwé woogoot. He left a while ago.
·Ch'u dziyáak áwé ishuwtusitee. We were expecting you a while ago

dzóox'

tiny clams (too small to eat)
·Éeñx' yéi teeý dzóox'. Small clams are found on the beach.

du dzúk

at his/her back; right behind him/her

,

Dictionary of Tlingit

« E/Ee/Ei »
É!

Check it out!; Wow!
This is an exclamation of pride, achievement, or wonder.
·É! Shahíký haa cháli çaatáa yéi daatooneiyí. Check it out! When we
are out trapping, our storehouse is full.

du ee~

him, her
This is a pronominal base which postpositions are added to,
resulting in the following forms:
du éet
du éeý
du eedé(i) / du éede(i)
·Háas' du éet yéi uwanéi yá yagiyee. He has been vomiting today.

Ée!

Yuck!; Eeeew!

eech

reef; large rock or boulder lying on the ocean floor
·Eech kát uwañúý wé yaakw. The boat ran over a reef.

eech kakwéiyi

fixed buoy
·Tlákw s'eenáa a káa yéi nateech eech kakwéiyi. There's always a light
on a fixed buoy.
·Point Retreat eech kakwéiyi áwé Point Retreat is a fixed buoy.

eech kwéiyi

floating buoy

éech'

something compact and very heavy
·Éech' akaawanóot' Yéil. Raven swallowed a stone.

éedaa

phosphorescence (sparks of light in ocean water); luminescence (on
rotten wood)
·Kadli.ít'ch éedaa xáanax'. The phosphoresence glows at night.

a eeçáa

waiting for it
·Wé sakwnéin éewu yan ça.eet eeçáa áwé ýa.áa. I am sitting, waiting for the bread to finish cooking.

a eeçayáak

the beach, shore below it (a town)
·Kóoshdaa haa eeçayáaknáý yan uwahín. The land otter swam through our beachfront.
·Aan eeçayáax' shóot awdi.ák. He made fire for himself below the town.

éeçi

from the woods onto the beach, shore

du éek'

her brother, cousin
·Aý éek' du aandaayaagú áwé. That is my brother's rowboat.
·Tsú yáa aý tláa ñu.aa Sheet'káx' áyá ñoowdzitee. Ña du éek' tsú

,

,

E/Ee/Ei

áa ñoowdzitee. My mother was born in Sitka. And her brother was also born there.

eeñ

copper

éeñ

beach; waterside; down on the beach, shore
éiñ
·Ý'al'daayéeji éeñt wujixeex. The sandpiper is running around the beach.
·Éeñx' yéi teeý dzóox'. Small clams are found on the beach.

eeñ háatl'i

verdigris

éeñ lukañées'i

low tide (point at which the tide will begin coming in)

een

(along) with, by means of; as soon as
tin, tín, teen, téen
·Aý éek' ña aý sáni al'óoni een át has na.átjin. My brother and my
paternal uncle used to accompany hunters.
·Góon dáanaa een áwé kawduwat'íý' aý jeeyís yá kées. This bracelet
was pounded out of a gold coin for me.

du een aa
éenaa
du éenee

his/her kinsman, moiety mate
scraper, as for scraping off bark from roots

his/her armpit
du éenyee, du éeni (C)

du éenee ýaawú

his/her armpit hair
du éenyee ýaawú, du éeni ýaawú (C)

éenwu

food taken home from a feast or dinner to which one was invited
éenu (TC)

du éesh

his/her father
·Ch'a yá Lingít yinaanáý ñu.aa áyá tléil ñaa éeshch áyú ñaa yádi
saa a yáý uteeyín. In our Tlingit culture, a father never names the children.
·Yá ñut'aayçáa gági ugootch yee éesh. During the warm season your
father would come out.

Eesháan!

Poor thing!
·Eesháank' kaltéelñ áwé haat wujixíx aý dachýánk'. Poor thing, my
grandchild ran over here shoeless.
·Eeshandéin tuwatee. He's feeling sad.

eet

room
·Haat has ñuwuteení yís áyá yan ýwasinéi yáa eet ká. I have reserved
this room for when they arrive.

a eetéenáý

lacking it; without it
·Éil' eetéenáy yatee wé taýhéeni. The broth needs salt.
·Kooxéedaa eetéenáy yatee wé shaatk'. The young girl needs a pencil.

,

Dictionary of Tlingit

a eetí

(in) place of it; place where it was; its imprint or aftermath
·Xein nageich ñutaan eetíx'. After the summer there are a lot of
spawned-out salmon.
·Laaxw eetí wé ñaa jeedáý atýá has du çaneiýíý wusitee. After the
famine, the food given to them became their salvation.

du eetí ká

(in) his/her room, bedroom
du eetí
·Du eetí a kaýyeet akawlis'íx'w ñaa yahaayí wé shaatk'átsk'u. The
young girl pasted a photo on the ceiling of her room.

éetkatlóoýu
éex

bullhead

downstream; south

eeý

oil, grease
eiý (C)
·A eeýí geiý yá chudéi dus.eeyí. There is a lot of oil in the tom cod when it's
cooked.
·Tsaa eeýí teen yak'éi at ý'éeshi. Seal oil is good with dryfish.

eeý kát sakwnein

fry bread, bannock
·Aý tláa jiyáý eeý kát sakwnéin ýasa.ée. I cook fry bread like my mom
does.

eey

bay

éil'

salt
·Éil' eetéenáý yatee wé taýhéeni. The broth needs salt.
·Éil' a kaadéi kanasxá wéi a kát yadu.us'ku át! Pour salt in the wash
basin!

éil'

ocean; salt water
éil' héen, éil' héeni
·Wé éil' héen diyáanaý.á adawóotl yáý áa at yatee. There is a war
going on across the ocean.
·Éil' kaadáý ýaat k'idéin aaý yixás' a kajeiçí! You all scrape the scales
off the fish from the salt water well!

éil' kahéeni

saltwater brine
·Éil' kahéeni káa yéi na.oo wé kaháakw. Put the fish eggs in the saltwater
brine.

Éits'k'!

Yum!

eiý (C)

oil, grease
eeý
·Tsaa eiýí teen áwé yak'éi t'á at ý'éeshi. Dry fish king salmon is good with
seal oil.
·Tsaa eiýí du daagú ágé a yanáaý yei at dutánch? Is a cover put on
when rendering seal oil?

,

,

éiý'

E/Ee/Ei

slough
·Kaldaaçéináý yaa gaýtooñóoý, tlél çwadlaan yá éiý' yík. We will
travel along slowly, it's not deep in this slough.

,

Dictionary of Tlingit

« G »
GAA
• yan akawligáa | yánde yaa akanalgéin | yaý aklagáa
s/he put up food | s/he is putting up food | s/he puts up food (regularly).
yan~ O-ka-S-l-gáa~ (ø motion)
for S to put up, store up, accumulate O (esp. food for winter); for S to finish
distributing things (esp. at party)

gáal'

cataract
wañgáal'

gáal'

clam
·Gáal' has akaháa. They are digging clams.

gaan

smokehole

1

GAAN

• át akaawagán | --- | áý akagaan
it's lit | --- | it lights (regularly).
P-t~ a-ka-ø-gaan~ (ø motion)
for P (light) to be on; for P (fire) to burn, catch alight
·S'eenáat akaawagán. The light is on.
• át akawligán | --- | áý aklagaan
s/he lit it | --- | s/he lights it (regularly).
P-t~ a-ka-S-l-gaan~ (ø motion)
for S to light, set fire to, cause P to shine; for S to turn on P (light)
·Toow s'eenáa át has akawligán. They lit a candle.
·Uýgannáas' tin áý akdulgaan. It is lit with a match.
• awdigaan | yei andagán | yei adagánch
it's sunny | it's getting sunny | it's sunny (regularly).
a-d-gaan~ (ça event)
for the sun to shine
·Awdagaaních áwé, dleit kaaý kalóoýjaa koolx'áasch hít kaadáý.
Because the sun is shining, the snow drips fast off the house.
·Yei andagán. The sun is beginning to shine.
• a kát kawdigán | --- | a káý kadagaan
it's shining on it | --- | it shines on it (regularly).
P-t~ ka-d-gaan~ (ø event)
for a light to shine on P

·Hít kageidí át kawdigán wé s'eenáa. The light is shining on the side of the house.
·Ñúnáý áwé ñ'asigóo i shaýaawú, a kát akawdagaaní. Your hair is really beautiful when the sun shines on it.

,

,

G

• kawdigán | --- | kadagáný
it's bright | --- | it brightens (regularly).
ka-d-gaan~ (ø event)
for something to shine, produce light by burning
• kei awsigán | kei anasgán | kei asgánch
s/he burned it up | s/he is burning it up | s/he burns it up (regularly).
kei O-S-s-gaan~ (ø motion)
for S to burn O up
A common use of this verb is in discussing the traditional practice of burning the clothes one was wearing when s/he passed away, as indicated in the example sentence.
·Ñaa naa.ádi kei dusgánch. They burn the person's clothes up.

gáan

outdoors; outside
·Gáande yaa nay.ádi wooch yáý x'wán anayl'eiý! Be sure to all dance alike when you walk out!
·Aawa.óos'i jiçwéinaa gáaný ashayaawatée. She hung the towel that she washed outside.

gáan

menstrual discharge; period
Gáan aawa.oo "she had her period".

gaan ká

smokehole

gaan woolí

opening of smokehole
·Gaan woolí a kaháadi áa kei aawatée. He put the cover for the smoke hole up there.

gaan ý'aháadi

smokehole cover

GAAS'

• aadé wligáas' | --- | aadé yoo ligás'k

s/he moved there | --- | s/he moves there (regularly).

P-dé O-l-gáas'~ (na motion)

for O to move household (with future plans unspecified) to P

• át wuligás' | --- | áý lagáas'

s/he moved there | --- | s/he moves there (regularly).

P-t~ O-l-gáas'~ (ø motion)

for O to move household (with future plans unspecified) to P

·Anóoshi Aanídáý áyá yaa San Fransiscot has wuligás'. They had
moved to San Fransisco from Russia.

• a kát sh wudligás' | --- | a káý sh ilgáas'

he/she/it leapt on it | --- | he/she/it leaps on it (regularly).

P-t~ sh S-d-l-gáas'~ (ø motion)

for S to leap, pounce on P

·Yóot sh wudligás' a ñoowúdáý. It charged out of its den.

·A wándáý áwé a yíkt sh wudligás' wé yéil. The raven leapt into it from
the edge.

,

G

Dictionary of Tlingit

• yan yaawagás' | --- | yaý yagáas'
s/he fell on his/her face | --- | s/he is nodding off, falling asleep while sitting.
yan~ O-ya-ø-gáas'~ (ø motion)
for O to fall on face; for O to nod off, fall asleep while sitting up
·Daýdahéen yan yaawagás'. He fell on his face twice.

gáas'

house post

gaaw

bell
·Wé ý'agáax' daakahídi gaawú iñnáach' teen wududliyéý The church
bell is made of brass.

gaaw

time
·Yat'éex'i gaaw a tóonáý yiyagút. You walked through that period of hard
time.
·X'oon gaawx' sá? At what time?

gaaw

drum

gaaw

clock

GAAW
• sawligaaw | saligaaw | kei salagaawch
he/she/it was loud-voiced | he/she/it is loud-voiced | he/she/it gets loud-voiced
(regularly).
O-sa-l-gaaw (ga state)
for O to be loud-voiced, noisy in speech
Note a related verb with a similar meaning: ý'aligaaw "s/he
has a loud, powerful voice."
·Aanñáawu Çeeyx' áwé has saligaaw ñúnáý wé kaçeet. The loons are
really loud in Ankau Bay.

gaawáñ
gaaw ítx'

serviceberry; saskatoonberry
late; after the appointed time
gaaw ít (C)

Gaawt'añ.aan
gaaw ý'áak

Hoonah
hour

gaaw yáý

on time; in time
gaaw yéý (T)

gáaxw

duck
·Héen wát át has wusikwaan wé gáaxw. The ducks are swimming around
at the mouth of the river.
·Du séek' yageeyí kayís áwé gáaxw awsi.ée. She cooked a duck for her
daughter's birthday.

,

,

G

GAAX'
• sh

káa ý'awdigáx' | sh káa ý'adagáax' | sh káa
ý'adagáx'ý
s/he prayed | s/he prays; s/he is praying | s/he prays (regularly).
sh káa ý'e-S-d-gáax'~ (ø act)
for S to pray
·Çaneiý káý sh káa ý'awdigáx'. She prayed for his salvation.
·Dikée aannáawu du yéet ítý na.aadí has du een sh káa
ý'awdigáx'. Jesus prayed with his disciples.

gági

from hiding into open
·Yá ñut'aayçáa gági ugootch yee éesh. During the warm season your
father would come out.

gán

firewood
·Xáshaa yéi ndu.eich gán yéi daaduneiyí. A saw is used to work on
wood.
·Wé aantñeení woosh ji.een gán has aawaxásh. The townspeople cut
wood together.

ganaltáak

in the fire
·Ganyal'óot' ganaltáakdáý kéi wjitúk. The flame shot up out of the fire.

ganaswáan

worker; crew

gandaa

around the fire
gaan daa
·Gandaax' té áa has akaawachák. They piled rock around the fire.
·Gandaat has ñéen. They are sitting around the fire.

gandaadagóogu

woodpecker
·Gandaadagóogu wéit wudiñeen. A woodpecker is flying around there.
·Gandaadagóogu kayéik ýaa.áých. I can hear the sound of a woodpecker.

gandaas'aají

bee; wasp
·Gandaas'aají ñ'eikaxwéin ýoot kawdliyeech. Bees are flying around
among the flowers.
·A kúdi daat wudiñeen wé gandaas'aají. There is a bee flying around the
nest.

gandaas'aají háatl'i (T)

honey
gendaas'aají háatl'i (C)

gandaas'aají kúdi

bee's nest
·Wé s'eek gandaas'aají kúdi aawat'ei. The black bear found a bee's nest.

gánde nagoodí

feces
·Tléiñw x'aakeidí áwé ts'ítskw gánde nagoodí tóox' yéi nateech.
Berry seeds are found in bird poop.

,

Dictionary of Tlingit

gan eetí

ashes
·Gan eetí kél't' ñugáas' yáý yatee. Ashes from the fireplace are gray.

gangook

fireside; by the fire, facing the fire
·Áat' jiyeet, gangookt ñukawdik'ít'. People crowded close around the fire because of the cold weather.
·Wé ñáa dzísk'u shaayí gangooknáý as.eeyín. He used to cook moose head next to the campfire.

gangukçáýi

fish heads cooked on ground around fire
·Gangukçáýi ñúnáý has du ý'é yak'éi. The fish heads cooked around the fire are very tasty to them.
·Gangukçáýi has du sitgawsáan atýaayí áwé. The fish heads cooked around the fire are their lunch.

ganigeidí

smoke spreaders (board suspended horizontally above

smokehouse fire)

gán kañás'ti

kindling
·Gán kañás'ti akawliýóot' wé ý'aan yís. He chopped kindling for the fire.
·Gán kañás'ti ñóok tóox' neil awsi.ín. He brought the kindling inside in a box.

gán láý'i

dead wood that's wet on the outside
·Yat'éex' át akawdusgaaní gán láý'i. It is hard to burn the wet outer part of firewood.
·Ch'a áa yan awli.át wé gán láý'i. He just left the wet outer part of firewood there.

gántiyaakw

steamboat; riverboat
gántinyaakw
·Gántiyaakw kaadé yís gán has aawaxaash. They cut wood to put on the steamboat.

·Has aawanéegwál' wé gántiyaakw. They painted the steamboat.

Gántiyaakw Séedi

Petersburg
·Gántiyaakw Séedidáý Lingít áwé. That is a Tlingit from Petersburg.
·Gántiyaakw Séedix' yaakw tlein yíý aawa.aat. People boarded the big boat at Petersburg.

gantutl'úk'ýu

woodworm
gentutl'úk'ýu (C)
·Gantutl'úk'ýu tléil daa.usýáaw. Woodworms are not furry.

gantuxoogú
gán tl'áak'

dry inner part of firewood
wet firewood

ganyal'óot'

flame
·Wé ganyal'óot' s'oow yáý yatee. That flame is green.
·Ganyal'óot' ganaltáakdáý kéi wjitúk. The flame shot up out of the fire.

,

,

gán yátx'i

G

small pieces of firewood; kindling

gawdáan

horse
·Du gawdáani aadé woo.aadi yé, a niyaadé çunéi wjixíx. He started running in the direction his horses went.
·Wé ñáa du dachýánk'i yís gawdáan aawa.oo. The man bought his grandchild a horse.

gawdáan yádi

colt
·Wé gawdáan yádi át wujik'éin. That colt is jumping around.

gé

[interrogative marks yes-no questions]
·Duýá gé çeey kanaý ñutées'? Are ratfish edible?
·Yaa indashán óosh gé! If only you were getting old!

a géek

stern (of a boat)
a gík
·Yées washéen a géekt satéen wé yaakw. A new motor sits at the stern of
that boat.
·A géekde yadál wé yaakw. The boat is stern heavy.

a geení

its tail flippers
·Tsaa geení aankadushxit át teen akawshixít. She took a picture of the
seal tail flippers with a camera.
·Aaý awlixaash a geení wé tsaa. He cut the tail flippers off of the seal.

geesh

kelp
·Geesh ýoot wootlóox' wé yáxwch'. The sea otter is rolling around in the
kelp.
·Geesh tóot uwañúý wé yaakw. The boat drove in among the kelp.
1

GEET

• aadé wdzigeet | --- | aadé yoo dzigítk
he/she/it fell there | --- | s/he falls there (regularly).
P-dé O-d-s-geet~ (na motion)
for O (live creature) to fall into P
·Té ý'áakde wdzigeet. He fell in the crevice.
• anaý yei wdzigít | --- | --s/he fell over it | --- | ---.
P-náý yei O-d-s-geet~ (ø motion)
for O (live creature) to fall down, trip over P
·X'éedadi kaanáý yéi aý wudzigít at gutóox'. I fell over a stump in the
woods.
• át wudzigít | --- | --he/she/it fell against it | --- | ---.
P-t~ O-d-s-geet~ (ø motion)
for O (live creature) to fall into, against P
·Diyée aanñáawu jeet wudzigít. He fell into satan's hands.

,

Dictionary of Tlingit

• daak wudzigít | --- | daak isgítch
he/she/it fell | --- | s/he falls (regularly).
daak O-d-s-geet~ (ø motion)
for O to fall (of live creature)(esp. off of something)
·T'óok' ýoodé daak aý wudzigít. I fell into the stinging nettles.
·Yaa ntoo.ádi áwé, daak wudzigít yaý akaawaýích wutuwa.ini
kaneilts'ákw. When we were walking along, she fell down and spilled all the
swamp currants we picked.
• kei awsigít | --- | kei asgítch
s/he woke him/her up | --- | s/he wakes him/her up (regularly).
kei O-S-s-geet~ (ø motion)
for S to wake O up, rouse O from sleep
• kei wdzigít | --- | --s/he woke up | --- | ---.
kei O-s-geet~ (ø motion)
for O to wake up
·Ts'ootaat kei aý wudzigít. I woke up in the morning.
• ñut wudzigeet | --- | ñut kei isgítch
s/he got lost | --- | s/he gets lost (regularly).
ñut O-d-s-geet~ (ga motion)
for O to lose oneself, be lost, usure of one's location
·Wé wanadóo yádi ñut wudzigeet. The lamb got lost.
2

GEET

• at géit wudzigít | at géide yaa nasgít | --s/he did something wrong | s/he is doing something
wrong | ---.
at géit~ S-d-s-geet~ (ø event)
for S to violate, break (law or custom), do something wrong
·At géit wudzigít wé ñáa átx'i aawutáawu. He went against the law when
he stole the man's belongings.

géewaa

beer

1

GEI

• --- | digéix' | ----- | they're big | ---.
d-géix' (ga state)
for (plural) objects to be big
·Haadaaçoojí a ooýú dañdigéix'. Lion teeth are large.
• --- | kadigéix' | ----- | they're big | ---.
ka-d-géix' (ga state)
for plural, usually spherical objects to be big
·Dañkadigéix' du guk.ádi. Her earrings are big.

• --- | kayagéi | ----- | it's big | ---.
ka-ø-gei~ (na state)

,

,

G

for a singular, usually round, spherical object to be big
·Nás'k a doogú x'óow áwé du káa kakçwagéi k'oodás' sákw, wé ñáa
tlein. It will take three leather blankets for the big man's shirt.
• --- | ligéi | ----- | he/she/it is big | ---.
O-l-gei~ (na state)
for O (esp. live creature or building) to be big, tall
• woogéi | yagéi | --it was big; there were many | there are many | ---.
ø-gei~ (na state)
for a solid mass or abstracts to be big (in quantity), be lots, many, plenty
·Ýaatl' áwé yagéi Jilñáatx'. There is a lot of algae in the Chilkat.
·Héen ý'ayaaý yagéi kaxwéiý. There are a lot of highbush cranberries
along the river.
• yéi kaawagéi | yéi koogéi | --it got this big; there were this many | it's this big; there are this
many | ---.
(yéi) k-u-ya-gei~ (na state)
for a thing to be (so) big; for things to be (so) many
·Wáa sá koogéi wé k'wát'? How many eggs are there?
·A ñín aý jee koogéi wé k'oodás' yeidí. I have less than the price of that
shirt.
• --- | yéi kwdigéi | ----- | they're that big | ---.
(yéi) + ka-u-d-gei~ (na state)
for (plural) objects to be (so) big
·Woosh çuwanyáade kwdigéi túlx'u. Drill bits come in different sizes.
• --- | yéi kwdzigéi | ----- | they're small | ---.
(yéi) ka-u-d-s-gei~ (ga state)
for grain-like objects to be small
·Yéi kwdzigeiyi aa ñákwx' áwé akooshtánin yéi daané aý léelk'w.
My grandmother loved to make those little baskets.
2

GEI

• du

daa yaa ñushuwsigéi | du daa yaa ñushusigéi | du
daa kei yaa ñushusagéich
s/he understood | s/he understands | s/he understands (regularly).
N daa yaa ñu-shu-s-géi (ga state)
for N to understand, comprehend
·Aý ýooní Lingít tlél du daa yaa ñushusgé. My friend doesn't understand
Tlingit.

a géit~

against it; wrongly, improperly
·Haat kanadaayí géide kei nañúý. She is going against the current.
·Té géit kaawagwátl wé kooch'éit'aa. The ball rolled against a rock.

,

G

géxtl'

aluminum
·Du ñ'wádli géxtl'iý sitee. Her pots are made of aluminum.
·Géxtl' tléil udál. Aluminum is not heavy.

gí

perhaps; I guess, it would seem

gijook

kind of hawk
kijook
·Gijook wéit kawdliyeech. Hawks are flying around there.
·Dañkáx' "Golden Eagle" gijook yóo tuwasáakw. In the Inland, we call the Golden Eagle "gijook".

Ginjichwáan

Canadian, British
Ginjoochwáan
·Ginjichwáan k'isáani áwé, wéix' has at shí. The young British men are singing there.
·Ginjichwáan aanídáý áwé wé shaatk'. That young woman is from Canada.

Ginjoochwáan

Canadian, British
Ginjichwáan

gis'óoñ

northern lights; aurora borealis
·Ñúnáý woo.aat gis'óoñ yá xáanaa. The Northern Lights are really moving about this evening.
·Ý'aan yáý teeyí gis'óoñ, tlél dultíný When the northern lights are red, they aren't to be looked at.

gishoo

pig
·Gishoo a kígi aý jeet wududzitáa. I was given half of a pig.
·K'idéin layéý yá ñ'anáaýán wé gishoo daaká yís! Build this fence well around those pigs!

gishoo taayí

bacon
·Atýá daakahídix' gishoo taayí ña k'wát' awdziçáaý. She ordered bacon and eggs at the restaurant.
·Gishoo taayí ña dleey wóosh teen akawlis'úk. She fried the meat with bacon.

Giyañw

Aleut
·Giyañw Ñwáan yoo ý'atángi ñóox' altóow. He is teaching people the Alutiq language.
·Giyañw Ñwáaný sitee aý ýooní, Russell. My friend Russell is Alutiq.
1

GOO

• ñ'awsigóo | ñ'asigóo | --it was fun | it's fun | ---.
ñ'a-s-góo (ga state)
for something to be enjoyable, fun, make one happy (esp. of speeches or songs at party); for something to be appealing to the eye
·Ñúnáý áwé ñ'asigóo i shaýaawú, a kát akawdagaaní. Your hair is

,

,

G

really beautiful when the sun shines on it.
·Ñ'asigóo kaltéelñ l'éiw kát át wusheex. It's fun running around barefoot in the sand.
• du toowú wsigóo | du toowú sigóo | --s/he was happy | s/he is happy | ---.
N toowú s-góo (ga state)
for N to be happy, glad
• du tuwáa wsigóo | du tuwáa sigóo | --s/he wanted it | s/he wants it | ---.
N tuwáa S-s-góo (ga state)
for N to want, like, desire S; for S to be pleasing to N
·Çuwakaan at xáshdi téel aý dachýánk' jeeyís aý tuwáa sigóo. I would like deer skin moccasins for my grandchild.
·Áý akawdudlis'eiçi ishñeen du tuwáa sagóowun aý éesh. My dad used to like smoked black cod.
2

GOO

• anaý

has yaawagóo | anaý yaa (ha)s yanagwéin |
anaý yoo (ha)s yaagwéik
they traveled through it | they are traveling through it | they travel through it (regularly).

P-náy̌ ya-S-ø-goo~ (na motion)
for S (a group of cars, fleet of boats) to travel through P together (by motor); for
a school of sea mammals to swim through P together
·Yú sgóon tl'átgi tlein, a góonnáy̌ day̌yanaagóo wé káa. The cars are
traveling on the isthmus of the big school yard.

• át has yaawagoo | --- | --they are traveling around; they traveled around | --- | ---.
P-t ya-ø-goo~ (na motion)
for S (a group of cars, fleet of boats) to travel around at P (by motor); for a
school of sea mammals to swim around at P
·Yaakwdáatx' áwé yakwyádi kát át ñuyaawagoowún héen kát.
People used to travel around in flat-bottomed canoes in the rivers in Yakutat.
• át yawsigóo | --- | áy̌ yasagoo
they swam to it | --- | they swim to it (regularly).
P-t~ ya-s-goo~ (ø motion)
for sea mammals to swim in a school to P
·Áa atoosçeiwú yé áwé kéet haa daat yawsigóo. The killer whales came
around where we were gillnetting.

gooch

small hill; mound, knoll
·Gooch shakéex' wutusiteen wé sheech dzísk'w. We saw the cow moose
on top of the hill.
·Gooch litká aadé duwatéen wé çooch. The wolf on the ridge of the hill is
visible.

,

G

GOOK
• awshigóok | ashigóok | --s/he learned how to do it | s/he knows how to do it | ---.
O-S-sh-góok (ga state)
for S to know, learn how to do O
·K'idéin ashigóok kakúxaa layeiý. He knows how to build bailers really
well.
·Náakw yís kayaaní ashigóok, áx' ñu.aa akwdliýéitl' ñaa ý'éiý aa
wuteeyí. He knows medicinal plants but he is afraid to give them to anyone.
GOOŇ
• aadé

(ha)s loowagooñ | aadé yaa (ha)s lunagúñ | aadé
yoo (ha)s luwagúñk
they ran there | they are running there | they run there (regularly).
P-dé O-lu-ø-gooñ~ (na motion)
for (plural) O to run toward P
·Yóode loowagooçu dzísk'w a ítde akñwal'óon. I will go hunting those
moose that ran over that way.

• át

has luwagúñ | aadé yaa (ha)s lunagúñ | áý has
loogook

they ran to it | they are running to it | they run to it (regularly).
P-t~ O-lu-ø-gooñ~ (ø motion)
for (plural) O to run to P
·Kéi dañinji s'áaxw tlein a tayeet ñaa luwagúñ séew tóodáý. People
ran under the big umbrella out of the rain.
• has loowagooñ | yaa has lunagúñ | yoo has luwagúñk
they ran | they are running | they run (regularly).
O-lu-ø-gooñ~ (na motion)
for (plural) O to run
·Jáaji kát yaa has lunagúñ. They are running on snowshoes.
·Yaa ñaa lunagúçu a kayéik has aawa.áý. They heard the sound of
people running.
• a ítý has loowagooñ | a ítý yaa (ha)s lunagúñ | a ítý

yoo (ha)s luwagúñk
they ran after it | they are running after it | they run after it (regularly).
N ítý O-lu-ø-gooñ~ (na motion)
for (plural) O to run after N
·Watsíx ítý yaa lunagúñ wé çooch. The wolves are chasing after the
caribou.

goon

spring (of water)

·Aý éek' si.áat'i héen goondáý ayáayin. My brother used to pack cold water from a spring.

góon

gold
·Wé ñáa góon awsiteen héenák'w táade. The man saw gold at the bottom of the creek.

,

,

G

·Góon dáanaa een áwé kawduwat'íý' aý jeeyís yá kées. This bracelet was pounded out of a gold coin for me.

a góon

portage, passage across it; its isthmus

du góos

privates (of female); vulva; vagina

góos'

cloud cover; sky, cloudy sky
·Góos' tóonáý ayatéen. She sees it through the clouds.
·Tlél góos' ñuwustee tatgé. There weren't clouds yesterday.

GÓOS'
• ñoowligóos' | ñuligóos' | kei ñulagóos'ch
it was cloudy | it's cloudy | it gets cloudy (regularly).
ñu-l-góos' (ga state)
for the sky to be cloudy

goos' shú

horizon
gus'shú
·Gus'shóode duwatéen wé çagaan. The sun is visible on the horizon.
·Gus'shóode ýaatéen wé watsíx. I see the caribou on the horizon.

du goosh

his/her thumb
·Du goosh awlichún. He hurt his thumb.
·Wudix'ís' du goosh. His thumb is swollen.

a gooshí

its dorsal fin (of killerwhale)
·Ch'as a gooshí duwatéen wé kéet. Only the dorsal fin of the killerwhale is visible.
·Jinkaat kéet gooshí ayatéen wé ñáa shaan. The old man sees ten killerwhale dorsal fins.

gooshúçunáý

nine (people)

gooshúññáý

gooshúñ

nine
·Gooshúñ dáanaa yéi ý'alitseen wé x'úx'. The book costs nine dollars.
·Gooshúñ yatee du keidlx'í. He has nine dogs.
1

GOOT

• aadáý woogoot | aadáý yaa nagút | aadáý yoo yagútk
he/she/it left there | he/she/it is leaving there | he/she/it leaves there (regularly).
P-dáý S-ø-goot~ (na motion)
for (singular) S to walk, go (by walking or as general term) away from P
·Ñaa yat'éináý hít yeedáý woogoot. He left the house when no one was looking.
• aadé woogoot | aadé yaa nagút | aadé yoo yagútk
he/she/it went there | he/she/it is going there | he/she/it goes there (regularly).
P-dé S-ø-goot~ (na motion)
for (singular) S to walk, go (by walking or as general term) toward P
·Hoon daakahídidéi nagú káaxweiçáa! Go to the store for some coffee!

,

Dictionary of Tlingit

·Hinyaa Ñwáan ýánde woogoot wé shaawát. The woman went to visit
the Klawock people.
• aaçáa woogoot | aaçáa yaa nagút | aaçáa yoo yagútk
s/he went to get it | s/he is going to get it | s/he goes to get it (regularly).
P-çaa S-ø-goot~ (na motion)
for (singular) S to go after P, go seeking P (on foot)
Note that -çaa takes the opposite tone of the final syllable of
the noun that it attaches to. Hence: kanat'áçaa "(going) after
blueberries", but shaawçáa "(going) after gumboots".
·Was'x'aan tléiçuçáa woogoot aý tláa. My mom walked to get
salmonberries.
• anaý yaawagút | anaý yaa wunagút | anaý yaa gútch
he/she/it walked through it | he/she/it is walking through it | he/she/it walks
through it (regularly).
P-náý ya-u-S-ø-goot~ (ø motion)
for (singular) S to walk, go (by walking or as general term) through P
This verb can be used metaphorically to indicate that
someone has pulled through an illness: A tóonáý yaawagút "s/he
got through it (an illness, eg.)".
·Yat'éex'i gaaw a tóonáý yiyagút. You walked through that period of hard
time.
• át uwagút | aadé yaa nagút | áý goot
he/she/it arrived there | he/she/it is going there | he/she/it goes there (regularly).
P-t~ S-ø-goot~ (ø motion)
for (singular) S to arrive at P, go to P (by walking or as general term)
·Nukshiyáan çaatáa ý'éit ugootch. The mink walks into the mouth of the
trap every time.
·Du séek' du ýánt uwagút. Her daughter came to her.
• át woogoot | --- | át yoo yagútk
he/she/it is walking around there; he/she/it walked around there | --- | he/she/it
walks around there (regularly).
P-t S-ø-goot~ (na motion)
for (singular) S to walk, go (by walking or as general term) around at P
·X'at'daayéejayi héenák'w át nagútch. The black turnstone walks around
in shallow water.
·Héen wantóot woogoot wé gus'yadóoli. The sandpiper is walking around
the riverbank.
• áý woogoot | áý yaa nagút | áý yoo yagútk
he/she/it walked along it | he/she/it is walking along it | he/she/it walks along it
(regularly).
P-ý S-ø-goot~ (na motion)
for (singular) S to walk, go (by walking or as general term) along P
·Yá neechý yaa neegúdi yei kçisatéen yá katóok. As you walk along
this shoreline you will see this cave.
·Yeedát ñuyak'éi çaatáa yéi daané yís yá kaxwaan káý yaa nagúdi.
Today the weather is good for walking out on the frost to check the traps.

,

• ayawdigút | yaa ayandagút | awudagútý
s/he turned back | s/he is turning back | s/he turns back (regularly).
a-ya-u-S-d-goot~ (ø motion)
for (singular) S to turn back, go back (by walking or as general term)

• daak uwagút | daak yaa nagút | daak gútch
he/she/it walked into the open | he/she/it is walking into the open | he/she/it walks
into the open (regularly).
daak S-ø-goot~ (ø motion)
for (singular) S to walk, go (by walking or as general term) into the open

·Wé ñaa sháade háni ñaa ýáni daak uwagút. The leader came out to the
people.

·Has du yáa daak uwagút wé xóots tlein kanat'á has a.éeni. While
they were picking blueberries, the brown bear came face to face with them.

• gági uwagút | gági yaa nagút | gági gútý
he/she/it emerged | he/she/it is emerging | he/she/it emerges (regularly).
gági S-ø-goot~ (ø motion)
for (singular) S to emerge, walk out into the open

·Yá ñut'aayçáa gági ugootch yee éesh. During the warm season your
father would come out.

• héide yaawagút | héide yaa wunagút | héide yaa

gútñ
s/he moved over that way | s/he is moving over that way | s/he moves over that
way (regularly).
héide ya-u-S-ø-goot~ (ø motion)
for (singular) S to move over (away from speaker)

• a ítý woogoot | a ítý yaa nagút | --he/she/it followed it | he/she/it is following it | ---.
N ítý yaa S-ø-goot~ (ga motion)
for (singular) S to follow N (on foot)
Note that the preverb yaa does not occur in the perfective
form.

·Wéiý yaa na.ádi watsíx, xóots a ítý yaa nagút. A grizzly bear is
walking behind the herd of caribou going that way.

·Wé yées ñáa du húnýw ítý yaa nagút. The young man's older brother is
walking along behind him.

• ñut woogoot | ñut kei nagút | ñut kei gútch
s/he got lost | s/he is getting lost | s/he gets lost (regularly).
ñut S-ø-goot~ (ga motion)
for (singular) S to get lost (on foot)

• a náñ woogoot | a náñ yaa nagút | a náñ yoo yagútk
s/he left it behind | s/he is leaving it behind | s/he leaves it behind (regularly).
P-náñ S-ø-goot~ (na motion)
for (singular) S to leave P behind, walk away from P

·Çalsaayít áwé du yéi jineiyí a náñ woogoot. She went away from her
work so that she could rest.

G

·A náñ yaa nagúdi yaa shukanashéen. She is singing as she is leaving it behind.
• --- | yaa nagút | ----- | s/he is walking along | ---.
yaa S-ø-gút (ga motion)
for (singular) S to be walking along, going along (by walking or as a general term)
This is an example of a progressive epiaspectual paradigm
(Leer, 91), which basically means that all forms are based on the
progressive aspect. The progressive epiaspect is characterized by:
1)having the yaa preverb in all forms, 2)having no perfective form,
and 3)denotes semantically a continuous transition from one
location or state to another.
·Áa agaýtool'oon yé yinaadé yaa gagú! Walk toward the place we will hunt!
·A wáný áwé yaa gagútch wé kaxéel' teen. He walks on the edge of trouble.
• yaaý woogoot | --- | yaaý yei gútch
s/he went aboard | --- | s/he goes aboard (regularly).
yaaý S-ø-goot~ (ça motion)
for (singular) S to go aboard (a boat)

gootl

bump, lump, hump, mound
·Gootl kát áa wé çáý. The rabbit is sitting on a mound.
·Gootl kanaý yawjik'én wé naaças'éi. The red fox jumped over a mound.

a goowú

its stump, butt end (of tree or other plant)
·Wé aas goowú káa woonook. She sat on that tree stump.
·Wé aas goowú aaý aawas'úw. He chopped off that tree stump.

gooý

slave
·Gooý ñaa jeex' yéi téeyin. People used to have slaves.
·Ch'áakw gooý shayadahéinin. There were lots of slaves long ago.

a gúgu

its antenna (of radio)
·Yóo tliyaa aasdéi ksaxát wéi kaxées' aý at shí ñóok gúgu yís! Attach
the wire to that tree over there for my radio antenna!

du gúk

his/her ear

·Ñínaa teen aawatáñ du gúk. She pierced her ear with a quill.
·Du gúkx' tsú yéi aa wduwa.oo wéi s'aañ ñ'anooý. They put the small bone labret in his ear too.

guk kajaash

earring
·A k'ishataaçaní yéi ndu.eich guk kajaashí yís. Its quills are used for earrings.
·Guk kajaash yéi aya.óo. She is wearing earrings.

gukkudayáat'

donkey
·Yaa at nayáan wé gukkudayáat'. The donkey is packing things.

,

,

a gukshatú

G

(in) the corner of it

a gukshitú (An)

gúkshi

corner
·Gúkshi yan sa.ín wé kañáshýi a káa yéi tuwa.oowu káast! Put the barrel we put the steamed berries in in the corner!

a gukshitú (An)

(in) the corner of it
a gukshatú
·Du hídi gukshitú niyaadé áwé aas anaý akaawahaa. He planted the tree toward the corner of his house.
·Wé hít gukshitúdáý kasixát wé kaxées'. The wire runs from the corner of that house.

guk tl'éinýw

earring; yarn dangling from the ears that sways during

dancing

du gukyikk'óoý'u

his/her earwax

guk.át

earring
guk.édi (C)
·Du guk.ádi yaayí ñut akaawaçéex'. She lost one of her earrings.
·Aý léelk'w jeeyís áyá kaýwaa.oo yá kanéist guk.át. I bought these cross earrings for my grandmother.

gúñl'

swan
gáñl'
·Gúñl' wéit wusikwaan. Swans are swimming around there.
·Gúñl' dleit yáý daçaatee. Swans are white.

Gunalchéesh!

Thank you!
·Gunalchéesh aý ý'éit yeeysa.aaýí. Thank you all for listening to me.
·Wé haa sháade háni "gunalchéesh" haa jeeyís yéi yanañéich. Our leader says "thank you" for us.

gúnl'

growth on the trunk of a tree, burl
·Gúnl' aaý aawaxaash. He cut the burl off.
·Gúnl' yéi aawa.oo nadáakw aýlayeiýít. He used a burl to make a table.

gunýaa

abalone
·Gunýaa yaka.óot' aawa.oo. She bought abalone buttons.
·Gunýaa yaka.óot' du l.uljíni kát akaawañáa. She sewed the abalone buttons on her vest.

gus'k'iñwáan l'oowú

oak
·Gus'k'iñwáan l'oowú teen wududliyéý wé nadáakw. The table is made of oak.

Gus'k'iyee ñwáan

White, European, Caucasian (man or person)

Gus'k'eeñwáan

,

Dictionary of Tlingit

gus'yadóoli

sandpiper
·Gus'yadóoli taakw.eetíx' haaý kalyeech. Sandpipers fly here in the early summer.
·Héen wantóot woogoot wé gus'yadóoli. The sandpiper is walking around the riverbank.

gus'yé kindachooneidí

pigeon or dove
·Tusconx' áwé aa saýwaa.áý gus'yé kindachooneidí. I heard some doves in Tuscon.

gút

dime
·Tléix' gút akaawahées'. He borrowed one dime.
·Gút akawdit'ei. She found herself a dime.

Gutéiý'

Chugach Eskimo

at gutú

woods; bush; brush, underbrush
at gatú (T), et getú (C)
·Wé çaatáa yéi daanéiyi at gutóodáý daak uwagút. The trapper came out of the bush.
·Wéi Sheet'kaadáý adátx'i at gutóox' áwé has du ée at dultóow. The kids from Sitka are taught out in the wilderness.

at gutu.ádi

thing of the woods
·Wáa yateeyi yéix' at gutu.ádi çalsháatadiý dulyéých. Sometimes wild animals are held captive.

gútl

blunt arrow for stunning
·Yées aa gútl du jeet wududzitán. He was given a new blunt arrow.
·Gútl teen al'óon woogoot. He went hunting with a blunt arrow.

guwáatl'

short

gúx'aa

cup; can
gúx'waa
·Wé shaatk' gúx'aa kát cháayoo aý jeet awsi.ín. The young girl gave me tea in a cup.
·Gúx'aa kat'óott kaawadáa wé cháayoo. The cup is filled part way up with tea.

gu.aal

I hope; would that
·Gu.aal kwshé iwulýéidliñ. Bless you. (Lit: I hope you get lucky.)

,

,

Gw

« Gw »
gwáa

[expression of strong surprise]
gu.áa

GWAAL
• aawagwaal | agwáal | --s/he beat it | s/he beats it; s/he is beating it | ---.
O-S-ø-gwaal~ (ga act)
for S to beat O (esp. drum); for S to ring O (bell); for S to stab O
·Ch'a hú du woowká aawagwál. He pounded his own chest.
·Du ý'ás' aawagwál wé ñáa. That man socked him on the jaw.
• ayaawagwál | --- | ayagwálý
s/he hit him/her in the face | --- | s/he hits him/her in the face (regularly).
O-ya-S-ø-gwaal~ (ø event)
for S to hit O in the face (with fist), punch O
• sh wudigwál | sh dagwáal | sh dagwálý
it rang | it's ringing | it rings (regularly).
sh da-gwaal~ (ø act)
for a telephone or bell to ring
GWAAS'
• ñoowdigwás' | yaa ñundagwás' | ñudagwás'ý
it's foggy; it was foggy | it's getting foggy | it gets foggy (regularly).
ñu-d-gwáas'~ (ø event)
for the weather to be foggy
GWAATL
• át kaawagwátl | aadé yaa kanagwátl | áý kagwaatl
it rolled to it | it's rolling to it | it rolls to it (regularly).
P-t~ ka-ø-gwáatl~ (ø motion)
for a spherical object to roll to P
·Té géit kaawagwátl wé kooch'éit'aa. The ball rolled against a rock.

gwál

perhaps
·Gwál tleiñáa ýʼoos áwé a kaýyeedé. It must be twenty feet to the ceiling.

gwálaa

dagger; machete, long knife
·Yées aa gwálaa aawaýooý. He asked for a new dagger.
·Gwálaa teen chʼáalʼ aawasʼúw ñaa ýʼoos deiyí kaaý. He chopped
willows off the foot trail with a machete.

gwéil

bag; sack
·Nadáakw kát téen wé xʼúxʼ gwéil. The paper bag is lying on the table.
·Du jeeçáa koodáal du gwéili. He can handle the weight of his backpack.

,

Dictionary of Tlingit

a gwéinli

its hoof
·T'ooch' yáý yatee a gwéinli wé dzísk'w. The moose's hoof is black.
·S'igeidí çeiwú yís a gwéinli aaý awlixaash, wé watsíx. He cut the
hooves off the caribou for a beaver net.

,

,

Ç

« Ç »
çaa
-çaa

enough, acceptably
(distributed) in the area of; (going) after, (waiting) for; about the

time of
-çáa
The tone on the postposition -çaa is the opposite of that on
the final syllable of the noun which it attaches to.
·Ý'aan yáý kakéinçaa neelhoon! Go buy me some red yarn!
·Ñuk'éet' áwé gaýtoo.áat kalchaneit tléiçuçáa. We are going to pick
mountain ash berries.

çáach

mat, doormat; rug
·Wé du tuwáa sigóowu çáach aawa.oo. She bought the rug she wanted.
·Ý'aan yáý kawdiyés' wé çáach. The rug is colored red.

çaañ

lynx

Çaanaýteidí

Gaanaxteidí, locally called "Frog"; a clan of the Raven
moiety whose principal crest is the Frog

ÇAAS'
• --- | kadliçáas' | ----- | it's striped | ---.
ka-d-l-çáas' (state)
for something to be striped
This verb only occurs in the imperfective.

·Haadaadóoshi kadliçáas'. Tigers are striped.

çaat

sockeye salmon; red salmon
·Ñúnáý yak'éi wé çaat. The sockeye salmon is really good.
·Jikañáas' káý ashayaawatée wé çaat atx'aan hídi yeex'. She hung the
sockeye salmon on the stick in the smokehouse.

çaatáa

trap (esp. steel trap)
·Nukshiyáan çaatáa ý'éit ugootch. The mink walks into the mouth of the
trap every time.
·Yeedát ñuyak'éi çaatáa yéi daané yís yá kaxwaan káý yaa nagúdi.
Today the weather is good for walking out on the frost to check the traps.

çaatáa yéi daanéiyi

trapper
·Aý éesh çaatáa yéi daanéiyiý satéeyin. My dad was a trapper.
·Wé çaatáa yéi daanéiyi at gutóodáý daak uwagút. The trapper came
out of the bush.

,

Ç

çáatl

pilot bread
·Wé çáatl aý tuwáa sigóo. I want the pilot bread
·Çáatl aawak'ít'. He finished the pilot bread.

çáax'w

herring eggs
·Wé s'íx' çáax'w a káa yéi yatee. There are herring eggs on that plate.
·Haaw héende awli.aat çáax'w káý. She put branches in the water for herring eggs.

çaaý

crying, weeping
·çaaý shí teen áwé yaawaxeex wé ñu.éex'. A cry song took place at the potlatch.

ÇAAÝ
• awdziçáaý | asçáaý | yei asçáaých
s/he asked for it | s/he is asking for it | s/he asks for it (regularly).
O-S-d-s-çaaý (ça act)
for S to cry for, ask for O
·Atýá daakahídix' gishoo taayí ña k'wát' awdziçáaý. She ordered bacon and eggs at the restaurant.
• kawdiçaaý | kadaçáaý | --he/she/it cried out | he/she/it is crying out | ---.
ka-S-d-çaaý~ (ga act)
for S to cry loudly (of child, or person in great pain), to cry out or scream (in fear or pain)
·Wé dóosh kadaçáaý. The cat is crying.
• wooçaaý | çáaý | kei çáých
s/he cried | s/he cries; s/he is crying | s/he cries (regularly).
S-ø-çaaý~ (ga act)
for (singluar) S to cry

a çádzi

its hindquarters; thigh
·Dzísk'u çádzi yaa anayéin. He is packing a moose hindquarter.
·Watsíx çádzi yei akanaxásh. She is cutting up a caribou hindquarter.

çagaan

sun
·Wé çagaan kei yaséich wé ñeiý'ét ñuwuhaayí. The sun lifts its face when dawn breaks.
·Çagaan daak uwaxíx wé séew ítdáý. The sun came out after the rain.

çagaan kas'úkwýu

sun-dried

çagaan ý'usyee

sunbeam; ray of sunlight
·Wé ts'ats'ée çagaan ý'usyeet .áa. That song bird is sitting in the ray of sunlight.
·Wé shaa shakéede duwatéen wé çagaan ý'usyee. The ray of sunlight can be seen on the mountain top.

,

,

Ç

çákw

dried and hard; stiff (as canvas, dry fish)
·Wé ýaat çákw yáý uwaxúk. That fish is dried stiff.
·Wé yées xwaasdáa çákw yáý yatee. The new tent is stiff.

çalçaañu

wilderness; the bush
katñaañú, çwalçañú (At), kalçañú (T)

çalsháatadi

captive
çalsháatedi (C)
·Wé ñáa neech káx' áwé çalsháatadiý wududliyéý. The man was made captive for nothing.
·Wáa yateeyi yéix' at gutu.ádi çalsháatadiý dulyéých. Sometimes wild animals are held captive.

çaltú

pocket
·Al'óon wugoodí uýgannáas' du çaltóode ayaawa.oo. When he was going hunting, he put matches in his pocket.

çaltulítaa

pocket knife
ñatltulítaa (AtT), galtulítaa (C)
·Yées aa çaltulítaa du léelk'w jeeyís aawa.oo. He bought his grandpa a new pocketknife.
·Yalik'áts' du çaltulítayi. His pocketknife is sharp.

Çalyáý Ñwáan

people of Kaliakh River (Cape Yakataga to Controller
Bay)
·Çalyáý Ñwáan áwé Yaakwdáat ñwáan ýoox' yéi s yatee. The Kaliakh
River people live among the Yakutat people.
·Çalyáý Ñwáan áwé Çalyáý Kaagwaantaaný has sitee. The Kaliakh
River people are the Kaliakh River Kaagwaantaan.

çánch

tobacco
·Hoon daakahídidáý çánch has aawa.oo. They bought tobacco from the
store.
·Çánch áwé aan yéi daaduné wéi kat'éý'aa yeit. He uses the mortar for
pounding his tobacco.

çaneiý

recovery; salvation
·Lingít ý'éináý yoo ý'atánk a.áýji çaneiý yáý áwé du ée yatee.
Hearing the Tlingit language is like salvation to her.
·Laaxw eetí wé ñaa jeedáý atýá has du çaneiýíý wusitee. After the
famine, the food given to them became their salvation.

çanook

petrel
·Wé çanook has du déint wudiñeen. The petrel is flying around near them.
·Tléil yá dañkáx' yéi utí wé çanook. Here in the Inland we don't have any
petrels.

du çáts

his/her buttocks, thighs
·Du çáts kalshúk'ý. His thighs cramp regularly.
·Du çátsiçáa wootee yá kawáat. There are tumors all over her thigh.

'

Ç

Dictionary of Tlingit

du çatsý'áak

his/her crotch; between his/her legs

çáý

rabbit
·Wé çáý dleit yáý ýasitee. The rabbit is white.
·Xáanaa atýaayí yís çáý akawlis'úk. She fried rabbit for dinner.

çayéis'

iron, tin
çiyéis', iñyéis'
·Kaduch'áak'w lítaa sákw yak'éiyi aa çayéis' neil tí! Bring home a good
piece of iron for a carving knife!
·Çayéis' ñ'wátl dañyadál. Iron pots are heavy.

çayéis' háatl'i

rust
·Çayéis' a háatl'iý yóo siteek. Iron rusts.

çayéis' hít

jail
çiyéis' hít
·Ch'áakw yéi kdunéek çayéis' hítdáý áwé haa ýoot yawduwaýáa
Anóoshi. It is told that long ago, Russians were brought among us from jail.
·Çayéis' hítde kawduwanáa. He was sent to jail.

çayéis' layeiýí

blacksmith
çiyéis' layeiýí, çiyéis' leyeiýí (C)
·Çayéis' layeiýí jeedé ý'awditaan du éet çadasheet. She telephoned the
blacksmith to help her.
·Çayéis' layeiýíý naýsateeyít sgóoni yoo uwagút. He went to school to
become an engineer.

çayéis' tíx'

cable
çiyéis' tíx'
·Wé çayéis' tíx' áwé du jín táakt yawdiçích. The steel cable poked him in
the hand.
·Çunayéide kwditlawu çayéis' tíx' du jeewú. He has steel cables of
different sizes.

çayéis' t'éiý'i

blacksmith
·Çayéis' t'éiý'i sháade háni haat ñuwatín tatgé. The chief blacksmith traveled here yesterday.
·Çayéis' t'éiý'íý naýsateet áwé. She is becoming a blacksmith.

ÇEECH
• aadé yawdiçeech | --- | aadé yoo yadiçíchk
it pierced it | --- | it pierces it (regularly).
P-dé ya-d-çeech~ (na motion)
for a sharp object to pierce, enter, prick P; for an animal to bite P
·Táax'ál' x'aan áwé aý tl'eiñ tóode yawdiçeech. The needle point poked my finger.
• át yawdiçích | --- | áý yadaçeech
it pierced it | --- | it pierces it (regularly).
P-t~ ya-d-çeech~ (ø motion)

,

,

Ç

for a sharp object to pierce, enter, prick P; for an animal to bite P
·Wé çayéis' tíx' áwé du jín táakt yawdiçích. The steel cable poked him in the hand.
·Du tl'eiñt yawdiçiji sheey kañáas'i áx' wudliñít'. It got infected where the splinter poked her finger.
• át yawdliçích | --- | áý yalçeech
they peirced it | --- | they pierce it (regularly).
P-t~ ya-d-l-çeech~ (ø motion)
for (plural) sharp objects to pierce, enter, prick P
·Wé ýalak'ách' ýaawú aý keidlí ý'éit yawdliçích. The porcupine quills stuck in my dogs mouth.

çéechadi

windfall; tree lying in the woods
·Dei kát la.ádi çéechadi aaý yéi awsinei. He removed the windfall lying in the road.
·Gán yís akaawaxaash wé çéechadi. She cut up the dead trees for firewood.

çeeçách'

swing; hammock
·Tíx' ña x'óow tin çeeçách' awliyéý t'ukanéiyi jeeyís. She made a hammock for the baby with rope and a blanket.
·Dzaas áwé yéi akçwa.oo çeeçách' akawusneiyí. She will use string when she crochets a hammock.

çéejadi

windfall; dead tree(s) or brush that has fallen
çéejedi (C)

ÇEEL
• yaawdiçíl | yaa yandaçíl | yadaçílý
it's dull | it's getting dull | it gets dull (regularly).
ya-d-çeel~ (ø event)
for an edge to be blunt, dull
·Yaawdiçíl du túlayi. His drill became dull.
ÇEEL'
• ayaawaçíl' | ayaçéel' | ayaçíl'ý
s/he sharpened it | s/he is sharpening it | s/he sharpens it (regularly).
O-ya-S-ø-çéel'~ (ø act)
for S to sharpen O (with a grindstone)
·Du t'eiýí ayaawaçíl'. He sharpened his fish hooks.
ÇEET
• aawaçéet | --- | yóo ayaçéetk
it's pouring rain; it poured rain | --- | it pours rain (regularly).
a-ø-çéet (na event)
for rain, hail, snow to fall (often hard, in dark rainstorm)
·Ñúnáý ýat wuditl'ák', kaklahéen áyá aawaçéet. I'm so wet - wet snow
is coming down hard.

,

Ç

Dictionary of Tlingit

• ñukawjiçít | yaa ñukanashçit | ñukashçítý
it's dark | it's getting dark | it gets dark (regularly).
ñu-ka-j-çéet~ (ø event)
for the sky to be dark
The ñu- prefix refers to weather or the sky in general.
Without the ñu- prefix, this verb can also refer to darkness of a
room. For example: kawjiçít "it's dark".
·Wé kóoñ a yee kawjiçít. It is dark inside the cellar.
ÇEEX'
• akaawaçéex' | --- | yoo akayaçix'k
s/he donated it | --- | s/he donates it (regularly).
O-ka-S-ø-çéex' (na event)
for S to donate O (esp. money); for S to load O (gun), put bullet in; for S to shoot
O (basketball)
To include the recipient of the donation in the sentence,
you would use: du jeet "to him/her", as in: Du jeet akaawaçéex'.
"S/he donated it to him/her." If the recipient is an organization,
you would use: a kagéi yís "to it", replacing the a with the name of
the organization. For example, Wé Salvation Army kagéi yís
akaawaçéex'. "S/he donated it to the Salvation Army."
• át kawdiçíx' | --- | áý kadaçéex'
s/he contributed to it | --- | s/he contributes to it (regularly).
P-t~ ka-S-d-çéex'~ (ø motion)
for S to donate, contribute, add to P
·A ýoonéet kaýwdiçíx'. I added to it.
• kawdiçéex' | yaa kandaçíx' | yoo kdiçíx'k
s/he contributed | s/he is contributing | s/he contributes (regularly).
ka-S-d-çéex'~ (na event)
for S to donate, contribute
• kei akaawaçíx' | --- | kei akaçíx'ch
s/he threw it | --- | s/he throws it (regularly).
kei O-ka-S-ø-çéex'~ (ø motion)
for S to throw O (esp. ball) up in the air
·Kei kawduwaçix'i té du káak't kaawaxíx. The rock that was thrown hit
him on the forehead.
• ñut aawaçéex' | ñut kei anaçíx' | ñut kei açíx'ch
s/he lost it | s/he is losing it | s/he loses it (regularly).
ñut O-S-ø-çéex'~ (ga motion)
for S to lose O
• ñut akaawaçéex' | --- | ñut kei akaçíx'ch
s/he lost it | --- | s/he loses it (regularly).
ñut O-ka-S-ø-çéex'~ (ga motion)
for S to lose O (round, spherical object)
·T'áa kát ñushí aý jeeyís - ñut kaýwaaçéex' aý kawóot ka.íshayi!

,

,

Ç

Look on the floor for me - I lost my needle!
·Du guk.ádi yaayí ñut akaawaçéex'. She lost one of her earrings.

çeey

bay
çeiy (TC)
·Aanñáawu Çeeyx' áwé has saligaaw ñúnáý wé kaçeet. The loons are
really loud in Ankau Bay.

çeey kanaý ñutées'

ratfish
·Tléil ýwasakú çeey kanaý ñutées' yóo duwasáagu ýáat. I don't know
the fish called ratfish.
·Duýá gé çeey kanaý ñutées'? Are ratfish edible?

çeey tá

head of the bay
·Çeey tá héen yaa nalt'íx'. The water at the head of the bay is freezing.
·Çeey tá déilit awsiñúý du yaagú. She drove her boat to the head of the
bay.

a çei

enclosed within (the folds of) it, between the folds, covers,
walls of it
·X'aa çeiyí niyaadé kei ayawli.át. He steered (his boat) toward the inside of
the point.
·Wé x'aa çei xóon tléil aan utí. The North Wind does not bother the shelter
of the point.

ÇEI
• kawliçéi | kaliçéi | kei klaçéich
he/she/it was fancy | he/she/it is fancy | he/she/it gets fancy (regularly).
O-ka-l-çéi (ga state)
for O to be fancy, prominent (esp. in appearance), conspicuous, attracting
attention
·Kalaçéi nooch aasgutú yeist ñuwuhaayí. The forest is brilliant when
fall comes.
• --- | shakliçéi | ----- | she is pretty | ---.
O-sha-ka-l-çéi (ga state)
for O to be pretty, cute
This verb is used to describe a beautiful woman or
something cute such as a puppy or kitten. It isn't generally used
to describe pretty objects such as beadwork.
• --- | sh tukdliçéi | ----- | s/he is proud | ---.
sh tu-ka-S-d-l-çéi (ga state)

for S to be proud (esp. of oneself), conceited; for S to be particular, picky, snooty
This verb only occurs in the imperfective. Note that it can
have a negative connotation, meaning "to be conceited." It can
also be used to indicate that one is proud of something or
someone by inserting N kaaý "of N" into the sentence. Usually the
N represents something or someone that the individual has a

,

personal stake in. For example: A kaaý sh tukdliçéi du dachýánx'iyán. "She is proud of her grandchildren." Otherwise, another verb is used: Du toowú kliçéi du kaadáý. "She is proud of him."
·A kaaý sh tukdliçéi du tsaa doogú at xáshdi téel. She is proud of her seal skin moccasins.
• du

toowú kawliçéi | du toowú kliçéi | du toowú kei klaçéich

s/he became proud | s/he is proud | s/he gets proud (regularly).
N toowú ka-l-çéi (ga state)
for N to be proud of, highly pleased with
To add who one is proud of in the sentence, use: N kaadáý
"of N". For example: Mary toowú kliçéi John kaadáý. "Mary is proud of John."

çeiçách'

swing, hammock
çeeçách' (T)

ÇEIN
• aadé awdliçein | --- | --he/she/it looked there | --- | ---.
P-dé a-S-d-l-çein~ (na motion)
for S to look in the direction of P
-çeen~ (An)
·Gáandei aneelçein çayéis'çaa! Look outside for some iron!
·I léelk'u keekándei aneelçein - ýaat yéi adaané! Go check on your grandpa - he's working on fish!

çeitl'

thick mucus, phlegm

ÇEIWOO
• awdziçeiwú | asçeiwú | --s/he seined | s/he is seining | ---.
a-S-s-çeiwú (na act)
for S to fish with net, seine
·Atoosçeiwú atyátx'i latíni ýaný has çañéech aý yátx'i. When we are gillnetting my children stay with a babysitter.
·Áa atoosçeiwú yé áwé kéet haa daat yawsigóo. The killer whales came around where we were gillnetting.

çeiwú

fish net; seine net

çeiwóo (C)
·Kawdis'éil' aý çeiwú. My net is all torn up.
·Çeiwú wooch yáý awsinei tle daak ashakaawañúý. She straightened
the net out and then she set it.

a çeiwú

its web (of spider)

,

,

Ç

a çeiyí

its edible part (of clam)
·Gáal' çeiyí duýá. Someone is eating clam muscles.
·Wé gáal' çeiyí aan nagú i léelk'w ýánde! Go with the clams to your
grandparent!

çeiy (TC)

bay
çeey

çíñs

fish hung over the fire to cook
·Ýáat yádi çíñs yís akaawaxaash. She cut the whitefish to barbeque over
the fire.
·Yées t'á çíñsi sitgawsáanx' has aawaýáa. They ate fresh king salmon
barbequed over the fire at noon.

çíñsaa (T)

fish roasted whole, strung up by its tail over the fire and
twirled periodically
çíñsi (AtT)

çíl'

cliff
·Çíl' yáý kanaadaa wé héen. The water is flowing down the face of the rock
cliff.
·Çíl' yáý kei naltl'ét' wé yadák'w. The young boy is climbing the cliff face.

çíl'aa

grindstone
·K'wát' yáý kaaxát du çíl'ayi. His grindstone is shaped like an egg.

·Du gwéili tóode aawatee wé çíl'aa. He put the grindstone in his bag.

çítçaa

pine needles, spruce needles
·Çítçaa ayaýsaháa yóode woogoot. She went over there to gather spruce needles.
·Náakw yís awsitáa wé çítçaa. He boiled the pine needles for medicine.

çíý'jaa ñóok

organ, piano
·Sh tóo awdlitóow çíý'jaa ñóok al.áýji. He taught himself to play the piano.
·Ý'agáax' daakahídix' ali.áých wé çíý'jaa ñóok. He plays the organ at the Church.

ÇOO
• awliçoo | alçéikw | yei alçwéich
s/he wiped it | s/he wipes it; s/he's wiping it | s/he wipes it (regularly).
O-S-l-çoo~ (ça act)
for S to wipe, mop, clean O by wiping
·Wé ýéel' du jíndáý awliçoo. She wiped the slime off her hands.
·Aaý gatí wéi kaxíl'aa kadushxeet t'áa yá çalçú! Pick up the eraser and clean the chalkboard!

çooch

wolf
·Watsíx áa káa daak has awlikél' wé çooch. The wolves chased the caribou out onto the lake.

,

Ç

·Gooch litká aadé duwatéen wé çooch. The wolf on the ridge of the hill is visible.

a çóot

without it; lacking it
·A çóot woogoot du s'áaxu. He went without his hat.
·Tléiñw çóot awsi.ée du sakwnéini. She cooked her bannock without berries.

ÇOOTL
• akaawaçútl | akaçóotl | akaçútlý
s/he mashed it | s/he is mashing it | s/he mashes it (regularly).
O-ka-S-ø-çootl~ (ø act)
for S to mash O by squeezing in the hand; for S to squeeze O tightly
·Du jintáak teen akaçútlý wé tléiñw. She mashes the berries with the palm of her hand.

Çunaaýoo Ñwáan

people of Dry Bay
·Yaakwdáatx' yéi has yatee yeedát Çunaaýoo Ñwáan. The Dry Bay people now live in Yakutat.
·Çunaaýoo Ñwáaný has sitee wé lingít. Those people are Dry Bay people.

çunakadeit

legendary sea monster
·Çunakadeit daat tlaagú daýñudzitee. There are legends about sea monsters.
·Tléil yáax' yéi aa utí çunakadeit. There are no sea monsters here.

Çunanaa

Athabaskan (Indian)
·Ýaldleit kinaa.át yéi aya.óo wé Çunanaa ñáa. That Athabaskan man is wearing a white fox overcoat.
·A ýoo aa Lingít Çunanaa has du ýoo ñuya.óo. Some Tlingits live among the Athabascans.

çunanaa tetl

punk wood, decayed dry wood

a çunayáade

differently from it
a çunayáadei, a çuwanyáade (An), a çunáade (C)

·Aadéi keenik yé çunayáade ýaatéen. I see it differently from the way you tell it.
·Wé naakéedáý lingít çunayáade yóo has ý'ali.átk. The people from the north speak differently.

çunayéi

beginning
çunéi
·Ñukawduyéil'i áwé Galyéýdei çunayéi uñooých wéi yaakw tlein.
The big boat would start traveling to the Kahliyet River when the weather was calm.

çunayéide

different
çunayéidei
·Çunayéide kwditlawu çayéis' tíx' du jeewú. He has steel cables of

,

,

Ç

different sizes.
·Çunayéide a daat sh tudinook yeedát. He feels differently about it now.

çunéi

start, begin
·Taan áa awsiteeni yé a niyaadé çunéi uwañúý. He started motoring in the direction he had seen the sea lion.
·Ñee.á shukát áwé çunéi gaýtooñóoý. We will start traveling before dawn.

du çushká

(on) his/her lap
·Wé shaawát du çushkáa yan awsi.ín du s'íx'i. The woman put her plate on her lap.
·Du dachýánk' du çushkáa kei awsinúk. He lifted his grandchild up onto his lap.

çuwakaan

deer
ñuwakaan (TC), ñuyakaan (At)
·Çuwakaan at xáshdi téel aý dachýánk' jeeyís aý tuwáa sigóo. I would like deer skin moccasins for my grandchild.
·Çuwakaan taayí kas'úkýu yís akaawaxaash. She cut up deer fat for frying.

çuwakaan yádi

fawn
·Çuwakaan yádi kajikáx'ý. A fawn is spotted.
·Wé çuwakaan yádi a tláa teen yóode yaa nashíx. The fawn is running over that way with its mother.

a çuwanyáade (An)

differently from it
a çunayáade, a çunáade (C)
·A çuwanyáadé ágé iyatéen? Do you see the difference?

,

« Çw »
çwáal'

fart
1

ÇWAAT'

• át wudiçwáat' | --- | át yoo diçwát'k
s/he is crawling around there; s/he crawled around there | --- | s/he crawls
around there (regularly).
P-t S-d-çwáat'~ (na motion)
for S (esp. child) to crawl around on hands and knees at P
·I yádi aý ý'usyeet wudiçwáat'. Your child is crawling around under my
feet.
• daañ wudiçwát' | --- | daañ daçwát'ch
s/he crawled away (from the open) | --- | s/he crawls away (from the open)
(regularly).
daañ S-d-çwáat'~ (ø motion)
for S (esp. child) to crawl up (from beach), away (from open) on hands and knees
·Tléi a x'aant áwé daañ wudiçwát' wé yadák'w. The young boy crawled
out the limb.

,

,

H

« H »
haa

our [possessive]
·Haa tláa hás ñútl'giçáa has na.átch has du ñ'eikaxwéini yís. Our
mothers send us for soil for their flowers.
·Haa kagéide yaa ana.át. People are coming toward us.

haa

us [object]
·Tle yeedát yáatý haa kaguýdayáa. We need to leave from here right now.

HAA
• akaawahaa | akahéiý | yoo akayaheiýk
s/he planted it | s/he is planting it | s/he plants it (regularly).
O-ka-S-ø-haa~ (na act)
for S to plant O
·Du hídi gukshitú áa akaawahaa wé ñ'eikaxwéin. She planted the

flowers at the corner of her house.

·Anahoo has akanahéijin. They used to plant turnips.

• akaawahaa | akahéiý | yoo akayaheiýk

s/he gardened | s/he is gardening | s/he gardens (regularly).

a-ka-S-ø-haa~ (na act)

for S to garden, dig

• akaawaháa | akaháa | --s/he dug it | s/he is digging it | ---.

O-ka-S-ø-háa~ (ø act)

for S to dig O

·Gáal' has akaháa. They are digging clams.

• át has yawdiháa | --- | áý has yadahaa

they crowded the place | --- | they crowd the place (regularly).

P-t~ O-ya-d-haa~ (ø motion)

for O (large numbers, esp. people, birds) to move in, come around to P

·K'isáani át yawdiháa. There's a crowd of young men there.

·Ldakát wooch ýoot has yawdiháa. Everybody came together.

• át ñuwaháa | aadé yaa ñunahéin | áý ñoohaa

it's time for it | it's getting to be time for it | the time comes for it (regularly).

P-t~ ñu-ø-haa~ (ø motion)

for the time to come for P

·Xáats'de yaa ñunahéin. It is becoming twilight.

·Shayadihéin tl'áxch' táakwde yaa ñunahéini. There are a lot of dead branches when it becomes winter.

• ayawsiháa | ayasahéiý | --s/he gathered it | s/he's gathering it | ---.

O-ya-S-s-haa~ (ø act)

'

for S to gather up, pick up, take up O
·Çítçaa ayaýsaháa yóode woogoot. She went over there to gather spruce needles.
·Ñ'áach' ayawsiháa. She gathered ribbon seaweed.
• du

éet ñuwaháa | du eedé yaa ñunahéin | du éeý
koohaa

it's his/her turn | his/her turn is coming up | s/he gets a turn (regularly).
N éet~ ñu-ø-haa~ (ø motion)
for N to have a turn
• du éet yaan uwaháa | --- | du éeý yaan haa
s/he is hungry | --- | s/he gets hungry (regularly).
N éet~ yaan ø-haa~ (ø event)
for N to be hungry
• kei akaawaháa | kei akanahéin | --s/he dug it up | s/he is digging it up | ---.
kei O-ka-S-ø-haa~ (ø motion)
for S to dig O up
·Tle hít tuwán áwé kóoñ áa kei has akaawaháa. Right next to the house they dug a pit.
·Kei akaawahaayi góon, aawahoon. He sold the gold that he mined.
• shayawdihaa | shayadihéin | --there got to be a lot | there are a lot | ---.
O-sha-ya-d-haa~ (na state)
for O to be many, plenty, lots
·Sgóonwaan atyátx'i has shayadihéin Yaakwdáatx'. There are a lot of school children in Yakutat.
·Wasóos wé akahéiýi jee shayadihéin. The farmer has lots of cows.
• --- | tlél gooháa | ----- | it's obvious | ---.
tlél ga-u-ø-háa (ga state)
for something to be obvious, clearly visible
Note that this verb is unique in that it requires the conjugation prefix (ga-) in all modes and only occurs in the negative. The negative imperfective tlél gooháa "it's obvious" is the most common form, although the negative future has also been documented.
·Tlél gooháa aadéi k'idéin dañéis'i yé. It's obvious how well she sews.

haadaadóoshi

man-eating feline; mountain lion; tiger, leopard
·Haadaadóoshi teen yéi jiné wé ñáa. That man is working with tigers.
·Haadaadóoshi kadliçáas'. Tigers are striped.

haadaaçoojí

man-eating animal; lion; tiger; man-eating wolf
·Haadaaçoojí éil' héen diyáanaý.áx' dul'óon. People hunt lions across

the ocean.
·Haadaaçoojí a ooýú dañdigéix'. Lion teeth are large.

,

,

H

1

HAAN

• --- | hán | ----- | s/he is standing | ---.
S-ø-hán (position)
for (singular) S to be standing
This verb only occurs in the imperfective. Note that a noun
phrase with (-t) postposition is used to indicate where one is
standing, but this noun phrase is not required by the verb. For
example, one could say: hán "s/he is standing", or: át hán "s/he is
standing there."
·A ý'anaa áwé át eehán. You are standing in its way.
·Du wañkas'óox' áwé át eehán. You're blocking his view.
• wudihaan | kei ndahán | kei dahánch
s/he stood up | s/he is standing up | s/he stands up (regularly).
S-d-haan~ (ga event)
for (singular) S to stand up, rise
·Ch'a çéçaa aaý kei dahánch. He tries to stand up from there (but is unable
to).
·Gunalchéesh yéi yanñañaat áyá ýwdihaan. I stood up to say thank you.
• yan uwahán | --- | yaý haan
s/he remained standing | --- | s/he keeps standing (regularly).
yan~ S-ø-haan~ (ø motion)
for (singular) S to keep standing
·I yoo ý'atángi káa yan hán! Stand on your words!
·A yaadéi nagú a tuwánx' yan hán! Walk to the face of it and stand beside
it!

haandé

hand it here, bring it here
haandéi
Although it has the postposition -dé and therefore looks like
an adverb, this word is unique in that it functions syntactically as
a predicate, replacing a verb in the sentence.
·Haandé wé ách at dusýa át! Hand me the fork!

HAAS'
• uwahás' | --- | yahás'kw
s/he is vomiting; s/he vomited | --- | s/he vomits (regularly).
O-ø-háas'~ (ø event)
for O to vomit

háas'

vomit; urge to vomit
·Háas' yáý sh tudinook. He feels like vomiting.
·Háas' du éet yéi uwanéi yá yagiyee. He has been vomiting today.

HAASH
• át wulihaash | --- | át yoo liháshk
it's floating around; it floated around | --- | he/she/it floats around (regularly).
P-t O-l-haash~ (na motion)

,

Dictionary of Tlingit

for O to float, drift around at P
·Héen shóot wulihaash wé kayaaní. The leaf floated around the edge of
the water.
• át wulihásh | aadé yaa nalhásh | áý lahaash
he/she/it drifted to it | he/she/it is drifting to it | he/she/it drifts to it (regularly).
P-t~ O-l-haash~ (ø motion)
for O to float, drift to P
·Heentu.eejí kát wulihásh du yaagú. Her boat drifted onto a reef.
·Tleidahéen áwé Yaakwdáatt aa wlihásh wé kanóox'. One time a turtle
floated to Yakutat.
• daak wulihásh | --- | --he/she/it drifted out to sea; he/she/it is drifting out to sea | --- | ---.
daak O-l-haash~ (ø motion)
for O to float, drift out to sea
·Du jináñ daak wulihásh wé ch'áal'. The willow drifted out away from
him.

haat~

hither, toward speaker
·Gus'yadóoli taakw.eetíx' haaý kalyeech. Sandpipers fly here in the early
summer.
·Eesháank' kaltéelñ áwé haat wujixíx aý dachýánk'. Poor thing, my
grandchild ran over here shoeless.

haat

current, tide
·Haat kei wudaayí tléil uýsatínch. He has not seen the tide rise yet.
·Haat kanadaayí géide kei nañúý. She is going against the current.

haat kool

whirlpool
·Haat kool héen yíkde duteen nooch. Whirlpools are visible in rivers.
·Éil' héenx' yéi daçaateeyi haat kool dañdigéix'. Whirlpools in the ocean
are large.

háatl'

feces; dung

haaw

bough, branch with needles on it, especially of hemlock
·Haaw héende awli.aat çáax'w káý. She put branches in the water for
herring eggs.
·Haaw yan awli.át a káa nçataayít. He put branches down so he could
sleep on them.

Haa yátx'u ée!

Poor baby!
This exclamation is used when a child hurts himself/herself
or when a child is upset.

Hadláa!

Good grief!
This exclamation is used in association with things
exaggerated or overdone, including an overdressed person, too
much food on a plate, or an exaggerated story.

,

,

H

has

they [subject]
s (optionally, after a vowel)
·Watsíx áa káa daak has awlikél' wé çooch. The wolves chased the
caribou out onto the lake.
·Nás'k yagiyee a kaanáý has yaawa.át. They walked for three days.

has

them [object]
s (optionally, after a vowel)
·K'idéin has jiduñéi katíý'aa s'aatí Dzántik'i Héenix'. Jailers are paid
well in Juneau.
·Gáanu hás, i yeeçáaý has sitee. They are outside waiting for you.

hás

[plural marker for kinship terms]
This word is categorized as an adjective in that it modifies a
noun. Hás is the plural marker for kinship terms.
·Haa tláa hás ñútl'giçáa has na.átch has du ñ'eikaxwéini yís. Our
mothers send us for soil for their flowers.
·Hoon daakahídidé has woo.aat aý séek' hás. My daughters have gone
to the store.

hás

they [independent]
·Gáanu hás, i yeeçáaý has sitee. They are outside waiting for you.

has du

their [possessive]

·Haa tláa hás ñútl'giçáa has na.átch has du ñ'eikaxwéini yís. Our mothers send us for soil for their flowers.

·Yeeytéen has du téiý' tóotý áyá toodé has yee uwaxích haa ñu.éex'i. You all can see that our hosts thank you from their hearts.

Ha.é!

[exclamation toward someone who is putting on airs in order to impress others]

hé

this/that (over here), the other
héi

HEEK
• ashawlihík | yaa ashanalhík | ashalahíký
s/he filled it | s/he is filling it | s/he fills it (regularly).
O-sha-S-l-heek~ (ø event)
for S to fill O (with solids or abstracts)
·Tláakw ashawlihík wé kadádzaa yeit. She filled the berry basket quickly.
·Ýáat teen áwé shawdudlihík wé kaxwénaa. The brailer bag was filled with salmon.
• shaawahík | yaa shanahík | shahíký
he/she/it is full | he/she/it is getting full | he/she/it gets full (regularly).
O-sha-ø-heek~ (ø event)
for O to be filled, be full (general and abstract)
·Haa a tóox' at dult'ix' át shaawahík dzísk'u dleeyí teen. Our freezer is full of moose meat.

,

Dictionary of Tlingit

·É! Shahíký haa cháli çaatáa yéi daatooneiyí. Check it out! When we
are out trapping, our storehouse is full.
• yan ashawlihík | --- | --s/he finished it | --- | ---.
yan~ O-sha-S-l-heek~ (ø motion)
for S to finish, complete O
·Yan ashawlihík yá haa tláach. This mother of ours has completed
everything.
·Ñaa ooý yéi daanéiyi yís sgóon yan ashawlihík She finished dentistry
school.
1

HEEN

• du éek' aawaheen | du éek' ayaheen | --s/he believed him/her | s/he believes him/her | ---.
N éek' a-S-ø-heen~ (ga state)
for S to believe, trust, believe in N
·Dikée aanñáawu du éek' atuwaheen. We believe in God.
2

HEEN

• yan uwahín | yánde yaa nahín | yaý heen
it swam ashore | it's swimming to shore | it swims ashore (regularly).
yan~ ø-heen~ (ø motion)
for sea animal to swim ashore
·Kóoshdaa haa eeçayáaknáý yan uwahín. The land otter swam through
our beachfront.

héen

water
·Aý éek' si.áat'i héen goondáý ayáayin. My brother used to pack cold
water from a spring.
·Ch'as héen ák.wé a kaadéi yóo yadudzixéik yá kat'ákýi? Is water all
that was put on these dried berries?

héen

river, stream, creek
·Héen kát jinaskwanchi át áwé wé atxaayí. The centipede swims on top
of the water.
·Héent wushiý'íl'. He slipped into the water.

héenák'w

creek; small stream
·X'at'daayéejayi héenák'w át nagútch. The black turnstone walks around
in shallow water.

·Wé ñáa góon awsiteen héenák'w táade. The man saw gold at the bottom of the creek.

héen gúx'aa
héeni

water dipper; ladle

into water

héen kanadaayí

current; tidal action
·Héen yík héen kanadaayí wáa yateeyi yéix' kuliýéitl'shán nooch. Sometimes currents in a river are dangerous.

,

,

H

héen sháak

head of river, stream
·Wé héen sháakx' áwé atx'aan hídi áa awliyéý. He built a smokehouse at the head of the river.
·Daýadooshú kaay yéi kunaaléi wé aan, héen sháakdáý. The town is seven miles from the head of the river.

héen shú

edge of body of water
hinshú (At)
·Héen shú át hán wé dzísk'w. That moose is standing at the edge of the water.
·Héen shóot wulihaash wé kayaaní. The leaf floated around the edge of the water.

héen táak

in the water; in the river
·Té tlénx' héen táakde duwatéen. Big rocks are visible on the bottom of the river.
·Héen táatý ák.wé du.een wéi kantáñw? Is the lupine picked from the water?

héen wantú

edge of river channel
·Lingít kóoxu aaý du.eenín héen wantú. Wild rice used to be picked along the riverbank.

·Héen wantóot woogoot wé gus'yadóoli. The sandpiper is walking around the riverbank.

héen wát

mouth of river, stream
·Héen wát át has wusikwaan wé gáaxw. The ducks are swimming around at the mouth of the river.
·Héen wátt uwax'ák wé t'ási. The grayling swam to the mouth of the river.

héený

into water

héen ý'aká

on (top of) the water, river
·Óoxjaa héen ý'akát uwaxíx. Wind has hit the surface of the water.

héen ý'ayaaý

riverside
·Wé héen ý'ayaaý chál wutuliyéý. We built a storehouse on the edge of the river.
·Héen ý'ayaaý yagéi kaxwéiý. There are a lot of highbush cranberries along the river.

héen yík

(in the) river valley
·Héen yíkde wooñooý wé yaakw. The boat went up the river.
·Héen yíkde aawa.aat al'óon. People went up the river hunting.

HEES'
• aawahées' | ahées' | kei ahées'ch
s/he borrowed it | s/he is borrowing it | s/he borrows it (regularly).
O-S-ø-hées' (ga act)
for S to borrow O
·Wé ñáa aý éesh jeedáý aankayéýaa aawahées'. The man borrowed a

,

plane from my Dad.
·Aawahées' du káani yaagú. He borrowed a boat from his brother-in-law.
• akaawahées' | akahées' | kei akahées'ch
s/he borrowed it | s/he is borrowing it | s/he borrows it (regularly).
O-ka-S-ø-hées' (ga act)
for S to borrow O (esp. round, spherical object)
·Tléix' gút akaawahées'. He borrowed one dime.
• du éet aawahís' | --- | du éeý ahées'
s/he lent it to him/her | --- | s/he lends it to him/her (regularly).
P-t~ O-S-ø-hées'~ (ø motion)
for S to lend O to P
·Tleiñáa dáanaa aý éet hís'! Lend me twenty dollars!
HEIN
• aawahéin | ayahéin | --s/he claimed it | s/he claims it | ---.
O-S-ø-héin (ga state)
for S to own, claim O (esp. clan property)
·Yaa L'úx yinaanáý yá saa áyá yaa L'úx áyá has aawahéin. They
claimed the name Mt. Edgecumbe as their crest.
·Xíxch' at óowu woosh jeedé duhéin nooch. The frog crest is claimed by
more than one clan.

héiýwaa

sympathetic magic, charm
·Héiýwaa yéi daadunéiyin ch'áakw. People used to use magic long ago.

HÉIÝWAA
• aawahéiýwaa | ahéiýwaa | --s/he performed rites | s/he is performing rites | ---.
S-ø-héiýwaa (na act)
for S to make magic, perform rites to bring desirable results in nature or give
youngsters power and confidence
·Al'óon kaadé aawahéiýwaa du keidlí. He used magic on his dog for
hunting.

hinshú (At)

end of body of standing water
héen shú

hintaak xóodzi

polar bear
hintakxóodzi
·Hintaak xóodzi akawshixít. She photographed a polar bear.
·Hintaak xóodzi has aawal'óon. They hunted polar bears.

hintaak x'óosi

coral

hintakx'óosi

·Hintaak x'óosi tléil yáax' yéi aa utí. There is no coral here.
·Hintakx'óosi nóox'u kayat'éex' Coral shells are hard.

hintakx'úxi

coral

,

,

hintakx'wás'çi

H

bufflehead (duck)

hintu.ejí

underwater reef; large rock or boulder lying under the water
heentu.ejí
·Heentu.ejí kát wulihásh du yaagú. Her boat drifted onto a reef.
·Héen kawulkuxú duteen nooch wé hintu.ejí. When the water level
drops, the reef can always be seen.

hinýuká

on (top of) the water, river
héen ýuká

Hinyaa Ñwáan

people of Klawock
·Hinyaa Ñwáan ýánde woogoot wé shaawát. The woman went to visit the
Klawock people.
·Hinyaa Ñwáan Celebrationx' has aawal'eiý. The Klawock people danced
at Celebration.

hinyikgáaxu

kind of duck
·Hinyikgáaxu kúdi awsiteen. She saw a golden eye duck's nest.
·Hinyikgáaxu kindachooneit ýoot wusikwaan. Golden eye ducks are
swimming around among the Mallard ducks.

hinyikl'eiýí

dipper; water ouzel

hít

house; building
·Yaa Aangóont áyá la.áa haa hídi Aanx'aagi Hít yóo duwasáakw.
Our clan house standing in Angoon is called Aanx'aagi Hít.
·Héen t'iká át la.áa du hídi. His house sits beside the river.

hít da.ideidí

house timbers

hít ká

roof
·Wé hít ká áa yéi jiduné. Someone is working on that roof.
·Çayéis' du hídi kát akawsix'óo. He nailed tin on his roof.

hít kagaadí

rafters (modern)

hít kaságu

rafters (large roof beams)
·Yan uwaneiyi hít kaságuçáa kawduwañaa. He was sent for ready-made rafters.
·Hít kaságu yaa anasxát'. He is dragging rafters along.

hít kat'áayi

shingle(s)
·Hít kat'áayi yóox' dulyéiý. They manufacture shingles over there.
·Hít kat'áayi yátx'i wé sée hídi káa yéi awa.oo. He put the small shingles on that doll house.

hít kax'úx'u

bark roofing material; tarpaper
hít kex'úx'u (C)
·T'ooch' yáý yatee wé hít kax'úx'u. That roofing is black.

,

Dictionary of Tlingit

hít s'aatí

head of a clan house; master of the house
·Aý éesh haa hít s'aatíý satéeyin. My dad was the head of our house.
·Wé hít s'aatí John yóo duwasáakw. That house leader's name is John.

hít shantú

upstairs; attic
·Hít shantóode akaawajeil wé x'óow. She took the blankets upstairs.
·Hít shantú k'idéin awsinei. She cleaned upstairs.

hít tayeegáas'i

piling, foundation post; floor joist
hít teyeegáas'i (C)
·Hít tayeegáas'i yís aas aawas'úw. He chopped down trees for pilings.
·Hít tayeegáas'i káa awliyéý du hídi. He built his house on pilings.

HOO
• yan uwahóo | yánde yaa nahú | yaý hoo
he/she/it waded ashore | he/she/it is wading ashore | he/she/it wades ashore
(regularly).
yan~ S-ø-hoo~ (ø motion)
for (singular) S to wade ashore
·Wé áa kaanáý yan uwahóowu watsíx a ítnáý yan uwañúý wé
yaakw. The boat followed behind the caribou that swam the lake.

Hóoch!

That's all!; All gone!; No more!; All done!
Hóochk'!

hoon

sale
hun
·Nas'gadooshú ch'iyáash kaýwaach'ák'w hun yayís. I carved eight sea
otter hunting canoes to sell.
·Hoon yís aswáat gishoo. He raises pigs to sell.

HOON
• aawahoon | ahóon | yoo ayahúnk
s/he sold it | s/he is selling it | s/he sells it (regularly).
O-S-ø-hoon~ (na act)
for S to sell O
·Kei akaawahaayi góon, aawahoon. He sold the gold that he mined.
·Ñaa ji.eetí wéix' duhóon. They are selling handmade crafts there.

• awlihóon | yaa analhún | --s/he went peddling it | s/he is peddling it | ---.
O-S-l-hoon~ (na event)
for S to go selling, peddle, hawk O
• wudlihoon | yaa nalhún | yoo dlihúnk
s/he went shopping | s/he is shopping | s/he goes shopping (regularly).
S-d-l-hoon~ (na event)
for S to go spending, go shopping
·Ace Hardwaredé neelhoon kas'éet katíý'aaçáa! Go to Ace Hardware
and buy a screwdriver!

,

,

H

·Lowesdéi neelhoon a káa dul.us'ku átçaa! Go to Lowes and buy a
washboard!

hoon daakahídi

store
·Hoon daakahídidé has woo.aat aý séek' hás. My daughters have gone
to the store.
·I dlaak' kajúxaa kát kanaljoox hoon daakahídidé. Take your sister to
the store in the wheel barrow.

hoon s'aatí

merchant; seller
·Wé hoon s'aatí een yóo ý'ali.átk aý aat. My paternal aunt is talking with
the storekeeper.
·Wé hoon s'aatí jeeyís yéi jiné wé shaatk'. The young girl is working for
that storekeeper.

hú

he, she [independent]
·Hú áwé aý éet wudishée. It is he who helped me.
·Hú áwé ý'añçeewóos'. It is he that you will ask.

Hú!

Ouch!

du húnýw

his older brother, cousin
·Aý húnýw ya.áakdáý woonú! Make room for my older brother!
·Wé yées ñáa du húnýw ítý yaa nagút. The young man's older brother is
walking along behind him.

Húsh!

Shame on you! [reprimand]

,

I

Dictionary of Tlingit

« I »
i

your (singular) [possessive]
·I léelk'u keekándei aneelçein - ýáat yéi adaané! Go check on your grandpa - he's working on fish!
·I tuñ'atáali i daaý yei jeekanaxíx. Your pants are falling down.

ii-

you (singular) [subject]
eeyou (singular) [object]
·Ikawdzitíý'. You're crooked (wicked).

du iñká

top of his/her foot

Iñkaa

Ahtna, Copper River Athabascan
·Wé shaawát Iñkaa aa lingítý sitee. That woman is a Copper River Athabascan person.

iñnáach'

brass
·Wé ý'agáax' daakahídi gaawú iñnáach' teen wududliyéý The church bell is made of brass.
·Iñnáach'ý sitee wé lítaa sákwti. The handle of that knife is brass.

iñyéis'
Ilí!
Ilí s'é!

iron, tin
çayéis'
Don't!; Stop it!
Lí!, Ihí!
Wait!
Ilí s'á!

ín

flint
·Ín tléil du jee yéi aa utí. He doesn't have any flint.
·Ínçaa ñushée. He is looking for flint.

ín x'eesháa

bottle; jug
·Wé at x'aakeidí ín x'eesháa tóox' yéi na.oo! Put the seeds in a bottle!
·Yaawat'aayi káaxwei ín x'eesháa tóot haat awsi.ín. She brought hot coffee in a bottle.

ísh

fishing hole; hole in stream, river, creek
·Ísh yíkde ýáat ayatéen. She sees salmon in the deep hole in the creek.
·Ísh yíkde shalýóot'. She is casting into the deep water hole.

ishñeen

black cod
·Áý akawdudlis'eiçi ishñeen du tuwáa sagóowun aý éesh. My dad used to like smoked black cod.

,

,

I

·Áý akawdudlis'eiçi ishñeen aa ýwaa.oo. I bought some smoked black cod.

a ít

after it
·Ý'éishx'w áwé nageich ñutaan ítdáý. After the summer is over there are a lot of bluejays
·S'íx' kawtoo.óos'i ítnáý agaýtoolñáa. After we have washed the dishes we will play cards.

du ít

(following) him, her, it
·Wé yées ñáa du húnýw ítý yaa nagút. The young man's older brother is walking along behind him.

a ít aa

the next one, the following one

du ítý nagoodí

his/her follower, disciple
·Dikée aanñáawu du yéet ítý nagoodí Peter yóo duwasáakw. Peter is the name of Jesus' disciple.

du ítý na.aadí

his/her followers, disciples
du ítý na.aatx'í, du ítý ne.aatx'í (C)
·Jinkaat ña déiý yatee Dikée aanñáawu du yéet ítý na.aadí. There
are twelve disciples of Jesus.
·Dikée aanñáawu du yéet ítý na.aadí has du een sh káa ý'awdigáx'.
Jesus prayed with his disciples.

ít'ch

glass (the substance)
·Ít'chi s'íx' ñ'áatl' du jeewú. She has a glass plate.
·Ít'ch s'íx' du jeet ýwaatán. I gave her a glass dish.

íxde

(toward) downstream
íxdei
·Dliwkát sh eeltín íxde yaa neeñúýu yáa kanaadaayi héen káx'.
Watch yourselves going down this river.

ixkée

downstream; south; lower 48 states, (locally: down south)
·Yáa ñutaanx' aadé ñugaýtootéen ixkée ch'a çaaýtusatéen wé sháa.
This summer we are going to travel down south just to see the girls.
·Aý sée du kacháwli áwé ixkéex' yéi yatee. My daughter's sweetheart
lives down south.

íýt'

shaman; medicine man
·Yanéegu lingít ýánde wuduwaýooý wé íýt'. The medicine man was
called to the sick person.
·Wé íýt'ch du een akaawaneek wáa sá at guçwaneiyí. The medicine
man told him what was going to happen.

,

J

Dictionary of Tlingit

« J »
JAA
• ashukaawajáa | ashukoojeis' | ashukajeiý
s/he instructed him/her | s/he is instructing him/her | s/he instructs him/her
(regularly).
O-shu-ka-S-ø-jaa~ (ø act)
for S to instruct, show O (by word); for S to advise, give advice to, counsel O
·Aý tláak'wch áa ýat shukaawajáa, aadé yéi daadunei yé. My
maternal aunt taught me how to make it.

jáa

honey!

jáaji

snowshoe
·Du jáaji a dzaasí yei nasháash. The thongs of his snowshoes are wearing
thin.
·Jáaji kát yaa has lunagúñ. They are running on snowshoes.

JAAÑ
• aawajáñ | yaa anajáñ | ajáñý
s/he killed him/her/it | s/he is (in the process of) killing it | s/he kills it (regularly).
O-S-ø-jaañ~ (ø event)
for S to kill (singular) O; (fig.) for S to let go of O without expecting any return
(at party)
·Táach ýat guçajáañ. I'm going to fall asleep. (Lit: Sleep is going to kill me.)
·Wé ñáa watsíx aawajáñ. That man killed a caribou.

jaañúý

canoe of caribou skins

1

JAAÑW

• aawajáañw | ajáañw | yoo ayajáañwk
s/he beat him/her up | s/he's beating him/her up | s/he beats him/her up
(regularly).
O-S-ø-jáañw (na act)
for S to beat up, assault, violently attack O

jánwu

mountain goat
jénu (C), ján (T), jánu (T)

·Du ýikshá káý yaa anayéin wé jánwu. He is carrying the moutain goat on his shoulder.
·Jánwu dleeyí aatlein yak'éi, gwál wé a s'óoçu. Mountain goat meat is really good, especially the ribs.

du jee

in his/her possession
·Diyée aanñáawu jeet wudzigít. He fell into satan's hands.

,

,

J

·Laaxw eetí wé ñaa jeedáý atýá has du çaneiýíý wusitee. After the famine, the food given to them became their salvation.
1

JEE

• yoo akaawajeek | yoo akaajeek | yoo akayajeek
s/he wondered about it | s/he is wondering about it | s/he wonders about it (regularly).
O-ka-S-ø-jeek (na act)
for S to wonder, be curious, anxious about O
·Yoo akaajeek a kaayí wé a káý yaa nagudi dei. He is wondering about the measure of the road he's walking on.
2

JEE

• kawlijée | kalijée / kulijée | --it looked terrible | it looks terrible | ---.
O-ka-(u)-l-jée (ga state)
for O to be awful, terrible, eerie (in appearance), unattractive
Note that in classical Tlingit, this verb had a thematic prefix (u-) which is slowly falling out of modern day speech. This is indicated in the Leer-Edwards theme as (u)-. Either imperfective form given here is acceptable: kalijée / kulijée.
·Du shax'ées'i kulijée. His matted hair is unattractive.

du jeeçáa

(big) enough for him/her to have or use; adequate for him/her
·Du jeeçáa yatee du yéi jineiyí. He is capable of handling his work.
·Du jeeçáa koodáal du gwéili. He can handle the weight of his backpack.

du jeeyís

for him/her
du jís

·Yéil x'óow aawañáa du ýán aa jeeyís. She sewed a Raven blanket for her husband.
·Wé haa sháade háni "gunalchéesh" haa jeeyís yéi yanañéich. Our leader says "thank you" for us.

a jeiçí

its scale (of fish)
·Wé ýáat a jeiçí teen yaý ayawlixásh. She cut up the fish with the scales on.
·Wé ýáat a jeiçí wé s'íx' kaaý aawa.óos'. She washed the scales of her fish off the plate.

JEIL
• aadé

akaawajeil | aadé yaa akanajél | aadé yóo
akayajélk
s/he carried it all there | s/he is carrying it all there | s/he carries it all there (regularly).
P-dé O-ka-S-ø-jeil~ (na motion)
for S to carry, take O to P (esp. to one place, making several trips)
·Hít shantóode akaawajeil wé x'óow. She took the blankets upstairs.

,

Dictionary of Tlingit

• aadé

at kaawajeil | aadé yaa at kanajél | aadé yoo at
kayajélk

s/he carried stuff there | s/he is carrying stuff there | s/he carries stuff there
(regularly).
P-dé at ka-S-ø-jeil~ (na motion)
for S to carry, take things to P (esp. to one place, making several trips)
·Haadéi at kagaýdujéil, a ya.áak x'wán yéi nasné! Make sure you make
room, they will be bringing it all!
• anaý yaawajél | --- | --s/he reached his/her hand through it | --- | ---.
P-náý ya-u-S-ø-jeil~ (ø motion)
for S to reach a hand through P
·Du kasánnáý áwé yaawajél, çunéi has aawal'éý. He put his hand
around her waist and they began dancing.

du jigúnl'i

his/her wrist
·Du jigúnl'i akaawas'ít. He bandaged his wrist.

du jiçei

crook of his/her arm; in his/her embrace
·Du tláa jiçeix' táach uwaján wé t'ukanéiyi. The baby fell asleep in his
mother's arms.
·Du jiçeiý yaa anasnúk du séek'. He is carrying his daughter in his arms.

jiçei.át

wrist guard
jiçei.ét (C), jika.át

jiçwéinaa

towel, hand towel
·Yées jiçwéinaa du léelk'u jeet yéi awsinei. He gave his grandmother new
towels.
·Aawa.óos'i jiçwéinaa gáaný ashayaawatée. She hung the towel that she
washed outside.

du jiká

back of his/her wrist
·Du jiká awlichún, ách áwé jika.át yéi aya.óo. She hurt her wrist. That's
why she's wearing a wrist guard.

jikañáas'

long smokehouse pole(s)
·Jikañáas' káý ashayaawatée wé çaat atx'aan hídi yeex'. She hung the
sockeye salmon on the stick in the smokehouse.

jikawáach

wristwatch

jika.át

wrist guard
jiçei.át, jiçei.ét (C)
·Du jiká awlichún, ách áwé jika.át yéi aya.óo. She hurt her wrist. That's
why she's wearing a wrist guard.
·Ñunáagu jeedáý jika.át yéi aya.óo. He is wearing a wrist guard from the
doctor.

du jiklix'ées'

his/her wrist

,

,

J

du jikóol

back of his/her hand
·Du jikóol wudiý'íý'. The back of his hand was burned.
·Du jikóol kawdiyés' The back of her hand is bruised.

du jín

his/her hand
·Wé ýeel' du jíndáý awliçoo. She wiped the slime off her hands.
·I jín wulich'éý'w. Your hands are dirty.

jinaháa

fate; bad luck
jineháa (C)
·Tléil áyáý at wuneiyí, jinaháa áwé yóo kdulneek. When something bad
happens they say it's bad luck.
·"Tliyéix', jinaháa haa kát çwaaxeex," yóo ý'ayañá du tláa. Her
mother says, "Behave, bad luck might befall us!"

du jináñ

away from it, leaving it behind (taking something away from him/her)
·Du keidlí du jináñ ñut wujixeex. His dog ran away from him.
·Aý jináñ ñut wujixeex. He ran away from me.

a jíni

its paw
a jín
·Wé dóosh du jín dleit kaaý kínde alshát. That cat is holding its paw up off the snow.
·Wé dóosh jín dleit kaaý kínde alshát. The cat is holding its paw up off the snow.

a jíni

it's sleeve (of shirt, coat)

jinkaadináý

ten (people)

jinkaatnáý

jinkaat

ten
·Jinkaat dáanaa yéi ý'alitseen wé x'óow. That blanket costs ten dollars.
·Jinkaat çanook has ayatéen. They see ten petrels.

jinkaat ña tléináý

eleven (people)

jinkaat ña tléix'

eleven
·Jinkaat ña tléix' du katáagu wé shaatk'. That girl is eleven years old.

du jintáak

his/her palm (of hand)
·Du jintáak teen akaçútlý wé tléiñw. She mashes the berries with the palm of her hand.
·Du jintáax' jiwduwanáñ. He was put in charge of it. (Lit: It was left in his hands).

du jintakyádi

his/her palm (center)

du jintú

his/her grip

·Du jintóoý kasixát wé tíx'. The rope is in his grip.

,

J

du jís

for him/her
du jeeyís

a jiseiyí

shelter of it (especially a tree)
·Wé x'aa jiseiyínáý yan uwañúý wé yaakw. The boat moored in the shelter of the point.
·A jiseiyít añéen aas tlénx'. People are sitting in the shelter of the big trees.

jishagóon

tool, tools
jishegóon (C)
·Yaakw ña çeiwú asçeiwú jishagóoný sitee. A boat and a net are a seine fisherman's tools.
·Wé ñáa du jishagóoni ñut kaawasóos. The man's tools are lost.

du jiwán

outer edge of his/her hand
·Du jiwán aawañ'ék'w. He cut the outside edge of his hand.
·Du jiwán wudiý'íý'. The outside edge of her hand was burned.

du jiýán

near him/her, by him/her (at hand, for him/her to work with)
·Du jiýánx' yan satán wé shunaýwáayi! Leave the axe near him!
·Du jiýáni yan tí wé lítaa, dleey aan akçwaxáash! Leave the knife near her, she will cut meat with it!

du jiyagéiý

against it, wrong (so as to foul up what s/he had done)

du jiyáý

according to the way s/he does it
·Aý tláa jiyáý eeý kát sakwnéin ýasa.ée. I cook fry bread like my mom does.
·Wé shaatk' du léelk'w jiyáý dañéis'. That young girl sews the way her grandmother does.

du jiyee

ready, waiting for him/her to use

The postposition -x' has an alternate form -ø (unmarked),
which explains the discrepancy between the forms: du jiyee and du
jiyeex' in the examples given. Either form is acceptable in either
sentence.
·Du jiyeex' yan awsitée du gwéili. He placed her bag within her reach.
·Du jiyee yan aawatée wé atóowu x'úx'. She placed the book he was
reading near him.

a jiyeet

under the burden, weight of it; belabored or suffering
from it (a burden, hardship)
·Toowú néekw jiyeet çáaý wé shaawát. The woman is crying under the
burden of sadness.
·Áat' jiyeet, gangookt ñukawdik'ít'. People crowded close around the fire
because of the cold weather.

du ji.een

working with him/her; helping him/her work or do something
·Wé aantñeení woosh ji.een gán has aawaxásh. The townspeople cut
wood together.

,

,

J

·Wé aantñeení woosh ji.een gán has aawaxásh. The townspeople cut
wood together.

du ji.eetí

his/her handiwork, artifact
·Aý ji.eetíçaa áyá ñuýashée. I'm looking for my handiwork.

JOOX
• aadé akawlijoox | --- | aadé yoo aklijúxk
s/he wheeled it there | --- | s/he wheels it there (regularly).
P-dé O-ka-S-l-joox~ (na motion)
for S to wheel O to P
·I dlaak' kajúxaa kát kanaljoox hoon daakahídidé. Take your sister to
the store in the wheel barrow.
• át akawlijúx | --- | áý aklajoox
s/he wheeled it to it | --- | s/he wheels it to it (regularly).
P-t~ O-ka-S-l-joox~ (ø motion)
for S to wheel O to P
·Haat kalajúx wé t'ooch'! Wheel the coal over here!
• kaawajóox | yaa kanajúx | kei kajúxch / kei kajooxch
it's running; it ran | it's running | it runs for a while (and then quits).
ka-ø-joox~ (ga event)

for a wheel to roll, spin; for an engine to start, run
A noun derived from this verb is: kayajuxti át "thing that
starts right away, runs well". Note that both repetitive
imperfective forms given here are acceptable to speakers: kei
kajúxch and kei kajooxch both mean "it runs for a while (and then
quits)".
·Yaa kanajúx wé toolch'án. The top is spinning.

júý'aa

sling
jóoý'aa (At)
·Júý'aa awliyéý. She made a sling.
·Júý'aa tóot astán du jín. He has his arm in a sling.

,

K

Dictionary of Tlingit

« K »
a ká

the (horizontal) surface of it; on it; on top of it; in it (a dish;
a path)
·Laañ'ásk gé aý ooý káwu? Do I have seaweed on my teeth?
·Wé x'ees du kaanáý yatee. The boil is too much for him.
1

KAA

• --- | oodzikaa | ----- | s/he is lazy | ---.
a-u-S-d-s-kaa (ga state)
for S to be lazy, slow
·Oodzikaayi ñáa áyá táakwx' guçwaláaxw. A lazy man will starve in the
winter.

káa

car, automobile
·Héen yáý kawdiyés' has du káayi. Their car is dark blue-gray in color.
·Wéide wooñooýu káa a ítde kñwagóot. I will go after that car that went
that way.

a káa dul.us'ku át

washboard
kát dul.us'ku át
·Aý jeet satán a káa dul.us'ku át! Hand me the washboard!
·Lowesdéi neelhoon a káa dul.us'ku átçaa! Go to Lowes and buy a
washboard!

Kaagwaantaan

Kaagwaantaan, locally called "Wolf"; a clan of the
Eagle moiety whose principal crest is the Wolf
·Çalyáý Ñwáan áwé Çalyáý Kaagwaantaaný has sitee. The Kaliakh
River people are the Kaliakh River Kaagwaantaan.

KAAK
• wusikaak | sikaak | kei sakaaký
it became thick | it's thick | it gets thick (regularly).
s-kaak (ga state)
for something to be thick (cloth, board, food, etc.)
• yéi kawsikaak | yéi kwsikaak | yéi kwsakáký
it got that thick; it thickened | it's that thick | it gets that thick (regularly).
(yéi) ka-u-s-kaak~ (na state)
for a board, cloth, etc. to be (so) thick

·Ñáa dzísk'w a doogú yéi kwsikaak. The hide of a bull moose is this thick.

du káak

his/her maternal uncle
·Has du ý'áakt wuhaan du káak. His maternal uncle stood between them.
·Du káak du ée at latóow. His maternal uncle is teaching him.

'

'

K

du káak'

his/her forehead
·Kei kawduwaçix'i té du káak't kaawaxíx. The rock that was thrown hit him on the forehead.
·Du káak' wudix'ís' ña kawdiyés'. His forehead is swollen and bruised.

a káa ñududziteeyi yoo ý'atánk

law, words one lives by
·Tléil oowaa wé aan káa ñududziteeyi yoo ý'atánk géide ñudunoogú. It is wrong to act against the law of the land.

du káalk'w

her fraternal niece, nephew, cousin
·Du káalk'w gán du jeeyís aawaxásh. Her nephew cut wood for her.

du káani

his/her brother-in-law, sister-in-law
·Aangóondáý áwé aý káani du daakanóox'u. My sister-in-law's ancestors are from Angoon.
·Du káani ji.een xáanaa atýaayí awsi.ée. She cooked the evening meal with her sister-in-law.

káast

barrel
·Wé káast kaadéi lít wé a x'éix'u! Throw the gills in the barrel!
·Gúkshi yan sa.ín wé kañáshýi a káa yéi tuwa.oowu káast! Put the barrel we put the steamed berries in in the corner!

káas'

ocean algae
·Káas' léin káa yéi nateech. There is always algae on the riverbank.

kaat

long, flat loosely woven basket for pressing out herring oil

káat'

sharpened stick (for digging up clams, roots, etc.); gardening fork

at kaawaxúkw

dried thing, esp. food

káaxwei

coffee
káxwei
·Hoon daakahídidéi nagú káaxweiçáa! Go to the store for some coffee!

káax'

spruce grouse, spruce hen; chicken
·Dunáñ kawdliyeech wé káax'. The grouse flew away from him.
·Káax' akawlis'úk. She fried chicken.

káa ýeýx'u yeit

bed
·Káa ýeýx'u yeit káa yan awsinúk du séek'. She put her daughter down on the bed.
·Shayeit a kát satéen káa ýeýx'u yeit . The pillow is lying on the bed.

kaay

measuring stick
·Tleidooshú ñaa ý'oos yéi kwliyáat' wé kaay. That measuring stick is six feet long.

kaay

measure; mile
·Daýadooshú kaay yéi kunaaléi wé aan, héen sháakdáý. The town is seven miles from the head of the river.

,

K

·Du hídidáý kaay shoowú yéi kunaaléi hoon daakahídi. The store is a half mile from her house.

káayaçijeit

chair
káayañijeit, ñáakejeit (C)
·Wé káayaçijeit káa çanú! Sit on that chair!
·Káayaçijeit anéegwál'. He is painting the chair.

at kaayí

cord (of wood)
et kaayí (C)

a kaayí

pattern, model, template for it; measure of it; measurement for it
·Daax'oon ñaa ý'oos a kaayí wé nadáakw. That table measures four feet.
·Yoo akaajeek a kaayí wé a káý yaa nagudi dei. He is wondering about the measure of the road he's walking on.

du kacháwli

his/her sweetheart
·Aý sée du kacháwli áwé ixkéex' yéi yatee. My daughter's sweetheart lives down south.

at kach'áak'u

carver
kadach'áak'u

kach'ák'waa

rounded carving chisel
·Kach'ák'waa teen akaawach'ák'w wé kootéeyaa. He carved a totem pole with a chisel.
·Yées aa kach'ák'waa aawa.oo. He bought himself a new chisel.

kadádzaa yeit

basket or pan used to collect berries by knocking them off the bush
·Kadádzaa yeit teen woogoot yóode. She went over there with a berry basket.
·Tláakw ashawlihík wé kadádzaa yeit. She filled the berry basket quickly.

kadánjaa

dust; pollen
·Wás' kadánjaa áwé tláakw ñuya.óo. People are overcome by the pollen.

kadás'

hail
·Kadás' daak wusitán. It is hailing.
·Wáa yateeyi yéix' kadás' kakandagéix'ch. Sometimes hail stones are big.

kadéix'

shame, embarrassment
kedéix' (C)
·Kadéix' du yát uwaxíx tatgé. Shame fell on him yesterday.
·Yéi daayaduñá, "Tlél kadéix' haa káý sheeteeñ!" He is told "Don't bring shame on us!"

a kádi

its head (of spear)
·A kádi yalik'áts'. The spear head is sharp.
·Yées aa a kádi awliyéý. He made a new spear head.

a kadíx'i

its stem (of plant); pith (of tree)

'

'

kadooheiý.aa

K

currants

kadúkli

fish smoked for a short time with the backbone taken out
·Kadúkli atx'aan hídidé yéi awsinei. She put the fish in the smokehouse.
·Aawsi.ée wé kadúkli atx'aan hídi yeedáý. She cooked some of the fish from the smokehouse.

kadulçóok s'eenáa

flashlight
kadulçúký s'eenáa
·Kadulçóok s'eenáa teen áý yaa nagút. He is walking along with a flashlight.

·Haayí wé kadulçóok s'eenáa! Hand over that flashlight!

kadulçúký s'eenáa

flashlight
kadulçóok s'eenáa

kadushxit t'aa yá

blackboard, chalkboard
kadushxeet t'aa yá
·Aaý gatí wéi kaxíl'aa kadushxeet t'áa yá çalçú! Pick up the eraser and clean the chalkboard!

kadútlýi

fish cleaned and hung to dry

kadu.uxýu át

balloon
·Du jintáak teen at'ácht wé kadu.uxýu át. She is slapping the balloon with the palm of her hand.

kagán

light
·Wé dís kagáni káax' yéi jiné. He works by moonlight.
·Kagán shaa kát uwaxíx. Light fell on the mountain.

du kagé

meeting, encountering, intercepting it; (arriving) at the same place or time as it
·Haa kagéide yaa ana.át. People are coming toward us.

a kageidí

side of it (house, building, animal); slab of meat covering its ribcage
·Hít kageidí át kawdigán wé s'eenáa. The light is shining on the side of the house.
·A kageidéex' áwé ýwaa.ún wé çuwakaan tlein. I shot the big deer in its side

kaçáak

mouse, deer mouse; vole
kaçák

kaçádaa

cheesecloth, loose-woven cloth; netting, screen
·Kaçádaa hoon daakahídidáý aawa.oo. He bought cheesecloth from the
store.
·Akawsitaayi tléiñw kaçádaa tóonáý akawlicháa. He strained the boiled
berries through cheesecloth.

,

K

Dictionary of Tlingit

kaçák

mouse
·Kaçák wududziteen. Someone saw a mouse.

kaçakl'eedí

yarrow; (locally) rat's tail
·Kaçakl'eedí ldakát yéix' kanas.éich. Yarrow grows all over.
·Kaçakl'eedí náakwý dulyéiý. Yarrow is used for medicine.

kaçeet

common loon
·Aanñáawu Çeeyx' áwé has saligaaw ñúnáý wé kaçeet. The loons are really loud in Ankau Bay.
·Ýáat yís áwé has akawliník Yéilch, wé kéidladi ña kaçeet. Raven talked the seagull and loon out of the salmon.

kaçít

darkness
·Wé kaçít tóoý yaa ntoo.ádi awdlidées. As we walked along in the darkness, the moon shined bright.
·Áa akwdliýéitl' wé kaçít tú. He is afraid of the dark.

kaçútlýi

mashed berries

a kaháadi

its covering; cover (over a large opening or something without an opening)
·Du gáni a kaháadi yís áwé xwaasdáa aawa.oo. He bought a tarp to cover his firewood.
·Wé té tlein a kaháadi káa yan tán! Put that large rock on top of its cover!

kaháakw

roe, eggs (of fish)
·Kaháakw daax' yéi jiduneiyí, xén tlél ushk'é. Using plastic to prepare salmon eggs is not good.
·L'ook kaháagu áyá yak'éi kanat'á kanéegwál' sákw. Coho salmon eggs are good for blueberry sauce.

at kahéeni

juice
·Tlei déiý ñ'ateil yáý áwé wutusineiý shákw kahéeni. We just saved
two gallons of the strawberry juice.

a kajeiçí

its scales (of fish)
a kajeeçí (T)
·Wé ýáat a kajeiçí aaý yéi awsinei. She took the scales off the fish.
·Ý'áakw hél a kajeiçí ñoostí. The freshwater sockeye doesn't have any
scales.

kajúxaa

flywheel; wheelbarrow; wagon; hand truck
·I dlaak' kajúxaa kát kanaljoox hoon daakahídidé. Take your sister to
the store in the wheel barrow.

kakatáx'aa

pliers
·Aadéi dutlákw yé áyá, kakatáx'aa teen yawduwadlaañ. As the story
goes, he was defeated by a pair of pliers.
·Kakatáx'aa aý jeet tí, Chýánk'! Hand me the pliers, Grandson!

,

,

K

kakéin

yarn; wool
·Aý léelk'w jeedáý kakéin l'ée x'wán áyá aý tuwáa sigóo. I like the
yarn socks from my grandmother.
·Ý'aan kakéin haat yéi ýwsiné kasné yís. I brought some red yarn for
knitting.

kakéin k'oodás'

sweater
·Xeitl kakéin k'oodás' aý yageeyí kaadéi áa ñaa jikaawañaa aý
léelk'wch. My grandmother commissioned a Thunderbird sweater for my
birthday.
·Ñusi.áat' gáan - kakéin k'oodás' yéi na.oo! It's cold out - wear a
sweater!

kaklahéen

wet snow; slush
kuklahéen

·Ñúnáý ýat wuditl'ák', kaklahéen áyá aawaçéet. I'm so wet - wet snow is coming down hard.

·Tláakw áyá haa kçwatée wult'éex'i yá kaklahéen. We will be in tough shape if this wet snow freezes.

kakúxaa

bailer

·K'idéin ashigóok kakúxaa layeiý. He knows how to build bailers really well.

·Tlél a káý yiseix'aaçúñ wé yaakw kakúxaa! Don't you all forget the bailer for the boat!

kak'dakwéiy s'aatí

captain; person in charge

·Aý éesh kak'dakwéiy s'aatíý sitee, x'úx' awuýáax'un. As a captain, my father used to haul mail.

·Aý éesh kak'dakwéiy s'aatíý wusitee s'ísaa yaakw káx'. My father became the captain of the sailboat.

kak'kakwéiy s'aatí (At)

captain (in the navy)

kak'kwéiy s'aatí (TC)

du kak'ýaawú

his/her bangs
du kek'ýaawú (C)

kañáshýi

steamed berries put up in soft grease

·Gúkshi yan sa.ín wé kañáshýi a káa yéi tuwa.oowu káast! Put the barrel we put the steamed berries in in the corner!

·Ñu.éex'dei nasýóot' yá kañáshýi! Pack the steamed berries to the potlatch!

kalchaneit

mountain ash

·Tlél kalchaneit áa koo.éiý Yaakwdáat. Mountain ash doesn't grow in Yakutat.

kalchaneit tléiçu

mountain ash berry

·Ñuk'éet' áwé gaýtoo.áat kalchaneit tléiçuçáa. We are going to pick mountain ash berries.

,

kaldaaçákw

bare; naked

kaldaaçéináý

slowly
·Shux'áanáý kaldaaçéináý áwé dugwáal yá shí. The drumming starts out slow in this song.
·Kaldaaçéináý yaa gaýtooñóoý, tlél çwadlaan yá éiý' yík. We will travel along slowly, it's not deep in this slough.

kaldáal'i

typist
kaldáal'
·Wéix' yéi jiýaneiyí kaldáal'iý áwé ýat satéeyin. I was a typist when I worked there.
·Yasátk aadéi ashigóogu yé wé kaldáal'. The typist knows how to type fast.

kaldáanaañ

broke; penniless; without money
·Kaldáanaañ áwé yaakwt wujixíx. He jumped aboard the ship without money.
·At tooý'áan áyá táakwni yís, kaldáanaañý haa nasteech. We are smoking fish for the winter because we are usually without money.

kalóox'jaa

fast drip, leak
kalóoýjaa

du kalóox'shani

his/her bladder
·Du kalóox'sháni néegooch áwé du daa yawdudzi.aa. He is being examined because of his bladder pain.
·Náakw du ý'éiý wuduwatee du kalóox'sháni néegooch. She was given medicine for her bladder pain.

kalóoýjaa

fast drip, leak
kalóox'jaa
·Awdagaaních áwé, dleit kaaý kalóoýjaa koolx'áasch hít kaadáý.
Because the sun is shining, the snow drips fast off the house.

·Héen sákw wé dleitdáý kalóoýjaa tayeex' yan tán! Set that below the snow drip for our water!

kals'éesjaa

dust cloud; snow cloud
·Kals'éesjaa wéiý yaa nals'ís. Dust is blowing along there.
·Táakwx' dleit kals'éesjaa duteen nooch. You can see blowing snow in the winter time.

kals'áak (T)

squirrel
kanals'áak
·Sakwnéin áwé du ý'éiý ýateeý wé kals'áak. I feed bread to the squirrel.
·Ch'áakw duýáa noojín wé kals'áak. They used to eat squirrels long ago.

kaltásk

berrying basket
kaltálk
·Ñuk'éet' yís áwé yéi daaduné wé kaltálk. The berrying basket is made for picking berries.

'

'

K

kaltéelñ

barefoot; shoeless
·Eesháank' kaltéelñ áwé haat wujixíx aý dachýánk'. Poor thing, my grandchild ran over here shoeless.
·Ñ'asigóo kaltéelñ l'éiw kát át wusheex. It's fun running around barefoot in the sand.

kanaadaayi héen

river; stream; creek
·Dliwkát sh eeltín íxde yaa neeñúýu yáa kanaadaayi héen káx'. Watch yourselves going down this river.

kanágaa

stretcher, form for shaping
·At xáshdi téel sákw áwé kanágaa akaawach'ák'w aý jeeyís. He carved a form for making moccasins for me.
·Ñúnáý dugóogun kanágaa layeiý. People really used to know how to make a moccasin-shaping form..

kanals'áak

red squirrel
kals'áak (T)

kanályi

steamed berries

kanas.aadí
kanashú

crawling insect; spider
drunkenness; inebriation; giddiness

kanat'á

blueberry; huckleberry
·Kanat'á a ýoo yéi nateech kaxwéiý. Blueberries are usually in the midst
of cranberries.
·L'ook kaháagu áyá yak'éi kanat'á kanéegwál' sákw. Coho salmon
eggs are good for blueberry sauce.

kanat'á kahéeni

blueberry juice; purple
·Wé ýaat kanat'á kahéeni káa yéi gaýtoo.oo. We will put the roots in the
blueberry juice.
·Du ooý kanat'á kahéeni yáý kawdiséñ'w. Her teeth are the color of
blueberry juice.

kanéegwál'

dish made with berries and salmon eggs
·Shaaý a.éen haa hídi daatý kanéegwál' sákw. She is picking gray
currants from around our house for a berry and salmon egg dish.
·L'ook kaháagu áyá yak'éi kanat'á kanéegwál' sákw. Coho salmon
eggs are good for blueberry sauce.

kaneilts'ákw

black currants or swamp currants
kanalts'ákw (T), kaneilts'íkw (At), kaneilts'ook (T)
·Yaa ntoo.ádi áwé, daak wudzigít yaý akaawaýích wutuwa.ini
kaneilts'ákw. When we were walking along, she fell down and spilled all the
swamp currants we picked.
·Tsaa Éiý' kaadáý áwé yawtuwadlaañ ch'a k'ikát wé kaneilts'ákw.
We finally managed to get some swamp currants from Seal Slough.

,

Dictionary of Tlingit

kaneilts'íkw (At)

black currants or swamp currants
kaneilts'ákw, kanalts'ákw (T), kaneilts'ook (T)

kanéist

cross
·Aý léelk'w jeeyís áyá kaýwaa.oo yá kanéist guk.át. I bought these
cross earrings for my grandmother.
·Ýáay een áwé ýwaliyéý wé kanéist. I built that cross out of yellow cedar.

kanóox'

turtle
tadanóox', tanóox', tadanóox'u (At)
·Tleidahéen áwé Yaakwdáatt aa wlihásh wé kanóox'. One time a turtle
floated to Yakutat.
·Kanóox' áwé kéi anasýít. He is breeding turtles.

kantáñw

lupine
kentáñw
Warning: some lupine species contain toxic alkaloids, be
certain of species before use.
·Héen táatý ák.wé du.een wéi kantáñw? Is the lupine picked from the
water?

du kasán

his/her waist
·Du kasánnáý áwé yaawajél, çunéi has aawal'éý. He put his hand
around her waist and they began dancing.
·Ñaa kasán tayeet shukatáni áwé yak'éi wéi s'él' kinaak.át. A
raincoat that hangs below the waist is the best.

kasanka.át

corset

a kaséiñ'u

its color
·A kaséiñ'u ý'éishx'w kayaaý sitee. The color is in the likeness of a
bluejay.

kaséiñ'w

neck cord worn for dance

kaséñ'ýu

dye
·Yán aas daadáý kayeiý áwé átý gaçilayéiý s'agwáat kaséñ'ýu
sákw. Shavings from a hemlock tree is what you will use for the brown dye.

kasçaaý

mourning, wailing, loud weeping or crying; wail, groan, moan

kasiyaayi héen

liquor; booze; alcoholic beverage

kasiyéiyi s'eiñ

marijuana
kasiyéiyi s'eeñ

kasné

knitting, crocheting
·Ý'aan kakéin haat yéi ýwsiné kasné yís. I brought some red yarn for
knitting.

kast'áat'

cotton; cotton blanket, quilt
·Ñóok yígu aý kast'áat'i - aý jeet .áý. My quilt is in the box - give it to me.

,

,

K

·Kast'áat' tlein áwé wóoshde añéis' aý yádi jeeyís. She is sewing
together a big quilt for my child.

kast'áat' x'óow

quilt; cotton blanket

kas'éet

screw
·Wéi yaakw yaýak'áaw kas'éet áa yéi du.oowú, k'idéin yéi
aguýlasháat. If a screw is put in the thwart of the boat, it will hold pretty well.

kas'éet kagwádlaa

wrench
kas'éet kaçúkwaa; kas'éet kakéigwaa
·Craftsman kas'éet kagwádlaa áwé Sears Roebuckdáý ýwaa.oo. I
bought a Craftsman wrench from Sears Roebuck.
·Yaakw yíx' yan tí wéi kas'éet kagwádlaa. Leave the wrench in the boat.

kas'éet kaçúkwaa

wrench
kas'éet kagwádlaa, kas'éet kakéigwaa

kas'éet katíý'aa

screwdriver
kas'éet katéý'aa (C)
·Kas'éet katíý'aa tlein áyá yaakwt kaýatéen. I have a big screwdriver
lying in the boat.
·Ace Hardwaredé neelhoon kas'éet katíý'aaçáa! Go to Ace Hardware
and buy a screwdriver!

kas'ígwaa yeit (A)

frying pan, skillet
kas'úgwaa yeit (TC)

a kas'úkýu

fried food
·Çuwakaan taayí kas'úkýu yís akaawaxaash. She cut up deer fat for
frying.

kas'úwaa

chopper
·Yá kas'úwaa teen a yíkdáý ýút'! Chip the inside out with this chopper!
·Yax'át yá kas'úwaa aý jeeyís! Sharpen this chopper for me!

kashéek'w gwéil

heating pad

kashéeý'

praise, glorification
·Ý'agáax' daakahídix' áwé at kashéeý' shí áa dushí. Songs of praise
are sung in church.

kashóok'

electricity

kashóok' gwéil

heating pad
·Wéi kashóok' gwéil aý ýeek káa yan satí! Set the heating pad on my
upper arm!
·Náakw s'é áa yéi kñwa.oo aý keey aaçáa tsá wéi kashóok' gwéil. I
will put medicine on my knee first, then the heating pad.

kashóok' yoo ý'atánk

email

,

K

Dictionary of Tlingit

kashxeedí

writer; scribe; secretary
·Kashxeedíý sitee haa yéet. Our son is a scribe.

du katáagu

his/her age
·Tleiñáa ña tléix' áwé du katáagu. He is twenty-one years old.
·Jinkaat ña tléix' du katáagu wé shaatk'. That girl is eleven years old.

at katáx'aa

pliers

kát dul.us'ku át

washboard
a káa dul.us'ku át

at katé

bullet
·Du kwéiyi ñínt kaawaxíx wé at katé. The bullet fell short of his mark.

katéiý

soup, porridge
·Ýalak'ách' katéiýi aý ý'é yak'éi. Porcupine soup is delightful to my mouth.

katíý'aa

key
katéý'aa (C)
·A kát tsé iseix'áañw haa hít katíý'aayi! Don't forget our house key!
·Tléix' dáanaa yéi ý'alitseen katíý'aa x'úx' daakahídix'. A key costs one dollar at the post office.

katíý'aa s'aatí

keeper of the key; jailer; night watchman
·Katíý'aa s'aatíý ýat guýsatée yá keijín yagiyeedáý. After Friday I will be the jailer.
·K'idéin has jiduñéi katíý'aa s'aatí Dzántik'i Héenix'. Jailers are paid well in Juneau.

katñaañú

wilderness; the bush
galçaañu, çwalçañú (At), kalçañú (T)

katóok

cave
·A daat shkalneek ñudzitee yá katóok. There is a story about this cave.
·Yá neechý yaa neegúdi yei kçisatéen yá katóok. As you walk along this shoreline you will see this cave.

a kát sh kadultseýt át

bicycle

kát yadu.us'ku át

wash basin
·Yat'aayi héen a káa yéi nay.oo wéi a kát yadu.us'ku át! You all put hot water in the wash basin!
·Éil' a kaadéi kanasxá wéi a kát yadu.us'ku át! Pour salt in the wash basin!

kat'ákýi

half-dried, compressed food, esp. berries or seaweed
·Aatlein shákw áwé wutuwa.ín kat'ákýi yéi naýtusaneit. We picked a lot of strawberries so we can make dried berry patties.
·Ch'as héen ák.wé a kaadéi yóo yadudzixéik yá kat'ákýi? Is water all that was put on these dried berries?

'

'

K

kat'éex'

(plug of) chewing tobacco
·Wé shaawát çánch kat'éex' du jeet wuduwatée. The woman was given a plug of tobacco.

kat'éý'aa

pounder (for meat or grease)

kat'éý'aa yeit

mortar for pounding
·Çánch áwé aan yéi daaduné wéi kat'éý'aa yeit. He uses the mortar for pounding his tobacco.

kat'íshaa

three-cornered needle for sewing skin or leather
·Yá kat'íshaa at xáshdi téel aan ýañéis'. I sew moccasins with this leather needle.
·Kat'íshaa JoAnne Fabricsdáý ýwaa.oo dzísk'u doogú yís. I bought a leather needle from JoAnne Fabrics for (sewing) moose hide.

a kat'óot

partway up it; halfway up it (the inside of a vessel or container)
·Gúx'aa kat'óott kaawadáa wé cháayoo. The cup is filled part way up with tea.
·A kat'óott shalatl'ít', tlél kei kçwadál! Fill it halfway, then it won't be heavy!

katl'áak'

mica

katl'áak'

gold-rust; flecked with gold or rust

katl'úñjaa

drip, leak with dripping
·Taat kanaý ýat wusiýéñ wé katl'úñjaa. All night I was kept awake by that slow drip.

káts

pounded shell powder
·Wé káts táay káa yéi na.oo! Put the pounded shell powder on the garden!

katsóowaa

planting stick
·Aý jeet tán wéi katsóowaa! Hand me the planting stick!

kawáat

lump in the flesh; tumor
·Du çátsiçáa wootee yá kawáat. There are tumors all over her thigh.

kawóot

bead
·Aý al'eiý k'oodás'i ch'áagu kawóot áwé a daawú á. There are old beads on my dance shirt.
·Kawóot teen ñ'eikaxwéin a káa kañá! Embroider a flower on it with beads!

kawóot ka.íshaa

fine needle for stringing beads
·Tlél déi ýwateen aý kawóot ka.íshaa. I can't see my needle anymore.
·T'áa kát ñushí aý jeeyís - ñut kaýwaaçéex' aý kawóot ka.íshayi!
Look on the floor for me - I lost my needle!

,

kaxágwaa yeit

mortar for grinding
·Aý jeet tán wé kaxágwaa yeit, yáa s'áxt' aan yéi nñasaneiyít! Hand
me the mortar so I can use it on this devil's club!

kaxéel'

trouble; conflict
·A wáný áwé yaa gagútch wé kaxéel' teen. He walks on the edge of
trouble.
·Kaxéel' sháade hániý sitee wé shaatk'. The young girl is a troublemaker.

kaxées'

wire
·Wé hít gukshitúdáý kasixát wé kaxées'. The wire runs from the corner of
that house.
·Kaxées' teen wóoshdei kdudzixát du ý'ás'. His jaw is held together with
a wire.

kaxíl'aa

scrubber
·Aý yéi jineiyí áwé kaxíl'aa k'idéin daané. My job is to clean erasers.
·Aaý gatí wéi kaxíl'aa kadushxeet t'áa yá çalçú! Pick up the eraser and
clean the chalkboard!

kaxwaan

frost
·Yeedát ñuyak'éi çaatáa yéi daané yís yá kaxwaan káý yaa nagúdi.
Today the weather is good for walking out on the frost to check the traps.
·Tlél tlaý kooshý'íl'k yá kaxwaan. It's not very slippery with this frost.

kaxweitl

itch; rash
·Yak'éiyi náakw áwé yéi awsinei yá kaxweitl káa yéi aawa.oo. He
made some good medicine and put it on the rash.

kaxwéiý

high bush cranberry
·Kanat'á a ýoo yéi nateech kaxwéiý. Blueberries are usually in the midst
of cranberries.
·Kanéegwál' yís yéi daaduné kaxwéiý. Highbush cranberries are used for
the berry and salmon egg dish.

kaxwénaa

dipper, scoop, ladle; brailer bag
·Ýáat teen áwé shawdudlihík wé kaxwénaa. The brailer bag was filled with salmon.
·Kaxwénaa yee yís áwé ýwliyéý aý yaagú yíkx'. I built space for the brailer bags in my boat.

kax'áasjaa

trickle of water; steady drip or leak
·Tlei ult'íx'ch taatx' wéi hít daadáý kax'áasjaa. The water dripping from the house freezes at night.

kax'ás'aa

rip saw; double-handled saw for sawing lumber
·Kax'ás'aa teen áwé kçeexáash ldakát wéi t'áa! You will cut all those boards with a rip saw!
·Kax'ás'aa yax'áat áwé ashigóok. He really knows how to sharpen the rip saw.

,

,

K

kax'ás'ti

lumber
·Wé kóoñ kax'ás'ti a yanáa yan aawatán. He put plywood over the pit in the ground.
·Yóo diyáanaý.aadáý áwé haat yaýwaaýáa wéi kax'ás'ti haa hídi sákw. I hauled the lumber from across the other side for our house.

kax'ás'ti daakahídi

sawmill
·Kax'ás'ti daakahídi ýánt hán. He is standing next to the sawmill.

KÁX'Ý
• --- | kajikáx'ý | ----- | it's spotted | ---.
ka-j-káx'ý (ga state)
for something to be spotted, have polka-dots
-gáx'ý
This verb only occurs in the imperfective.
·Çuwakaan yádi kajikáx'ý. A fawn is spotted.

at káý adéli
kaýgáani yeit

a káýi

guard, watchman
frying pan, skillet

its sap, phloem

a kaýyee

its ceiling
·Dleit yáý wuduwanéegwál' wé kaýyee. The ceiling was painted white.
·Gwál tleiñáa ý'oos áwé a kaýyeedé. It must be twenty feet to the ceiling.

kaý'át'
kaý'ees

green, unripe berry
strong urine smell
keý'ees (C)

kaý'íl'aa

iron (for ironing)
·Ch'áagu aa kaý'íl'aa stoox káx' áwé yan dutéeych yaçat'aayít. The
irons of long ago were set on the stove to heat up.

a kayaa

something sort of like it; something not measuring up to it; where
one expects it to be
·A kaséiñ'u ý'éishx'w kayaaý sitee. The color is in the likeness of a
bluejay.

kayaaní

leaf, leaves; vegetation, plants, herbs, herbiage
·Héen shóot wulihaash wé kayaaní. The leaf floated around the edge of
the water.
·Çuwakaan ýaýooý nooch ñ'eikaxétl'k kayaaní teen. I always use a
bunchberry leaf to call deer.

kayáash

platform; porch
·Yéi áwé wduwasáa Kayáash Hít L'uknaý.ádich. The Coho Salmon tribe
has named it Platform House.

,

Dictionary of Tlingit

du kayádi

her fetus, unborn child
du keyédi (C)

a kayéik

sound, noise of it
·Washéen kayéik aawa.áý. She heard the sound of the machine.
·Gandaadagóogu kayéik ýaa.áých. I can hear the sound of a woodpecker.

kayéil'

peace, calm

kayeiý

wood shavings
·Yán aas daadáý kayeiý áwé átý gaçilayéiý s'agwáat kaséñ'ýu
sákw. Shavings from a hemlock tree is what you will use for the brown dye.

kayeiýtáçu (C)

wood chips; wood shavings
kayeiýtaçú (AtT)
·Aan áwé shóot aýwdi.ák wé kayeiýtáçu. I built a fire with the wood
shavings.
·Ýáay kayeiýtáçu a takáx' yéi na.oo! Put yellow cedar shavings in the
bottom of it!

a kayís

for it (a day, week; a dish)
·Du séek' yageeyí kayís áwé gáaxw awsi.ée. She cooked a duck for her
daughter's birthday.
·Woosh gaýdusháa a kayís áwé yées l'aak aawañáa. She sewed a new
dress for the wedding that was to take place.

a ka.aasí

its mast (of boat)

du keekán

coming to see him/her
·I léelk'u keekándei aneelçein - ýaat yéi adaané! Go check on your
grandpa - he's working on fish!

du kéek'

her younger sister; his younger brother; cousin
·Ts'ootsxánch uwasháa aý kéek'. A Tsimshian married my little sister.
·Du kéek' teen áwé ñuk'éet' has woo.aat. She went berry picking with her younger sister.

kéel

auklet or murrelet
·Sheishóoý áwé akaawach'ák'w, kéel a káa yéi aawa.oo. He carved a rattle and put a murrelet on it.

kées

bracelet
·Góon dáanaa een áwé kawduwat'íý' aý jeeyís yá kées. This bracelet was pounded out of a gold coin for me.
·Xeitl a káa kawduwach'ák'w yá kées. A Thunderbird is carved on this bracelet.

KEES'
• ayakawlikís' | --- | ayaklakís'ý
s/he put it out | --- | s/he puts it out (regularly).

,

,

K

O-ya-ka-S-l-kées'~ (ø event)
for S to put out, extinguish O (fire); for S to turn off O (light)
• yakawlikís' | yaa yakanalkís' | yaklakísý
it went out | it's starting to go out | it goes out (regularly).
ya-ka-l-kées'~ (ø event)
for a fire, light to go out
·Ý'aan yakawlikís'. Wé kél't' ñu.aa, ch'u uwat'áa. The fire has gone out but the ashes are still warm.

kéet

killerwhale
·Ch'as a gooshí duwatéen wé kéet. Only the dorsal fin of the killerwhale is visible.
·Áa atoosçeiwú yé áwé kéet haa daat yawsigóo. The killer whales came around where we were gillnetting.

du keey

his/her knee
·Náakw s'é áa yéi kñwa.oo aý keey aaçáa tsá wéi kashóok' gwéil. I

will put medicine on my knee first, then the heating pad.
·Du keey áwé wuduwaxaash. They cut into his knee.

du keey shakanóox'u

his/her kneecap
du kiyshakanóox'u, du kiyshakunóox'u (At), du
kiyshekenóox'u (C)
·Du keey shakanóox'u áwé tlei át nashý'íl'ch. His kneecap slides
around.

kei

up
kéi
·Haat kei wudaayí tléil uýsatínch. He has not seen the tide rise yet.
·Ánk'w áwé kéi has anaswát wéit lingítch. Those people are raising a
crybaby.

KEI
• akawsikei | aksakéikw | yei aksakéich
s/he untangled it | s/he is untangling it | s/he untangles it (regularly).
O-ka-S-s-kei~ (ça act)
for S to trail, follow tracks of O; for S to untangle O; for S to rip back, undo O
(sewing, knitting)
·Kaýsaké a kóon wé kinaak.át! Unravel the hem on the coat!

kéi dañinji s'áaxw

umbrella
·Kéi dañinji s'áaxw tlein a tayeet ñaa luwagúñ séew tóodáý. People
ran under the big umbrella out of the rain.
·Áa akwdliýéitl' wéi kéi dañinji s'áaxw. He is afraid of the umbrella.

kéidladi

gull, seagull
·Ýaat yís áwé has akawliník Yéilch, wé kéidladi ña kaçeet. Raven
talked the seagull and loon out of the salmon.
·Dei át has woo.aat wéi yées kéidladi. The young seagulls are already
walking around.

,

K

Dictionary of Tlingit

du keigú

his/her lungs
·Du keigú tóox' áwé kawáat aawasháat. He got lung cancer.

keijín

five
·Deisleenx' keijín has yatee ñaa sháade náñx'i. In Teslin there are five leaders.
·Keijín aý yaadéi kei jisataan! Give me five!

keijíninaý

five (people)

keijín yagiyee

Friday
·Katíý'aa s'aatíý ýat guýsatée yá keijín yagiyeedáý. After Friday I will be the jailer.

KEIL
• akawlikél | yaa akanalkél | aklakélý
s/he soaked it | s/he is soaking it | s/he soaks it (regularly).
O-ka-S-l-keil~ (Ø event)
for S to soak O

du kéilk'

his sororal niece, nephew
du kéilk'w
·Asiýán áwé du kéilk'. He loves his nephew.
·Du kéilk' du ý'eis at wusi.ée. His niece cooked for him.
1

KEIL'

• daak awlikél' | daak analkél' | daak alkél'ch
he/she/it chased it into the open | he/she/it is chasing it into the open | he/she/it chases it into the open (regularly).
daak O-l-keil'~ (ø motion)
for S to chase O into the open, out to sea
This verb is often used to describe the practice used by net fishermen of running the boat along the net to chase fish into it.
·Watsíx áa káa daak has awlikél' wé çooch. The wolves chased the caribou out onto the lake.

keishísh

alnus alder (beach or mountain alder)
·Keishísh áwé lats'áa nooch ñutaanx'. Alder always smells good in the summer.

kéit'u

pick, pickaxe
·Jishagóon áwé kéit'u. A pick is a tool.

keitl

dog
·Wé ýalak'ách' ýaawú aý keidlí ý'éit yawdliçích. The porcupine quills stuck in my dogs mouth.
·Igayeiñ tsá wé keitl! Don't let the dog bite you!

kélaa

dish; platter
kílaa
·Kílaa yáý i yá kaaxát. Your face is shaped like a platter.

'

'

K

kél't'

ash; ashes
·Kél't' tuwaakúý dulyéiý. They make tobacco out of wood ashes.
·Ý'aan yakawlikís'. Wé kél't' ñu.aa, ch'u uwat'áa. The fire has gone out but the ashes are still warm.

Kenasnoow

Killisnoo
·Kenasnoow áa ñoowdzitee wé ñáa. That man was born in Killisnoo.

ketllóox'u

yellow
·Ketllóox'u yáý yatee wé ñ'eikaxwéin. The flower is light yellow.

Kichýáan

Ketchikan
·Deikeenaa ña Ts'ootsxán áa shayadihéin Kichýáan. There are a lot of Haida and Tsimshian people in Ketchikan.

kichý.anagaat

rainbow
·Kichý.anagaat daat shkalneek tlél wuduskú. There aren't any stories known about rainbows.

kichyát

tern
·Kichyaat ilk'wát'ý sít' yáx'. Terns lay eggs by glaciers.

a kígi

half of it (something cut or broken in half); one side of it (a symmetrical object)
·Gishoo a kígi aý jeet wududzitáa. I was given half of a pig.

a kíji

its wing
·Du kíji áwé wool'éex' wé ts'ítskw, ách áwé tlél át wudañeen. The songbird's wing broke, that's why it doesn't fly around.

kijook

kind of hawk
gijook
·Kijook s'áaxw ñudzitee. There is a hawk hat.

du kík

one side of his/her torso
·Ch'a du kíkt uwagút. He walked by his side.
·Du kíkt hán wé du yéet. His son is standing beside him.

a kík

alongside it; catching up with it

a kíknáý

in addition to it; along with it; to the side of it; besides that
·Du kíknáý kei ý'anatán. He is talking while someone else is talking.

Kiks.ádi

Kiks.ádi, locally called "Frog"; a clan of the Raven moiety whose principal crest is the Frog

du kikyádi

his/her twin
du kikyédi (C)
·Déiý wooch kikyátx'i aý jeewú. I have two sets of twins.

kík'i aa

younger one
·Xóots ý'us.eetí áwé awsiteen wé kík'i aa. The younger one saw the bear tracks.

,

kílaa

dish; platter
kélaa
·Kílaa aý jeewú, tlél ñu.aa átý uýlayeiý I have a platter but I don't use it.
·Tlé kílaa kát áwé ñaa ý'éiý has at wootee. They fed the people from platters.

a kináak

above it
·Shaa kináakdei yaa nagút. He is walking to the top of the mountain.
·Du hídi kináak áwé át wulis'ees wé aan kwéiyi. The flag is blowing around above his house.

kinaak.át

coat, overcoat
kinaa.át, kinaa.ét (C)
·Atýa átch áwé uwaýáa aý kinaak.ádi. A moth ate my coat.
·Ñaa kasán tayeet shukatáni áwé yak'éi wéi s'él' kinaak.át. A raincoat that hangs below the waist is the best.

kinaa.át

coat, overcoat
kinaak.át, kinaa.ét (C)
·Ýaldleit kinaa.át yéi aya.óo wé Çunanaa ñáa. That Athabaskan man is wearing a white fox overcoat.

kindachooneit

mallard duck
·Kindachooneit kuña.óon xáanaa atýaayí yís. I will shoot a mallard duck for dinner.
·Hinyikgáaxu kindachooneit ýoot wusikwaan. Golden eye ducks are swimming around among the Mallard ducks.

kíndei

upward
kínde, dikíndei, dikínde
·Ñ'anashgidéi ñaa áwé kíndei alshát du shá. The poor man is holding his head high.
·Wé dóosh du jín dleit kaaý kínde alshát. That cat is holding its paw up off the snow.

kinguchwáan x'óowu

Hudson Bay blanket
·Kinguchwáan x'óowu du káý kawduwayaa. He was covered with a
Hudson Bay blanket.

kít'aa

pry; stick or tool for prying; crowbar
·Kít'aa áwé átý has alyeiýín haa léelk'u hás. Our grandparents used to
use a peavey.

du kiyshá

end of his/her knee

du kiyshakanóox'u

his/her kneecap
du keey shakanóox'u, du kiyshakunóox'u (At), du
kiyshekenóox'u (C)

,

,

K

2

KOO

• awsikóo | yaa anaskwéin | askweiý
s/he knows it | s/he's beginning to learn it | s/he realizes it (regularly).
O-S-s-koo~ (ø event)
for S to know, be acquainted with, make known O (esp. people, facts); for S to
learn O (esp. facts)
·Has çaduskóot áwé koogéinaa yéi s aya.óo. They are recognizable by
the sash that they wear.
·Tléil ýwasakú çeey kanaý ñutées' yóo duwasáagu ýáat. I don't know
the fish called ratfish.

kóoch'

noiseless fart

kooch'éit'aa

ball
kooch'éet'aa
·Kooch'éit'aa áwé aan has ash koolyát wé atyátx'i. The children are
playing with a ball.
·Té géit kaawagwátl wé kooch'éit'aa. The ball rolled against a rock.

koogéinaa

sash (worn over shoulder)
koogwéinaa
·Has çaduskóot áwé koogéinaa yéi s aya.óo. They are recognizable by
the sash that they wear.

koojúxaa (TC)

wheelbarrow; hand truck, dolly
koojúxwaa (An), koojíxwaa (At)
·Koojúxaa káx' áwé has akaawachák wé gán. They hauled the firewood
in the wheel barrel.

koojúxwaa (An)

wheelbarrow; hand truck, dolly
koojúxaa (TC), koojíxwaa (At)

at kookeidí

parable

kookíts'aa

seesaw
kookéets'aa (At)
·Ldakát school áwé kookíts'aa áa yéi duwa.óo A seesaw is put at every
school.

kook'énaa

sandhopper
·Át wujik'éin wé kook'énaa. The sandhopper is hopping around.

kóoñ

pit; hole dug in the ground; cellar
·Tle hít tuwán áwé kóoñ áa kei has akaawaháa. Right next to the house
they dug a pit.
·Wé kóoñ a yee kawjiçít. It is dark inside the cellar.

kooñénaa

messenger; angel
·Kooñénaach áwé has du een kaawaneek yá aaçáa ñoowdziteeyí yé
haa Dikée aanñáawu. The messenger told them when our Lord was born.
·Du kooñénayi ñut wujixeex. His messenger ran away.

,

K

Dictionary of Tlingit

du kool

his/her navel, bellybutton
·Du kool áwé kawlixwétl. His navel itches.

kooléiý'waa

walrus
·Kooléiý'waa dleey gé duýá? Is walrus meat eaten?

du kóon

hem of his/her coat, shirt, dress

kóon

northern flicker
·Kóon t'aawú yéi ndu.eich al'eiý yís. Flicker feathers are used in dancing.

a kóon

its hem, bottom edge (of coat, dress, shirt); rim (of hat)
·Kaýsaké a kóon wé kinaak.át! Unravel the hem on the coat!

kóoshdaa

land otter; river otter
·Kóoshdaa haa eeçayáaknáý yan uwahín. The land otter swam through our beachfront.
·Aas t'éik áwé áa awdlisín wé kóoshdaa. The land otter hid behind a tree.

kóoshdaa náagu

liniment

kootéeyaa

totem pole
·Du ý'ayáý awliyéý wé kootéeyaa. He made the totem according to his instructions.
·Kootéeyaa gaýdulyeiýí ýáay yéi ndu.eich. When a totem is made it is yellow cedar that is used.

koot'áax'aa

marble
·Koot'áax'aa ash katoolyát noojín. We always used to play with marbles.

kootl'éit'aa
koow

tern

slippers (shell creature)

a koowú

its tail (of bird or fish)
·Ch'u tle a koowú teen ýwaaýáa. I ate the tail and all.

KOOX
• kawlikoox | yaa kanalkúx | yoo klikúxk
it drained out | it's draining out | it drains out (regularly).
ka-l-koox~ (na event)
for a kettle, container etc. to drain out, go dry
·Héen kawulkuxú duteen nooch wé hintu.eejí. When the water level
drops, the reef can always be seen.
• shaawakúx | --- | shakúxý
s/he is thirsty | --- | s/he gets thirsty (regularly).
O-sha-ø-koox~ (ø event)
for O to be thirsty; for O to be dry

kóox

rice; Kamchatka lily root
·Kóox een dus.ée tl'aañ'wách'. Wild rice is cooked with wild rhubarb.
·Kóox daakeit káa yéi du.úýx'. Rice is put into a container.

'

'

K

kooxéedaa

pencil; pen; brush
·Kooxéedaa eetéenáý yatee wé shaatk'. The young girl needs a pencil.
·Wéit tin x'úx' áwé a káa yan kaysatán i kooxéedayi! Put your pencil
on top of that book laying there!

kooxídaa (At)

fish spear with a long pole and detachable gaff hook

Kooya Ñwáan

Kuiu Island people

a kúdi

nest (of animal)
·Hinyikgáaxu kúdi awsiteen. She saw a golden eye duck's nest.

kuhaankée
kúñdlaa

orphan

bubbles, esp. from whale
gúñdlaa

kúñjaa

fast drip with bubbles

kunaçeey

cove; bight
kunaçeiy

kusakaak

thick

kút

nest
·A kúdi daat wudiñeen wé gandaas'aají. There is a bee flying around the
nest.

kutlá
kuts'een
kuwáat'
kux

stout
mouse; rat
long
aground, into shallow water

,

Dictionary of Tlingit

« Kw »
kwaan

smallpox

KWAAN
• át has wusikwaan | --- | --they are swimming around there; they swam around there | --- | ---.
P-t s-kwaan~ (na motion)
for birds to swim around on surface of water at P
·Héen wát át has wusikwaan wé gáaxw. The ducks are swimming around
at the mouth of the river.
·Gúñl' wéit wusikwaan. Swans are swimming around there.
• át jiwsikwaan | --- | --it is swimming around there; it swam around there | --- | ---.
P-t ji-s-kwaan~ (na motion)
for a bird or insect to swim around on surface of water at P (esp. aimlessly or in
circles)
·Héen kát jinaskwanchi át áwé wé atxaayí. The centipede swims on top
of the water.

Kwaashk'i Ñwáan

Kwaashk'i Kwáan, locally called "Humpback
Salmon"; a clan of the Raven moiety whose principal crest is the Humpback
Salmon

kwéiy

marker; mark, sign
·Du kwéiyi ñínt kaawaxíx wé at katé. The bullet fell short of his mark.

kwshé

Eh?; I wonder
kwshéi, kushé, kushéi
·Gu.aal kwshé iwulýéidliñ. Bless you. (Lit: I hope you get lucky.)

kwshéi

maybe; I'm not sure; [expression of uncertainly]
kwshé, gushéi, gushé

-k'

little; precious; [diminutive suffix]
Adding -k' to the end of a noun indicates small size. When
added to a kin term, it serves as a term of endearment.
·Eesháank' kaltéelñ áwé haat wujixíx aý dachýánk'. Poor thing, my
grandchild ran over here shoeless.

,

,

K'

« K' »
k'aagán

stickleback

K'AAN
• awshik'aan | ashik'áan | --s/he hated him/her/it | s/he hates him/her/it | ---.
O-S-sh-k'aan~ (ga state)
for S to hate O
This is the only known stative verb with ga- conjugation
prefix and a variable stem. All other stative verbs with gaconjugation prefix have invariable stems.

k'ákw

owl without ear tufts
·Tlél aa ñwasatínch wé k'ákw yóo duwasáagu aa tsísk'w. I have never
seen the bird they call the owl without ear tufts.
·Taatx' áwé has al'óon wé k'ákw. Owls hunt at night.

K'ÁTS'
• yawlik'áts' | yalik'áts' | kei yalak'áts'ch
it got sharp | it's sharp | it gets sharp (regularly).
ya-l-k'aats'~ (ga state)
for an edge to be sharp
·Nóosk ýaagú ñúnáý yalik'áts'. Wolverine claws are really sharp.
·Yalik'áts' du çaltulítayi. His pocketknife is sharp.

k'eeljáa

chinook wind; south wind
k'eiljáa
·K'eeljáa tóonáý yaa nañúý. He is driving through a storm.
·K'eeljáa teen áyá séew haat ayawditée. Rain came with the storm.

K'EET'
• aadé

(ha)s kawdik'éet' | aadé yaa (ha)s kandak'ít' |
aadé yoo (ha)s kadak'ít'k
the group went there | the group is going there (in stages) | the group goes there
(regularly).
P-dé O-ka-di-k'éet'~ (na motion)
for O (group of people) to all go or come to P
·Aan kaadé ñukawdik'éet'. Everyone went uptown.

• át

has kawdik'ít' | aadé yaa (ha)s kandak'ít' | áý has
kadak'éet'
the group went to it | the group is going to it (in stages) | the group goes to it
(regularly).
P-t~ O-ka-d-k'éet'~ (ø motion)
for O (group of people) to all leave, go or come to P

,

K'

Dictionary of Tlingit

·Áat' jiyeet, gangookt ñukawdik'ít'. People crowded close around the fire
because of the cold weather.
• ñoowak'ít' | ñuk'éet' | ñuk'ít'ý
s/he picked berries | s/he is picking berries | s/he picks berries (regularly).
ñu-S-ø-k'éet'~ (ø act)
for S to pick berries (esp. pick in quantity to take home)
·Ñuk'éet' gaýtoo.áat ch'eeý'çaa. We are going to pick thimbleberries.
·Aý dlaak' tín Xunaadé ñugaýtootéen kanat'á ñuk'éet' yís. We are
going to travel to Hoonah to pick blueberries with my sister.

k'éets'an

false azalea (fruitless bush)
·Ch'as k'éets'an áyá yáaçaa wootee. There's nothing but false azalea
around here.

K'EEÝ'
• yanaý wushik'éeý' | --- | yanaý kei shak'íý'ch
he/she/it got hung up | --- | he/she/it gets hung up (regularly).
P-náý O-sh-k'éeý'~ (ga motion)
for O to get delayed, stuck, hung up at P
-k'éiý'
·Wáançaneensx' yanaý kei shak'íý'ch aý yoo ý'atángi. Sometimes my
words get hung up.

a k'eeyí

its base (of tree or other plant); the lower part of its trunk or stem
·Aas k'eeyéet ash aawatán du óonayi. He leaned his rifle against the tree
trunk.

K'EI
• awlik'éi | kei analk'éin | kei alk'éich
s/he improved it | s/he is improving it | s/he improves it (regularly).
O-S-l-k'éi~ (ga event)
for S to improve O; for S to make peace, make up with O (after quarrel)
• ñoowak'ei | ñuwak'éi | yei ñuk'éich
the weather became good | the weather is good | the weather becomes good
(regularly).
ñu-ø-k'ei~ (ça state)
for the weather to be good
·Yeedát ñuyak'éi çaatáa yéi daané yís yá kaxwaan káý yaa nagúdi.
Today the weather is good for walking out on the frost to check the traps.
• du toowú wook'éi | du toowú yak'éi | du toowú kei

k'éich
s/he was happy | s/he is happy | s/he gets happy (regularly).
N toowú ø-k'éi (ga state imperf. -k'éi/-k'é)

for N to be glad, happy, feel fine

·Ñúnáý wé yee woo.éex'i aa tsú yee ýoo yéi kçwatée toowú k'é
teen. Your hostess will welcome you all as well. (Lit: Your hostess will be among you all with good feelings.)

·Ña ýát tsú aý toowú yak'éi yaa a káa yéi ýat guçwateeyí yaa

,

,

K'

Lingítý ýat sateeyí. And I too am thankful that I'm part of this being that I'm Lingít.

• tlél wushk'é | tlél ushk'é | tlél kei ushk'éich
he/she/it was bad | he/she/it is bad | he/she/it gets bad (regularly).

tlél O-sh-k'éi~ (ga state)
for O to be bad, evil, no good

Some fluent speakers consider this a taboo word to use in reference to another person, while others find it acceptable. For speakers who find it acceptable, here is an example: Tlél ushik'éiyi ñáa áwé. "That man is no good."

·Lushik'éiyi át ákwé atxaayí? Is the centipede poisonous?

·Tlél ushik'éiyi aa yoo ý'atánk áwé tsá a.aýji nooch . She always only hears the bad talk.

• wook'éi | yak'éi | kei k'éich
he/she/it was good; he/she/it got better | he/she/it is good | he/she/it gets better (regularly).

O-ø-k'éi (ga state)
for O to be good, fine, pretty

·L'ook at ý'éeshi áwé yak'éi. Coho salmon dryfish is good.

·L'ook kaháagu áyá yak'éi kanat'á kanéegwál' sákw. Coho salmon eggs are good for blueberry sauce.

• du ý'é wook'éi | du ý'é yak'éi | --s/he liked the taste of it | s/he likes the taste of it | ---.

N ý'é ø-k'éi (ga state)
for N to like the taste of something

·Çáý dleeyí gé i ý'é yak'éi? Does rabbit meat taste good to you?

·Gangukçáýi ñúnáý has du ý'é yak'éi. The fish heads cooked around the fire are very tasty to them.

k'eiljáa

chinook wind; south wind
k'eeljáa

K'EIN
• át wujik'éin | --- | --he/she/it is jumping around; he/she/it jumped around | --- | ---.

P-t S-j-k'éin~ (na motion)
for (singular) S to jump around at P

·Át wujik'éin wé kook'énaa. The sandhopper is hopping around.

·Wé gawdáan yádi át wujik'éin. That colt is jumping around.

• kei has kawduwak'én | kei (ha)s kanduk'én | kei

kaduk'éný
they jumped | they're getting ready to jump | they jump (regularly).
kei O-ka-du-ø-k'éin~ (ø motion)
for (plural) O to jump
·Tlákw kaduk'énx' wé cheech. The porpoise always jump.

,

(ha)s

K'

Dictionary of Tlingit

k'eit

young salmonberry bush shoots (edible)
·K'eit duýáayin. Young salmonberry bush shoots used to be eaten.

K'EIÝ'
• ashaawak'éý' | --- | ashak'éý'ý
s/he hooked it in the head | --- | s/he hooks it in the head (regularly).
O-sha-S-ø-k'éiý'~ (ø event)
for S to hook O (fish) in the head
-k'éeý'~ (An)

du k'í

his/her rump; the flesh around his/her hips
·Ch'a tlákw .áa áwé yanéekw du k'í. His rump hurts from sitting all the
time.
·Aý k'í wulix'wás'ñ. My rump is numb.

a k'í

the base or foot of it (a standing object)

du k'idaaká

next door to him/her/it
·Yee k'idaaká ñu.óowu gaysaýán! Love your neighbor!

k'idaaká aa

neighbor
·Haa k'idaaká ñu.óowu taat kanaý has at wooshee. Our neighbors
sang all night long.

k'idaañwáani

neighbors

k'idéin

well
·K'idéin aaý xásh wé t'áa at ý'aýéedli! Cut the trimming off the board
good!
·K'idéin gé sh eeltín? Are you taking good care of yourself?

du k'iñl'án

his/her palate

du k'iñl'én (C)

k'inashóo

pneumonia
·K'inashóo néekw áyá aawasháat. She caught pneumonia.

k'inchéiyi

rose
·K'inchéiyi áwé aý tláa jeeyís ýwaa.oo. I bought a rose for my mother.

k'inchéiyi tléiçu

rosehip
·K'inchéiyi tléiçu teen wududzi.ée yóo kanat'á. Those blueberries were
cooked with rosehips.

k'ínk'

aged fish head
·Yak'éi k'ínk' ýoox' ýáat yik.ádi. The fish guts are good in fermenting stink
heads.
·K'ínk'i tséegi ñúnáý yak'éi. Barbecued fermented salmon heads are very
good.

k'isáani

boys, young men
·K'isáani át yawdiháa. There's a crowd of young men there.

,

,

K'

·K'isáanich gán du jeeyís has aawaxásh. The young men cut wood for
him.

a k'ishataaçaní

quills on rear end of it (porcupine)
a k'ishetaaçaní (C)
·A k'ishataaçaní yéi ndu.eich guk kajaashí yís. Its quills are used for
earrings.

k'íý'aa

gaff hook; grappling hook
k'éý'aa

a k'iyee

near the base of it; at the foot of it; the back, rear or it
(house); behind it (house); under the shelter of it (a standing object or structure)
·Wé aas k'iyeet áwé has ñéen. They're sitting beneath the tree.

k'oodás'

shirt
goodás', k'oodés' (C)
·Nás'k a doogú x'óow áwé du káa kakçwagéi k'oodás' sákw, wé ñáa
tlein. It will take three leather blankets for the big man's shirt.
·Aý al'eiý k'oodás'i ch'áagu kawóot áwé a daawú á. There are old
beads on my dance shirt.

a k'óol'

its back end; stern (of boat)
a k'óol'i
·A k'óol'de kaychák! You all pack it in the stern!
·A k'óol'i has çaaçañee wé at yátx'i. Let the children sit in the stern.

du k'óol'

his/her tailbone; bottom of his/her spine

K'OOTS
• awlik'oots | --- | yoo alik'útsk
s/he broke it | --- | s/he breaks it (regularly).
O-S-l-k'oots~ (na event)
for S to break O (esp. rope-like objects)
·A x'éix'u áwé yoo dudlik'útsk wé ýáat. One breaks the gills of the fish.

k'óox

marten
·K'óoxçaa al'óon áwé has woo.aat. They went hunting for marten.

k'óox dísi

Venus

k'óoý'

gum; lead
·Gút yéi ý'alatseenín k'óoý'. Gum used to cost a dime.

k'óoý' létl'k
k'óoý' tíx'i
k'ul'kaskéxkw

soft lead

leadline (of net)
beetle

k'únts'

potato
·Wé akahéiýi jeedáý k'únts' has aawa.oo. They bought potatoes from the farmer.

,

K'

Dictionary of Tlingit

a k'únts'i

its testicles (of moose, caribou)

k'uwaaní

deer cabbage, lily-of-the-valley

,

,

K'w

« K'w »
k'wálý

fiddlehead fern (with edible rhizome)

k'wát'

egg (of bird)
·Wáa sá koogéi wé k'wát'? How many eggs are there?
·K'wát' X'áadidé gaýtooñóoý kéidladi k'wádiçáa. We are going to Egg
Island for seagull eggs.

du k'wát'

his testicles

K'WÁT'
• awdlik'wát' | --- | alk'wát'ý
it laid an egg | --- | it lays eggs (regularly).
a-d-l-k'waat'~ (ø event)
for birds to lay eggs, nest
Note that the verb in the example sentence here: ilk'wát'ý is
the intransitive repetitive form, while the repetitive form given
above: alk'wát'ý is transitive. The difference is that the transitive
form focuses more on the object (in this case, the egg). For
example, alk'wát'ý could be translated as "it lays eggs" while
ilk'wát'ý could be translated as "it reproduces (in the form of an
egg)".
·Kichyaat ilk'wát'ý sít' yáx'. Terns lay eggs by glaciers.

,

Ñ

Dictionary of Tlingit

« Ñ »
ña

and
·S'igeidí l'eedí yawúý' ña ñ'áatl' yáý yatee. A beaver's tail is wide and
flat.
·T'ooch' ña tl'áatl' yáý daçaatée gandaas'aají. Bees are black and yellow.
1

ÑAA

• áa ajikaawañaa | --- | áa yoo ajikaayañéik
s/he gave him/her orders | --- | s/he gives him/her orders (regularly).
áa O-ji-ka-(u)-S-ø-ñaa~ (na event)
for S to instruct, give O orders (to do)
Note that in classical Tlingit, this verb had a thematic prefix
(u-) which is slowly falling out of modern day speech. This is
indicated in the Leer-Edwards theme as (u)-. Alternate forms
given online show one form with the thematic (u)- and one
without, both of which are acceptable in modern speech.
·Aan adul'eiý aýáa kañach'áak'wt áyá áa ýat jikawduwañaa. I have
been commissioned to carve a dance paddle.
·Xeitl kakéin k'oodás' aý yageeyí kaadéi áa ñaa jikaawañaa aý
léelk'wch. My grandmother commissioned a Thunderbird sweater for my
birthday.
• akaawañaa | --- | yoo akayañéik / yoo akuwañéik
s/he sent him/her on an errand | --- | s/he sends him/her on an errand (regularly).
O-ka-(u)-S-ø-ñaa~ (na event)
for S to send O (esp. on a mission or errand, or to deliver a message)
Note that in classical Tlingit, this verb had a thematic prefix
(u-) which is slowly falling out of modern day speech. This is
indicated in the Leer-Edwards theme as (u)-. Alternate forms
given above show one form with the thematic (u)- and one without,
both of which are acceptable in modern speech.
·Yan uwaneiyi hít kaságuçáa kawduwañaa. He was sent for ready-made
rafters.
• --- | yéi adaayañá | ----- | s/he tells him/her that | ---.
(yéi) O-daa-ya-S-ø-ñá (act)
for S to tell O (that)
This verb only occurs in the imperfective.
·Yéi daayaduñá, "Tlél kadéix' haa káý sheeteeñ!" He is told "Don't
bring shame on us!"
• yéi yaawañaa | yéi ý'ayañá | yoo ý'ayañeik
s/he said that | s/he is saying that | s/he says that (regularly).
(yéi) (ý'a)-ya-S-ø-ñaa~ (na act)
for S to say (a certain thing); for S to confess, acknowledge, declare (a certain

,

,

Ñ

thing)
Note that the imperfective forms and prohibitive forms
require the thematic prefix ý'a- which refers to the mouth. Also
note that some speakers use yóo instead of yéi, as in: yóo
yaawañaa "s/he said that".
·Ý'agáax' áwé litseen yéi yaawañaa aý léelk'w. My grandparent said
that prayer is powerful.
·"Tliyéix', jinaháa haa kát çwaaxeex," yóo ý'ayañá du tláa. Her
mother says, "Behave, bad luck might befall us!"
• yoo ayawsiñaa | yoo ayanasñá | yoo ayasiñéik
s/he told him/her that | s/he is telling him/her that | s/he tells him/her (regularly).
(yoo) O-ya-S-s-ñaa~ (na event)
for S to tell, say (that) to O; for S to ask O to do (that)
·"Iýsiýán," yoo ayawsiñaa du yadák'u. She told her boyfriend, "I love
you."
·At géide ayawsiñaa du kéek' tatgé. She spoke wrongly against her
younger sister yesterday.
2

ÑAA

• aawañáa | añéis' | --s/he sewed it | s/he is sewing it | ---.
O-S-ø-ñaa~ (ø act)
for S to sew O
·Yá aý l'eiý k'oodás' a wán shóot at ñá! Sew something to the edge of my
dance shirt!
·Yá kat'íshaa at xáshdi téel aan ýañéis'. I sew moccasins with this
leather needle.
• a káa akaawañáa | a káa akañéis' | a káa akañéiý
s/he embroidered it on it | s/he's embroidering it on it | s/he embroiders it on it
(regularly).
O-ka-S-ø-ñaa~ (ø act)
for S to sew beads, embroider O
To indicate what the design was embroidered onto, use: N
káa "on N". For example: Yéil du luljíni káa akaawañáa. "S/he
embroidered a raven on his/her vest." This is not required with
this verb, however, and therefore is not given in the Leer-Edwards
theme. This sentence is also acceptable: Yéil akaawañáa. "S/he
embroidered a raven."
·Gunýaa yaka.óot' du l.uljíni kát akaawañáa. She sewed the abalone
buttons on her vest.
·Kawóot teen ñ'eikaxwéin a káa kañá! Embroider a flower on it with
beads!
• a kát akawliñáa | a kaadé yaa akanalñéin | a káý

aklañéiý
s/he sewed it on it | s/he is sewing it on it | s/he sews it on it (regularly).

P-t~ O-ka-S-l-ñaa~ (ø motion)
for S to sew O on P

,

Ñ

• wudiñáa | dañéis' | --s/he sewed | s/he sews; s/he is sewing | ---.
S-d-ñaa~ (ø act)
for S to sew
·Tl'iñnaa.át een duñéis'. A thimble is used for sewing.
·Tlél gooháa aadéi k'idéin dañéis'i yé. It's obvious how well she sews.
3

ÑAA

• awdliñáa | alñáa | --s/he gambled | s/he is gambling | ---.
a-S-d-l-ñáa (na act)
for S to gamble (by means of gambling sticks, dice, etc.); for S to play cards
·S'íx' kawtoo.óos'i ítnáý agaýtoolñáa. After we have washed the dishes we
will play cards.

ñáa

man; male; person, people
·Nás'k a doogú x'óow áwé du káa kakçwagéi k'oodás' sákw, wé ñáa
tlein. It will take three leather blankets for the big man's shirt.
·Sagú yáý ñaa yayík du.aýji nooch héendei yaa ana.ádi. Men's voices
would always sound happy when they went to the sea.

ñaa at oohéini

possession; that which is claimed
·Çooch Yanyeidí ñaa at oohéini áwé. The Wolf crest is the property of the
Yanyeidí Clan.
·S'igeidí Deisheetaan ñaa at oohéini áwé. The Beaver is the property of
the Deisheetaan Clan.

ñaa at óowu

possession(s); that which is owned (by them)
ñaa et óowu (C)
·X'átgu áwé Shangukeidí has du at óowuý sitee. The dogfish is an
artifact of the Thunderbiird people.
·Shayadihéini at óow wéide yaa ndusxát'. They are hauling lots of
someone's possessions over that way.

Ñaachýana.áak'w

Wrangell
·Ñaachýana.áak'wde daak uwañúý wé yaakw. The boat set out for
Wrangell.
·Ñaachýana.áak'wdáý haat aawa.át. People walked here from Wrangell.

Ñaach.ádi

Kaach.ádi, locally called "Sockeye"; a clan of the Raven
moiety whose principal crest is the Sockeye

ñaa daakeidí

coffin; casket
·Ñaa daakeidí wududliyéý. Someone built a casket.

ñaadaaxaashí

surgeon
·Ñaadaaxaashí ýánde kawduwanáa. He was sent to the surgeon.
·Dr. Smith yóo duwasáakw wé ñaadaaxaashí. The surgeon's name is
Dr. Smith.

ñaa daa yaséiýi

doctor

,

,

Ñ

ñaa ji.eetí

handiwork, handmade crafts
·Ñaa ji.eetí wéix' duhóon. They are selling handmade crafts there.
·Ñúnáý yak'éi áyá ñaa ji.eetí. This is really good handiwork.

ñaa kanaýñáa

snob; person who considers himself/herself better than

others
ñaa kenaýñáa (C)

ñáakwt~

accidentally, wrongly
·Áa ñúý teedataan wé ñáakwt iwuneiýí! Think back to the time when you
got hurt!

ÑAAÑ
• wujiñaañ | --- | yei ishñáñch
he/she/it squatted | --- | he/she/it squats (reguarly).
S-j-ñaañ~ (ça event)
for (singular) S to squat, sit down low; for (singular) S to sit down quickly, squat
down; for (singular) S to land (of waterfowl, plane)
·Aý tl'eiñ káa wjiñaañ digitgiyáa. A hummingbird landed on my finger.

ñaañýwdaagané (A)

accident; unfortunate mistake or mishap
ñaañýwdaganée (T)

ñaanaawú tl'átgi

graveyard
·Ñaanaawú tl'átgi kaadéi yakñwaýáa ñ'eikaxwéin. I will transport flowers to the graveyard.

ñaankak.eetx' (T)

in public; at a potlatch, feast
ñaankageetx' (T), ñaank'egeex' (C)
·Ñaankak.eetx' yoo ý'eiwatán. He spoke in public.
·Ñaankak.eetx' has at wooshee ña (ha)s aawal'eiý. They sang and danced in public.

ñaa ooý layeiýí

dentist
ñaa ooý leyeiýí (C)

ñaa ooý yei daanéiyi

dentist
·Du yéet ñaa ooý yéi daanéiyiý sitee. His son is a dentist.
·Du ée yan at wududlitóow ñaa ooý yéi daanéiyi yís. She completed dentistry school.

ñáas'

match; stick
·A ý'éináý áwé kadul.eesh wé ñáas' kaadéi wé saak. Those hooligan are strung through the mouth on the stick.
·Al'óon wugoodí uýganñáas' du çaltóode ayaawa.oo. When he was going hunting, he put matches in his pocket.

ñaa s'aatí

boss
·Wuduwaýooý yóode wé ñaa s'aatí. The boss was called to go over there.

du ñáash

his/her pelvis, hip

,

Ñ

ñaa sháade háni

leader
ñaa sháade héni (C)
·Wé ñaa sháade háni ñaa ýani daak uwagút. The leader came out to the people.
·Wé haa sháade háni "gunalchéesh" haa jeeyís yéi yanañéich. Our leader says "thank you" for us.

ñaa sháade náñx'i

leaders
·Deisleenx' keijín has yatee ñaa sháade náñx'i. In Teslin there are five leaders.
·Nás'gináý has yatee wé Yéil naa sháade náñx'i. There are three Raven Clan leaders.

ñáa shaan

old man
·Wé gán aan nagú wé ñáa shaan du shóot açida.aagít! Go with the wood to build a fire for the elderly man!
·Jinkaat kéet gooshí ayatéen wé ñáa shaan. The old man sees ten killerwhale dorsal fins.

ñaa shaksayéigu

comb

ñaa shaksayíñs'i

hair pendant

ñaashashýáaw

dragonfly
·Ñaashashýáaw taakw.eetíx' haaý kalyeech. The dragonflies come in the summer time.
·Ñaashashýáaw tláakw át nadañínch. The dragonfly flies around fast.

ñaashaxáshaa

scissors
·Ñaashaxáshaa aý jeet katí! Hand me the scissors!
·Wé ñaashaxáshaa yalik'áts' The scissors are sharp.

ñaatoowú

chickadee
ñaatook'ú (C)
·Ñaatoowú yáax' shayadihéin ñukawult'éex'i. There are lots of chickadees here when it's still icy.
·Wáa yateeyi yéix' yáax' yéi aa nateech táakw kanaý wé ñaatoowú. Sometimes some chickadees stay here through the winter.

ñaa toowú lat'aa

comfort
ñaa toowú let'aa (C)
·Ñaa toowú lat'aa yáý du ée yatee wé kinaak.át ñusa.áat' tóox'. The coat is a comfort to him in the cold.
·Ñaa toowú lat'aa áwé ý'aan. The fire is a comfort.

du ñaatl

his/her flank, side of his/her belly

du ñáawu

his/her husband's clan brother; his/her man, boyfriend,
husband
·Yat'aayi héen du ñáawu ý'éit awsi.ín. She gave her husband's clan brother coffee.

,

,

Ñ

ñáax'w

men
·Nás'gináý ñáax'w áwé hít káa yéi jiné. There are three men working on that house.

ñaaý

merganser
·Ñaaý haaý kalyeech. Mergansers migrate here.
·Ñaaý aawa.ún. He shot a merganser.

ñaa ý'a.eetí

leftovers, food scraps
·Ñaa ý'a.eetí awsit'áa. She warmed up the leftovers.
·Ñaa ý'a.eetí keitl ý'éiý aawatee. He fed the scraps to the dog.

ñaa ý'éidáý kashxeedí

secretary (stenographer)
ñaa ý'éitý kashxeedí
·Ñaa ý'éidáý kashxeedí yáý yéi jiné. She works as a secretary.
·Aý ýooní ñaa ý'éidáý kashxeedí áwé. My friend is a secretary.

ñaa ý'oos

foot (measurement)
·Tléix' ñaa ý'oos yéi kwliyáat' wé tíx'. That rope is one foot long.
·Gwál tleiñaa ý'oos áwé a kaýyeedé. It must be twenty feet to the ceiling.

ñaa ý'oos deiyí

foot path
ñaa ý'usdeiyí
·Gwálaa teen ch'áal' aawas'úw ñaa ý'oos deiyí kaaý. He chopped
willows off the foot trail with a machete.
·Shaanáý yaawashóo wé ñaa ý'oos deiyí. The foot trail extends through
the valley.

ñaa yakçwahéiyagu

spirit
·Ý'agáax' tóonáý ñaa yakçwahéiyagu litseen. Through prayer, a
person's spirit is strong.
·Du yakçwahéiyágu tléil ultseen. His spirit is weak.

ñaayaku.óot'i (At)

button
ñaayuka.óot'i (T)

ñaa yat'éináý

in secret (where nobody can see); away from people's
view
·Ñaa yat'éináý hít yeedáý woogoot. He left the house when no one was
looking.
·Ñaa yat'éináý x'wán daasa.áýw wé ñóok! Wrap that box when no one is
looking now!

ñaayuka.óot'i x'óow (T)

button blanket
yuka.óot' x'óow, ñaayaku.óot'i x'óow (At), ñaakóot'i x'óow
(T), kaakóot'i x'óow (C)

ñachoo

actually; in fact; contrary to what was thought
ýachoo

ñákw

basket
·Ñákw yéi daané yís áwé yéi daaýané yá sháak. I am collecting this

,

timothy grass for making baskets.
·Dáñde ñákw aawayaa i léelk'w. Your grandmother died. (Lit: Your grandmother took her basket into the woods).

ñashde

I thought
ñashdei

du ñatlyá

his/her flank, side of his/her body between the ribs and the hip
·Aý ñatlyát wujiýín wé ýáaw tlein. That big log fell on my side.
·Du ñatlyá awlichún. He hurt his side.

ÑEE
• --- | has ñéen | ----- | they are sitting | ---.
S-ø-ñee~ (position)
for (plural) S to be seated
This verb only occurs in the imperfective. Note that a noun phrase with (-t) postposition is used to indicate where one is sitting, but this noun phrase is not required by the verb. For example, one could say: has ñéen "they are sitting", or: át has ñéen "they are sitting there".
·Wé aas chéý'i tayeet áwé tooñéen. We are sitting in the shade of the tree.
·Dáýnáý a géekt añéen wé yaakw. There are two people sitting at the stern of the boat.
• has wooñee | yei (ha)s nañéen | yei has ñéech
they sat down | they are sitting down | they sit down (regularly).
S-ø-ñee~ (ça event)
for S to sit down
·Atoosçeiwú atyátx'i latíni ýáný has çañéech aý yátx'i. When we are gillnetting my children stay with a babysitter.
·A k'óol'i has çaaçañee wé at yátx'i. Let the children sit in the stern.

ñéech'

scab

ÑEEN
• át wudiñeen | --- | át yoo diñéenk
he/she/it is flying around; he/she/it flew around | --- | he/she/it flies around (regularly).
P-t S-d-ñeen~ (na motion)
for (singular) S (bird, or persons in a plane) to fly around at P
·Du kíji áwé wool'éex' wé ts'ítskw, ách áwé tlél át wudañeen. The songbird's wing broke, that's why it doesn't fly around.
·Gandaadagóogu wéit wudiñeen. A woodpecker is flying around there.

ñées'

flood; tide

ñées' shuwee

high tide line
ñées' shuyee

,

,

Ñ

ÑEET'
• wudliñít' | yaa nalñít' | ilñít'ý
it's infected | it's getting infected | it gets infected (regularly).
d-l-ñéet'~ (ø event)
for a wound to be infected, have pus
Note that both forms given in the perfective habitual are
acceptable to all speakers consulted for this project.
·Du tl'eiñt yawdiçiji sheey kañáas'i áx' wudliñít'. It got infected where
the splinter poked her finger.

ñéet'

pus; discharge (from a sore, wound); sore, wound that discharges pus
·A daa át kas'ít déi wéi ñéet'! Wrap something around the pus now!

Ñéeý'

Kake
Ñéiý'

ñeeý'é

dawn, daybreak
ñee.aý'é, ñei.ý'é (An), ñee.á, ñei.á
·Ñeeý'é shukát áwé shoodanookch aý léelk'w. My grandfather wakes up
before dawn.

Ñéeý' Ñwáan

people of Kake

ñee.á

dawn, daybreak
ñei.á, ñeeý'é, ñeiý'é (An), ñee.aý'é
·Ñee.á shukát áwé çunéi gaýtooñóoý. We will start traveling before dawn.

ÑEI

• ajeewañéi | ajiñéi | yóo ajiyañéik
s/he paid him/her | s/he pays him/her; s/he is paying him/her | s/he pays him/her
(regularly).
O-ji-S-ø-ñéi (na act)
for S to pay O (esp. a person, for work done); for S to pay for O
·Jiduñéi at wuskóowuý sateeyéech. He is paid because he is a
knowledgeable person.
·K'idéin has jiduñéi katíý'aa s'aatí Dzántik'i Héenix'. Jailers are paid
well in Juneau.

ñéich'ál'

seam

Ñéiý'

Kake
Kéeý'
·Du daat shkalneek ñudzitee Ñéiý'dáý ñ'atýáan. There is a story about
the coward from Kake.
·Ñéiý'dei naýtooñooý shaawçáa. Let's travel to Kake for some gumboots.

ñeiý'é (An)

dawn, daybreak
ñee.aý'é, ñeeý'é, ñei.á, ñee.á
·Wé çagaan kei yaséich wé ñeiý'ét ñuwuhaayí. The sun lifts its face
when dawn breaks.

,

Ñ

ñei.á

dawn, daybreak
ñee.á, ñee.aý'é, ñeeý'é, ñeiý'é (An)

ñénaa

long feather; quill (of bird)
ñínaa

ñín

brant (small goose)

a ñín

less than it; (reaching, falling) short of it; not (big or
far) enough for it
·A ñín kaawagei. There wasn't enough.
·A ñín aý jee koogéi wé k'oodás' yeidí. I have less than the price of that
shirt.

ñínaa

long feather; quill (of bird)
ñénaa
·Ñínaa teen aawatáñ du gúk. She pierced her ear with a quill.

ÑOO
• wudliñoo | ilñú | yoo iliñúk
s/he vomited | s/he vomits; s/he is vomiting | s/he vomits (regularly).
S-d-l-ñoo~ (na act)
for S to vomit, throw up

ñóo at latóowu (T)

teacher
ñóo at latéewu (At), ñóo et letóowu (C)
·Ñóo at latóowu yís áwé du ée at wududlitóow. He was taught to be a
teacher.

ñóok

box
·Ñóok shutú aawatséý. She died. (Lit: S/he kicked the edge of the box.)
·Tl'aadéin áwé át tán wé ñóok. The box is sitting sideways.

ñoon sh kalneegí

storyteller; preacher
·Haa ñoon sh kalneegí áwé ñúnáý tuli.aan. Our preacher is very kind.

ÑOOTL'
• kawshiñútl' | kashiñútl'k | kashañútl'ý
it got muddy | it's muddy | it gets muddy (regularly).
ka-sh-ñóotl'~ (ø state)
for a road, etc. to be muddy
·Kashiñútl'k wé héen táak. The bottom of that river is muddy.

ñoowajaçi aa

murderer
·Wé ñoowajaçi aa du daach kalneek x'úx' káa yéi yatee. There is a
story about the murderer in the paper.

a ñoowú

its den, lair (of animal, undergound)
·Yóot sh wudligás' a ñoowúdáý. It charged out of its den.
·Tléil awuskú xóots ñoowú káý wugoodí. He did not know that he had
walked over a grizzly bear den.

'

'

Ñ

a ñóox'

in the midst of it (a crowd, an activity or event involving
several people); in the hubbub
·Yaa ñu.éex' ñóox' ñu.aa áyá aý yaawdudlit'áa yá saa Ñaajaañwtí.
Though during potlatches they call me this name, Ñaajaañwtí.
1

ÑOOÝ

• aadé awsiñooý | aadé yaa anasñúý | aadé yoo asiñúýk
s/he drove it there | s/he is driving it there | s/he drives it there (regularly).
P-dé O-S-s-ñooý~ (na motion)
for S to drive O (boat, car) to P
• aadé wooñooý | aadé yaa nañúý | aadé yoo yañúýk
s/he drove there | s/he is driving there | s/he drives there (regularly).
P-dé S-ø-ñooý~ (na motion)
for S to travel, go toward P (in a boat, car)
·Héen yíkde wooñooý. He went up the river (by boat).
·A kayéikçaa áwé ñuntoos.áých shtéen káa haadé yaa nañúýu. We
always listen for the sound of the steam engine when it's coming.
• át awsiñúý | aadé yaa anasñúý | áý asñooý

s/he drove it to it | s/he is driving it to it | s/he drives it to it (regularly).

P-t~ O-S-s-ñooý~ (ø motion)

for S to drive O (boat, car) to P

·Çeey tá déilit awsiñúý du yaagú. She drove her boat to the head of the bay.

• át uwañúý | aadé yaa nañúý | áý ñooý

s/he drove to it | s/he is driving to it | s/he drives to it (regularly).

P-t~ S-ø-ñooý~ (ø motion)

for S to travel, go to P (by boat, car)

·Dzeit shuyeet uwañúý wé yaakw. The boat motored to the landing.

·Geesh tóot uwañúý wé yaakw. The boat drove in among the kelp.

• át wooñooý | --- | át yoo yañúýk

s/he is driving around; s/he drove around | --- | s/he drives around (regularly).

P-t S-ø-ñooý~ (na motion)

for S to travel, go around at P (by boat, car)

·Yaakw áa kát wooñooý. A boat is cruising around on the lake.

·Ñutý.ayanahá káax' át has nañúých. They navigate by the stars.

• awsiñooý | yaa anasñúý | yoo asiñúýk

s/he drove it | s/he is driving it | s/he drives it (regularly).

O-S-s-ñooý~ (na motion)

for S to drive O (car); for S to skipper O (boat)

·Wé ñáa a géeknáý áwé yaa anasñúý du yaagú. The man is driving his boat from the stern.

• ayawdiñúý | --- | awudañúýý

s/he turned back | --- | s/he turns back (regularly).

a-ya-u-S-d-ñooý~ (ø motion)

for S to turn back, return (by boat, car)

,

Ñ

• daak uwañúý | daak nañúý | daak ñúých
s/he went out to sea | s/he is going out to sea | s/he goes out to sea (regularly).
daak S-ø-ñooý~ (ø motion)
for S to go out to sea (in a boat); for S to move into the open (in a boat, car)
·Ñaachýana.áak'wde daak uwañúý wé yaakw. The boat set out for
Wrangell.
• a daaý yaawañúý | a daaý yaa nañúý | a daaý yaa

ñúých
s/he drove around it | s/he is driving around it | s/he drives around it (regularly).
N daaý ya-u-S-ø-ñooý~ (ø motion)
for S to circle, drive around N (by boat, car)
·X'aa daaý yaawañúý wé yaakw. The boat motored around the point.
• çunéi uwañúý | --- | çunéi ñooýý
s/he started driving | --- | s/he starts driving (regularly).
çunéi S-ø-ñooý~ (ø motion)
for S to begin traveling, going (by boat, car)
·Taan áa awsiteeni yé a niyaadé çunéi uwañúý. He started motoring in
the direction he had seen the sea lion.
·Ñee.á shukát áwé çunéi gaýtooñóoý. We will start traveling before
dawn.
• ñut wooñooý | ñut kei nañúý | ñut kei ñúých
s/he got lost | s/he is getting lost | s/he gets lost (regularly).
ñut S-ø-ñooý~ (ga motion)
for S to get lost (going by motorized vehicle)
• a tóonáý yaawañúý | a tóonáý yaa nañúý | a tóonáý

yaa ñúých
s/he drove through it | s/he is driving through it | s/he drives through it
(regularly).
P-náý ya-u-S-ø-ñooý~ (ø motion)
for S to travel, go through P (by boat, car)
·K'eeljáa tóonáý yaa nañúý. He is driving through a storm.
• wooñooý | yaa nañúý | yoo yañúýk
s/he went (by motorized vehicle) | s/he is going (by motorized vehicle) | s/he goes
(by motorized vehicle) (regularly).
S-ø-ñooý~ (na motion)
for S to travel, go (by boat, car)
·Yaa nañúý stéen káa ý'anaat áwé hán wé dzísk'w tlein. The big
moose was standing in the way of the steam train.
• --- | yaa nañúý | ----- | s/he is going along (by boat, car) | ---.
yaa S-ø-ñooý~ (ga motion)
for S to be going, traveling along (by boat, car)
This is an example of a progressive epiaspectual paradigm
(Leer, 91), which basically means that all forms are based on the
progressive aspect. The progressive epiaspect is characterized by:
1)having the yaa preverb in all forms, 2)having no perfective form,

,

,

Ñ

and 3)denotes semantically a continuous transition from one location or state to another.
·Kaldaaçéináý yaa gaýtooñóoý, tlél çwadlaan yá éiý' yík. We will travel along slowly, it's not deep in this slough.
• yan uwañúý | yánde yaa nañúý | yaý ñooý
s/he went ashore | s/he is going ashore | s/he goes ashore (regularly).
yan~ S-ø-ñooý~ (ø motion)
for S to go ashore (in a boat); for S to come to a rest, stop (in a boat, car)
·Wé áa kaanáý yan uwahóowu watsíx a ítnáý yan uwañúý wé yaakw. The boat followed behind the caribou that swam the lake.
·Aan eeçayáaknáý yan uwañúý wé yaakw. The boat landed below the town.

ñugáas'

gray; fog
ñugwáas'
·Gan eetí kél't' ñugáas' yáý yatee. Ashes from the fireplace are gray.

ñugóos'

cloud(s)

ñukadlénýaa

temptation, trial

ñukahín

crankiness; irritation; petulance
Ñukahínt uwanúk "s/he's acting irritated, cranky".

ñukalt'éex' ká

spring (AT)

ñulagaaw

fighting; war, conflict
ñulegaaw (C)
·Ñulagaaw yinaa.át yéi aya.óo. He is wearing war clothes.

ñúlk

very rotton wood

ñunáagu

healer; doctor; nurse
·Ñunáagu jeedáý jika.át yéi aya.óo. He is wearing a wrist guard from the
doctor.

ñúnáý

very
·Nóosk ýaagú ñúnáý yalik'áts'. Wolverine claws are really sharp.
·Ñúnáý wé yee woo.éex'i aa tsú yee ýoo yéi kçwatée toowú k'é teen.
Your hostess will welcome you all as well. (Lit: Your hostess will be among you
all with good feelings.)

ñusaýañwáan

tribe of cannibals, man-eaters

ñusaýán

love (of people)
·X'éiçaa átý sitee ñusaýán. Love is true.

ñusa.áat'

cold weather
ñuse.áat' (C)
·Ñaa toowú lat'aa yáý du ée yatee wé kinaak.át ñusa.áat' tóox'. The
coat is a comfort to him in the cold.

,

Ñ

ñusa.áat' néekw
ñustí
ñus.ook'

chest cold

life; way of living
plaything

ñut

astray, getting lost
·Aý jináñ ñut wujixeex. He ran away from me.
·Wé ñ'wátl yana.áat'ani ñut ýwaataan. I misplaced the lid for the pot.

ñutaan

summer
·Xéen áwé woogéi yá ñutaan. There were a lot of blue bottle flies this
summer.
·Yáa ñutaanx' aadé ñugaýtootéen ixkée ch'a çaaýtusatéen wé sháa.
This summer we are going to travel down south just to see the girls.

ñutí
ñútý

weather
too much

ñutý.ayanahá

star
ñutý.anaháa (AtT), ñutý'anaháa (T)
·Ñutý.ayanahá káax' át has nañúých. They navigate by the stars.

ñutl'ídaa

shovel

ñútl'kw

mud
·Haa tláa hás ñútl'giçáa has na.átch has du ñ'eikaxwéini yís. Our
mothers send us for soil for their flowers.
·L'éý'kw, ñútl'kw nasteech séew daak wustaaní Soil turns to mud when
it rains.

ñuwakaan (TC)

deer

çuwakaan

ñuxaak
ñuý

dry weather; clear day
(returning) back

ñuý dak'óol'een

backwards
·Ñuý dak'óol'een áwé kát adatéen du k'oodás'i. He's wearing his shirt
backwards.
·Ldakát át áwé ñuý dak'óol'in ýwaasáakw. I said everything backwards.

ñu.aa

however
ñu.a
·Ý'aan yakawlikís'. Wé kél't' ñu.aa, ch'u uwat'áa. The fire has gone out
but the ashes are still warm.
·Náakw yís kayaaní ashigóok, áx' ñu.aa akwdliýéitl' ñaa ý'éiý aa
wuteeyí. He knows medicinal plants but he is afraid to give them to anyone.

ñu.áých

hearing

'

'

ñu.áýji

hearing aid

ñu.eení

murderer

Ñ

ñu.éex'

feast, potlatch; party
·çaaý shí teen áwé yaawaxeex wé ñu.éex'. A cry song took place at the
potlatch.
·Atýá tlein áyá ñu.éex'de yakñwaýáa. I am going to haul a lot of food to
the potlatch.

ñu.oo

people; community
·Ana.óot ñu.oo haa ýánt has uwa.át. Aleut people came to see us.
·A ýoo aa ñu.oo woolnáý wooshñáñ has al'óon. Some people hunt the
wren.

,

Dictionary of Tlingit

« Ñw »
ñwaañý daañ

by mistake, wrongly

a ñwáan

person or people from that place
·Ch'a a ñwáanch áwé yéi uwasáa Deishú. The local people gave Haines its name.
·Deishú ñwáan has at shí ña has al'eiý. The Haines People are singing and dancing.

,

,

Ñ'

« Ñ' »
ñ'áach'

ribbon seaweed
·Ñ'áach' du tuwáa sigóo. She wants ribbon seaweed.
·Ñ'áach' ayawsiháa. She gathered ribbon seaweed.

ñ'aakanéi

large rectangular tub for soaking skins while tanning them

ñ'aan

dolphin
·Ñ'aan du tuwáa sigóo aatlein aý dachýánk'. My granddaughter really likes dolphins.
·Ñ'aan yahaax'ú wutuwa.oo du jeeyís. We bought her pictures of dolphins.

ñ'áatl'

thin (flat object)
·S'igeidí l'eedí yawúý' ña ñ'áatl' yáý yatee. A beaver's tail is wide and flat.

ñ'alkátsk

razor clam
·Ñ'alkátsk yáxwch'ich yaý yawsiýáa haa aaní kaadáý. The sea otter

has devoured the yellowneck clams on our land.
·Ñ'alkátsk kahaa yís léinde gaýtoo.áat yá xáanaa. This evening we are
going yellowneck clam digging.

ñ'anáaýán

fence
·Yanshukáx' áwé k'idéin wutuliyéý yá ñ'anáaýán. We built the fence
really well out here in the wilderness.
·K'idéin layéý yá ñ'anáaýán wé gishoo daaká yís! Build this fence well
around those pigs!

ñ'anashgidéi ñáa

poor man
·Ñ'anashgidéi ñáa áwé kíndei alshát du shá. The poor man is holding
his head high.
·Ñ'anashgidéi ñáaý satéeyin. He used to be a poor man.

ñ'anooý

labret, small lip plug
·Du gúkx' tsú yéi aa wduwa.oo wéi s'aañ ñ'anooý. They put the small
bone labret in his ear too.
·S'aañ áwé shux'áanaý átý wududliyéý aý léelk'w du ñ'anooýú yís.
My grandmother's first labret was made out of bone.

ñ'anooý eetí

labret hole

a ñ'anooýú

its whiskers, beard (of fish)
·Tléil a ñ'anooýú ñoostí daleiyí. Lake trout do not have beards.
·Chudéi áwé a ñ'anooýú áwu. Tom cod have a beard.

,

Ñ'

ñ'ateil

pitcher; jug
·Wé ñ'ateil xákwti aý jeet tán!. Hand me the empty pitcher!
·Ñ'ateil tóodei yanasxá k'idéin ý'adíx'! Pour it in the jug and cork it up!

ñ'atýáan

coward
·Du daat shkalneek ñudzitee Ñéiý'dáý ñ'atýáan. There is a story about
the coward from Kake.
·Ch'a çóot yéidei yéi jiné has du jeeý dutee wéi ñ'atýáan. Cowards
are given different jobs to perform.

ñ'eikaxétl'k

bunchberry
·Çuwakaan ýaýooý nooch ñ'eikaxétl'k kayaaní teen. I always use a
bunchberry leaf to call deer.

ñ'eikaxwéin

flower; blossom
·Ketllóox'u yáý yatee wé ñ'eikaxwéin. The flower is light yellow.
·Kawóot teen ñ'eikaxwéin a káa kañá! Embroider a flower on it with
beads!
1

Ñ'EIK'W

• aawañ'ék'w | --- | añ'ék'wý
s/he cut it | --- | s/he cuts it (regularly).
O-S-ø-ñ'éik'w~ (ø event)
for S to cut O (human body), usually accidentally; for S to wound O with a sharp
instrument
·Du jiwán aawañ'ék'w. He cut the outside edge of his hand.
• sh wudiñ'ék'w | --- | sh dañ'ék'wý
s/he cut himself/herself | --- | s/he cuts himself/herself (regularly).
sh S-d-ñ'éik'w~ (ø event)
for S to cut himself/herself, usually accidentally;
for S to wound himself/herself with a sharp
instrument

ñ'eiñ'w

tern
·Ha yéi áwé has duwasáakw Ñ'eiñ'w Sháa Xunaadáý. They are called
the Sea Pigeon gals from Hoonah.

ñ'éiñ'w

cut; knife wound

ñ'eildaháak'u

pretending; make-believe

ñ'eishkaháagu

bog cranberry; low bush cranberry
·Tl'átgi káa yéi nateech ñ'eishkaháagu. Low bush cranberries are on the
ground.

,

,

Ñ'w

« Ñ'w »
ñ'wátl

pot, cooking pot
·Ñ'wátl kaadé yéi adaané wé gáal'. She is putting clams into the cooking
pot.
·Wé ñ'wátl yana.áat'ani ñut ýwaataan. I misplaced the lid for the pot.

,

L

Dictionary of Tlingit

« L »
1

LAA

• áý woolaa | áý yei naléin | --the tide went out from under it | the tide is going out from under it | ---.
P-ý ø-laa~ (ça motion)
for the tide to ebb, go out from under P
·Du yaagú yeiý woolaa. The tide went out from under his boat.
• wuliláa | yaa nalléin | laléiý
it melted | it's melting | it melts (regularly).
l-laa~ (ø event)
for something to melt, dissolve, thaw
• yan uwaláa | yánde yaa naléin | yaý laa
the tide is low | the tide is going out | the tide goes out (regularly).
yan~ ø-laa~ (ø motion)
for the tide to go out, be low

laañ'ásk

dulse (type of seaweed)
·Laañ'ásk gé aý ooý káwu? Do I have seaweed on my teeth?
·Lidzée kayaaní a kaadéi kawuls'éesi wé laañ'ásk. It's frustrating when leaves are blown onto the black seaweed.

du láaw

privates (of male); penis and testicles

laaxw

famine; starvation
·Laaxw eetí wé ñaa jeedáý atýá has du çaneiýíý wusitee. After the famine, the food given to them became their salvation.

LAAXW
• uwaláxw | yaa naláxw | --he/she/it starved | he/she/it is starving | ---.
O-ø-laaxw~ (ø event)
for O to be starving, starved
·Oodzikaayi ñáa áyá táakwx' guçwaláaxw. A lazy man will starve in the winter.

laaý

red cedar
·Laaý teen áwé has awliyéý wé hít kat'áayi. They made those shingles out of cedar.

láaý

dead dry tree, still standing

du laayiçágu
lagaaw

his/her ring finger

noise

,

,

laçwán

bow (ribbon tied into a bow)

du laká

inside of his/her mouth

du lak'éech'

his/her occiput; nape of neck; back of head

du lak'eech'kóoçu
lak'eech'wú
láñt

L

pit at base of his/her skull

scooter duck

bentwood box

lanáalý

wealth; prosperity; riches

latseen

strength, power
·S'eiñ ýaat xáas'i áwé yak'éi çaltóot idateení latseen sákw at
eel'óoni. When you're out hunting a piece of smoked fish skin in your pocket is
good for energy.

Lawáak

Klawock

lawúý

young seagull

lawúý

gray

láý'

heron; Canada crane

a láý'i

its sapwood; its sappy inner bark (of a tree)

láý' loowú

swamp blueberry
The name derives from the similar gray-bluish color of the
heron's beak.

at layeiý s'aatí

carpenter
et leyeiý s'aatí (C)

at la.át

baggage, luggage; things, stuff packed up for carrying
et le.ét (C)

ldakát

all; every
·Kax'ás'aa teen áwé kçeexáash ldakát wéi t'áa! You will cut all those
boards with a rip saw!
·Ldakát wooch ýoot has yawdiháa. Everybody came together.

ldakát át

everything
·Awdagaaní yáa yagiyee, ldakát át kaadáý kaguýlax'áas. When it
sunshines today everything will be dripping off.
·Ldakát át áwé ñuý dak'óol'in ýwaasáakw. I said everything backwards.

ldakát yé

everywhere

ch'a ldakát yé
·Kaçakl'eedí ldakát yéix' kanas.éich. Yarrow grows all over.

du léelk'w

his/her grandparent
·Yaa aý léelk'w aý tláa yinaanáý Ñéin yóo dusáagun yaa

'

Dictionary of Tlingit

Xutsnoowúdáý. My grandmother on my mother's side was called Ñéin, from Angoon.
·I léelk'u keekándei aneelçein - ýáat yéi adaané! Go check on your grandpa - he's working on fish!

Léelk'w!

Grandmother!; Grandfather!
This is the form used to address one's grandparent.

LEET
• át aawalít | --- | áý aleet
s/he threw it to it | --- | s/he throws it to it (regularly).
P-t~ O-S-leet~ (ø motion)
for S to throw O (usually with force so that object scatters) to P
Note that in the example sentence below, the postposition
-dé (káast kaadé "in the barrel") occurs with the imperative form:
lít "throw it", where we would expect the postposition -t (as in
káast kát). Both forms are acceptable, this being a peculiarity of
this particular verb.
·Wé káast kaadéi lít wé a x'éix'u! Throw the gills in the barrel!

léet'

roots or vines used in basket decoration

LEI
• yéi kaawalei | yéi kunaaléi | --it became that far | it's that far | ---.
(yéi) ka-u-ø-lei~ (na state)
for something to be (so) far, distant (in time or space)
-lee~
The perfective form: yéi kaawalei "it was that far" is
commonly used in situations where one just fell short of making it
to a destination. In other words, "I almost made it, it was just that
far away".
·Daýadooshú kaay yéi kunaaléi wé aan, héen sháakdáý. The town is
seven miles from the head of the river.
·Du hídidáý kaay shoowú yéi kunaaléi hoon daakahídi. The store is
a half mile from her house.

du leikachóoý'u

his/her windpipe; pharynx
du leikechóoý'u (C)

léikwaa
léiñ'w

Easter bread; communion bread
red rockfish; red snapper

léin

tide flats
·Ñ'alkátsk kahaa yís léinde gaýtoo.áat yá xáanaa. This evening we are
going yellowneck clam digging.
·Káas' léin káa yéi nateech. There is always algae on the riverbank.

leineit shál

sheep or goat horn spoon

,

,

du leitóoý

L

his/her throat

léiý'w

crimson red; face paint

leiyís

fir

lékwaa

fighting spirit

du lidíý'

back of his/her neck
du ludíý'
·Xéesh áwé du lidíý' yéi yatee. He has a rash on his neck.

lingít

person
·Ý'éidei kakçilatiý' yé ch'a yeisú lingít áwu. There are still people in the
place you are locking.
·Wáa yateeyi lingít sáwé wa.é? What kind of person are you?

Lingít

Tlingit

·Ña ýát tsú aý toowú yak'éi yaa a káa yéi ýat guçwateeyí yaa
Lingítý ýat sateeyí. And I too am thankful that I'm part of this being that I'm
Lingít.
·Lingít ý'éináý kashxeet áwé ashigóok. He knows how to write in the
Tlingit language.

lingít aaní
lingít k'únts'i

world
water hemlock

lingít shákw

wild strawberry
used in comparison to the commercial strawberry, "shákw"

lingít x'áax'i

crabapple

lítaa

knife
·K'idéin yax'át wé lítaa x'aan! Sharpen the tip of the knife good!
·Ýáat jeiçí du lítayi kaaý aawa.óos'. She washed fish scales off her knife.

lítaa eetí

knife wound

a litká

(on) the back of it (fish); on the crest, ridge, backbone of
it (hill, ridge, point)
·Gooch litká aadé duwatéen wé çooch. The wolf on the ridge of the hill is
visible.
·Shaa litká aadé daýduwatéen wé watsíx. The caribou are visible on the
mountain ridge.

lit.isdúk
l ñool.áýji
l ñooshtéeni

black bass
deaf person
blind person

lñ'ayáak'w ý'us.eetí

Milky Way

,

L

Dictionary of Tlingit

lookanáa

person who acts crazy or possesssed

lóol

fireweed

lóol

pink

loon

dry woody outer bark

lóot'

eel

a loowú

its beak
·Ch'áak' lú yóo katán. A bald eagle's beak is curved.
·Dagwatgiyáa lú yayát' ña yéi kwlisáa. A hummingbird's beak is long and skinny.

du lóox'u

his/her urine

l s'aatí shaawát
Ltu.aa

widow

Lituya Bay

a lú

its point (of a long thin pointed object)
·Wé tséek a lú yalik'áts'. The point of the barbeque stick is sharp.
·Du tséegi a lú akaawayéý. He sharpened the point of his barbecue stick.

du lú

his/her nose
·Aý lú tukawlixwétl. My nose tickled (inside).

du ludíý'

back of his/her neck
du lidíý'

lugán

tufted puffin
lugén (C)

du lugóoch'
luçeitl'

lobe of his/her nostril
snot

luçwéinaa

handkerchief

a lukatíx'i

its bowstay

lukat'íshaa

leather needle

lukshiyáan

mink
nukshiyáan

l ulitoogu Ñaa Yakçwahéiyagu
lunás

Holy Spirit

nose ring

l ushk'é

evil, sin

du lutú

inside of his/her nose

,

,

L

a lututúñl'i

his/her nose cartilage
·Wé dzísk'w a lututúñl'i a kaaý kéi akaawas'él'. She tore (the membrane) off the soft bone in the moose nose.
·Watsíx a lututúñl'i tléil tlaý ugé. The soft bone in a caribou nose is not very big.

du lut'aañ

side of his/her nose

l uwaxwachgi néekw
a lux'aa

paralysis; polio

its tip, point

at lux'aañáawu

troublemaker
et lux'aañáawu (C)
·At lux'aañáawu áwé yéi yatee wé shaatk'. That young girl is a troublemaker.

l yaa ñooshgé

foolishness; recklessness

l yoo ñ'eishtángi

mute; person who cannot speak
l yoo ñ'eishténgi (C)

l.uljíni

vest; sleeveless top
·Gunýaa yaka.óot' du l.uljíni kát akaawañáa. She sewed the abalone buttons on her vest.

,

L'

Dictionary of Tlingit

« L' »
du l'aa

his/her breast

l'aak

dress
·Woosh gaýdusháa a kayís áwé yées l'aak aawañáa. She sewed a new
dress for the wedding that was to take place.

l'áañw

old, worn-out boat

l'áaý'

grayish; blond (hair)

l'açakáý
l'ákwti

fallen tree

l'át'aa

tongs

l'aýkeit
l'ée

west wind

dance regalia
l'eýkeit
wool blanket (used as potlatch gift or for dancing)

a l'eedí

its tail (of animal)
·S'igeidí l'eedí yawúý' ña ñ'áatl' yáý yatee. A beaver's tail is wide and
flat.
·S'eek l'eedí tléil ulyát'. A black bear's tail is short.

L'eeneidí

L'eeneidí, locally called "Dog Salmon"; a clan of the Raven
moiety whose principal crest is the Dog Salmon

·Tsu tsá yá naaý satí ñu.aa áyá yaa téel' áyá haa shukáý sitee,
L'eeneidí. Also the dog salmon is our clan crest, L'eeneidí.

L'EEX̱'
• aawal'éex' | --- | yoo ayal'íx'k
s/he broke it | --- | s/he breaks it (regularly).
O-S-ø-l'éex'~ (na event)
for S to break O (general, solid object)
This verb would be used to talk about breaking such things
as a tooth, leg, board, or a stick.
• awlil'éex' | --- | yoo alil'íx'k
s/he broke it | --- | s/he breaks it (regularly).
O-S-l-l'éex'~ (na event)
for S to break O (often by bending) (usually long objects)
·Du woosáani awlil'éex'. He broke his spear.
• wool'éex' | --- | yoo yal'íx'k
it broke | --- | it breaks (regularly).

,

,

L'

ø-l'éex'~ (na event)
for a general, solid object to break
·Du ýeek áwé wool'éex'. His upper arm is broken.
·Du kíji áwé wool'éex' wé ts'ítskw, ách áwé tlél át wudañeen. The
songbird's wing broke, that's why it doesn't fly around.
• wulil'éex' | --- | yoo lil'íx'k
it broke | --- | it breaks (regularly).
l-l'éex'~ (na event)
for a long object to break
·Aatý wulil'éex' wé nadáakw ý'oosí. The table leg broke off.

l'ée x'wán

sock(s)
·Du jeeýís l'ée x'wán kaýwsinei. I knitted socks for her.
·Aý léelk'w jeedáý kakéin l'ée x'wán áyá aý tuwáa sigóo. I like the
yarn socks from my grandmother.

l'éiw

sand; gravel
·Du ýaakw eetí áwé wé l'éiw káwu. His fingernail markings are in the
sand.
·Ñ'asigóo kaltéelñ l'éiw kát át wusheex. It's fun running around barefoot
in the sand.

l'eiwú

wood, piece of wood; wood chip

l'éiw x'aayí

sand point

l'éiw yátx'i

fine sand or gravel

L'EIÝ
• aawal'eiý | al'eiý | yoo ayal'éýk
s/he danced | s/he dances; s/he is dancing | s/he dances (regularly).
a-S-ø-l'eiý~ (na act)
for S to dance
·Has ançal'eiý ñaa shukát wé atyátx'i. Let the children dance before
everyone.
·Jilñoot Ñwáan has al'eiý. The Chilkoot people are dancing.
• daak aawal'éý | daak anal'éý | daak al'éých
s/he danced out | s/he is dancing out | s/he dances out (regularly).
daak S-ø-l'eiý~ (ø motion)
for S to dance out into the open
·Tlék'çaa áwé anaý daak has aawal'éý. One by one they danced out.
• çunéi aawal'éý | --- | çunéi al'éýý
s/he started dancing | --- | s/he starts dancing (regularly).
çunéi S-ø-l'eiý~ (ø motion)
for S to begin dancing
·Du kasánnáý áwé yaawajél, çunéi has aawal'éý. He put his hand
around her waist and they began dancing.

,

L'

Dictionary of Tlingit

l'éý'kw

soil; dirt
·L'éý'kw, ñútl'kw nasteech séew daak wustaaní Soil turns to mud when it rains.

du l'íli

his penis

l'ook

coho salmon; silver salmon
·L'ook at ý'éeshi áwé yak'éi. Coho salmon dryfish is good.
·L'ook kaháagu áyá yak'éi kanat'á kanéegwál' sákw. Coho salmon eggs are good for blueberry sauce.

L'OON
• aawal'óon | al'óon | yoo ayal'únk
s/he hunted it | s/he hunts it; s/he is hunting it | s/he hunts it (regularly).
O-S-ø-l'óon~ (na act)
for S to hunt O (wild game)
·A ýoo aa ñu.oo woolnáý wooshñáñ has al'óon. Some people hunt the wren.
·Yóode loowagooçu dzísk'w a ítde akñwal'óon. I will go hunting those moose that ran over that way.
• aawal'óon | al'óon | yoo ayal'únk
s/he hunted | s/he is hunting | s/he hunts (regularly).
a-S-ø-l'óon~ (na act)
for S to hunt
·Áa agaýtool'oon yé yinaadé yaa gagú! Walk toward the place we will hunt!
·Taatx' áwé has al'óon wé k'ákw. Owls hunt at night.

du l'óot'

his/her tongue

l'oowú

wood, piece of wood; wood chip

l'oowú táñl
l'óoý

mallet, wooden hammer

silty, murky water

L'ukaaý.ádi

L'ukaax.ádi, locally called "Sockeye"; a clan of the Raven
moiety whose principal crest is the Sockeye

L'uknaý.ádi

L'uknax.ádi, locally called "Coho"; a clan of the Raven
moiety whose principal crest is the Coho
·Yéi áwé wduwasáa Kayáash Hít L'uknaý.ádich. The Coho Salmon tribe
has named it Platform House.

l'ut'tláañ

snake

,

,

N

« N »
naa

nation; moiety; clan; band of people
·Yaa uháan haa naaý sitee, Yéil áyá haa shukáý sitee. For our clan,
Raven is our main crest.
·Xeitl naaý has sitee Shangukeidí. The Shangukeidí are Thunderbird.
2

NAA

• awdináa | adaná | adanáaý
s/he drank it | s/he drinks it; s/he is drinking it | s/he drinks it (regularly).
O-S-d-naa~ (ø act)
for S to drink O
·Tléiñw kahéeni awdináa. He drank berry juice.
• at wudináa | at daná | --s/he drank | s/he drinks, is drinking | ---.
at S-d-naa~ (ø act)
for S to drink
3

NAA

• aadé

akaawanáa | aadé akoonáa | aadé yoo
akayanáakw

s/he sent him/her there | s/he is sending him/her there | s/he sends him/her there (regularly).

O-ka-u-S-ø-náa~ (na act)

for S to order (esp. to go), send, command O; (fig.) for S to give O (esp. in accordance with clan relationship)

·Ñaadaaxaashí ýánde kawduwanáa. He was sent to the surgeon.

·Çayéis' hítde kawduwanáa. He was sent to jail.

a náa

(draped) over it, covering it

naadaayi héen

river; stream; creek

·Tláakw naadaayi héen kuliýéitl'shán. A fast river is dangerous.

naaças'éi

fox; red fox

·Du ñoowú tóode wujixéex wé naaças'éi. The red fox ran into his den.

·Gootl kanaý yawjik'én wé naaças'éi. The red fox jumped over a mound.

naa káani

master of ceremonies, elder of the opposite clan consulted
conducting a ceremony

naakée

upstream; north

·Wé naakéedáý lingít çunayáade yóo has ý'ali.átk. The people from the north speak differently.

·Ñukawduwayél' áyá - naakéede naýtooñooý. It's calm out - let's go up the bay.

,

náakw

medicine
·Náakwý awliyéý aasdaak'óoý'u. She made medicine out of pitch.
·Kaçakl'eedí náakwý dulyéiý. Yarrow is used for medicine.
1

NAAÑ

• --- | has náñ | ----- | they are standing | ---.
S-ø-náñ (position)
for (plural) S to be standing
This verb only occurs in the imperfective. Note that a noun
phrase with (-t) postposition is used to indicate where one is
standing, but this noun phrase is not required by the verb. For
example, one could say: has náñ "they are standing", or: át has
náñ "they are standing there".
• yan has uwanáñ | --- | yaý has naañ
they kept standing; they stood | --- | they stay standing (regularly).
yan S-ø-naañ~ (ø motion)
for (plural) S to stand, stay standing
·A yáa yan yináñ! You all stand in front of it!
2

NAAÑ

• ajeewanáñ | --- | ajináñý
s/he let it go | --- | s/he lets it go (regularly).
O-ji-S-ø-naañ~ (ø event)
for S to let go, release, relinquish O; for S to leave, desert O; for S to hand over,
deliver up O
·Déiý ýaat haa jeex' ajeewanáñ. He left two salmon for us.
·Du jintáax' jiwduwanáñ. He was put in charge of it. (Lit: It was left in his
hands).

naañw

rotten wood

1

NAAÑW

• yawdináñw | yadanáñws' | yadanáñwý
s/he baited hooks | s/he is baiting hooks | s/he baits hooks (regularly).
ya-S-d-naañw~ (ø act)
for S to bait hooks, put bait on fish hooks
·Yadanáñws' cháatlçaa. He is baiting hooks for halibut.

náañw

octopus; devilfish
·Shayadihéin has du tl'eeçí wé náañw. Octopus have a lot of tentacles.

NÁALÝ
• wulináalý | lináalý | --s/he got rich | s/he's rich | ---.
O-l-náalý (ga state)
for O to be rich, wealthy, profitable

,

,

N

·Yéi át aýwdishée iwulnáalýi. I wish you wealth.
·Ast'eiý tlél ulnáalýin. Trolling didn't used to be profitable.

naanyaa kanat'aayí

huckleberry; blueberry

naasa.áa

large cannister

du naasí

his/her intestines, guts

naa shuklaçeeyí
náaw

the life of the party

liquor; booze; alcoholic beverage

náaw éesh

alcoholic

náaw s'aatí

drunk; drunkard

naaxein

Chilkat blanket
·Teey woodí naaxeiný dulyéiý. Yellow cedar bark is used to make a chilkat robe.

náayadi

half-dried salmon (smoked)
·A xáas'i teen áwé duxáash náayadi sákw. Half smoked fish is cut with the fish skin intact.

naa.át

clothes, clothing; garment
naa.ét (C)
·A déinde aa du naa.ádi aaý awli.aat. She picked up the rest of her clothes.
·Yak'éiyi naa.át aaý du.óow wé hoon daakahídi. Good clothing can be bought from that store.

naa.át kaxít'aa

clothes brush
naa.ét kexít'aa (C)

nadáakw

table
·Nadáakw káx' yéi na.oo! Put it on the table!
·Wéidu çánch gwéili nadáakw káa yan satí! Put that bag of tobacco on the table!

nakwnéit

priest; pastor; minister

nakws'aatí

witch

a náñ

(going, taking something) away from it
·Çalsaayít áwé du yéi jineiyí a náñ woogoot. She went away from her work so that she could rest.
·A náñ yaa nagúdi yaa shukanashéen. She is singing as she is leaving it behind.

nalháashadi
naná

driftwood

death

,

Dictionary of Tlingit

nas'gadooshóonáý

eight (people)

nas'gadooshú

eight
·Nas'gadooshú ch'iyáash kaýwaach'ák'w hun yayís. I carved eight sea otter hunting canoes to sell.

nas'gidahéen

three times

nás'k dahéen

nás'giçáa

three at a time, three by three

nás'gináý

three (people)
·Nás'gináý has yatee wé Yéil naa sháade náñx'i. There are three Raven Clan leaders.

nás'k

three
·Nás'k a doogú x'óow áwé du káa kakçwagéi k'oodás' sákw, wé ñáa tlein. It will take three leather blankets for the big man's shirt.
·Nás'k yagiyee a kaanáý has yaawa.át. They walked for three days.

nás'k jinkaat

thirty

nás'k jinkaat ña tléix'
náxw

thirty one

halibut hook (made of wood)

-náý

along, via; including the time of
Some nouns and relational nouns undergo changes in vowel

length and/or tone when combined with -náý:

á "it, there" + -náý = anaý "through it; through there"

a ká "its surface" + -náý = a kanáý / a kaanáý "through (the surface of) it; throughout it"

a yá "its face" + -náý = a yanaý / a yáanáý "through (the face of) it"

a tú "its inside" + -náý = a tóonáý "through (the inside of) it"

·Yat'éex'i gaaw a tóonáý yiyagút. You walked through that period of hard time.

·Nás'k yagiyee a kaanáý has yaawa.át. They walked for three days.

né

hairy grass, seaweed on which herring spawn

neech

shoreline; beach

·Ýeil neech káa yéi nateech xóon wudunoogú. Foam is on the beach when the north wind blows.

·Yá neechý yaa neegúdi yei kçisatéen yá katóok. As you walk along this shoreline you will see this cave.

neechkayádi

fatherless child; bastard
nichkayádi (An)

néegwál'

paint

·A yáanáý áwé kayliséñ'w yá néegwál'. You tinted this paint too much.

·Ch'áak' loowú yáý néegwál' ýwaa.oo. I bought some dark yellow paint.

,

,

N

NÉEGWÁL'
• aawanéegwál' | anéegwál' | yoo ayanéegwál'k
s/he painted it | s/he is painting it | s/he paints it (regularly).
O-S-ø-néegwál' (na act)
for S to paint O
·Ý'aan yáý wutuwanéegwál' a yá. We painted the side of it red.
·Has aawanéegwál' wé gántiyaakw. They painted the steamboat.

neek

news; gossip, rumor
·Neek ash atláx'w yaa ñudzigéiyi ts'ats'ée. Pigeons carry messages.

NEEK

• akaawaneek | akanéek | yóo akaaníkk

s/he told about it | s/he tells about it; s/he is telling about it | s/he tells about it (regularly).

O-ka-S-ø-neek~ (na act)

for S to tell about, report about, give facts about O; for S to witness to, tell about, testify about O

To indicate who the listener is, use: N een. For example,

Mary een akaawaneek. "S/he told Mary about it." This is not required with this verb however, and is therefore not included in the Leer-Edwards theme.

·Aadéi keenik yé çunayáade ýaatéen. I see it differently from the way you tell it.

·Wé íýt'ch du een akaawaneek wáa sá at guçwaneiyí. The medicine man told him what was going to happen.

• akawlineek | aklaneek | yoo akliníkk

s/he told the story of it | s/he tells the story of it; s/he is telling the story of it | s/he tells the story of it (regularly).

O-ka-S-l-neek (na act)

for S to tell the story of O; for S to talk into O

·Tléil áyáý at wuneiyí, jinaháa áwé yóo kdulneek. When something bad happens they say it's bad luck.

• a káý akawliník | --- | --s/he talked him/her out if it | --- | ---.

N káý O-ka-S-l-neek~ (ø event)

for S to defraud, talk O out of N

·Ýaat yís áwé has akawliník Yéilch, wé kéidladi ña kaçeet. Raven talked the seagull and loon out of the salmon.

• sh kawdlineek | sh kalneek | --s/he told a story | s/he is telling a story | ---.

sh ka-S-d-l-neek (na act)

for S to preach, narrate, tell a story

To include in the sentence what the story is about, use: N daat "about N". To include who the story is being told to, use: N een "to N". For example: Mary áwé John een sh kawdlineek wé naaxein daat. "Mary told John a story about the Chilkat robe."

,

Dictionary of Tlingit

·Yéi sh kadulneek a yahaayí ñudzitee dáanaa. They say money has a spirit.
·Ha wáa sás sh kadulneek? What's the latest news?

neek s'aatí (T)

gossip; rumormonger

niks'aatí

neek shatl'éñx'u

gossip; rumormonger
neek shetl'éñx'u (C)

NEEKW
• woonéekw | yanéekw | kei néekwch
s/he got sick | s/he's sick | s/he gets sick (regularly).
O-ø-néekw (ga state)
for O to be sick; for O to hurt, be in pain
·Du díý' néekw nooch. His back always hurts.
·Du çáts daçaanéekw. His thighs are sore.

néekw

sickness; illness; disease
nóokw
·Néekwch at ash yaawa.aat. Sickness is trying to get him.
·Náakw du ý'éiý wuduwatee du kalóox'sháni néegooch. She was given medicine for her bladder pain.

nées'

sea urchin

NEEX'
• awsiníx' / awdziníx' | asinéex' | asníx'ý
s/he smelled it | s/he smells it | s/he smells it (regularly).
O-S-(d)-s-néex'~ (ø act)
for S to smell O
·Wé xóots awusnéex'i a yinaadé wjixeex haa keidlí. Our dog is running toward the brown bear it smelled.

néeý'

marble
néiý'

NEI
• aaý yéi awsinei | --- | aaý kei yéi asneich
s/he picked them up off of it | --- | s/he picks them up off of it (regularly).
P-dáý yéi O-S-s-nei~ (ga motion)
for S to pick up, lift up, take (plural) O (objects) up off of P
-nee~ (An)
·Atýá aaý yéi awusneiyi yé, dáanaa a eetíx' yan akaawatée. She put
money in place of the food she picked up.
·Dei kát la.ádi çéechadi aaý yéi awsinei. He removed the windfall lying
in the road.
• akawsinei | aksané | --s/he knitted it | s/he is knitting it | ---.
O-ka-S-s-nei~ (na act)

,

,

N

for S to make O (cloth of any kind) (by weaving, knitting, or crocheting); for S to
make or mend O (net)
·Du jeeyís l'ée x'wán kaýwsinei. I knitted socks for her.
·Dzaas áwé yéi akçwa.oo çeeçách' akawusneiyí. She will use string
when she crochets a hammock.
• du jeet yéi awsinei | --- | du jeeý yéi asnei
s/he gave them to him/her | --- | s/he gives them to him/her (regularly).
N jeet~ yéi O-S-s-nei~ (ø motion)
for S to give, take, hand (plural) O to N
-nee~ (An)
·Yées jiçwéinaa du léelk'u jeet yéi awsinei. He gave his grandmother
new towels.
• kawdzinéi | kasné | --s/he knitted | s/he is knitting; s/he knits | ---.
ka-S-d-s-néi~ (ø act)
for S to knit, weave, or crochet
• ñáakwt uwanéi | --- | ñáakwý nei
s/he had an accident | --- | s/he has accidents (regularly).
ñáakwt~ O-ø-nei~ (ø motion)
for O to have an accident, get hurt; for something bad to happen to O
-nee~ (An)
·Áa ñúý teedataan wé ñáakwt iwuneiyí! Think back to the time when you
got hurt!
• du wañshiyeex' yéi awsinei | --- | ñaa wañshiyeex' yoo

asineik
s/he demonstrated it to him/her | --- | s/he demonstrates it to people (regularly).
N wañshiyeex' yéi O-S-s-nei~ (na event)
for S to demonstrate, perform publicly, show N how to do O by action
-nee~ (An)
·Aý wañshiyeex' yéi nasné! Show me how it's done!
• wooch yáý awsinei | wooch yáý yaa anasnéin | --s/he straightened it out | s/he is
straightening it out | ---.
wooch yáý O-S-s-nei~ (na event)

for S to straighten out O, smooth O over (literal or abstract)
-nee~ (An)
·Çeiwú wooch yáý awsinei tle daak ashakaawañúý. She straightened
the net out and then she set it.
• du yáa ayaawanéi / du yáa awuwanéi | du yáa kei

ayananéin | --s/he respects him/her | s/he is beginning to respect him/her | ---.
N yáa a-ya-u-S-ø-néi (ga act)
for S to respect, regard highly, think highly of N
• yan awsinéi | yánde yaa anasnein | yáý asnei
s/he finished it | s/he is finishing it | s/he finishes it (regularly).
yan~ O-S-s-nei~ (ø motion)

,

Dictionary of Tlingit

for S to finish, complete O
-nee~ (An)
·Yan awsinéi du s'ís'aa hídi eetí. He fixed up the place for his tent.
• yan sh wudzinéi | yánde yaa sh nasnein | yaý sh isnei
s/he is dressed up | s/he's getting dressed up | s/he gets dressed up (regularly).
yan~ sh S-d-s-nei~ (ø event)
for S to dress up
-nee~ (An)
·Yan sh wudzinéi. She's all dressed up.
• yan uwanéi | yánde yaa nanein | yaý nei
he/she/it is ready | he/she/it is getting ready | he/she/it is always ready.
yan~ O-ø-nei~ (ø motion)
for O to be permanent, happen for good; for O to be finished, complete, ready;
for O to be prepared, ready
-nee~ (An)
·Yan uwanéi ágé wé tléix' aa yáý? Is it ready like the other one?
·Yan uwaneiyi hít kaságuçáa kawduwañaa. He was sent for ready-made
rafters.
• yan yéi akawsinéi | --- | yaý yéi aksanei
s/he put them down | --- | s/he puts them down (regularly).
yan~ yéi O-ka-S-s-nei~ (ø motion)
for S to put down, leave O (plural round objects)
-nee~ (An)
·Atýa át náagu a ýoo yan yéi ksané! Put some moth balls among it!
• --- | yéi adaanéi | ----- | s/he does it; s/he is doing it | ---.
(yéi) O-daa-S-ø-nei~ (na act)
for S to do, perform O (a particular action); for S to work on O
·Aý tláak'wch áa ýat shukaawajáa, aadé yéi daadunei yé. My
maternal aunt taught me how to make it.
·Aý yéi jineiyí áwé kaxíl'aa k'idéin daané. My job is to clean erasers.
• yéi at woonei | --- | yéi at yaneik
that's what happened | --- | that's what happens (regularly).
(yéi) at ø-nei (na event)
for something to happen
-nee~ (An)
·Tleidahéen, yéi at woonei. Once upon a time, this happened.
·Tléil áyáý at wuneiyí, jinaháa áwé yóo kdulneek. When something
bad happens they say it's bad luck.
• yéi awsinei | yéi yaa anasnéin | yéi yoo asineik
s/he fixed it | s/he is fixing it | s/he fixes it (regularly).
(yéi) O-S-s-nei~ (na event)
for S to do (that) to O; for S to fix, cause (that) to happen to O
-nee~ (An)
·K'idéin nasné wé nadáakw! Clear and clean the table!
·Hít shantú k'idéin awsinei. She cleaned upstairs.

,

,

N

• yéi jeewanei | yéi jiné | yéi yoo jiyaneik
s/he worked | s/he works; s/he is working | s/he works (regularly).
yéi ji-S-ø-nei~ (na act)
for S to work; for S to do
·Seiçán gé i tuwáa sigóo aý een yéi jiyineiyí? Do you want to work with
me tomorrow?
·Yan yéi jiwtooneiyí a ítnáý tsá gaýtoo.áat. After we have finished work,
then we will go.
• yéi woonei | yéi yaa nanein | yéi yoo yaneik
that happened to him/her/it | that's happening to him/her/it | that happens to
him/her/it (regularly).
(yéi) O-ø-nei (na event)
for (that) to happen, occur to O
-nee (An)

neigóon

nagoonberry, lagoonberry, dwarf nagoonberry

neil~

inside, into the house, home
·Kaduch'áak'w lítaa sákw yak'éiyi aa çayéis' neil tí! Bring home a good
piece of iron for a carving knife!
·Gán kañás'ti ñóok tóox' neil awsi.ín. He brought the kindling inside in a
box.

neil

home
·Xít'aa een du neilí axít'gi nooch. He always sweeps his house with a
broom.
·L s'eiñý usiteeyi neil áyá. This is a smoke-free home.

neil yee táax'ayi
neilyeetéeli

housefly
slipper(s); house shoe(s)

néil'

basket of woven red cedar bark

neis'

oil, grease (for coating skin or rubbing); lotion; liniment

du néix'i

his/her inheritance; possessions of deceased given to him/her at

a feast
NEIÝ
• awsineiý | --- | yei asneiých
s/he saved him/her/it | --- | s/he saves him/her/it (regularly).
O-S-s-neiý (ça event)
for S to save O; for S to heal, cure O
·Aankanáagu tín sh wudzineiý. She healed herself with medicine from the land.
·Tlei déiý ñ'ateil yáý áwé wutusineiý shákw kahéeni. We just saved two gallons of the strawberry juice.
• wooneiý | yei nanéý | yei néých
s/he recovered | s/he is beginning to recover | s/he recovers (regularly).

,

Dictionary of Tlingit

O-ø-neiý~ (ça event)
for O to be saved; for O to be healed, cured, recover; for O to be satisfied
·Wuwtunéekw jeedáý áwé wooneiý. She was saved from tuberculosis.

néý'w
niks'aatí

yellow cloudberry
gossip, rumormonger
neek s'aatí (T)

nisdaat

last night

a niyaa

in its way; keeping it away; protecting, shielding,
screening from it; blocking it
·Aý dayéen hán xóon niyaa. He is standing facing me, shielding me from
the North Wind.

a niyaadé

in the direction or general area of it; (headed) toward it
a niyaadéi, a yinaadé, a yinaadéi
·Áa niyaadé yaa nagút. He is walking toward the lake.
·A niyaadé yaa nagút. He is walking toward it.

niyaháat

body armor, breastplate

nooch

always; [auxiliary]
nuch
The auxiliary nooch follows a verb and is used in the
imperfective habitual aspect, giving the verb a habitual meaning
"always".
·Ñaa tuk'éi nooch çagaan duteení. People are always happy when they see
the sun.
·Tlél ushik'éiyi aa yoo ý'atánk áwé tsá a.aýji nooch . She always only
hears the bad talk.
1

NOOK

• áa wdinook | --- | --the building was situated there (suddenly as if overnight) | --- | ---.
d-nook~ (ça event)
for a building to be situated
• át awsinook | --- | át yoo asinúkk
s/he is carrying him/her/it around; s/he carried him/her/it around | --- | s/he carries him/her/it around (regularly).
P-t O-S-s-nook~ (na motion)
for S to carry, take O (live creature) around at P
• awsinook | --- | yei asnúkch
s/he seated him/her | --- | s/he seats him/her (regularly).
O-S-s-nook~ (ça event)
for S to seat O
• awsinook | yaa anasnúk | yoo asinúkk
s/he carried him/her/it | s/he is carrying him/her/it | s/he carries him/her/it (regularly).

,

,

N

O-S-s-nook~ (na motion)
for S to carry, take O (live creature)
·Du jiçeiý yaa anasnúk du séek'. He is carrying his daughter in his arms.
• kei awsinúk | --- | kei asnúkch
s/he lifted him/her/it up | --- | s/he lifts him/her/it up (regularly).
kei O-S-s-nook~ (ø motion)
for S to lift up O (live creature)
·Du dachýánk' du çushkáa kei awsinúk. He lifted his grandchild up
onto his lap.
• shawdinúk | --- | shadanúký
s/he got up | --- | s/he gets up (regularly).
sha-S-d-nook~ (ø event)
for (singular) S to get up, rise
·Ts'ootaat shaýwdinúk. I got up in the morning.
·Ñeeý'é shukát áwé shoodanookch aý léelk'w. My grandfather wakes up
before dawn.
• woonook | --- | yei núkch
s/he sat down | --- | s/he sits down (regularly).
S-ø-nook~ (ça event)
for (singular) S to sit, sit down (esp. act of sitting)
·At ýéidi yax'aat a shóox' çanú! Sit down and do some arrow-head
sharpening!
·Wé aas goowú káa woonook. She sat on that tree stump.
• yan awsinúk | --- | yaý asnook
s/he put him/her/it down | --- | s/he puts him/her/it down (regularly).
yan~ O-S-s-nook~ (ø motion)
for S to put down O (live creature)
·Káa ýeýx'u yeit káa yan awsinúk du séek'. She put her daughter down
on the bed.
2

NOOK

• jée awdinúk | jée adinook | jée adanúký
s/he felt it | s/he's feeling it | s/he feels it (regularly).
jée O-S-d-nook~ (ø state)
for S to feel, touch O (esp. with hands)
This verb is commonly used in
reference to labor pains. For
example: Jée gé idinook? "Are you
feeling it (contractions)?"
• wuduwanúk | yaa ndunúk | dunúký
it blew; it's blowing | it's starting to blow | it blows (regularly).
du-ø-nook~ (ø event)
for the wind to blow, be felt (esp. a breeze, light wind)
·Xóon wuduwanúk. A north wind is blowing.
·Ýeil neech káa yéi nateech xóon wudunoogú. Foam is on the beach
when the north wind blows.

,

Dictionary of Tlingit

• x'áant uwanúk | x'áande yaa nanúk | x'áaný nook
s/he's angry | s/he's getting angry | s/he gets angry (regularly).
x'áan-t~ S-ø-nook~ (ø motion)
for S to be angry
• ý'éi awdinúk | ý'éi adinook | x'éi adanúký
s/he tasted it | s/he tastes it | s/he tastes it (regularly).
ý'éi O-S-d-nook~ (ø state)
for S to taste, sample O
• yéi ñoowanook | yéi ñuwanóok | --s/he did it | s/he is doing it | ---.
(yéi) ñu-S-ø-nook~ (na act)
for S to behave, do, act (in a certain way)
-neekw
·Tléil oowaa wé aan káa ñududziteeyi yoo ý'atánk géide
ñudunoogú. It is wrong to act against the law of the land.
·L át yáý ñoonook. He doesn't act normal.
• yéi sh tuwdinook | yéi sh tudinook | --s/he felt that way | s/he feels that way | ---.
(yéi) sh tu-S-d-nook~ (na act)
for S to feel (that way) (esp. physical sensation)
·Háas' yáý sh tudinook. He feels like vomiting.
·Çunayéide a daat sh tudinook yeedát. He feels differently about it now.

nóosk

wolverine
nóoskw
·Nóosk káý çaatáa yan awli.át. He set traps for wolverine.
·Nóosk ýaagú ñúnáý yalik'áts'. Wolverine claws are really sharp.

nóoskw
nóosh

wolverine
nóosk
dead salmon (after spawning)

NOOT'
• akaawanóot' | --- | yoo akayanút'k
s/he swallowed it | --- | s/he swallows it (regularly).
O-ka-S-ø-nóot'~ (na event)
for S to swallow O (pill, etc.)
·Éech' akaawanóot' Yéil. Raven swallowed a stone.
1

NOOTS

• at kaawanúts | at kanútst | --s/he is grinning; s/he grinned | s/he is trying to grin | ---.
at ka-S-ø-nóots~ (ø act)
for S to smile at something (often knowingly or sarcastically), grin

·At kadunuts nuch aý saayí çadu.áýín. T'aaw Chán. They always grin
when they hear my name, T'aaw Chán.

,

,

noow

fort

noow

flat-topped island with steep sides; low flat island or hill

noow çei

N

in a fort, shelter, cove

nóox'

shell; shell-like chip or flake; china; carapace
·Nóox' tóodáý aawaxás' wé ýeel'. He scraped the slime out of the shell.
·Hintakx'óosi nóox'u kayat'éex' Coral shells are hard.

nóox'

eggshell

nukshiyáan

mink
lukshiyáan

núkt

blue grouse

NÚKTS
• wulinúkts | linúkts | --it was sweet | he/she/it is sweet | ---.
O-l-núkts (ga state)
for O to be sweet

,

Oo

« Oo »
oolxéis'

wish; prayer

óonaa

gun, rifle
·Aas k'eeyéet ash aawatán du óonayi. He leaned his rifle against the tree trunk.

óonaa eetí
óos'i

gunshot wound

laundry

Óos'k'!

Cute!
Óots'k'!
This exclamation is used in association with little, cute things such as babies, puppies, or small objects.

óosh

as if; if only; even if
·Yaa indashán óosh gé! If only you were getting old!

óot'

rock pile fish trap

a óot'i

its sucker (devilfish)

óoxjaa

wind
·Aan kwéiyi óoxjaa tóot wulis'ees. A flag is blowing in the wind.
·Wé litseeni óoxjaa géide áwé yaa has na.át. They are walking against the strong wind.

a óoxu

spray of air exhaled through its blowhole (of sea mammal)

du óox'u

his/her shoulderblade; scapula

du ooý

his/her tooth
·Laañ'ásk gé aý ooý káwu? Do I have seaweed on my teeth?
·Du ooý kanat'á kahéeni yáý kawdiséñ'w. Her teeth are the color of blueberry juice.

ooý katsáçaa

toothpick

du ooýk'i.eetí

his/her missing tooth

a ooýú

its tooth
·Haadaaçoojí a ooýú dañdigéix'. Lion teeth are large.

,

,

S

« S »
sá

[interrogative - marks WH-questions]
·Wáa yateeyi lingít sáwé wa.é? What kind of person are you?
·X'oon gaawx' sá? At what time?

saa

name
·Aý tláa saayí ñu.aa áyá Shaaxeidí Tláa yóo áwé wduwasáa. My mother's name was Shaaxeidi Tláa.
·Ý'aháat kináak áwé át akawsix'óo, du saayí. He nailed his name above the door.
1

SAA

• --- | yéi kwlisáa | ----- | it's narrow | ---.
yéi ka-u-l-saa~ (state)
for something (esp. container) to be narrow

This verb occurs in the imperfective only.

·Dagwatgiyáa lú yayát' ña yéi kwlisáa. A hummingbird's beak is long and skinny.

2

SAA

• yéi aawasáa | --- | --s/he named him/her/it that | --- | ---.
O-S-ø-saa~ (ø event)
for S to name O; for S to nominate O
The difference between: yéi aawasáa "s/he named
him/her/it that" and yéi aawasáakw "s/he called him/her/it that"
is one of repetition. The former denotes a one-time event in which
someone or something was given a name, while the latter depicts
repeatedly calling someone or something by a name. Note that the
latter form: yéi aawasáakw has the iterative suffix (-kw), which
generally denotes a repeated action.

·Aý tláa saayí ñu.aa áyá Shaaxeidí Tláa yóo áwé wduwasáa. My
mother's name was Shaaxeidi Tláa.

·Yéi áwé wduwasáa Kayáash Hít L'uknaý.ádich. The Coho Salmon
tribe has named it Platform House.

• yéi aawasáakw | yéi ayasáakw | --s/he called him/her/it that | s/he calls him/her/it that | ---.
O-S-ø-sáakw (na state)
for S to call O by a certain name
The difference between: yéi aawasáa "s/he named
him/her/it that" and yéi aawasáakw "s/he called him/her/it that"
is one of repetition. The former denotes a one-time event in which
someone or something was given a name, while the latter depicts

,

repeatedly calling someone or something by a name. Note that the
latter form: yéi aawasáakw has the iterative suffix (-kw), which
generally denotes a repeated action.
·Yaa aý léelk'w aý tláa yinaanáý Ñéin yóo dusáagun yaa
Xutsnoowúdáý. My grandmother on my mother's side was called Ñéin, from
Angoon.
·Ldakát át áwé ñuý dak'óol'in ýwaasáakw. I said everything backwards.
3

SAA

• wudlisáa | (tlákw) yaa nalséin | ulséiý
s/he rested; s/he's resting | s/he is (always) resting | s/he rests (regularly).
S-d-l-saa~ (ø event)
for S to rest
·Aas seiyí áa wdlisáa. He rested in the shelter of the tree.
·Çalsaayít áwé du yéi jineiyí a náñ woogoot. She went away from her
work so that she could rest.

saak

eulachon; candlefish; hooligan
·A ý'éináý áwé kadul.eesh wé ñáas' kaadéi wé saak. Those hooligan
are strung through the mouth on the stick.

saak eeýí
sáanáý

hooligan oil
wind (blowing) from the south

du saayee

underside of his/her knee; (inside of) his/her lower leg

du saayí

his/her name; his/her namesake

sadaat'aay

neck scarf; kerchief
·Du gúk káý ayaawayeesh du sadaat'aayí. She pulled her scarf down
over her ears.

sagú

joy; happiness

·Sagú yáý ñaa yayík du.aýji nooch héendei yaa ana.ádi. Men's voices would always sound happy when they went to the sea.

at saçahaayí

will; wish(es)
et seçahaayí (C)

saka.át

necktie

sákw

future (noun), (noun) to be, for (noun)
·Nás'k a doogú x'óow áwé du káa kakçwagéi k'oodás' sákw, wé ñáa tlein. It will take three leather blankets for the big man's shirt.
·L'ook kaháagu áyá yak'éi kanat'á kanéegwál' sákw. Coho salmon eggs are good for blueberry sauce.

sakwnéin

flour; bread
·Tléiñw çóot awsi.ée du sakwnéini. She cooked her bannock without berries.
·Sakwnéin áwé du ý'éiý ýateeý wé kals'áak. I feed bread to the squirrel.

,

,

S

sakwnéin éewu

(loaf of) bread
·Wé sakwnéin éewu yan ça.eet eeçáa áwé ýa.áa. I am sitting, waiting for the bread to finish cooking.

sakwnéin katéiýi

porridge

sakwnéin kaý'eiltí

bread crumbs

a sákwti

its handle (stick-like); its shaft (of spear, etc.)
a sáxwdi, a síxwdi (AtT), a súxdi (T), a súxti (TC)
·Iññáach'ý sitee wé lítaa sákwti. The handle of that knife is brass.

sáñs

bow

du sáni

his/her paternal uncle, cousin
·Aý éek' ña aý sáni al'óoni een át has na.átjin. My brother and my
paternal uncle used to accompany hunters.

sankeit

armor made of tough hide or wooden rods

Sanyaa Ñwáan

people of Cape Fox, Saxman

SÁTK
• woosátk | yasátk | kei sátkch
he/she/it was fast | he/she/it is fast | he/she/it gets fast (regularly).
O-ø-sátk (ga state)
for O to be fast (at doing things)
·Yasátk aadéi ashigóogu yé wé kaldáal'. The typist knows how to type
fast.

du satú

his/her voice

a sáxwdi

its handle (stick-like); its shaft (of spear, etc.)
a síxwdi (AtT), a súxdi (T), a súxti (TC)

sáx'

cambium, sap scraped from inner bark

at saýán
du sé

love (of things, of everything)
his/her voice

sée

doll
·Hít kat'áayi yátx'i wé sée hídi káa yéi awa.oo. He put the small shingles
on that doll house.

du sée

his/her daughter, cousin
·Yóo áyú aawasáa du sée aý tláa. That's what my mother named her daughter.
·Du séek' du ýánt uwagút. Her daughter came to her.
1

SEEK

• yaawasík | --- | woosíký
s/he is delayed | --- | s/he gets delayed (regularly).

'

S

Dictionary of Tlingit

O-ya-ø-seek~ (ø event)
for O to be delayed, prevented, held back from plans (often due to inclement
weather)

séek

belt

SEEN
• awdlisín | --- | --he/she/it hid; s/he's hiding | --- | ---.
a-S-d-l-seen~ (ø event)
for S to hide oneself, remain out of sight
·Awdlisín chéý'i tóox'. He is hiding in the shadows.
·X'éedadi tóox' awdlisín. She hid in a tree stump.
• awlisín | --- | alsíný
s/he hid it; s/he's hiding it | --- | s/he hides it (regularly).
O-S-l-seen~ (ø event)
for S to hide, conceal, put O out of sight

seet

dug-out canoe designed to go through shallow waters
·Dúñ een dulyéiý seet yaakw. The canoe is made out of cottonwood.

séet

draw, gully, box canyon

séew

rain
sóow (C)
·Wé aas seiyít wujixíx séew tóodáý. She ran to the shelter of the tree to get
out of the rain.
·Ýat wulixwétl wé séew. I'm tired of the rain.

séew kooshdaneit

swallow

seiçán

tomorrow
seiçánin
·Seiçán gé i tuwáa sigóo aý een yéi jiyineiyí? Do you want to work with
me tomorrow?
·Áx' ñaa ée at dultóow yé áa yéi ýat guçwatée seiçán. I will be in
school tomorrow.

seiçánin

tomorrow
seiçán

seiçatáanaa

berrying basket or can hung around the neck, resting on

the chest
SEIÑ'W
• akawliséñ'w | aklaséñ'w | aklaséñ'wý
s/he dyed it | s/he is dying it | s/he dyes it (regularly).
O-ka-S-l-séiñ'w~ (ø act)
for S to stain, dye, color the surface of O
·A yáanáý áwé kayliséñ'w yá néegwál'. You tinted this paint too much.

,

,

S

·Tléiñw kahéeni áwé átý dulyéiý kalséñ'ýu yís. Berry juices are used
for dyeing.
• kawdiséñ'w | --- | kadaséñ'wý
it's dyed | --- | it's dyed (regluarly).
O-ka-d-séiñ'w~ (ø event)
for O to be stained, dyed
·Du ooý kanat'á kahéeni yáý kawdiséñ'w. Her teeth are the color of
blueberry juice.

séiñ'w
seit

the quick (the flesh under the outer skin)
necklace

a seiyí

the shelter of it; the lee of it; the (beach) area below it (a

mountain, hill, etc.)

sgóon

school
·Çayéis' layeiýíý naýsateeyít sgóoni yoo uwagút. He went to school to
become an engineer.
·Yú sgóon tl'átgi tlein, a góonnáý daýyanaagóo wé káa. The cars are
traveling on the isthmus of the big school yard.

sgóonwaan

student; pupil; scholar
·Sgóonwaan atyátx'i has shayadihéin Yaakwdáatx'. There are a lot of school children in Yakutat.

sitgawsáan

noon
·Gangukçáýi has du sitgawsáan atýaayí áwé. The fish heads cooked around the fire are their lunch.
·Yées t'á çíñsi sitgawsáanx' has aawaýáa. They ate fresh king salmon barbequed over the fire at noon.

sít'

glacier
·Kichyaat ilk'wát'ý sít' yáx'. Terns lay eggs by glaciers.

sít' tuxóodzi

glacier bear

si.áat'i héen

cold water
·Aý éek' si.áat'i héen goondáý ayáayin. My brother used to pack cold water from a spring.
·Si.áat'i héen ín x'eesháa tóode akawsixaa. She poured cold water into the bottle jug.

si.áax'u át
sooñ

pepper

peat moss
1

SOOS

• ñut akaawlisóos | --- | ñut kéi aklasóosch
s/he lost them | --- | s/he loses them (regularly).
ñut O-ka-S-l-sóos (ga motion)
for S to lose (plural) O

,

S

Dictionary of Tlingit

• ñut has kaawasóos | --- | ñut kei has kasóosch
they are lost; they got lost | --- | they get lost (regularly).
ñut O-ka-ø-sóos (ga event)
for (plural) O (objects, people) to be lost
·Wé ñáa du jishagóoni ñut kaawasóos. The man's tools are lost.

sóow (C)

rain
séew

stoox

stove
·Ý'aan yeenayát'ch wé yées stoox tóox'. The fire lasts in the new stove.
·Stoox káa yan sa.ín wé at téiýi! Set the broth on top of the stove!

sú

bull kelp

Suñteeneidí

Sukteeneidí, locally called "Dog Salmon"; a clan of the
Raven moiety whose principal crest is the Dog Salmon

suñtéitl'

goose tongue

,

,

S'

« S' »
s'aach

shield fern

s'aaçitunéekw (AtT)

rheumatism

s'aaçitunóok (TC)

s'aañ

bone
·Du gúkx' tsú yéi aa wduwa.oo wéi s'aañ ñ'anooý. They put the small
bone labret in his ear too.
·S'aañ áwé shux'áanáý átý wududliyéý aý léelk'w du ñ'anooýú yís.
My grandmother's first labret was made out of bone.

at s'aan.aýw dzáas
s'áas'

spear which binds rope around seal

goldfinch, canary

du s'aatí

his/her boss, master
·Yées ñáa áwé has du s'aatí. Their boss is a young man.

s'áaw

dungeness crab
·Goosú á yana.áat'ani wé s'áaw a kát isa.eeyi ñ'wátl? Where is the
cover for the pot you're cooking the crab in?

s'áaxw

hat
·Kijook s'áaxw ñudzitee. There is a hawk hat.
·A çóot woogoot du s'áaxu. He went without his hat.

s'aaý

hoary marmot; groundhog, whistler

s'áaý'

ling cod

s'agwáat

brown
·Yán aas daadáý kayeiý áwé átý gaçilayéiý s'agwáat kaséñ'ýu
sákw. Shavings from a hemlock tree is what you will use for the brown dye.

s'agwáat

flaky surface of the outer bark of conifers, especially hemlock

a s'añshutúñl'i

cartilage, gristle at the end of its bones

s'añtu.eeýí

his/her bone marrow
s'añtu.eiýí (C)

a s'añtu.eeýí

its bone marrow
a s'añtu.eiýí (C)

a s'añý'áak túñl'i
s'áx

cartilage, gristle between its bones

starfish

,

Dictionary of Tlingit

s'áxt'

devil's club
·Aý jeet tán wé kaxágwaa yeit, yáa s'áxt' aan yéi nñasaneiyít! Hand me the mortar so I can use it on this devil's club!

s'é

clay; alluvial silt

s'é

first
·Náakw s'é áa yéi kñwa.oo aý keey aaçáa tsá wéi kashóok' gwéil. I will put medicine on my knee first, then the heating pad.

du s'ee

his/her eyebrow
du s'ei

s'eek

black bear
·S'eek l'eedí tléil ulyát'. A black bear's tail is short.
·Wé s'eek gandaas'aají kúdi aawat'ei. The black bear found a bee's nest.

s'eeñ

smoke
s'eiñ

s'eeñ kawóot

light bluish-gray trade bead(s)

s'eenáa

lamp
·Uýganhéen s'eenáa káax' has dañéis'in. They used to sew by kerosene lamp.
·S'eenáat akaawagán. The light is on.

s'eenáa yaakw

gas-powered boat

S'EES

• aadé kawdlis'ées | aadé yaa kanals'ís | --it's blowing in the wind there | it's blowing in the wind there | ---.
P-dé ka-l-s'ées~ (na motion)
for an object to be blown in the wind to P
·Lidzée kayaaní a kaadéi kawuls'éesi wé laañ'ásk. It's frustrating when leaves are blown onto the black seaweed.
• át wulis'ees | --- | --it's blowing around; it blew around | --- | ---.
P-t O-l-s'ees~ (na motion)
for O to be blown around at P (by wind), to sail
·Aan kwéiyi óoxjaa tóot wulis'ees. A flag is blowing in the wind.
·Du hídi kináak áwé át wulis'ees wé aan kwéiyi. The flag is blowing around above his house.
S'EET
• akaawas'ít | akas'éet | akas'ítý
s/he bandaged it | s/he is bandaging it | s/he bandages it (regularly).
O-ka-S-ø-s'eet~ (ø act)
for S to bind up, wrap around, bandage O

,

,

S'

·Du keitl jíni akaawas'ít. He bandaged his dog's paw.
·Du jigúnl'i akaawas'ít. He bandaged his wrist.

s'eex

dirt; scrap(s); rubbish, trash, clutter; lint

S'EEX
• wulis'íx | yaa nals'íx | las'íxý
it aged | it's aging | it ages (regularly).
l-s'eex~ (ø event)
for animal matter to age, spoil to stage where still firm, but smelly
·Wé ýeel' wuls'eexí lichán. When the slime rots it stinks.

s'éex'át

shrimp

S'EEX'W
• át akawlis'íx'w | --- | áý aklas'éex'w
s/he stuck it to it | --- | s/he sticks it to it (regularly).
P-t~ O-ka-S-l-s'éex'w~ (ø motion)
for S to stick O (esp. paper) to P
·Du eetí a kaýyeet akawlis'íx'w ñaa yahaayí wé shaatk'átsk'u. The young girl pasted a photo on the ceiling of her room.

du s'ei

his/her eyebrow
du s'ee

s'eiñ

smoke
s'eeñ
·S'eiñ ýáat xáas'i áwé yak'éi çaltóot idateení latseen sákw at
eel'óoni. When you're out hunting a piece of smoked fish skin in your pocket is
good for energy.
·L s'eiñý usiteeyi neil áyá. This is a smoke-free home.

S'EIÑ
• áý akawlis'eiñ | --- | áý aklas'éñý
s/he tanned it | --- | s/he tans it (regularly).
áý a-ka-S-l-s'eiñ~ (na event)
for S to tan, smoke, cure something by placing in smoke
-s'eeñ~ (An)
·Áý akawdudlis'eiçi ishñeen du tuwáa sagóowun aý éesh. My dad
used to like smoked black cod.
·Téil yéi aya.óo at doogú aklas'éñýi yís. She is using dry wood for
smoking that hide.
• sh ý'awdis'eiñ | sh ý'adas'eiñ | yoo sh ý'adis'eiñk
s/he smoked | s/he's smoking | s/he smokes (regularly).
sh ý'a-S-d-s'eiñ (na act)
for S to smoke (cigarettes, etc.)
·Sh ý'áýdas'eiñ. I smoke.

s'eiñ daakahídi

smokehouse (with smoke piped in from outside)
s'eiñ hídi, s'eiñ daakéedi (C)

,

Dictionary of Tlingit

·Awdziçeiwu çaat s'eiñ hídi yeeý ash ayaawatée. She hung the sockeye
salmon that she netted in the smokehouse.

s'eiñdaakeit

pipe (for tobacco)

S'EIL'
• aawas'éil' | yaa anas'él' | yoo ayas'él'k
s/he tore it | s/he's tearing it | s/he tears it (regularly).
O-S-ø-s'éil' (na event)
for S to tear O
• akaawas'éil' | akas'él't | yei akas'éil'ch
s/he tore it | s/he is tearing it | s/he tears it (regularly).
O-ka-S-ø-s'éil' (ça act)
for S to tear, tear up, rip off O; for S to peel off O (bark from a tree)
• aý'eiwas'él | aý'as'él'ý | --s/he held it open | s/he is holding it open | ---.
O-ý'a-S-ø-s'éil'~ (ø act)
for S to tear O away (from hook); for S to stretch or hold O (opening) open
With this verb, it is best to name the thing being held open.
For example: gwéil aý'eiwas'él' "s/he held the bag open".
Otherwise, it sounds like someone is holding their mouth open
with their hands.
·A ý'é áwé aawasháat wé ñáa tlein, tle aý'éiwas'él'. The big man
grabbed its mouth and tore it apart.
• kawdis'éil' | --- | yei kdas'él'ch
it's torn | --- | it gets torn (regularly).
ka-d-s'éil' (ça event)
for something to be torn up
·Kawdis'éil' aý çeiwú. My net is all torn up.
• ýaat awlis'él' | ýaat als'éil' | ýaat als'éil'ý
s/he pulled up spruce roots | s/he pulls up spruce roots; s/he is pulling up spruce
roots | s/he pulls up spruce roots (regularly).
O-S-l-s'éil'~ (ø act)
for S to tear up, pull up O (roots)
·Ýaat áyá gaýtulas'éil'. We're going to dig spruce roots.

s'éil'

wound

s'éil' tsáax'

rubber gloves

s'éiýwani

lichen that hangs down from trees

s'éiýwani

yellow

s'élasheesh

flathead duck

s'él'

rubber
·Ñaa kasán tayeet shukatáni áwé yak'éi wéi s'él' kinaak.át. A
raincoat that hangs below the waist is the best.

,

,

s'éý

S'

swamp hemlock

s'igeeñáawu yaagí

red mussel

s'igeidí

beaver
s'ikyeidí
·S'igeidí ña yáay a káa kashaxít wé at doogú x'óow! Draw a Beaver
and whale design on the leather blanket!
·S'igeidí káý çaatáa héen táakde awsitee. He set a trap underwater for
beaver.

s'igeidí áayi
s'igeidí ýaayí

beaver dam
beaver's den

s'içeeñáawu

ghost
s'igeeñáawu (T)

s'içeeñáawu tléiçu

various odd looking, tasteless, or otherwise

undesirable berries, some poisonous; meaning varies locally, incl. twistedstalk (Streptopus species), snowberry (Symphoricarpos albus), fool's huckleberry (Menziesia ferruginea), etc.

s'íksh

false hellebore
Warning: extremely poisonous

s'ikshaldéen

Hudson Bay tea
Warning: the similar bog-rosemary (Andromeda polifolia),
and bog-laurel (Kalmia microphylla subspecies occidentalis) are
toxic, they lack brown rusty hairs under the leaves and have pink
flowers)

s'iñdaakeit

tobacco pipe
s'eiñdaakeit

s'ín

carrot
·Anahoo s'ín teen wudustaayí yak'éi. Turnip boiled with carrots is good.

s'ísaa

cloth; sailcloth
·S'ísaa gwéil tóox' duhoonín kóox. Rice used to be sold in cloth bags.
·S'ísaa ñáas' hoon daakahídidáý aawa.oo. She bought a yard of fabric from the store.

s'ísaa hít

tent
·Yan awsinéi du s'ís'aa hídi eetí. He fixed up the place for his tent.

s'ísaa yaakw

sailboat
·Aý éesh kak'dakwéiy s'aatíý wusitee s'ísaa yaakw káx'. My father became the captain of the sailboat.
·Anóoshi aan kwéiyi áwé át wududziyíñ wé s'ísaa yaakw ýuká. They raised a Russian flag on the deck of that sailboat.

,

S'

s'íx'

dish; plate
·Wé s'íx' çáax'w a káa yéi yatee. There are herring eggs on that plate.
·S'íx' ýoot ilt'ách déi! Wash up the dishes now! (Lit: Slap (up) the dishes now).

s'íx'çaa

moss

s'íx' ñ'áatl'

plate
s'íx' t'áal' (C)
·Ít'chi s'íx' ñ'áatl' du jeewú. She has a glass plate.

du s'óoçu

his/her rib
·Jánwu dleeyí aatlein yak'éi, gwál wé a s'óoçu. Mountain goat meat is
really good, especially the ribs.

s'ook

barnacle

S'OOK
• akawlis'úk | aklas'úk | aklas'úký
s/he fried it | s/he's frying it | s/he fries it (regularly).
O-ka-S-l-s'ook~ (ø act)
for S to toast O (bread); for S to fry O (usually till crisp)
O-ka-S-l-s'éekw~ (ø act)
·Gishoo taayí ña dleey wóosh teen akawlis'úk. She fried the meat with
bacon.
·Xáanaa atýaayí yís çáý akawlis'úk. She fried rabbit for dinner.

s'óos'
s'óos'ani
s'oow

pole(s) on which fish are hung for drying in smokehouse
pine cone, spruce cone
s'óos'eni (C)
greenstone

s'oow

green, light blue

·Wé ganyal'óot' s'oow yáý yatee. That flame is green.

S'OOW
• aawas'úw | as'úw | --s/he chopped it | s/he's chopping it; s/he chops it | ---.
O-S-ø-s'óow~ (na act)
for S to chop O (esp. chopping down trees, chopping off branches)
Can also be used metaphorically to mean to terminate
something.
·Aasdaaçáadli aaý aawas'úw. He chopped off the tree fungus.
·Hít tayeegáas'i yís aas aawas'úw. He chopped down trees for pilings.

s'oow ýút'aa
s'uñkasdúk

stone adze
solid-ribbed brown bear

,

,

s'ús'
s'úwaa

harlequin duck
awl; chopping block

,

S'

Dictionary of Tlingit

« Sh »
du shá

his/her head
du shán
·Ñ'anashgidéi ñáa áwé kíndei alshát du shá. The poor man is holding his head high.

a shá

its head
·Wé ñáa dzísk'u shaayí gangooknáý as.eeyín. He used to cook moose head next to the campfire.

shaa

mountain
·Wé shaa dayéen áayáý uwahán. He turned around to face the mountain.
·Shaa litká aadé daýduwatéen wé watsíx. The caribou are visible on the mountain ridge.
1

SHAA

• aawasháa | --- | --s/he married him/her; s/he is married | --- | ---.
O-S-ø-shaa~ (ø event)
for S to marry O
·Sheet'kaadé ñu.aa áyá wdusháayin Teiñweidéech áyá. She was married to a man from Sitka from Teikweidí clan.
·Sheendé! Táach ikçwasháa. Get up! You're going to oversleep. (Lit: Sleep will marry you.)
• wooch has wudisháa | --- | --they married each other | --- | ---.
wooch S-d-shaa~ (ø event)
for S (two people) to marry each other
Either wooch or woosh can be used with this verb.
• wuduwasháa | --- | --s/he got married | --- | ---.
O-du-ø-shaa~ (ø event)
for O to get married

sháa

women
·Yáa ñutaanx' aadé ñugaýtootéen ixkée ch'a çaaýtusatéen wé sháa. This summer we are going to travel down south just to see the girls.
·Ha yéi áwé has duwasáakw Ñ'eiñ'w Sháa Xunaadáý. They are called the Sea Pigeon gals from Hoonah.

sháach'

young herring

a shaadí

its sprouts, fleshy leaves growing toward the top of the stem
(e.g. of bear root)

,

,

Sh

sháak

timothy grass (used for basket decoration)
·Ñákw yéi daané yís áwé yéi daaýané yá sháak. I am collecting this
timothy grass for making baskets.

shaañ

snag; driftlog, driftwood

sháal

fish trap

shaan

old age

shaan

old person

SHAAN
• wudishán | yaa ndashán | --s/he is old | s/he's getting old | ---.
O-d-shaan~ (ø event)
for O to show signs of old age (esp. grey hair), for O to become old, age
·Yaa indashán óosh gé! If only you were getting old!

shaanák'w

(little) old person

shaanáý

mountain valley; valley
·Shaanáý yaawashóo wé ñaa ý'oos deiyí. The foot trail extends through
the valley.

shaa seiyí

the shelter of a mountain, area on the beach below a

mountain
SHAASH
• woosháash | yei nasháash | yei sháashch
it wore out | it's wearing out | it wears out (regularly).
ø-sháash (ça event)
for something to wear out by continuous friction
·Yá washéen katáçayi woosháash. This connecting rod wore out.
·Du jáaji a dzaasí yei nasháash. The thongs of his snowshoes are wearing
thin.

shaa shakée

mountaintop; on top of the mountain
shaa shekée (C)
·Wé shaa shakéede duwatéen wé çagaan ý'usyee. The ray of sunlight
can be seen on the mountain top.

SHAAT
• aawasháat | --- | kei ashátch
s/he caught it | --- | s/he catches it (regularly).
O-S-ø-sháat~ (ga event)
for S to catch O; for S to grab, take hold of, snatch O; for S to arrest O; for S to
trap O
·S'eiñ ash daa dleeyí aawasháat. S/he's addicted to smoking. (Lit: Smoke
took hold of his/her body.)
·Ñúnáý haa téiý' aawasháat. It really caught our hearts.

,

Dictionary of Tlingit

• át ayawashát | aadé yaa ayanashát | --the wind hit it in gusts | the wind is hitting it in gusts | ---.
P-t~ a-ya-ø-shát (ø motion)
for the wind, weather to move in gusts to P
·Haa kát ayawashát wé xóon. The north wind hit us in gusts.
• awlisháat | alshát | yei alshátch
s/he held it | s/he is holding it | s/he holds it (regularly).
O-S-l-sháat~ (ça act)
for S to hold, retain O in one's grasp; for S to capture, hold O captive
·Wé dóosh du jín dleit kaaý kínde alshát. That cat is holding its paw up
off the snow.
·Wéi yaakw yaýak'áaw kas'éet áa yéi du.oowú, k'idéin yéi
aguýlasháat. If a screw is put in the thwart of the boat, it will hold pretty well.

shaatk'

young woman (not married)
·Ginjichwáan aanídáý áwé wé shaatk'. That young woman is from
Canada.
·Kaxéel' sháade hániý sitee wé shaatk'. The young girl is a troublemaker.

shaatk'átsk'u

girl
shaatk'iyátsk'u, shaatk'iyétsk'u (C)
·Shaatk'átsk'uý ýat siteeyí aý ý'é k'éiyin wé tl'aadéin.aa. When I was
a little girl, I used to love turnips.
·Ñúnáý ánk'w áwé wé shaatk'átsk'u. The young girl is a real crybaby.

du shaatk'í

his/her girlfriend
·Wé yées shaawát du shaatk'íý sitee. That young woman is his girlfriend.

shaatk'iyátsk'u

girl
shaatk'iyétsk'u (C), shaatk'átsk'u

shaaw

gumboots; chiton
·Ñéiý'dei naýtooñooý shaawçáa. Let's travel to Kake for some gumboots.

du shaawádi

his old lady (wife)
du shaawadí (TC)

shaawát

woman
·Ch'a yóo Anóoshi Aaníx' yaa German shaawát áyá du ýánx' yéi
wootee. While in Russia he was with a German woman.
·Wé yées shaawát du shaatk'íý sitee. That young woman is his girlfriend.

du sháawu

his/her clan sister

shaax'wsáani

girls, young women
·Wáa yateeyi aa shaax'wsáani sá ash koodlénýaa? What kind of girls
does he find tempting?

shaaý

gray currant, stink currant
·Shaaý a.éen haa hídi daatý kanéegwál' sákw. She is picking gray
currants from around our house for a berry and salmon egg dish.

,

,

Sh

·Aatlein shaaý kanéegwál' yéi ýwsinei. I made a lot of gray currant berry
sauce.

shaayáal

kind of hawk

shaa yadaa

mountainside; around the mountain

sháchgi tléiçu

swamp berries
·A yee.ádi gataan sháchgi tléiçu yís! Carry a container for swamp berries!

sháchk

swamp
·Sháchgi káa ka.éiý dáxw. Lowbush cranberries grow in the meadow.

sháchk kaý'wáal'i

sháchk ka.aasí
shach'éen

stunted tree in swamp; jackpine, swamp spruce

hair ribbon

a shadaa

around the top of it (object with rounded top)

du shadaadoogú
shadaa.át
shadakóoý'

cottongrass, Alaska cotton, swamp cotton

his/her scalp

headscarf, kerchief covering the head
ceremonial woven root hat with a stack of basket-like

cylinders on top

a shagóon

its what it is (to be) made of; its parts, components, materials

du shagóon

ancestor(s) of his/her clan or nation; his/her background,

heredity

du shakakóoch'i

his/her curly hair
du shekekóoch'i (C)

shákdéi

perhaps, probably

a shakée

top of it (something with a rounded top, as a
mountain); above it; (elevated) over it
·Gooch shakéex' wutusiteen wé sheech dzísk'w. We saw the cow moose
on top of the hill.
·Daax'oonínáý ñáa shaa shakéede al'óon has woo.aat. Four men went
up on the mountain hunting.

shakee.át

headdress, dance hat
·A ý'adaadzaayí áwé átý dulyéiý shakee.át daax'. Its whiskers are used
for a headdress.

shakéil'

dandruff
·Dleit yáý yatee i shakéil'i. Your dandruff is white.

shákw

strawberry
shíkw
·Aatlein shákw áwé wutuwa.ín kat'ákýi yéi naýtusaneit. We picked a

,

lot of strawberries so we can make dried berry patties.
·Tlei déiý ñ'ateil yáý áwé wutusineiý shákw kahéeni. We just saved two gallons of the strawberry juice.

shak'áts'

double-ended dagger

shak'únts'
shál

deer sprouting horns

spoon

shalas'áaw

deer with full-grown antlers

du shaláý'

back of his/her head at the base

shals'áaw

deer or other ruminant with full-grown horns
shalas'áaw

shaltláaý

nucleus of emerging river island; reef above high tide level

du shanáa

over his/her head; covering his/her head

shanaýwáayi

axe
shanýwáayi

shanaýwáayi yádi

hatchet

Shangukeidí

Shangukeidí, locally known as "Thunderbird"; a clan of

the Eagle moiety whose principal crest is the Thunderbird
·X'átgu áwé Shangukeidí has du at óowuý sitee. The dogfish is an artifact of the Thunderbiird people.
·Xeitl naaý has sitee Shangukeidí. The Shangukeidí are Thunderbird.

du shashaaní

gray hair
du sheshaaní (C)

du shát

his wife

shataaçáa
du shátý

deer or other ruminant having a horn with only one point
her older sister, cousin

du shaýaawú

his/her hair
·Ý'aan ch'éen i shaýaawú káx' kei kçwak'éi. A red ribbon in your hair would be good.
·Ñúnáý áwé ñ'asigóo i shaýaawú, a kát akawdagaaní. Your hair is really beautiful when the sun shines on it.

shaýdáñw

man-eating shark (legendary)
shuýdáñw, shaýdáñ (At)

shaý'ée x'wál'

hair pin

at shaýishdi dzáas
shaý'út'aa

spear for clubbing

fishing rod

,

,

shaý'wáas' (T)
shayéen

Sh

bald spot; bald head

nail

shayéinaa

anchor

shayeit

pillow
·Shayeit a kát satéen káa ýeýx'u yeit . The pillow is lying on the bed.

sh daxash washéen

chainsaw

shé

blood
shí
·Shí anaý naadaa wé taan geení. There is blood coming from the sea lion's tail flippers.
·Shé a ýoodé ayatéen du ý'astóoýu. He sees blood in his sputum.

shé

[expression of mild surprise]
shéi
1

SHEE

• aaçáa

ñoowashee | aaçáa ñushée | aaçáa yoo ñuyasheek
s/he looked for it | s/he is looking for it | s/he looks for it (regularly).
P-çáa ñu-S-ø-shee~ (na act)
for S to search for, look for, hunt for, seek P
·Aý ji.eetíçaa áyá ñuýashée. I'm looking for my handiwork.
·Ínçaa ñushée. He is looking for flint.

• át awdishée | --- | --s/he hopes for it | --- | ---.
át a-S-d-shee~ (ø event)
for S to hope, desire and expect something
·Yéi át aýwdishée iwulnáalýi. I wish you wealth.
• át ñuwashée | át ñushée | --s/he searched there | s/he is searching there | ---.
P-t ñu-S-ø-shee~ (ø act)
for S to search at P
·T'áa kát ñushí aý jeeyís - ñut kaýwaaçéex' aý kawóot ka.íshayi!

Look on the floor for me - I lost my needle!
• át uwashée | --- | áý shee
s/he touched it | --- | s/he touches it (regularly).
át~ S-ø-shee~ (ø motion)
for S to touch, take, pick up
·Ch'a çóot ñáa at óowu, tléil áý ooshee. You don't touch another person's possessions.
• aý éet wudishée | aý eedé yaa ndashéen | aý éeý

dashee
he/she/it is helping me; s/he helped me | he/she/it is beginning to help me |

,

he/she/it helps me (regularly).
N éet~ S-d-shee~ (ø event)
for S (person, medicine, etc.) to help, give help to, assist N
·Hú áwé aý éet wudishée. It is he who helped me.
·Çayéis' layeiýí jeedé ý'awditaan du éet çadasheet. She telephoned the blacksmith to help her.
2

SHEE

• aawashee | ashí | --s/he sang it | s/he sings it; s/he is singing it | ---.
O-S-ø-shee~ (ga act)
for S to sing O
·Ý'agáax' daakahídix' áwé at kashéeý' shí áa dushí. Songs of praise are sung in church.
• at wooshee | at shí | --s/he sang | s/he sings; s/he is singing | ---.
at S-ø-shee~ (ga act)
for S to sing
·Daýnáý naa sháadi náñx'i wé at yátx'i has du jeeyís has at wooshee. Two chiefs sang for the children.
·Jilñáat Ñwáan has at shí. The Chilkat people are singing.

Shee At'iká Ñwáan

people of Sitka

Sheet'ká Ñwáan

sheech

female (animal)
shich
·Gooch shakéex' wutusiteen wé sheech dzísk'w. We saw the cow moose on top of the hill.
·Wé áak'w déint áwé át woogoot wé sheech dzísk'u tlein. The big cow moose was walking around in the vicinity of the pond.

Sh eelk'átl'!

Shut up!; Be quiet!

sheen

wooden bailer (for boat)

shéen

large wooden spoon

sheen ý'ayee

dipper (for dipping water)

Sheet'ká

Sitka
·Sheet'kaadé ñu.aa áyá wdusháayin Teiñweidéech áyá. She was
married to a man from Sitka from Teikweidí clan.
·Wéi Sheet'kaadáý adátx'i at gutóox' áwé has du ée at dultóow. The
kids from Sitka are taught out in the wilderness.

sheexw

close quarter bow and arrow

at shéex'i

singers, choir
et shéex'i (C)

,

,

sheey

stick
sheey kañáas'i

sheey
at shéeyi

Sh

limb, primary branch; limb knot
singer
et shéeyi (C)

sheey kañáas'i

splinter, sliver
·Sheey kañáas'i du jíndáý kei aawayísh. She pulled a splinter out of her
hand.
·Du tl'eiñt yawdiçiji sheey kañáas'i áx' wudliñít'. It got infected where
the splinter poked her finger.

sheey tukagoodlí
sheey woolí
a sheidí

limb knot

knot hole
its horn

sheishóoý

rattle (of shaman)
·Ch'eet sheishóoý áwé akaawach'ák'w. She carved a murrelet rattle.
·Sheishóoý áwé akaawach'ák'w, kéel a káa yéi aawa.oo. He carved a
rattle and put a murrelet on it.

sheixw

close quarter bow and arrow
sheexw

SHEIÝ'
• akaawashéý' | akashéiý' | --s/he praised him/her | s/he is praising him/her | ---.
O-ka-S-ø-shéiý' (ø act)
for S to praise, glorify O; for S to approve, commend O; for S to comment on O
-shéeý' (An)
·Kawduwashíý' haa sháade háni. Our leader was really praised.

shéiý'w

red alder

shéiý'w

orange (in color)

shéiyi

Sitka spruce

sheý'wtáax'i
Shçagwei

bright red or orange
Skagway

at shí

music, singing, song
et shí (C)
·Ginjichwáan k'isáani áwé, wéix' has at shí. The young British men are
singing there.
·A náñ yaa nagúdi yaa shukanashéen. She is singing as she is leaving it
behind.

,

Sh

Dictionary of Tlingit

shí

song
·Shí áwé shukñwalaýóoý. I'm going to compose a song.
·Ý'agáax' daakahídix' áwé at kashéeý' shí áa dushí. Songs of praise
are sung in church.

shich

female (animal)
sheech

at shí ñóok

radio, phonograph, stereo, music box, ipod; any device that
plays music
·Yóo tliyaa aasdéi ksaxát wéi kaxées' aý at shí ñóok gúgu yís! Attach
the wire to that tree over there for my radio antenna!
·Anóoshi ý'asheeyí at shí ñóok tóode too.áýjin. We used to hear Russian
songs on the radio.

a shís'ñ

its green wood (of tree)

a shís'ñ

its raw (flesh or meat); rare (meat)

sh kadax'áshti hít
sh kahaadí
sh kalneegí

sawmill

crazy; insane; disturbed; mentally unbalanced
preacher

shkalneek

story
·Ýéet' a daat shkalneek ñudzitee. There is a story about a giant clam.
·Tlél kei guýlats'áa i daat sh kalneek. Gossip about you is not going to
smell good.

sh kalyéiyi

prostitute

SHOO

• --- | áý çaashóo | ----- | it's hanging there | ---.
P-ý ø-shoo~ (ça motion)
for a bulky item to hang, extend down along P
This verb is one of a small set of motion verbs with
extensional imperfective forms (Leer, 1991). It is distinguished by
an imperfective form which requires the conjugation prefix, in this
case ça-.
·Du doonyaaý k'oodás'i áý çaashóo. His undershirt is hanging out.
• áý kei wlishóo | --- | --it extends up there | --- | ---.
P-ý kei l-shóo~ (ø motion)
for a complex object (esp. road) to extend up to P
·Dzeit áý kei wlishóo. The ladder extends up there.
• áý yaawashóo | --- | --it extends around it | --- | ---.
P-ý ya-u-ø-shoo~ (ø motion)

,

,

Sh

for a slender item (esp. road) to extend around, along P
·Héen t'ikáý yaawashóo ñaa ý'oos deiyí. The foot trail goes beside the
river.
·Shaanáý yaawashóo wé ñaa ý'oos deiyí. The foot trail extends through
the valley.

SHOOCH
• wudishúch | dashóoch | dashúchý
s/he bathed | s/he is bathing | s/he bathes (regularly).
S-d-shooch~ (ø act)
for S to take a bath
·Ús'aa een daa dushóoch People bathe with soap.

shóogunáý

(at) first; originally; in the beginning

SHOOK'
• kawdlishúk' | --- | kalshúk'ý
it cramped; it's cramping | --- | it cramps (regularly).
O-ka-d-l-shóok'~ (ø event)
for O to have cramps; for O to get shocked (by electricity)
·Aý ý'oos kawdlishúk'. My foot got a cramp.
·Du çáts kalshúk'ý. His thighs cramp regularly.

at shooñ

laughter

SHOOÑ
• at wooshooñ | at shooñ | --s/he laughed | s/he laughs; s/he is laughing | ---.
at S-ø-shooñ (na act)
for S to laugh; for S to smile (often with laughter)

a shoowú

part of it; half of it
·Du hídidáý kaay shoowú yéi kunaaléi hoon daakahídi. The store is a
half mile from her house.

shooý'
shóo yaý
Shtax'héen

robin-like bird
turning over endwise
Stikine River

shtéen káa

steam engine, train
·A kayéikçaa áwé ñuntoos.áých shtéen káa haadé yaa nañúýu. We
always listen for the sound of the steam engine when it's coming.

sh tuwáa kasyéiyi

tourist

a shú

the end of it
·Yá aý l'eiý k'oodás' a wán shóot at ñá! Sew something to the edge of my
dance shirt!

,

Sh

du shuká

in front of him/her; his/her geneology, history; his/her

ancestors

a shuká

front of it; ahead of it
·Cháatl tíx'i yaa (ha)s a shuká nañúý. They're setting halibut gear.
·Ñeeý'é shukát áwé shoodanookch aý léelk'w. My grandfather wakes up
before dawn.

shukalýaají

troller
shukelýaají (C)

shunaýwáayi

axe
·Du jiýánx' yan satán wé shunaýwáayi! Leave the axe near him!

du shutóoý'

outer side of his/her foot up to the anklebone

a shutú

(in) the corner, (on or along) the edge, end of it
·Ñóok shutú aawatséý. She died. (Lit: S/he kicked the edge of the box.)

a shuwadaa

around it (bypassing it, avoiding it); around the

end of it

a shuwee

the foot of it; below it (raised place); flat area at the
end of it (lake); down from the crest of it (slope); the end of it (dock)
a shuyee

shux'áanáý

(at) first, originally
·Shux'áanáý kaldaaçéináý áwé dugwáal yá shí. The drumming starts

out slow in this song.
·S'aañ áwé shux'áanáý átý wududliyéý aý léelk'w du ñ'anooýú yís.
My grandmother's first labret was made out of bone.

a shuyee

the foot of it; below it (raised place); flat area at the
end of it (lake); down from the crest of it (slope); the end of it (dock)
a shuwee

sh yáa awudanéiyi

respected person; gentleman; lady

'

'

T

« T »
-t

(resting) at; coming to, arriving at; moving about
-t has different meanings depending on what verb it occurs
with. With "sit" or "stand" it means "at"; with (ø-) conjugation
motion verbs it means "coming to, arriving at"; with na-conjugation
motion verbs it means "moving around, about".
·Gootl kát áa wé çáý. The rabbit is sitting on a mound.
·Háas' du éet yéi uwanéi yá yagiyee. He has been vomiting today.

tá

sleep
·Du taayí yoo ý'ayatánk. She talks in her sleep.
·Sheendé! Táach ikçwasháa. Get up! You're going to oversleep. (Lit: Sleep
will marry you.)
1

TAA

• wootaa | tá | teiý
s/he slept | s/he is sleeping | s/he sleeps (regularly).
S-ø-taa~ (na act)
for (singular) S to sleep, sleep alone
·Haaw yan awli.át a káa nçataayít. He put branches down so he could
sleep on them.
• a yáanáý yaawatáa | --- | --s/he overslept | --- | ---.
a yáanáý ya-u-S-ø-táa~ (ø motion)
for S to oversleep
·A yáanáý yaawatáa. She slept in.
3

TAA

• awsitáa | asteiý | asteiý
s/he steamed it | s/he is steaming it | s/he steams it (regularly).
O-S-s-taa~ (ø act)
for S to boil, steam O (food, esp. meat)
·Teey woodí dustéiý. Yellow cedar bark is boiled.
·Anahoo s'ín teen wudustaayí yak'éi. Turnip boiled with carrots is good.

a táak

the bottom of it (a cavity)
·Wé çayéis' tíx' áwé du jín táakt yawdiçích. The steel cable poked him in
the hand.

táakw

winter; year
·Shayadihéin tl'áxch' táakwde yaa ñunahéini. There are a lot of dead
branches when it becomes winter.
·Oodzikaayi ñáa áyá táakwx' guçwaláaxw. A lazy man will starve in the
winter.

,

Dictionary of Tlingit

taakw aanási

jellyfish

táakw niyís

(in preparation) for winter
·At tooý'áan áyá táakwni yís, kaldáanaañý haa nasteech. We are
smoking fish for the winter because we are usually without money.
·Táakw niyís kinaa.át áwé ýwaa.oo. I bought a coat for winter.

taakw.eetí

summer; early summer
·Gus'yadóoli taakw.eetíx' haaý kalyeech. Sandpipers fly here in the early
summer.
·Ñaashashýáaw taakw.eetíx' haaý kalyeech. The dragonflies come in the
summer time.
1

TAAÑ

• aawatáñ | --- | atáñý
s/he poked it | --- | s/he pokes it (regularly).
O-S-ø-taañ~ (ø event)
for S to spear, prod, poke, jab at O
·Ñínaa teen aawatáñ du gúk. She pierced her ear with a quill.
• yaakw daak ayawlitáñ | yaakw daak ayanaltáñ | --s/he pushed the boat out (with a pole) | s/
he's pushing the boat out (with a pole) |
---.
daak O-ya-S-l-taañ~ (ø motion)
for S to pole, push O (canoe, boat) out away from the shore with a pole
·Tsáçaa een yaakw daak has ayawlitáñ. They pushed the boat offshore
with a pole.

táal

flat open basket woven from wide strips of bark (for carrying fish, etc.);
large platter

taan

sea lion
·Shí anaý naadaa wé taan geení. There is blood coming from the sea lion's
tail flippers.
·Taan áa awsiteeni yé a niyaadé çunéi uwañúý. He started motoring in
the direction he had seen the sea lion.

TAAN
• aawataan | yaa anatán | kei atánch
s/he carried it | s/he's carrying it | s/he carries it (regularly).
O-S-ø-taan~ (ga motion)
for S to carry, take O (usually a container or hollow object)
·A yee.ádi gataan sháchgi tléiçu yís! Carry a container for swamp
berries!
·X'eesháa yaa anatán. She is carrying a bucket.
• áa yan shukaawatán | --- | --it ended there | --- | ---.
yan shu-ka-ø-taan~ (ø event)
for something to end

'

'

T

• áa yaý aawatán | --- | áa yaý atáný
s/he turned it over | --- | s/he turns it over (regularly).
áa yaý O-S-ø-taan~ (ø motion)
for S to turn O (usually container, hollow object) over
• akaawataan | yaa akanatán | yoo akayatánk
s/he bent it | s/he is bending it | s/he bends it (regularly).
O-ka-S-taan~ (na event)
for S to bend O (usually long, simple object) over
• --- | akwshitán | ----- | s/he's in the habit of doing it | ---.
O-ka-u-S-sh-tán (ga state)
for S to be in habit of doing O; for S to do O frequently because S enjoys doing it
In addition to hobbies, this verb can be used to describe
habits with a negative connotation. For example: Ñaa yat'éi yoo
ý'atánk akwshitán "S/he likes to talk behind people's backs" or:
Akwshitán ñaa yáý kei ý'adatánch "S/he likes to argue". In the
negative, this verb is used to indicate that someone doesn't like to
do something, and therefore doesn't do it often. For example: Tlél
akooshtán dañéis' "S/he doesn't like to sew (and therefore doesn't
do it often)".
·Yéi kwdzigeiyi aa ñákwx' áwé akooshtánin yéi daané aý léelk'w.
My grandmother loved to make those little baskets.
• át aawataan | --- | át yoo ayatánk
s/he is carrying it around; s/he carries it around | --- | s/he carries it around
(regularly).
P-t O-S-ø-taan~ (na motion)
for O to carry O (usually container or hollow object) around at P
• át aawatán | aadé yaa anatán | áý ataan
s/he carried it there | s/he's carrying it there | s/he carries it there (regularly).
P-t~ O-S-ø-taan~ (ø motion)
for S to carry, take O (usually a container or hollow object) to P
·Aas k'eeyéet ash aawatán du óonayi. He leaned his rifle against the tree
trunk.
• --- | át astán | ----- | s/he has it lying there | ---.
P-t O-S-s-taan (position)

for S to have O (usually long, complex object) lying at P

·Júý'aa tóot astán du jín. He has his arm in a sling.

• --- | át shukatán | ----- | it extends to it | ---.

P-t shu-ka-ø-tán (position)

for something to extend to, end at P

This verb only occurs in the imperfective.

·Ñaa kasán tayeet shukatáni áwé yak'éi wéi s'él' kinaak.át. A raincoat that hangs below the waist is the best.

,

T

Dictionary of Tlingit

• --- | át tán | ----- | it's sitting there | ---.
P-t ø-tán (position)
for a container or hollow object to sit at P
This verb only occurs in the imperfective.
·Tl'aadéin áwé át tán wé ñóok. The box is sitting sideways.
• a daa toowditaan | --- | --s/he made a decision about it | --- | ---.
(yéi) tu-S-d-taan~ (na event)
for (singular) S to decide, make up one's mind (that way)
• a daa yoo toowatán | a daa yoo tuwatánk | a

daa yoo

tuwatánk
s/he thought about it | s/he thinks about it; s/he is thinking about it | s/he thinks
about it (regularly).
N daa yoo tu-S-ø-taan~ (ø act)
for (singular) S to think over, consider, make up one's mind about N
• du éet ý'eiwatán | --- | du éeý ý'ataan
s/he spoke to him/her | --- | s/he speaks to him/her (regularly).
N éet~ ý'a-S-ø-taan~ (ø motion)
for S to speak, talk to N
·Tula.aan een du éet ý'eiwatán. He spoke to her with kindness.
• du jeedé ý'awditaan | --- | du jeedé yoo ý'aditánk
s/he called him/her on the phone | --- | s/he calls him/her on the phone
(regularly).
N jeedé ý'a-S-d-taan~ (na motion)
for S to call N on telephone
·Çayéis' layeiýí jeedé ý'awditaan du éet çadasheet. She telephoned the
blacksmith to help her.
• du jeet aawatán | du jeedé yaa anatán | du jeeý ataan
s/he gave it to him/her | s/he is giving it to him/her | s/he gives it to him/her
(regularly).
N jeet~ O-S-ø-taan~ (ø motion)
for S to give, take, hand O (usually container or hollow object) to N
·Wé ñ'ateil xákwti aý jeet tán!. Hand me the empty pitcher!
·Aý jeet tán wé kaxágwaa yeit, yáa s'áxt' aan yéi nñasaneiyít! Hand
me the mortar so I can use it on this devil's club!
• du jeet awsitán | --- | du jeex astaan
s/he gave it to him/her | --- | s/he gives it to him/her (regularly).
N jeet~ O-S-s-taan~ (ø motion)
for S to give, take, hand O (usually long, complex object) to N
·Yées aa gútl du jeet wududzitán. He was given a new blunt arrow.
·Aý jeet satán a káa dul.us'ku át! Hand me the washboard!
• du jeet ý'awditán | --- | du jeeý ý'adataan
s/he called him/her on the phone | --- | s/he calls him/her (regularly).

,

,

T

N jeet~ ý'a-S-d-taan~ (ø motion)
for S to call N on telephone
• du jikaadáý ayaawatán | --- | du jikaadáý yaa atánch
s/he moved it out of his/her way | --- | s/he moves it out of his/her way (regularly).
N jikaadáý O-ya-u-S-ø-taan~ (ø motion)
for S to move O (usually container or hollow object) out of N's way
• jiwsitaan | yaa jinastán | kei jisatánch
it's rough | it's getting rough | it gets rough (regularly).
ji-s-taan~ (na event)
for the ocean to be rough
• a kanaý jiyawsitán | a kanaý yaa jiyanastán | --waves washed over it | waves are washing
over it | ---.
N kanaý ji-ya-s-taan~ (ø motion)
for waves to wash over N
·Has du yaagú kaanáý jiyawsitán. Waves washed over their boat.
• kei awsitán | --- | kei astánch
s/he brought it out | --- | s/he brings it out (regularly).
kei O-S-s-taan~ (ø motion)
for S to bring out, unearth O (usually long, complex object)(esp. from a box or
other container or place which O is kept); for S to pick up, lift up O
·Du jín kei awsitán. She raised her hand.
• kei jiwsitán | --- | --s/he raised his/her hand | --- | ---.
kei ji-S-s-taan~ (ø motion)
for S to raise a hand
·Ñaa yáý kei jisatánch wáadishgaa. The priest blesses people.
·Keijín aý yaadéi kei jisataan! Give me five!
• ñut aawataan | --- | ñut kei atánch
s/he lost it | --- | s/he loses it (regularly).
ñut O-S-ø-taan~ (ga motion)
for S to lose, misplace O (usually a container or hollow object)
·Aý ñ'wádli yanáak aa tsé ñut gaytáan! Don't misplace my pot cover!
·Wé ñ'wátl yana.áat'ani ñut ýwaataan. I misplaced the lid for the pot.
• ñuý aawatán | --- | ñuý atánch
s/he returned it | --- | s/he returns it (regularly).
ñuý O-S-ø-taan~ (ø motion)
for S to return O (usually a container or hollow object)
• séew daak wusitán | séew daak nastán | séew daak

satáný
it's raining | it's starting to rain | it rains (regularly).
daak s-taan~ (ø event)
for rain, snow to fall
·L'éý'kw, ñútl'kw nasteech séew daak wustaaní Soil turns to mud when
it rains.

,

Dictionary of Tlingit

·Kaklahéen daak guýsataaní yáý ñuwatee. The weather looks like it will
snow (wet snow).
• ý'awditaan | yaa ý'andatán | yoo ý'aditánk
s/he spoke | s/he is speaking | s/he speaks (regularly).
ý'a-S-d-taan~ (na event)
for S to speak, talk, make a speech
·A yáanáý tsé ý'anidataan! Don't say too much now!
• yaaý aawataan | --- | yaaý yei atánch
s/he carried it aboard | --- | s/he carries it aboard (regularly).
yaaý O-S-ø-taan~ (ça motion)
for S to carry O (usually container or hollow object) aboard (a boat)
• yan aawatán | yánde yaa anatán | yaý ataan
s/he put it down | s/he is putting it down | s/he puts it down (regularly).
yan~ O-S-ø-taan~ (ø motion)
for S to put down, lay down, leave, place O (usually container or hollow object)
·Wé té tlein a kaháadi káa yan tán! Put that large rock on top of its
cover!
·Wé kóoñ kax'ás'ti a yanáa yan aawatán. He put plywood over the pit in
the ground.
• a yanáaý at wootaan | --- | a yanáaý yei at tánch
s/he covered it | --- | s/he covers it (regularly).
at S-ø-taan~ (ça event)
for S to cover (esp. pot) with something
·Tsaa eiýí du daagú ágé a yanáaý yei at dutánch? Is a cover put on
when rendering seal oil?
• yan akawsitán | --- | --s/he put it down | --- | ---.
yan~ O-ka-S-s-taan~ (ø motion)
for S to put down, lay down, leave, place O (usually quite small, stick-like object)
·Wéit tin x'úx' áwé a káa yan kaysatán i kooxéedayi! Put your pencil
on top of that book laying there!
• yan awsitán | --- | --s/he put it down | --- | ---.
yan~ O-S-s-taan~ (ø motion)
for S to put down, lay down, leave, place O (usually long, complex object)
·Du jiýánx' yan satán wé shunaýwáayi! Leave the axe near him!
• yan jiwsitán | --- | --s/he put his/her hand down | --- | ---.
yan~ ji-S-s-taan~ (ø motion)
for S to lower a hand
• yan jiwsitán | --- | --waves reached the beach | --- | ---.
yan~ ji-s-taan~ (ø motion)
for waves to reach the beach

,

,

• --- | yóo katán | ----- | it's bent | ---.

yóo ka-ø-tán (position)
for something to be bent
This verb only occurs in the imperfective.
·Yóo katán wé tuháayi. The nail is bent.
·Ch'áak' lú yóo katán. A bald eagle's beak is curved.
• yoo ý'eiwatán | yoo ý'ayatánk | yoo ý'ayatánk
s/he talked | s/he is talking | s/he talks (regularly).
yoo ý'a-S-ø-taan~ (ø act)
for S to talk, speak
·Ñaankak.eetx' yoo ý'eiwatán. He spoke in public.
·A géide yoo ý'ayatánk wé aadé át kadu.aañw yé. He is speaking out
against the proposed decision.

táanaa

spear (for devilfish)

du taaní (TC)

his/her umbilical cord
du taanú (AtT)

du taanú (AtT)

his/her umbilical cord
du taaní (TC)

taan ý'adaadzaayí
taashuká

horsetail

river flats; tidelands; mudflats

taat

night
·Haa k'idaaká ñu.óowu taat kanaý has at wooshee. Our neighbors
sang all night long.
·Taat kanaý oonñal'eiýín. I would have danced all night.

taat aayí adéli

night watchman

taat sitgawsáani
taat yeen

midnight

during the night; in the middle of the night

TAAW
• aawatáw | atáaw | atáawý
s/he stole it | s/he steals it | s/he steals it (regularly).
O-S-ø-táaw~ (ø act)
for S to steal O
·At géit wudzigít wé ñáa átx'i aawutáawu. He went against the law when he stole the man's belongings.

táaw s'aatí

thief

TAAX'
• ash wusitáax' | --- | kei ash satáx'ch
it bit him/her/it | --- | it bites him/her/it (regularly).

,

T

Dictionary of Tlingit

O-s-taax'~ (ga event)
for an insect to bite O
Note that ash wusitáax' and awsitáax' both have basically
the same meaning "it bit him/her/it". The difference is that the
object pronoun ash "him/her/it" is used when the referent is
prominent in the conversation.
·Xeitl táax'aa ýat wusitáax'. A horsefly bit me.
·Wanatíxch wusitáax' du wankach'eeñ. The ant bit his little finger.

táax'aa

mosquito

táax'aa ý'uskudayáat'

daddy long legs; mosquito eater

táax'ál'

needle
·Táax'ál' x'aan áwé aý tl'eiñ tóode yawdiçeech. The needle point poked
my finger.

táaý'

slug, snail

TAAÝ'W
• wootáaý'w | yei natáý'w | yoo
it sank | it's sinking | it sinks (regularly).
ø-táaý'w (na event)
for something to sink

yatáý'w

taay

fat; blubber
·Çuwakaan a taayí teen awsi.ée. She cooked deer with the fat on.
·Çuwakaan taayí kas'úkýu yís akaawaxaash. She cut up deer fat for
frying.

táay

garden; field
·Dákwtasi átý dulyéiý táay yíx'. Rendered fat is used in the garden.
·Wé káts táay káa yéi na.oo! Put the pounded shell powder on the garden!

táay kahéiýi

gardener

tadanóox'

turtle
kanóox', tanóox', tadanóox'u (At)

táçaa
taçanís

lancet
sapling; pole made from sapling

a taká

the inside surface of its bottom (of container, vessel)
·Ýáay kayeiýtáçu a takáx' yéi na.oo! Put yellow cedar shavings in the
bottom of it!

tañaadí

rockslide
teñaadí (C)

táñl

hammer

tás

thread; sinew

,

,

a tási

T

its sinew

tatgé

yesterday
·Çayéis' t'éiý'i sháade háni haat ñuwatín tatgé. The chief blacksmith
traveled here yesterday.
·At géide ayawsiñaa du kéek' tatgé. She spoke wrongly against her
younger sister yesterday.

tatóok
tawéi

cave
mountain sheep, bighorn sheep

tax'aayí

rock point

taýhéeni

soup broth; soup
·Éil' eetéenáý yatee wé taýhéeni. The broth needs salt.

Taýhéeni
tayashagoo
tayataayí

Takhini hot springs (north of Whitehorse, Yukon Territory)
small red sea anemone
sea anemone

a tayee

underneath it; beneath it; below it
·Wé aas chéý'i tayeet áwé tooñéen. We are sitting in the shade of the tree.
·Kéi dañinji s'áaxw tlein a tayeet ñaa luwagúñ séew tóodáý. People
ran under the big umbrella out of the rain.

tayees

stone axe

tayeidí

bladder rack; rock weed; yellow seaweed

té

stone; rock
·Téix' gwáa wégé átý dulyeiýín chooneit sákw. Little stones must have
been used to make arrows.
·Wé té tlein a kaháadi káa yan tán! Put that large rock on top of its cover!
1

TEE
•a

eetéenáý wootee | a eetéenáý yatee | a eetéenáý yoo
yateek
he/she/it needed it | he/she/it needs it | he/she/it needs it (regularly).

N eetéenáý O-ø-tee~ (na state)
for O to need, lack, require N
·Yées túlaa eetéenáý ýat yatee. I need a new drill.
·Kooxéedaa eetéenáý yatee wé shaatk'. The young girl needs a pencil.

• ñoowdzitee | ñudzitee | --it existed; s/he was born | it exists; s/he is alive | ---.
O-ñu-d-s-tee~ (ça state)
for O to be, be in existence, live; for O to be born
·Tsú yáa aý tláa ñu.aa Sheet'káx' áyá ñoowdzitee. Ña du éek' tsú
áa ñoowdzitee. My mother was born in Sitka. And her brother was also born
there.

,

Dictionary of Tlingit

·Tléil ýwasakú daañw.aa ýáat sá a ñ'anooýú ñusteeyí. I don't know
which fish have beards.
• (noun)-ý wusitee | (noun)-ý sitee | --s/he became a (noun) | s/he is a (noun) | ---.
P-ý O-s-tee~ (na state)
for O to be P (a member of a group); for O to become P
This verb requires that the preceding noun phrase have the
-ý postposition. In the forms given here, (noun) can be replaced
by any noun which makes sense. An example is the name of a
profession such as: asçeiwú "seiner" as in: asçeiwúý wusitee "s/he
became a seiner". Another example is the name of a moiety such
as: ch'áak' naa "eagle moiety" in the common phrase: Ch'áak' naaý
ýat sitee "I am of the Eagle moiety". Please see the example
sentences for more options.
·Ña ýát tsú aý toowú yak'éi yaa a káa yéi ýat guçwateeyí yaa
Lingítý ýat sateeyí. And I too am thankful that I'm part of this being that I'm
Lingít.
·L s'eiñý usiteeyi neil áýá. This is a smoke-free home.
• sh tóoçáa wditee | sh tóoçáa ditee | sh tóoçáa yoo

diteek
s/he was grateful | s/he is grateful | s/he is grateful (regularly).
sh tóoçáa O-d-tee~ (na state)
for O to be grateful, thankful, satisfied
·Sh tóoçáa wditee aý yoowú. My stomach was satisfied.
• tleiyéi yéi wootee | tleiyéi yéi yatee | tleiyéi yéi teeý
he/she/it became still | s/he is still | he/she/it is still (regularly).
tleiyéi yéi O-ø-tee~ (na state)
for O to be still, quiet; for O to stop (car, clock, e.g.)
·Wé yaakw tlein Aangóonx' tleiyéi yéi wootee. The big boat stopped in
Angoon.
• du wañshiyeex' yéi wootee | du wañshiyeex' yéi yatee

| du wañshiyeex' yéi teeý
he/she/it appeared before him/her | he/she/it is in front of his/her eyes | he/she/it
appears before him/her (regularly).
N wañshiyeex' yéi O-ø-tee~ (na state)
for O to appear to N; for O to be apparent to N
·I wañshiyeex' yéi yatee. It's in front of your eyes.
• du

ýánx' yéi wootee | du ýánx' yéi yatee | du ýánx' yéi
teeý

s/he was with him/her | s/he is with him/her | s/he stays with him/her (regularly).
P-x' yéi O-ø-tee~ (na state)
for O to be, stay, remain at P; for O to dwell, live at P
·Ch'a yóo Anóoshi Aaníx' yaa German shaawát áýá du ýánx' yéi
wootee. While in Russia he was with a German woman.

·Aý sée du kacháwli áwé ixkéex' yéi yatee. My daughter's sweetheart
lives down south.

,

,

T

• a yáý wootee | a yáý yatee | --he/she/it was like it | he/she/it is like it | ---.
N yáý O-ø-tee~ (na state)
for O to be like, similar to N
·Wé yées xwaasdáa çákw yáý yatee. The new tent is stiff.
·Gan eetí kél't' ñugáas' yáý yatee. Ashes from the fireplace are gray.
• yéi ñoowatee | yéi ñuwatee | yéi yoo ñuyateek
the weather was that way | the weather is that way | the weather is that way
(regularly).
(yéi) ñu-ø-tee~ (na state)
for the weather to be (that way)
To specify how the weather is, replace yéi with a weather
term + yáý. For example: séew yáý ñuwatee "it looks like rain". In
the negative, one can say: tlél áyáý ñootí "the weather looks bad".
·Kaklahéen daak guýsataaní yáý ñuwatee. The weather looks like it will
snow (wet snow).
• --- | yéi tuwatee | ----- | s/he feels that way | ---.
(yéi) O-tu-ø-tee~ (na state)
for O to want to do, feel like doing (that); for O to feel a certain way
·Eeshandéin tuwatee. He's feeling sad.
• yéi wootee | yéi yatee | yóo yateek
he/she/it was that way | he/she/it is that way | he/she/it is that way (regularly).
(yéi) O-ø-tee~ (na state)
for O to be (that way)
·Ña ýat tsú aý toowú yak'éi yaa a káa yéi ýat guçwateeyí yaa
Lingítý ýat sateeyí. And I too am thankful that I'm part of this being that I'm
Lingít.
·Wé al'óon tlél wáa sá wootee. The hunt went alright.
2

TEE

• aadé aawatee | aadé yaa anatéen | aadé yoo ayateek
s/he carried it there | s/he is carrying it there | s/he carries it there (regularly).
P-dé O-S-ø-tee~ (na motion)
for S to carry, take O (general, often compact object) to P
·Du gwéili tóode aawatee wé çíl'aa. He put the grindstone in his bag.
• aadé awsitee | aadé yaa anastéen | aadé yoo asiteek
s/he carried it there | s/he is carrying it there | s/he carries it there (regularly).
P-dé O-S-s-tee~ (na motion)
for S to carry, take O (solid, often complex object) to P
·S'igeidí káý çaatáa héen táakde awsitee. He set a trap underwater for
beaver.
• aaý aawatée | --- | aaý kei ateech

s/he picked it up off of it | --- | s/he picks it up off of it (regularly).
P-dáý O-S-ø-tee~ (ga motion)
for S to pick O (general, compact object) up off of P

,

Dictionary of Tlingit

·Aaý gatí wéi kaxíl'aa kadushxeet t'áa yá çalçú! Pick up the eraser and
clean the chalkboard!

• ashoowsitee | ashusitee | yoo ashusiteek
s/he expected him/her/it | s/he's expecting him/her/it | s/he expects him/her/it
(regularly).
O-shu-S-s-tee~ (na state)
for S to anticipate, foresee O; for S to expect, consider O likely to happen or
arrive
·Ch'u dziyáak áwé ishuwtusitee. We were expecting you a while ago
·Ch'u tliyaatgé áwé shuýwsitee. I was expecting it the other day.

• --- | át akatéen | ----- | s/he has it lying there | ---.
P-t O-ka-S-téen (positional)
for S to have (round, spherical) O lying at P
·Kas'éet katíý'aa tlein áyá yaakwt kaýatéen. I have a big screwdriver
lying in the boat.

• --- | át satéen | ----- | it's sitting there | ---.
P-t s-téen (position)
for a solid, often complex object to sit at P
This verb only occurs in the imperfective.
·Yées washéen a géekt satéen wé yaakw. A new motor sits at the stern of
that boat.

• awsitee | yaa anastéen | kei asteech
s/he carried it | s/he is carrying it | s/he carries it (regularly).
O-S-s-tee~ (ga motion)
for S to carry, take O (solid, often complex object)

• áý aawatee | --- | --s/he put it there | --- | ---.
P-ý O-S-ø-tee~ (ça motion)
for S to install, hang, place O at P

• áý ashayaawatée | --- | áý ashayateeý
s/he hung it there | --- | s/he hangs it there (regularly).
P-ý O-sha-ya-S-ø-tee~ (ø motion)
for S to hang up O at P (esp. to dry)
·Wé atx'aan hídi yee áwé áý ashayaawatée wé ýaat. She hung the fish
inside the smokehouse.
·Jikañáas' káý ashayaawatée wé çaat atx'aan hídi yeex'. She hung
the sockeye salmon on the stick in the smokehouse.

• ayawditee | yei ayandatéen | yei ayadateech
it's stormy | it's getting stormy | it gets stormy (regularly).
a-ya-d-tee~ (ça event)
for the weather to be stormy, rough
·Dákde át xóon áwé ayawditee. An offshore east wind is blowing.
·Ñúnáý k'eeljáa yéi ayaguýdatée ách áyá haa yaagú dáñde
tusaýút'x'. It's going to get stormy so we are dragging our boats up.

,

,

• héent ayaawatée | --- | héený ayatee
s/he baptized him/her | --- | s/he baptizes him/her (regularly).
héent~ O-ya-S-ø-tee~ (ø motion)
for S to baptize, immerse (singular) O in water or pour water upon O as a
religious rite
·Johnch héent ayaawatée haa Aannáawu. John baptised our lord.
• du jeet aawatée | --- | du jeeý atee
s/he gave it to him/her | --- | s/he gives it to him/her (regularly).
N jeet~ O-S-ø-tee~ (ø motion)
for S to give, take, hand O (general, esp. abstract object) to N
·Du gúk yís náakw du jeet wuduwatée. He was given medicine for his
ear.
·Ch'a çóot yéidei yéi jiné has du jeeý dutee wéi ñ'atýáan. Cowards
are given different jobs to perform.
• du jeet akaawatée | du jeedé yaa akanatéen | du jeeý

akatee
s/he gave it to him/her | s/he's giving it to him/her | s/he gives it to him/her
(regularly).
N jeet~ O-ka-S-tee~ (ø motion)
for S to give, take, hand O (round object) to N
·Haa léelk'u hás tuwáadáý áwé gútk haa jeet kawduwatée. If it
wasn't for our elders, we wouldn't be here. (Lit: Because of our elders, we were
given a dime.)
·Ñaashaxáshaa aý jeet katí! Hand me the scissors!
• --- | kát adatéen | ----- | s/he is wearing it | ---.
kát O-S-d-tee~ (position)
for S to wear O
This verb only occurs in the imperfective. For all other
modes, speakers use the verb: yéi aawa.oo 's/he wore it'.
·Ñuý dak'óol'een áwé kát adatéen du k'oodás'i. He's wearing his shirt
backwards.
• du kát ashuwatée | --- | du káý ashutee
s/he blamed it on him/her | --- | s/he blames it on him/her (regularly).
P-t~ O-shu-S-ø-tée~ (ø motion)
for S to bring O (abstract, esp. shame, blame, joy) onto P
This verb can be used with nouns such as joy, shame, but
note that when no noun is explicitly given, the meaning is "blame"
for this verb. N éet~ can replace N kát~ to give the same meaning.
For example, du éet ashuwatée "s/he blamed it on him/her". To
blame someone for eating something, use N ý'éit~, as in: du ý'éit
shuýwaatée "I blamed him for eating it". To blame someone for
doing something with the hands, use N jeet~, as in: du jeet
shuýwaatée "I blamed him for doing it".
·Yéi daayaduñá, "Tlél kadéix' haa káý sheeteeñ!" He is told "Don't
bring shame on us!"

,

Dictionary of Tlingit

• káý awditee | --- | káý yéi adateech
s/he put it on | --- | s/he puts it on (regularly).
káý O-S-d-tee~ (ça event)
for S to put on O (shirt, dress, etc.)
• kei aawatée | --- | kei ateech
s/he brought it out | --- | s/he brings it out (regularly).
kei O-S-ø-tee~ (ø motion)
or S to bring out, unearth O (general, often compact object)(esp. from a box or
other container or place which O is kept); for S to pick up, lift up O
·Gaan woolí a kaháadi áa kei aawatée. He put the cover for the smoke
hole up there.
• neil aawatée | --- | neilý atee
s/he brought it inside | --- | s/he brings it inside (regularly).
neil O-S-ø-tee~ (ø motion)
for S to carry, take O (general, often compact object) home, inside
·Kaduch'áak'w lítaa sákw yak'éiyi aa çayéis' neil tí! Bring home a
good piece of iron for a carving knife!
• du ý'éiý aawatee | --- | du ý'éiý ateeý
s/he fed it to him/her/it | --- | s/he feeds it to him/her/it (regularly).
N ý'éiý O-S-ø-tee~ (na event)
for S to feed O to N; for S to give O to N to eat
·Náakw du ý'éiý wuduwatee du kalóox'sháni néegooch. She was
given medicine for her bladder pain.
·Náakw yís kayaaní ashigóok, áx' ñu.aa akwdliýéitl' ñaa ý'éiý aa
wuteeyí. He knows medicinal plants but he is afraid to give them to anyone.
• du ý'éiý at wootee | du ý'éiý yaa at natéen | du ý'éiý

at teeý
s/he fed him/her/it | s/he is feeding him/her/it | s/he feeds him/her/it (regularly).
N ý'éiý at S-ø-tee~ (na event)
for S to feed N, give food to N (for immediate consumption)
·Tlé kílaa kát áwé ñaa ý'éiý has at wootee. They fed the people from
platters.
• yan aawatée | --- | yaý atee
s/he put it down | --- | s/he puts it down (regularly).
yan~ O-S-ø-tee~ (ø motion)
for S to put down, lay down, leave, place O (general, often compact object)
·Du jiýáni yan tí wé lítaa, dleey aan akçwaxáash! Leave the knife near
her, she will cut meat with it!
·Ch'áagu aa kaý'íl'aa stoox káx' áwé yan dutéeych yaçat'aayít. The
irons of long ago were set on the stove to heat up.
• yan akaawatée | --- | yaý akatee
s/he put it down | --- | s/he puts it down (regularly).
yan~ O-ka-S-ø-tee~ (ø motion)
for S to put down, lay down, leave, place O (round, spherical object)
·Du jintáak káa yan akaawatée du tl'iñkakéesi. He put his ring in the
center of his palm.

,

,

T

·Atýá aaý yéi awusneiyi yé, dáanaa a eetíx' yan akaawatée. She put money in place of the food she picked up.
• yan awsitée | --- | yaý astee
s/he put it down | --- | s/he puts it down (regularly).
yan~ O-S-s-tee~ (ø motion)
for S to put down, lay down, leave, place O (solid, often complex object)
·Wéi kashóok' gwéil aý ýeek káa yan satí! Set the heating pad on my upper arm!
·Wéidu çánch gwéili nadáakw káa yan satí! Put that bag of tobacco on the table!
3

TEE

• aý'eiwatee | aý'atee | yoo aý'ayateek
s/he imitated him/her | s/he's imitating him/her | s/he imitates him/her (regularly).
O-ý'a-S-ø-tee (na act)
for S to imitate O; for S to mimic O's speech; for S to quote O

teel

scar

téel

shoe(s)
·I téeli yee.át ý'usyeex' yéi na.oo! Put your shoes at the foot of the bed!
·Wooshdakádin ý'oosdé awdiyiñ du téeli. He put his shoes on the wrong feet.

téel daakeyéis'i (C)

shoe polish

téel iñkeidí

moccasin top

téel layeiýí

shoemaker, cobbler

téel tukanágaa

wooden form for shaping/stretching moccasins

téel kanágaa

téel ý'adzaasí

shoelace(s)
téel ý'akadzaasí, téel ý'agudzaasí
·Du téel ý'adzaasí akaawadúx'. She tied her shoelaces.

téel ý'agudzaasí

shoelace(s)
téel ý'adzaasí; téel ý'akadzaasí

téel ý'akadzaazí

shoelace(s)
téel ý'adzaasí, téel ý'agudzaasí

téel'

dog salmon; chum salmon
·Tsu tsá yá naaý satí ñu.aa áyá yaa téel' áyá haa shukáý sitee,
L'eeneidí. Also the dog salmon is our clan crest, L'eeneidí.

teen

(along) with, by means of; as soon as
téen, tin, tín, een
·Tsaa eiýí teen áwé yak'ei t'á at ý'éeshi. Dry fish king salmon is good with
seal oil.

,

·Du jintáak teen at'ácht wé kadu.uxýu át. She is slapping the balloon
with the palm of her hand.
TEEN
• aadé

ñoowateen | aadé yaa ñunatín | aadé yoo
ñuyateenk

s/he traveled there | s/he is traveling there | s/he travels there (regularly).
P-dé ñu-S-ø-teen~ (na motion)
for S to travel, go on a trip to P
·Haadé yaa s ñunatín Waashdan Ñwáan. The Americans are traveling
here.
·Yáa ñutaanx' aadé ñugaýtootéen ixkée ch'a çaaýtusatéen wé
sháa. This summer we are going to travel down south just to see the girls.
• át ñuwatín | --- | áý ñuteen
s/he traveled there | --- | s/he travels there (regularly).
P-t~ ñu-S-ø-teen~ (ø motion)
for S to travel, go on a trip to P
·Çayéis' t'éiý'i sháade háni haat ñuwatín tatgé. The chief blacksmith
traveled here yesterday.
·Yáa ñutaanx' aadé ñugaýtootéen ixkée ch'a çaaýtusatéen wé
sháa. This summer we are going to travel down south just to see the girls.
• awlitín | altín | altíný
s/he watched him/her/it | s/he is watching him/her/it | s/he watches him/her/it
(regularly).
O-S-l-teen~ (ø act)
for S to look at, gaze at, watch O; for S to watch, take care of, mind, look after O
·Ý'aan yáý teeyí gis'óoñ, tlél dultíný When the northern lights are red,
they aren't to be looked at.
·K'idéin gé sh eeltín? Are you taking good care of yourself?
• awsiteen | --- | --s/he sees it; s/he saw it | --- | ---.
O-S-s-teen~ (ça event)
for S to see, behold O (usually specific)
·Dzísk'w awusteení tle a dachóon kéi uwagút. When he saw the moose
he turned to walk straight towards it.
·Aaçáa tsá ýwsiteeni yé. It's about time I saw it; I finally saw it.
• --- | ayatéen | ----- | s/he can see it | ---.
O-S-ø-teen~ (ga state)
for S to see, perceive O (often abstract)
This verb only occurs in the imperfective.
·A çuwanyáadé ágé iyatéen? Do you see the difference?
·Yeeytéen has du téiý' tóotý áýá toodé has yee uwaxích haa
ñu.éex'i. You all can see that our hosts thank you from their hearts.
• --- | ñuwatéen / ñuyatéen | ñuwatíný
--- | s/he has sight | s/he recognizes people (regularly).

,

,

T

ñu-S-ø-téen (ga state)
for S to have sight (see people)
Note that this verb has the prefix ñu-, which often refers to
"people." The only form in which this specific meaning seems to
arise however, is the repetitive imperfective form, which translates
as "recognizes people." This verb is often used with the adverb
k'idéin, as in: tlél k'idéin ñooýateen "I don't see well."
• --- | tlél ñooshtéen | ----- | s/he is blind | ---.
tlél ñu-S-sh-téen (ga state)
for S to be blind
TÉES'SHÁN
• kawlitées'shán | kulitées'shán | --it was a sight to behold | it's a sight to behold | ---.
ka-u-l-tées'shán (ga state)
for something to be fascinating to watch, to be a wonderful sight
·Ý'eis'awáa l'eiýí kulitées'shan nooch. The dance of the ptarmigan is
always a wonder to behold.

teet

wave; swell
·Áa kaadé ýaatéen teet. I see waves on the lake.

teet ý'achálýi
téet'

foam (on waves); sponge

vein; tendon (inside body)

TEEÝ'
• kawdzitíý' | --- | kastíý'ý
it's crooked; s/he is crooked, wicked | --- | it gets crooked (regularly).
O-ka-d-s-téeý'~ (ø event)
for O to be crooked, wicked
-teiý'
·Tléi kawdzitíý' a yá shawtoot'éeý'i. It's face twisted when we clubbed it.
·Du toowú kawdzitíý' His inner thoughts are crooked.

téey

patch

du téey
téeyí

his/her chin
soaked dried fish

teey woodí

yellow cedar bark (for weaving)
teey hoodí (T)
·Teey woodí naaxeiný dulyéiý. Yellow cedar bark is used to make a chilkat robe.
·Teey woodí dustéiý. Yellow cedar bark is boiled.

teiñ

shawl; cape; poncho

,

Dictionary of Tlingit

Teiñweidí

Teikweidí, locally called "Brown Bear"; a clan of the Eagle
moiety whose principal crest is the Brown Bear
·Sheet'kaadé ñu.aa áyá wdusháayin Teiñweidéech áyá. She was
married to a man from Sitka from Teikweidí clan.
·Teiñweidí dachýán áyá ýát. I am a grandchild of the Teikweidí.

téil

pitch scab (where bark has been removed); pitchwood
·Ý'aan aan dulyéiý téil. Pitchwood is used to make fire.
·Téil dei yaaýt la.át. Scraps of pitchwood are lying along the road.

téiý

boiled food; broth
at téiýi, a téiýi
·Wé çuwakaan dleeyí at ý'aýéedli k'idéin aaý xásh, téiý sákw! Cut
the trimming off the deer meat well for the broth!

a téiýi

boiled food; broth
at téiýi, téiý
·Stoox káa yan sa.ín wé at téiýi! Set the broth on top of the stove!

TEIÝ'
• át akawlitíý' | aadé yaa akanaltíý' | áý aklatéeý'
s/he screwed it on it | s/he's screwing it on it | s/he screws it on it (reguarly).
P-t~ O-ka-S-l-téeý'~ (ø event)
for S to screw O into P
-téiý'~
·A ý'oosí k'idéin át kalatéý'! Screw the leg on it good!
• ý'éit akawlitíý' | ý'éide yaa akanaltíý' | ý'éiý aklatéeý'
s/he locked it | s/he's locking it | s/he locks it (regularly).
ý'éi-t~ O-ka-S-l-teeý'~ (ø event)
for S to lock O
-téiý'~
·Ý'éidei kakçilatiý' yé ch'a yeisú lingít áwu. There are still people in the
place you are locking.

du téiý'

his/her heart
·Yeeytéen has du téiý' tóotý áyá toodé has yee uwaxích haa
ñu.éex'i. You all can see that our hosts thank you from their hearts.
·Wé ñáa watsíx téiý'i akawlis'úk. The man fried caribou heart.

du teiyí

his/her bile

té kas'úgwaa yeit (T)
té ñáas'
té ñ'áatl'

cast-iron skillet

rock crevice; fissure in rock
wide, flat stone (used for cooking)

té shanaýwáayi
té tayee tlóoýu

sledgehammer
little bullhead (found under beach rocks)

'

'

té xóow

T

cairn; rock pile

tin

(along) with, by means of; as soon as
tín, teen, téen, een
·Dáanaa tín has akoodlénýaa. They tempted him with money.
·Aý dlaak' tín Xunaadé ñugaýtootéen kanat'á ñuk'éet' yís. We are
going to travel to Hoonah to pick blueberries with my sister.

tináa

copper shield
·Yadál wé tináa. The copper shield is heavy.

tínx

alpine bearberry, kinnikinnick
·Tínx kaxwéiý oowayáa tl'átgi káx' ñu.aa ka.éiý. Bearberries look like
cranberries but they grow on the ground.

tíx

flea

·Líl tíx eewustáax'iñ! Don't let the bedbugs bite! (Lit: Don't let the fleas bite you!)
·Eesháan, haa keidlí awsitáax' wé tíx. Our poor dog was bit by a flea.

tíxwjaa (At)

sound of stamping, pounding fists, clapping; sound of running quickly
túxjaa (TC)

tíx'

rope
·Cháatl tíx'i yaa (ha)s a shuká nañúý. They're setting halibut gear.
·Tíx' ña x'óow tin çeeçách' awliyéý t'ukanéiyi jeeyís. She made a hammock for the baby with rope and a blanket.

tíx' yádi
tíyaa

string
chisel

too-

we [subject]
tu·Tuháayi teen áwé át kawtusix'óo. We nailed it on it with a nail.

a tóo at dult'ix'ýi át

freezer
a tóo at dult'ix' át, a tóox' at dult'ix' át
·Haa a tóox' at dult'ix' át shaawahík dzísk'u dleeyí teen. Our freezer is full of moose meat.
2

TOOK

• kei wjitúk | --- | kei ishtúký
it exploded | --- | it explodes (regularly).
kei sh-tóok~ (ø event)
for something to explode, blow up
·Ganyal'óot' ganaltáakdáý kéi wjitúk. The flame shot up out of the fire.

tooñ
du tóoñ

needlefish
his/her buttocks, butt

,

Dictionary of Tlingit

toolch'án

top (spinning toy)
toolch'én (T), toolch'ánaa (At)
·Yaa kanajúx wé toolch'án. The top is spinning.

a tóonáx kadus'íñs' át

straw (for drinking)

tóonáý ñaateen

mirror
·Wé tóonáý ñaateen kaadé awsiteen du yahaayí. He saw his image in
the mirror.

tóos'

shark
·Tóos' hítdáý áwé du ýúý. Her husband is from the Shark house.

toow

tallow, hard fat

TOOW
• aawatóow | atóow | yoo ayatóowk
s/he read it | s/he reads it; s/he is reading it | s/he reads it (regularly).
O-S-ø-tóow (na act)
for S to read O
-teew (An)
·Du jiyee yan aawatée wé atóowu x'úx'. She placed the book he was
reading near him.
• du éex' at wulitóow | du éex' at latóow | --s/he taught him/her | s/he's teaching him/her | ---.
P-x' at S-l-tóow (ø act)
for S to teach P
With the noun phrase du ée "to him/her; in his/her
company", the postposition -x' has a variant form -ø (unmarked).
Therefore, you will notice that in some examples, the postposition
-x' is present, as in: du éex' at wulitóow "s/he taught him/her"
and in others it is not, as in: du ée at wulitóow "s/he taught
him/her". Both forms are acceptable and have the same meaning.
·Du káak du ée at latóow. His maternal uncle is teaching him.
·Du ée yan at wududlitóow ñaa ooý yéi daanéiyi yís. She completed
dentistry school.
• du éex' awlitóow | du éex' altóow | --s/he taught it to him/her | s/he is teaching it to him/her
| ---.
P-x' O-S-l-tóow (ø act)

for S to teach O to P
With the noun phrase du ée "to him/her; in his/her
company", the postposition -x' has a variant form -ø (unmarked).
Therefore, you will notice that in some examples, the postposition
-x' is present, as in: du éex' awlitóow "s/he taught him/her" and
in others it is not, as in: du ée awlitóow "s/he taught him/her".
Both forms are acceptable and have the same meaning.
·Giyañw Ñwáan yoo ý'atángi ñóox' altóow. He is teaching people the
Alutiq language.

,

,

T

• sh

tóo at wudlitóow | sh tóo at iltóow | sh tóo at
iltóowý
s/he studied | s/he studies; s/he is studying | s/he studies (regularly).
sh tóo at S-d-l-tóow (ø act)
for S to study, teach oneself

• sh tóo awdlitóow | sh tóo altóow | sh tóo altóowý
s/he studied it | s/he is studying it | s/he studies it (regularly).
sh tóo O-S-d-l-tóow (ø act)
for S to study, learn O; for S to practice, rehearse O
·Sh tóo awdlitóow çíý'jaa ñóok al.áýji. He taught himself to play the
piano.
• wuditóow | datóow | yoo ditóowk
s/he read | s/he reads; s/he is reading | s/he reads (regularly).
S-d-tóow (na act)
for S to read
-téew (An)

toow s'eenáa

candle
·Toow s'eenáa át has akawligán. They lit a candle.

du toowú

his/her inner being; mind; soul; feelings; intention
·I toowúch a yáý ákwé? Is it like you think?
·K'wáaý' yáý aý toowú yatee. I feel blah.

toowú klaçé

pride; self-esteem, feeling good about oneself
·Ñútý toowú klaçé tlél áýáý utí. Too much pride is not good.

toowú k'é

good thoughts; felicity; happiness

tuk'é

toowú latseen

strength of mind or heart; courage; resolve

toowú néekw

sorrow; sadness
toowú nóok
·Toowú néekw jiyeet çáaý wé shaawát. The woman is crying under the burden of sadness.
·Toowú néekw ñaa káa yéi teeyí, tlél oodul'eiý. When there is sorrow, there's no dancing.

toowú nóok

sorrow; sadness
toowú néekw

TOOÝ
• yóot ñ'awdzitúý | --- | yóoý ñ'astooý
s/he spat | --- | s/he spits (regularly).
yóot~ ñ'a-S-d-s-tooý~ (ø motion)
for S to spit, spit out

,

Dictionary of Tlingit

TOOÝ'
• --- | du ý'óol' kastóoý' | ----- | his/her stomach is growling | ---.
ka-s-tóoý' (ø act)
for the stomach to growl, gurgle
This verb only occurs in the
imperfective.
• du ý'óol' kawditóoý' | du ý'óol' kadatóoý'
his/her stomach growled | his/her stomach is growling | ---.
ka-d-tóoý' (ø act)
for the stomach to growl, gurgle
·Du ý'óol' kadatóoý'. His stomach is growling.

| ---

a tú

inside it
·Ý'áal' tóox' wutusi.ée. We cooked it in skunk cabbage.
·Yeeytéen has du téiý' tóotý áyá toodé has yee uwaxích haa
ñu.éex'i. You all can see that our hosts thank you from their hearts.

tudaxákw

basket with a rattle in the lid
tuñdaadaxákw

at tugáni

gunpowder
et tugáni (C)

tuháayi

nail
·Tuháayi teen áwé át kawtusix'óo. We nailed it on it with a nail.
·Yóo katán wé tuháayi. The nail is bent.

a tukayátx'i

its seeds (inside it, as inside a berry)
·Xéel'i kútý a tukayátx'i yagéi. Mossberries have too many seeds.

a tuñdaa

(around) the bottom of it
·Wuditláý a tuñdaa. The bottom of it is moldy.

tuñdaadaxákw

basket with rattle in the lid

tudaxákw

tuñdaa.át

diaper
·Tlél dé tuñdaa.át du.ús'k. Diapers aren't washed anymore.

túñl'

young spruce or hemlock
·Ch'u shóogu aan wududliyeýi túñl' áwé a kaýyee wéi ANB hall.
Those are the original young spruce they used to build the ceiling of the ANB hall.

a túñl'i

cartilage, gristle

du tuñ.woolí

his/her anus
du tooý'é (T)

,

,

T

tuñ'atáal

pants, trousers
·Tuñ'atáal ý'oosdé awdiyíñ. He put on his pants.
·I tuñ'atáali i daaý yei jeekanaxíx. Your pants are falling down.

túlaa

drill
·Yées túlaa eetéenáý ýat yatee. I need a new drill.
·Yaawdiçíl du túlayi. His drill became dull.

tula.aan

kindness; generosity of heart
tule.aan (C)
·Tula.aan een du éet ý'eiwatán. He spoke to her with kindness.

túlx'u

drill bit

·Woosh çuwanyáade kwdigéi túlx'u. Drill bits come in different sizes.

tunaýhinnadaa

pipe (for carrying water)

tundatáan

thought
tundetáan (C)
·I tundatáani kakçinéek. You will tell your thoughts.

tután

hope; intention; focus of hopes or thoughts

tuteesh

loneliness; boredom

a tuwáadáý

because of it; due to it; by virtue of it; on the strength of
it; encouraged by it
·Haa léelk'u hás tuwáadáý áwé gútk haa jeet kawduwatée. If it
wasn't for our elders, we wouldn't be here. (Lit: Because of our elders, we were
given a dime.)

tuwaakú

tobacco
·Kél't' tuwaakúý dulyéiý. They make tobacco out of wood ashes.

a tuwán

beside it, next to it
·Tle hít tuwán áwé kóoñ áa kei has akaawaháa. Right next to the house
they dug a pit.
·Tle a tuwán áwé atýá daakahídi áa wdudliyéý. They built a restaurant
next to it.

du tuwáx'

in his/her opinion; to his/her way of thinking, feeling
·I tuwáx' yeewooyáat' yóo ñu.éex'. You thought the potlach was long.

túxjaa

sound of stamping, pounding fists, clapping; sound of running

quickly
tíxwjaa (At)

·Wé ñu.éex' túxjaa duwa.áých aadé. Stamping and clapping was heard at the potlach.

tux'andaxeech

anxiety; wracked nerves; preoccupation; something weighing on one's mind
tux'endexeech (C)

,

T

Dictionary of Tlingit

du tuý'ax'aayí
at tuý'wáns'i

crack of his/her buttocks; his/her butt crack
buckshot; moccasin lining

tuý'wáns'i náakw

pepper
tuý'wáns'i náagu
·Tuý'wáns'i náagu átý dulyeiýín ch'áakw. Long ago they made medicine
out of pepper.

,

,

T'

« T' »
t'á

king salmon; chinook salmon; spring salmon
·Tsaa eiýí teen áwé yak'éi t'á at ý'éeshi. Dry fish king salmon is good with
seal oil.
·Yées t'á çíñsi sitgawsáanx' has aawaýáa. They ate fresh king salmon
barbequed over the fire at noon.

T'AA
• awsit'áa | ast'eiý | ast'eiý
s/he warmed it up | s/he is warming it up | s/he warms it up (regularly).
O-S-s-t'aa~ (ø act)
for S to warm O (water, etc.)
The form: ast'eiý gives both a basic imperfective meaning
"s/he is warming it up" and a repetitive imperfective meaning
"s/he warms it up (regularly)".
·Ñaa ý'a.eetí awsit'áa. She warmed up the leftovers.
• ñoowat'áa | ñuwat'áa / ñuyat'áa | --the weather got hot | the weather is hot | ---.
ñu-ø-t'aa~ (ø state)
for the weather to be warm, hot
This may be the only stative verb with a ø- conjugation
prefix.
• du toowú awlit'áa | du toowú alt'eiý | du toowú alt'eiý
he/she/it comforted him/her | he/she/it is comforting him/her | he/she/it comforts
him/her (regularly).
N toowú S-l-t'aa~ (ø act)
for S to comfort N
The form: du toowú alt'eiý gives both a basic imperfective

meaning "he/she/it is comforting him/her" and a repetitive
imperfective meaning "he/she/it comforts him/her (regularly)".
• uwat'áa | yaa nat'éin | --it's hot | it's getting hot | ---.
ø-t'aa~ (ø event)
for something to be warm, hot
·Wé áak'w héeni uwat'áa. The pond water is warm.
·Ý'aan yakawlikís'. Wé kél't' ñu.aa, ch'u uwat'áa. The fire has gone out
but the ashes are still warm.
• yaawat'áa | yaa yanat'éin | yat'éiý
it's hot | it's getting hot | it gets hot (regularly).
ya-ø-t'aa~ (ø event)
for something to be hot, heated
·Wé yaawat'aayi héençaa woogoot. He went to get some heated water.

,

T'

Dictionary of Tlingit

·Ch'áagu aa kaý'íl'aa stoox káx' áwé yan dutéeych yaçat'aayít. The irons of long ago were set on the stove to heat up.

t'áa

board
·K'idéin aaý xásh wé t'áa at ý'aýéedli! Cut the trimming off the board good!
·Kax'ás'aa teen áwé kçeexáash ldakát wéi t'áa! You will cut all those boards with a rip saw!

T'AACH
• aawat'ách | at'ácht | at'áchý
s/he slapped him/her/it | s/he is slapping him/her/it | s/he slaps him/her/it (regularly).
O-S-t'aach~ (ø act)
for S to slap O; for S to tag O (as in game of tag)
·Du jintáak teen at'ácht wé kadu.uxýu át. She is slapping the balloon with the palm of her hand.

du t'aaçí

his/her clan brother or sister, distant relative, comrade

t'áa jáaji

ski(s)

t'áa jáaji wootsaaçayí

ski pole(s)

du t'áak

behind him/her; back of him/her; at his/her back
·Ñaa t'áak áwé áa awliyéý du hídi. He built his house behind the village.
·Ñaa t'áak áwé áa uwaýée. She camped behind everyone.

a t'áak

behind it; back inland from it; on the landward side of it (something on the water)

t'áa ká

floor
·T'áa kát ñushí aý jeeyís - ñut kaýwaaçéex' aý kawóot ka.íshayi!
Look on the floor for me - I lost my needle!

t'áa kayéýaa

plane for scraping wood
t'áa keyéýaa (C)

T'AAKW
• héende awjit'ákw | --- | héende asht'ákwý
it dove into the water | --- | it dives into the water (regularly).
a-j-t'aakw~ (ø event)
for something to dive into the water; for something to slap tail down hard as
going down in water (esp. of killerwhale and beaver)
·Cháaý héen táade awjit'ákw. The grebe dove into the water.

a t'aañ
T'aañú

beside it, at its side
Taku

t'áa shukaayí

square (for marking boards)

,

,

t'áa shuxáshaa

T'

narrow saw used to cut corners off lumber; bevel saw

t'aaw

feather
·Kóon t'aawú yéi ndu.eich al'eiý yís. Flicker feathers are used in dancing.

t'aawáñ

Canada goose
·Yei googénk'i at ýéidi teen áwé ýwaat'úk wé t'aawáñ. I shot the
Canada goose with a small arrow.

t'aawáñ x'eesháa
T'aawyáat

tea kettle (originally with long curved spout)

American Indian

T'AAÝ'
• wusit'áaý' | --- | sat'áaý'ý
it's burning hot | --- | it burns hot (regularly).
s-t'áaý' (ø event)
for a fire, etc. to be hot, radiate, throw out heat
·Ý'aan wusit'áaý'. The fire is burning hot.

t'áaý'w

wart

t'aay

hot springs

t'áa yá

wall

t'aa yátx'i

shingles

t'aay néekw (AtT)

fever

t'aay nóok (TC)

T'añdeintaan

T'akdeintaan, locally called "Seagull"; a clan of the
Raven moiety whose principal crest is the Seagull

a t'añká

beside, alongside, next to it
·Wildflower Court wé hospital t'añkáa yéi yatee. Wildflower Court is
next to the hospital.

du t'añká
a t'áni

beside, alongside, next to him/her
its secondary branch

t'ási

grayling
·Héen wátt uwax'ák wé t'ási. The grayling swam to the mouth of the river.

t'áx'ýi

dentalia shells

t'éesh

tanning frame; frame for stretching skin

t'éesh kaayí

square

T'EEX'
• kaawat'íx' | kayat'éex' | kat'íx'ý
it hardened | it's hard | it hardens (regularly).

,

Dictionary of Tlingit

ka-ø-t'éex'~ (ga state)
for something to harden, cake up
·Hintakx'óosi nóox'u kayat'éex' Coral shells are hard.
• --- | kasit'éex' | ----- | it's hard | ---.
ka-s-t'éex'~ (ga state)
for something to be hard (esp. of round object)
• woot'éex' | yat'éex' | kei t'íx'ch
it was difficult | it's difficult | it gets difficult (regularly).
ø-t'éex' (ga state)
for something to be hard (abstract), difficult
·Yat'éex'i gaaw a tóonáý yiyagút. You walked through that period of hard time.
·Wé dleey yat'éex'. The meat is tough.
• wudlit'íx' | yaa nalt'íx' | ult'íx'ý
it's frozen; it froze | it's freezing | it freezes (regularly).
d-l-t'éex'~ (ø event)
for something to harden, solidify; for something to freeze
·Çeey tá héen yaa nalt'íx'. The water at the head of the bay is freezing.
·Tlei ult'íx'ch taatx' wéi hít daadáý kax'áasjaa. The water dripping from the house freezes at night.

t'éex'

ice

T'EEÝ'
• akaawat'éý' | akat'éiý' | akat'éý'ý
s/he pounded it | s/he is pounding it | s/he pounds it (regularly).
O-ka-S-ø-t'éiý'~ (ø act)
for S to smash O up by pounding; for S to mash O by pounding with something heavy; for S to pound, hammer on O
t'éeý'~ (An)
·Góon dáanaa een áwé kawduwat'íý' aý jeeyís yá kées. This bracelet was pounded out of a gold coin for me.

du t'eey

his/her elbow

1

T'EI

• aawat'ei | --- | kei at'eich
s/he found it | --- | s/he finds it (regularly).
O-S-ø-t'ei (ga event)
for S to find O (usually as the result of searching)
·Tlagu aan yaduxas' át aawat'ei. He found an old-time razor.

·Wé s'eek gandaas'aají kúdi aawat'ei. The black bear found a bee's nest.
• akaawat'ei | --- | kei akat'eich
s/he found it | --- | s/he finds it (regularly).
O-ka-S-ø-t'ei (ga event)
for S to find O (usually round, spherical object)

,

,

T'

a t'éik

behind it
·Aas t'éik áwé áa awdlisín wé kóoshdaa. The land otter hid behind a tree.

a t'einyaa

the inside of it (clothing, bedding); lining it
a t'einaa (C)

a t'einyaakawoowú (At)

its lining
a t'einyaakayoowú (T), a t'einyaakewoowú (C)

t'eiý

fish hook
·Du t'eiýí ayaawaçíl'. He sharpened his fish hooks.

T'EIÝ
• awdzit'eiý | ast'eiý | yoo adzit'eiýk
s/he fished (with a hook) | s/he is fishing (with a hook) | s/he fishes (with a hook)
(regularly).
a-S-d-s-t'eiý~ (na act)
for S to fish with hooks, catch on a hook, troll
·Aashát tlein awdzit'eiý. She hooked a big steelhead trout.
·Ast'eiý tlél ulnáalýin. Trolling didn't used to be profitable.

t'eiýáa (T)

fish hook
·T'eiýáa een áwé cháatl has aawasháat. They caught halibut with hooks.

a t'iká

beside it; out past it; out away from it; (on) the outskirts
of it (town)
·Héen t'ikáý yaawashóo ñaa ý'oos deiyí. The foot trail goes beside the
river.

·Héen t'iká át la.áa du hídi. His house sits beside the river.

du t'iyshú

tip of his/her elbow

t'ooch'

charcoal
·T'ooch' aa yéi nateech wé ý'aan eetí. There's charcoal where the fire was.
·Haat kalajúx wé t'ooch'! Wheel the coal over here!

t'ooch'

black
·T'ooch' yáý shasitee. She has black hair.
·T'ooch' ña tl'áatl' yáý daçaatée gandaas'aají. Bees are black and yellow.

t'ooch' eeýí

petroleum, oil

t'ooch'ineit

bottle; jug

t'ooch' ñáa

Black (man or person); African-American
·Tléináý t'ooch' ñáa haa ýoo yéi yatee. There's only one black man among us.

t'ooch' té

coal

t'ook

cradleboard; papoose carrier
·T'ook kát as.áa du yádi. He has his child seated on the papoose board.

,

T'

T'OOK
• aawat'úk | --- | at'úký
s/he shot it | --- | s/he shoots it (regularly).
O-S-ø-t'óok~ (ø event)
for S to shoot O (with bow and arrow); for S to choose O (in gambling with sticks)
·Yei googénk'i at ýéidi teen áwé ýwaat'úk wé t'aawáñ. I shot the Canada goose with a small arrow.
·Wé yadak'wátsk'u chooneit tín áwé aawat'úk wé ts'ítskw. The young boy shot the bird with a barbed arrow.

t'óok'

nettle
Warning: stinging hairs contain formic acid which causes rash and edema
·T'óok' ýoodé daak aý wudzigít. I fell into the stinging nettles.

t'ukanéiyi

baby
t'ookanéiyi (T)
·Goox' sáwé yéi has gaýdusñéi wé t'ukanéiyi? Where will they seat the babies?
·Tíx' ña x'óow tin çeeçách' awliyéý t'ukanéiyi jeeyís. She made a hammock for the baby with rope and a blanket.

,

,

Tl

« Tl »
TLAA
• --- | yéi kwditláa | ----- | it's that big around | ---.
(yéi) ka-u-d-tlaa~ (na state)
for something to be (so) big around, in girth
·Çunayéide kwditlawu çayéis' tíx' du jeewú. He has steel cables of different sizes.

du tláa

his/her mother
·Yaa aý léelk'w aý tláa yinaanáý Ñéin yóo dusáagun yaa Xutsnoowúdáý. My grandmother on my mother's side was called Ñéin, from Angoon.
·Yan ashawlihík yá haa tláach. This mother of ours has completed

everything.

tlaagú

myth; legend; children's tale
·Çunakadeit daat tlaagú daýñudzitee. There are legends about sea
monsters.

TLAAKW
• akaawatlaakw | yaa akanatlákw | yoo akayatlákwk
s/he's investigating it; s/he investigated it | s/he's (in the process of) investigating
it | s/he investigates it (regularly).
O-ka-S-ø-tlaakw~ (na event)
for S to investigate, make inquiry into, research O
·Ch'áakw aan galañú yaa kandutlákw. A flood from long ago is being
researched.
• ñoon aawatlákw | ñoon atláakw | --s/he told people a legend | s/he is telling people a legend
| ---.
O-S-ø-tlaakw~ (ø act)
for S to tell, recount, narrate O (legend, myth, fairy tale, etc.)
·Aadéi dutlákw yé áyá, kakatáx'aa teen yawduwadlaañ. As the story
goes, he was defeated by a pair of pliers.

tláakw

fast
·Tláakw aýáa du aandaayaagú. He is rowing his rowboat quickly.
·Tláakw naadaayi héen kuliýéitl'shán. A fast river is dangerous.

du tláak'w

his/her maternal aunt
·Aý tláak'wch áa ýat shukaawajáa, aadé yéi daadunei yé. My
maternal aunt taught me how to make it.

tláañ

sharp arrow for killing
·Tláañ du eedé ksixát. The arrow is stuck in his body.

,

Dictionary of Tlingit

tlaaý

mold
·Tlaaý áa yaa kana.éin. Mold is growing there.

TLAAÝ
• wuditláý | yaa ndatláý | ditláýkw
it's moldy; it got moldy | it's getting moldy | it molds (easily, regularly).
d-tlaaý~ (ø event)
for something to be moldy
·Wuditláý a tuñdaa. The bottom of it is moldy.

du tlagooñwansaayí

his/her namesake
du tlegooñwansaayí (C)
·Du léelk'w du tlagooñwansaayíý sitee. His grandparent is his namesake.

tlagu

old; from the past
·Aanñáawuch áwé woo.oo, wé tlagu hít tlein. A rich person bought the big old house.
·Wé tlagu hídi gáannáý wuduwanéegwál'. Someone painted the outside of the old house.

tlagu ñwáanx'i

people of long ago

tlagu ts'ats'éeyee

grey singing bird (sparrow or finch)

tlaçanís

pole; sapling
·Tlaçanís aan kwéiyi tugáas'iý has awliyéý. They made a flagpole out of a sapling.

du tlaçeiyí

his/her brain
du tleçeiyí (C)
·Átý layéý dé i tlaçeiyí! Use your brain now!

tlákw

always, all the time, constantly
·Tlákw kaduk'énx' wé cheech. The porpoise always jump.
·Tlákw s'eenáa a káa yéi nateech eech kakwéiyi. There's always a light on a fixed buoy.

Tlákw Aan

Klukwan
·Tlákw Aandáý haa shoow sitee. Our roots stem from Klukwan.
·Jilñáat Ñwáan Tlákw Aanx' has ñuya.óo. The Chilkat people live in Klukwan.

Tláp!

Oops!

tlaý

very
·Watsíx a lututúñl'i tléil tlaý ugé. The soft bone in a caribou nose is not very big.
·Tlél tlaý kooshý'íl'k yá kaxwaan. It's not very slippery with this frost.

tlaýaneis'

kingfisher

'

'

Tl

tle

just, simply; just then
tlei
·Tlei déiý ñ'ateil yáý áwé wutusineiý shákw kahéeni. We just saved two gallons of the strawberry juice.
·Çeiwú wooch yáý awsinei tle daak ashakaawañúý. She straightened the net out and then she set it.

tleidahéen

once, one time
tlex'dahéen, tleidehéen (C)
·Tleidahéen, yéi at woonei. Once upon a time, this happened.
·Tleidahéen áwé Yaakwdáatt aa wlihásh wé kanóox'. One time a turtle floated to Yakutat.

tleidooshóonáý

six (people)

tleidooshú

six
·Aý atx'aan hídi tleidooshú ñaa ý'oos ña daax'ooný sitee. My smoke house is six feet by four feet.
·Tleidooshú ñaa ý'oos yéi kwliyáat' wé kaay. That measuring stick is six feet long.

tleikatánk

red huckleberry
·Tleikatánk kanat'á een yak'éi. Red huckleberries are good with blueberries.
·Tleikatánk áwé kanat'áý ýoo yéi nateech. Red huckleberries are always among blueberries.

tléik'

no
tláyk'

tleiñáa

twenty
·Tleiñáa dáanaa aý éet hís'! Lend me twenty dollars!
·Gwál tleiñáa ý'oos áwé a kaýyeedé. It must be twenty feet to the ceiling.

tleiñáa ña tléináý

twenty one (people)

tleiñáa ña tléix'

twenty one
·Tleiñáa ña tléix' áwé du katáagu. He is twenty-one years old.

tleiñáanáý

twenty (people)

tléiñw

berry, berries
·Wé tléiñw daakeidí yís áyá. This is a container for the berries.
·Yeisú kadliý'át' wé tléiñw. The berries are still green.

tléiñw kahéeni

berry juice
·Tléiñw kahéeni awdináa. He drank berry juice.

·Aý ý'éit aa kaýích tléiñw kahéeni! Give me some juice! (Lit: Throw some juice at my mouth!)

tleiñw kahínti

watermelon berry, twisted stalk, wild cucumber

,

Dictionary of Tlingit

tléiñw wás'i

berry bush
tléñw wás'i
·Tléiñw wás'i áa kaawa.aa. Berry bushes are growing there.

tléil

no, none, not
tlél, l, hél
·Du tl'eñtlein áwé tlél á. His middle finger is missing.
·Kaldaaçéináý yaa gaýtooñóoý, tlél çwadlaan yá éiý' yík. We will
travel along slowly, it's not deep in this slough.

tlein

big
·Aý léelk'u hás jeeyís áwé wududliyéý wé atx'aan hídi tlein. That big
smoke house was built for my grandparents.
·Ñukawduyéil'i áwé Galyéýdei çunayéi uñooých wéi yaakw tlein.
The big boat would start traveling to the Kahliyet River when the weather was
calm.

tléináý

one (person)
·Tléináý t'ooch' ñáa haa ýoo yéi yatee. There's only one black man among
us.
·Tléináý ñáa áý yaa nagút. One person is walking along there.

tléix'

one
·Yan uwanéi ágé wé tléix' aa yáý? Is it ready like the other one?
·Tléix' ñ'ateil yáý áwé liyék wéi xén. That plastic container can hold one
gallon.

tléix' hándit
tleiyán

one hundred

shoreline

tleiyeekaadé

one kind, type; one way, direction
tleiyeekaadéi

tlék'çaa

one at a time, one by one
·Tlék'çaa áwé anaý daak has aawal'éý. One by one they danced out.

tlék'çaanáý

one (person) at a time
·Tlék'çaanáý áwé has wuduwaýooý. They called them one by one.

tléñw yádi

raspberry
tléiñw yádi
·Tléiñw yádi has aawa.ín. They picked raspberries.

tlél daa sá

nothing
tléil daa sá, hél daa sá

tlex'dahéen

once, one time
tleidahéen, tleidehéen (C)
·Ch'a tlex'dahéen du een kananeek! Just tell him once!

'

'

Tl

tl'iñkakées

ring
·Du jintáak káa yan akaawatée du tl'iñkakéesi. He put his ring in the center of his palm.

tliyaa

farther over; way over
·Tliyaa aani ñwáani haa ýánt has uwa.át. The people from that town have come to visit us.
·Yóo tliyaa aasdéi ksaxát wéi kaxées' aý at shí ñóok gúgu yís! Attach the wire to that tree over there for my radio antenna!

tliyaatgé

the other day; a few days ago
tliyaatatgé (At)

·Ch'u tliyaatgé áwé shuýwsitee. I was expecting it the other day.

TLOOX'
• aadé wootlóox' | --- | aadé yoo yatlúx'k
he/she/it crawled there on his/her/it's belly | --- | he/she/it crawls there on
his/her/its belly (regularly).
P-dé S-ø-tloox'~ (na motion)
for S to creep, crawl on hands and toes with body close to ground (usually when
stalking game) toward P
• át wootlóox' | --- | --he/she/it is crawling around on his/her/its belly; he/she/it crawled
around on
his/her/its belly | --- | ---.
P-t S-ø-tloox'~ (na motion)
for S to creep, crawl around on hands and toes with body close to ground
(usually when stalking game) at P; for S to squirm around on the ground at P
·Geesh ýoot wootlóox' wé yáxwch'. The sea otter is rolling around in the
kelp.

tlóoý

mud bullhead
·Tlóoý tlél tooýá. We don't eat bullhead.

,

Tl'

Dictionary of Tlingit

« Tl' »
tl'aadéin

sideways
·Tl'aadéin áwé át tán wé ñóok. The box is sitting sideways.

tl'aadéin.aa

turnip
·Shaatk'átsk'uý ýat siteeyí aý ý'é k'éiyin wé tl'aadéin.aa. When I was
a little girl, I used to love turnips.

TL'AAK'
• wuditl'ák' | yaa ndatl'ák' | datl'ák'ý
he/she/it is wet | he/she/it is getting wet | he/she/it gets wet (regularly).
O-d-tl'aak'~ (ø event)
for O to be wet (may be thoroughly wet, but not by actual immersion)
·Ñúnáý ýat wuditl'ák', kaklahéen áyá aawaçéet. I'm so wet - wet snow
is coming down hard.

tl'áak'

pale; pastel
·Tl'átgi káa yagéi wé tl'áak'. There are a lot of dead leaves on the ground.

tl'aañ'wách'

sourdock; wild rhubarb
Warning: leaves contain oxalic acid, possibly harmful in
large quantities
·Tl'aañ'wách' een áwé awsi.ée wé kaxwéiý. She cooked wild rhubarb with
cranberries.
·Kóox een dus.ée tl'aañ'wách'. Wild rice is cooked with wild rhubarb.

tl'áatl'

yellow
·Tl'áatl' aas yít wudiñeen. The small bird flew into the tree.
·T'ooch' ña tl'áatl' yáý daçaatée gandaas'aají. Bees are black and yellow.

tl'açáa

enough; adequate
·De tl'açáa áwé yakoogéi. There is enough.

tl'átk

earth; land, country; soil

tl'átgi, tl'étk (C)

·Tl'átgi káa yéi nateech ñ'eishkaháagu. Low bush cranberries are on the ground.

·Yú sgóon tl'átgi tlein, a góonnáý daýyanaagóo wé káa. The cars are traveling on the isthmus of the big school yard.

tl'áxch'

old, dead branch

·Shayadihéin tl'áxch' táakwde yaa ñunahéini. There are a lot of dead branches when it becomes winter.

,

,

Tl'

a tl'eeçí

its tentacle (of octopus)

a tl'eiçí (C)

·Shayadihéin has du tl'eeçí wé náañw. Octopus have a lot of tentacles.

tl'éek'at

sticks woven through the fish lengthwise after it has been filleted

for barbecuing

du tl'eeñ

his/her finger

du tl'eiñ

·Du tl'eeñ áwé aý yáa ash akaawliyén. He's shaking his finger at me.

TL'EET'

• ashawlitl'ít' | yaa ashanaltl'ít' | ashalatl'ít'ý

s/he filled it | s/he is filling it | s/he fills it (regularly).

O-sha-S-l-tl'éet'~ (ø event)

for S to fill O (with liquid)

·A kat'óott shalatl'ít', tlél kei kçwadál! Fill it halfway, then it won't be heavy!

tl'eex

filth, mess; trash, rubbish, garbage

·Gáande wé tl'eex! Put the dirt outside!

a tl'eiçí (C)

its tentacle (of octopus)

a tl'eeçí

du tl'eiñ

his/her finger
du tl'eeñ
·Táax'ál' x'aan áwé aý tl'eiñ tóode yawdiçeech. The needle point poked
my finger.
·Aý tl'eiñ káa wjiñaañ digitgiyáa. A hummingbird landed on my finger.

a tl'éili

its semen; its milt (of fish)

TL'EIT'
•a

daaý kei wdlitl'ét' | a daax kei naltl'ét' | a daax kei
iltl'ét'ch
he/she/it climbed up it | he/she/it is climbing up it | he/she/it climbs up it
(regularly).
N daaý kei S-d-l-tl'eit'~ (ø motion)
for S to climb up along N (tree, rope, etc.) by holding on tightly
·Aas daaý kei wdlitl'ét'. He climbed up the tree.

•a

yáý wudlitl'éit' | a yáý kei naltl'ét' | a yáý kei
iltl'ét'ch

he/she/it climbed the face of it | he/she/it is climbing the face of it | s/he climbs
the face of it (regularly).
N yáý S-d-l-tl'éit'~ (ga motion)
for S to climb up along the face of N (mountain, cliff, fence, etc.)
·Çíl' yáý kei naltl'ét' wé yadák'w. The young boy is climbing the cliff face.

,

Tl'

tl'éitl'

Dictionary of Tlingit

moonfish, suckerfish, blowfish
tl'étl'

du tl'eñshá

his/her fingertip
du tl'iñshá
·Du tl'eñshá áwé awliý'éý' wé stoox káx'. He burned his fingertip on the
stove.

du tl'eñtlein

his/her middle finger
du tl'iñtlein
·Du tl'eñtlein áwé tlél á. His middle finger is missing.

du tl'eñý'áak

between his/her fingers

tl'iñnaa.át

thimble
·Tl'iñnaa.át een duñéis'. A thimble is used for sewing.

du tl'iñshá

his/her fingertip
du tl'eñshá

du tl'iñtlein

his/her middle finger
du tl'eñtlein

tl'ildaaskeit

littleneck clams

du tl'óoçu

his/her liver
·Dzísk'u tl'óoçu ña a dáali aý ý'é yak'éi. I like to eat moose liver and its
tripe.
·Du tl'óoçu áwé ash kaawaxíl'. Her liver is bothering her.

tl'ooñ

rotting sore; gangrene; cancer
·Tl'ooñ du jín daa yéi yatee. There are sores on his hand.

tl'úk'ý

worm; larva; grub; caterpillar; snake
·Tl'úk'ý awsiwadi shaawát daatý shkalneek ñudzitee. There's a story about the woman who raised the worm.

,

,

Ts

« Ts »
tsá

only then
·Náakw s'é áa yéi kñwa.oo aý keey aaçáa tsá wéi kashóok' gwéil. I will put medicine on my knee first, then the heating pad.
·Tlél ushik'éiyi aa yoo ý'atánk áwé tsá a.aýji nooch . She always only hears the bad talk.

tsaa

hair seal
·A kaaý sh tukdliçéi du tsaa doogú at xáshdi téel. She is proud of her seal skin moccasins.
·Aaý awlixaash a geení wé tsaa. He cut the tail flippers off of the seal.

Tsaagweidí

Tsaagweidí; a clan of the Eagle moiety whose principal crests are the Seal and Killerwhale

tsaaçál'

spear
·Tsaaçál' átý dulyeiýín ch'áakw. Spears were used long ago.

TSAAÑ
• kei jiwlitsáñ | --- | kei jilatsáñý
s/he raised a hand | --- | s/he raises a hand (regularly).
kei ji-S-l-tsaañ~ (ø event)
for (singular) S to raise the hand (in voting, etc.)

tsáats

bear root, Indian potato

tsáçaa

pole (for boating, for pushing skin toboggan)
·Tsáçaa een yaakw daak has ayawlitáñ. They pushed the boat offshore
with a pole.

tsálk

arctic ground squirrel

tsé

be sure not to
This particle is used with the admonitive verb form, which
gives the meaning "be sure not to (verb)"; "see that you don't
(verb)".

TSEEK
• awlitsík | altséek | altsíký
s/he barbecued it | s/he's barbecueing it | s/he barbecues it (regularly).
O-S-l-tseek~ (ø act)
for S to broil O slowly, cook O directly over live coals, barbecue

tséek

spit, skewer, roasting stick, barbecue stick
·Tséek éen has awsi.ée wé cháatl. They barbecued the halibut.

,

Dictionary of Tlingit

·K'ínk'i tséegi ñúnáý yak'éi. Barbecued fermented salmon heads are very
good.
TSEEN
• tlél wultseen | tléil ultseen | tlél kei ultseench
he/she/it was weak | he/she/it is weak | s/he doesn't get stronger.
tlél O-l-tseen (ga state)
for O to be weak; for O to be mild (of weather); for O to be anemic
-cheen
·Du yakçwahéiyágu tléil ultseen. His spirit is weak.
• wulitseen | litseen | kei latseench
he/she/it became strong | he/she/it is strong | he/she/it gets strong (regularly).
O-l-tseen (ga state)
for O to be strong, powerful
·Wóoshnáý ý'akakéiýi tíx' yáanáý litseen. Chain is stronger than rope.
·Xunaa Ñáawu áwé ñúnáý has litseen. Hoonah people are very strong.
• ý'awlitseen | ý'alitseen | kei ý'alatseench
it was expensive | it's expensive | it gets expensive (regularly).
ý'a-l-tseen (ga state)
for something to be expensive, high-priced; for something to be precious, of great
value
·T'á ñúnáý ý'alitseen Dzantik'i Héenix'. King salmon is very expensive in
Juneau.
·Tléix' dáanaa yéi ý'alitseen katíý'aa x'úx' daakahídix'. A key costs
one dollar at the post office.

tseeneidi shál
tseený'é

handmade ladle

lizard, newt

TSEIÝ
• aawatséý | atséýt | atséýt
s/he kicked it | s/he's kicking it | s/he kicks it (regularly).
O-S-ø-tseiý~ (ø act)
for S to kick O; for S to stamp O, put foot down on O violently
The form: atséýt gives both a basic imperfective meaning
"s/he is kicking it" and a repetitive imperfective meaning: "s/he
kicks it (regularly)".
·Ñóok shutú aawatséý. She died. (Lit: S/he kicked the edge of the box.)

du tseiýí
tsín

his/her sweetheart
muskrat

tsísk'w

owl with ear tufts
·Xáanaax' áwé du.aýji nooch tsísk'w. Owls are heard at night.
·Tlél aa ñwasatínch wé k'ákw yóo duwasáagu aa tsísk'w. I have never
seen the bird they call the owl without ear tufts.

,

,

Ts

TSOOW
• çagaan át ý'oos uwatsóow | --- | --sun rays are shining on it | --- | ---.
çagaan P-t~ ý'oos ø-tsóow (ø
event)
for the sun rays to shine on P
·Çagaan át ý'oos uwatsóow. Sun rays are shining on it. (Lit: The sun is
poking its feet out.)

tsu

again; still; some more
tsoo
·Tsu yéi wunañá! You can say that again!

tsú

also, too, as well
·Du gúkx' tsú yéi aa wduwa.oo wéi s'aañ ñ'anooý. They put the small
bone labret in his ear too.
·Ñúnáý wé yee woo.éex'i aa tsú yee ýoo yéi kçwatée toowú k'é teen.
Your hostess will welcome you all as well. (Lit: Your hostess will be among you
all with good feelings.)

,

Ts'

Dictionary of Tlingit

« Ts' »
TS'AA
• wulits'áa | lits'áa | kei lats'áaych
he/she/it was fragrant | he/she/it is fragrant | he/she/it becomes fragrant (reguarly).
O-l-ts'áa (ga state)
for O to be fragrant, sweet-smelling
·Keishísh áwé lats'áa nooch ñutaanx'. Alder always smells good in the summer.
·Tlél kei guýlats'áa i daat sh kalneek. Gossip about you is not going to smell good.

ts'ak'áawásh

dried fish strips, dried necktie style
·Ts'ak'áawásh Deishúdáý has aawa.oo. They bought dried fish strips from Haines.

ts'áñl

black with dirt, filth, stain

ts'anéi

round basket made of split red cedar branches

ts'ats'ée

songbird; bird
ts'ets'ée (C)
·Ts'ats'ée áwé ýwaa.áý tatgé ts'ootaat. I heard a songbird yesterday morning.
·Wé ts'ats'ée çagaan ý'usyeet .áa. That song bird is sitting in the ray of sunlight.

ts'axweil

crow
·Ts'axweil át kawdliyeech. Crows are flying around.

ts'eeçéeni

magpie
ts'eiçéeni (T)

ts'éekáýk'w

alpine blueberry

·Ts'éekáýk'w has aawa.ín. They picked alpine blueberries.

a ts'éek'u

its muscles (of shell creature)

ts'eiçéeni (T)

magpie

ts'eeçéeni

ts'ésý'w
at ts'ík'wti

snail with shell
muscles of a shell creature; pincher; thing that pinches

,

,

Ts'

ts'ítskw

songbird; bird
·Du kíji áwé wool'éex' wé ts'ítskw, ách áwé tlél át wudañeen. The songbird's wing broke, that's why it doesn't fly around.

ts'ootaat

morning
·Ts'ats'ée áwé ýwaa.áý tatgé ts'ootaat. I heard a songbird yesterday morning.
·Ts'ootaat shaýwdinúk. I got up in the morning.

Ts'ootsxán

Tsimshian
Ts'ootsxén
·Deikeenaa ña Ts'ootsxán áa shayadihéin Kichýáan. There are a lot of Haida and Tsimshian people in Ketchikan.
·Ts'ootsxánch uwasháa aý kéek'. A Tsimshian married my little sister.

,

U

« U »
-u

is/are at
·Chudéi áwé a ñ'anooýú áwu. Tom cod have a beard.
·Gáanu hás, i yeeçáaý has sitee. They are outside waiting for you.

uháan

we [independent]
·Ldakát uháan haa wduwa.éex'. All of us were invited.

ús'aa

soap
·Ús'aa een daa dushóoch People bathe with soap.

útlýi

boiled fish
·Ý'áakw útlýi awsi.ée. She cooked freshwater sockeye soup.
·Ý'áax'w útlýi áwé yak'éi. Boiled ling cod is good.

uýganhéen

kerosene; coal oil
·Uýganhéen s'eenáa káax' has dañéis'in. They used to sew by kerosene lamp.

uýganñáas'

match
·Uýganñáas' tin áý akdulgaan. It is lit with a match.
·Al'óon wugoodí uýganñáas' du çaltóode ayaawa.oo. When he was going hunting, he put matches in his pocket.

uý kei

out of control; blindly

du uýk'idleeyí

his/her gums

,

,

W

« W »
wáachwaan

policeman; policewoman

wáadishgaa

priest
·Ñaa yáý kei jisatánch wáadishgaa. The priest blesses people.

du waañ

his/her eye
·Du waañnáý kaawaxeex. He's staring at it. (Lit: It fell through his eye.)

wáançaneens

sometimes, once in a while
·Wáançaneensx' yanaý kei shak'íý'ch aý yoo ý'atángi. Sometimes my
words get hung up.

wáa sá

how
·Wé íý'ch du een akaawaneek wáa sá at guçwaneiyí. The medicine
man told him what was going to happen.
·Wáa yateeyi lingít sáwé wa.é? What kind of person are you?

Waashdan Ñwáan

American
·Haadé yaa s ñunatín Waashdan Ñwáan. The Americans are traveling
here.

waat

armspan; fathom
·Tleiñáa waat yéi kçwaadláan. It's twenty fathoms deep.

WAAT
• awsiwát | aswáat | aswátý
s/he raised him/her/it | s/he raises him/her/it; s/he is raising him/her/it | s/he
raises him/her/it (regularly).
O-S-s-wáat~ (ø act)
for S to raise O (child, animal); for S to grow O (plant)
·Tl'úk'ý awsiwadi shaawát daatý shkalneek ñudzitee. There's a story
about the woman who raised the worm.
·Ánk'w áwé kéi has anaswát wéit lingítch. Those people are raising a
crybaby.
• kei uwawát | kei nawát | --s/he grew up | he/she/it is growing up | ---.

O-ø-wáat~ (ø event)
for O to grow up (size and maturity) (esp. of human and animal)
Note that the kei in: kei uwawát "he/she/it grew up" is
optional, and therefore is not given in the Leer-Edwards theme.
However, speakers generally prefer to use the verb with kei.
·Ana.óot ýoox' uwawát wé ñáa. That man grew up among the Aleut people.
·A tóodáý kei uwawát. He grew out of it.

,

wáa yateeyi yéix'

sometimes
·Wáa yateeyi yéix' yáax' yéi aa nateech táakw kanaý wé ñaatoowú.
Sometimes some chickadees stay here through the winter.
·Wáa yateeyi yéix' at gutu.ádi çalsháatadiý dulyéých. Sometimes wild
animals are held captive.

wañdáanaa

eyeglasses
·Wañdáanaa waañt akal.át. She has eyeglasses on. (Lit: She has glasses
lying on her eyes.)

wañdlóoñ

sleep in his/her eyes
·Wé i wañdlóoçu aaý na.óos'! Clean the sleep from your eyes!

du wañká

blocking his/her view; in his/her way (so that he/she can't see)
du wañkas'óox'

du wañkadoogú

his/her eyelid
du wañkedoogú (C)

wañkadóox'

blindfold
·Wañkadóox' du yáa yéi duwa.óo. He was blindfolded.

wañkals'ooý' gáaxw

scooter duck
·Gáaxw áwé yéi duwasáakw wañkals'ooý' gáaxw. That duck is called a
scooter duck.

du wañkas'óox'

blocking his/her view; in his/her way (so that he/she

can't see)
du wañká
·Du wañkas'óox' áwé át eehán. You're blocking his view.

du wañlatáak

inside of his/her eye
du wañltáak

du wañltáak

inside of his/her eye
du wañlatáak
·Du wañltáaknáý át wooxeex. Something fell in her eye.

du wañshiyee

before his/her eyes; where he/she can see (it)
du wañshee (C)
·Aý wañshiyeex' yéi nasné! Show me how it's done!
·I wañshiyeex' yéi yatee. It's in front of your eyes.

du wañshú

corner of his/her eye

a wán

edge of it; (to the) side of it
·Yá aý l'eiý k'oodás' a wán shóot at ñá! Sew something to the edge of my dance shirt!
·A wándáý áwé a yíkt sh wudligás' wé yéil. The raven leapt into it from the edge.

,

,

a wanáak

W

separate from it; on the edge, side of it; missing its

mark
a wanyáak
·A wanáax' yakoojél wé cháas'! Put the Humpback salmon separate from them!
·A wanáax' yéi inatí wé kaxéel'! Separate yourself from trouble!

wanadóo

sheep
wanedóo (C)
·Shaa yá daat na.átch wanadóo. Sheep walk the mountainsides.
·Al'óoni wé wanadóo ítý kei nagút. The hunter is following the sheep that

is going uphill.

wanadóo latíni

shepherd
wanedóo letíni (C)
·Wé wanadóo latíni táach uwaján. The shepherd fell asleep.

wanadóo yádi

lamb
wanedóo yédi (C)
·Wé wanadóo yádi ñut wudzigeet. The lamb got lost.

wanatíx

ant
·Ash wusitáax' wé wanatíx. The ant bit him.
·Wanatíxch wusitáax' du wankach'eeñ. The ant bit his little finger.

wanatóox

ant
wanatíx (T)

a wanká

on the edge, side of it (as a trail); on the shoulder of it
·A wankát has ñéen wé yéil. The ravens are sitting on the edge of it.

du wankach'eeñ

his/her little finger
du wankech'eeñ (C)
·Wanatíxch wusitáax' du wankach'eeñ. The ant bit his little finger.

wankashxéet

starry flounder
·Duýá wankashxéet. Starry flounders are eaten.

wasóos

cow
·Wasóos áwé a dleeyí yak'éi. Cow meat is good.
·Wasóos wé akahéiýi jee shayadihéin. The farmer has lots of cows.

wasóos l'aayí

cow's milk
·Wasóos l'aayí yak'éi wásh een. Cow milk is good with mush.

wás'

bush
·Wás' kadánjaa áwé tláakw ñuya.óo. People are overcome by the pollen.

Was'eeneidí

Was'eeneidí; a clan of the Eagle moiety whose principal
crests are the Wolf and Auklet

,

Dictionary of Tlingit

was'x'aan tléiçu

salmonberry
·Was'x'aan tléiçuçáa woogoot aý tláa. My mom walked to get
salmonberries.

du wásh
wásh

his/her cheek
mush, oatmeal, porridge

washéen

engine, motor
·Yées washéen a géekt satéen wé yaakw. A new motor sits at the stern of
that boat.
·Washéen kayéik aawa.áý. She heard the sound of the machine.

washéen katáçayi

engine cylinder connecting rod
·Yá washéen katáçayi woosháash. This connecting rod wore out.

du washká

(outside of) his/her cheek
·Ý'aan yáý yatee du washká. His cheek is red.

du washtú

inside of his/her cheek
·Du washtú áwé yanéekw. The inside of his cheek hurts.

a wát

mouth of it (a river, creek)
·Xóow héen wátx' yéi wdudzinei. They put a memorial pile of rocks at the
mouth of the water.

watsíx

caribou
·Watsíx dleeyí áwé ýwaaýáa. I ate caribou meat.
·Watsíx a lututúñl'i tléil tlaý ugé. The soft bone in a caribou nose is not
very big.

du waý'ahéeni

his/her tears
du wañhéeni
·Du waẏ'ahéeni wulilóoẏ. His tears flowed.

du waẏ'aẏéiẏ'u

his/her eyelash
du wañẏ'aẏéiẏ'u (C)
·Dliyát'x' du waẏ'aẏéiẏ'u. Her eyelashes are long.

wa.é

you (singular) [independent]
·Wáa yateeyi lingít sáwé wa.é? What kind of person are you?

wé

that (at hand)
wéi
·Ánk'w áwé kéi has anaswát wéit lingítch. Those people are raising a
crybaby.
·Tl'aadéin áwé át tán wé ñóok. The box is sitting sideways.

wéiksh

woman's curved knife

wéis'

louse, lice
·Wéis' du shaktóot uwa.át. She got lice in her hair.

'

'

W

wéiẏ'

bullhead, sculpin
·Wéiẏ' tlein aawasháat. She caught a big sculpin.
1

WOO

• aaçáa aawawóo | --- | aaçáa awéiẏ
s/he ordered it | --- | s/he orders it (regularly).
P-çáa a-S-ø-wóo~ (ø event)
for S to send for, order P (usually from a catalog)
·Cháanwaan atẏaayíçaa awóo! Order some Chinese food!

du wóo

his/her father-in-law
·Asçeiwú s'aatíý sitee aý wóo. My father-in-law is a master seiner.

wooch

together [object]
woosh
·Wooch ýoot wuduwa.át. People came together.
·Ldakát wooch ýoot has yawdiháa. Everybody came together.

wooch yáý yaa datóowch
wool

math

hole

WOOL
• --- | yawóol | ----- | it has a hole in it | ---.
ø-wóol (ga state)
for something to have a hole, outlet
·Yawóol yá deegáa. This 'dipnet has holes in it.

woolnáý wooshñáñ

wren
woolnáý wooshñáý
·A ýoo aa ñu.oo woolnáý wooshñáñ has al'óon. Some people hunt the wren.

woon

maggot

woosáani

spear for hunting
·Du woosáani awlil'éex'. He broke his spear.
1

WOOS'

• aý'eiwawóos' | aý'awóos' | yoo aý'ayawóos'k
s/he asked him/her | s/he's asking him/her | s/he asks him/her (regularly).
O-ý'a-S-ø-wóos' (na act)
for S to ask, question O
·Hú áwé ý'añçeewóos'. It is he that you will ask.

woosh

together [object]
wooch
·Wé aanñáax'u wéix' woosh ýoot has wudi.át. The chiefs gathered there.
·Kaxées' teen wóoshdei kdudzixát du ý'ás'. His jaw is held together with
a wire.

,

W

wooshdakádin

different directions
·Wooshdakádin ý'oosdé awdiyiñ du téeli. He put his shoes on the wrong feet.

woosh çunayáade

differently
woosh çuwanáade, woosh çuwanyáade

woosh çunayáade aa

different ones; variety
·Woosh çunayáade téel ýaatéen. I see a variety of different shoes.

woosh çuwanyáade

differently
woosh çunayáade, woosh çuwanáade
·Woosh çuwanyáade kwdigéi túlx'u. Drill bits come in different sizes.

wóoshnáý ý'akakéiýi

chain
·Wóoshnáý ý'akakéiýi tíx' yáanáý litseen. Chain is stronger than rope.

woosh yaayí

pair
·Woosh yaayí hél du jee. He doesn't have a pair.

wootsaaçáa

cane; walking stick; staff
yootsaaçáa (C)

du wóow

his/her chest
·Du wóow áwé káast yáý koogéi. His chest is as large as a barrel.

wóow

food, lunch, provisions taken along (on a trip, to work or school)
·Wóow yéi awsinei. He made lunch.

wóow daakeit

container for traveling provisions; lunch basket, lunch container
·Shakliçéiyi wóow daakeit áwé. That is a pretty lunch basket.

du woowká

(on) his/her chest
·Ch'a hú du woowká aawagwál. He pounded his own chest.

WOOÝ'
• --- | yawúý' | ----- | it's wide | ---.
ø-wúý' (ga state)
for something to be wide, broad
This verb only occurs in the imperfective.
·S'igeidí l'eedí yawúý' ña ñ'áatl' yáý yatee. A beaver's tail is wide and flat.

at wuskóowu

knowledgeable person
·Du léelk'w áwé at wuskóowuý wusitee . His grandfather was a knowledgeable man.
·Jiduñéi at wuskóowuý sateeyéech. He is paid because he is a knowledgeable person.

,

,

at wuskú daakahídi

W

school

wuwtunéekw

chest pain; tuberculosis
·Wuwtunéekw jeedáý áwé wooneiý. She was saved from tuberculosis.

,

« X »
XAA
• aadé akawsixaa | --- | aadé yoo aksixeik
s/he poured it out there | --- | s/he pours it out there (regularly).
P-dé O-ka-S-ø-xaa~ (na motion)
for S to pour O into P, pour O out at P; for S to dump, empty O in one mass (by turning over container) at P
·Naaliyéidei kanasxá wé ýaat yik.ádi! Dump the fish guts far away!
·Éil' a kaadéi kanasxá wéi a kát yadu.us'ku át! Pour salt in the wash basin!
• át akawsixáa | --- | áý aksaxaa
s/he poured it there | --- | s/he pours it there (regularly).
P-t~ O-ka-S-s-xaa~ (ø motion)
for S to pour, dump, empty O at P
·Héen áanjís kahéeni ýoot akawsixáa. He poured water in with the orange juice.
• a kaadé ayawsixaa | a kaadé yaa ayanasxéin | a

kaadé yoo ayasixéik
s/he poured it on there | s/he is pouring it on there | s/he pours it on there (regularly).
P-dé O-ya-S-s-xaa~ (na motion)
for S to pour O on/in P
·Ch'as héen ák.wé a kaadéi yóo yadudzixéik yá kat'ákýi? Is water all that was put on these dried berries?
·Ñ'ateil tóodei yanasxá k'idéin ý'adíx'! Pour it in the jug and cork it up!

du xaagú

his/her skeleton, bare bones
du xaagí
·Ch'as du xaagú áwé wuduwat'ei. Only his skeleton was found.

xáak

empty bivalve shell
·Xáak hél daa sá a tú. There is nothing in the bivalve shell.

xáanaa

evening
·Keil atyátx'i latíniý naýsatee yá xáanaa. Let Keil be the babysitter this evening.
·Ñ'alkátsk kahaa yís léinde gaýtoo.áat yá xáanaa. This evening we are going yellowneck clam digging.

xaas

bison, buffalo; ox, muskox; cow; horse
·Xaas al'óon woogoot. She went hunting for muskox.

,

,

X

XAAS'
• aawaxás' | axáas' | axás'ý
s/he scraped it | s/he is scraping it; s/he scrapes it | s/he scrapes it (regularly).
O-S-ø-xáas'~ (ø act)
for S to scrape O
·Nóox' tóodáý aawaxás' wé ýéel'. He scraped the slime out of the shell.
·Éil' kaadáý ýáat k'idéin aaý yixás' a kajeiçí! You all scrape the scales
off the fish from the salt water well!

a xáas'i

its skin (of fish)
·S'eiñ ýáat xáas'i áwé yak'éi çaltóot idateení latseen sákw at
eel'óoni. When you're out hunting a piece of smoked fish skin in your pocket is
good for energy.
·A xáas'i teen áwé duxáash náayadi sákw. Half smoked fish is cut with
the fish skin intact.

XAASH
• aawaxaash | axáash | yoo ayaxáshk
s/he cut it | s/he cuts it; s/he is cutting it | s/he cuts it (regularly).
O-S-ø-xaash~ (na act)
for S to cut O with knife; for S to saw O
·A xáas'i teen áwé duxáash náayadi sákw. Half smoked fish is cut with
the fish skin intact.
·Du keey áwé wuduwaxaash. They cut into his knee.
• aaý aawaxásh | aaý axáash | aaý axásht
s/he cut it off | s/he's cutting it off | s/he cuts if off (regularly).
O-S-ø-xaash~ (ø act)
for S to cut, saw O (esp. cutting something off or cutting wood)
·K'idéin aaý xásh wé t'áa at ý'aýéedli! Cut the trimming off the board
good!
·K'isáanich gán du jeeyís has aawaxásh. The young men cut wood for
him.
• akaawaxaash | yei akanaxásh | yei akaxáshch
s/he cut it up | s/he is cutting it up | s/he cuts it up (regularly).
O-ka-S-ø-xaash~ (ça event)
for S to cut O in several pieces; for S to carve O (on surface); for S to slice O
(e.g., bread)
·Watsíx çádzi yei akanaxásh. She is cutting up a caribou hindquarter.
·Çuwakaan taayí kas'úkýu yís akaawaxaash. She cut up deer fat for
frying.
• awlixaash | alxáash | yoo alixáshk

s/he cut it | s/he's cutting it | s/he cuts it (regularly).
O-S-l-xaash~ (na act)
for S to cut O (esp. rope-like object)
·S'igeidí çeiwú yís a gwéinli aaý awlixaash, wé watsíx. He cut the
hooves off the caribou for a beaver net.
·Aaý awlixaash a geení wé tsaa. He cut the tail flippers off of the seal.

,

• wudixaash | daxáash | yoo dixáshk
s/he cut | s/he cuts; s/he is cutting | s/he cuts (regularly).
S-d-xaash~ (na act)
for S to cut
1

XAAT

• aadé akawsixát | --- | aadé aksaxáty̓
s/he connected it there | --- | s/he connects it there (regularly).
P-dé O-ka-S-s-xaat~ (ø event)
for S to connect, attach O to P
·Yóo tliyaa aasdéi ksaxát wéi kaxées' ay̓ at shí ñóok gúgu yís!
Attach the wire to that tree over there for my radio antenna!
·Kaxées' teen wóoshdei kdudzixát du y̓'ás'. His jaw is held together with
a wire.
• --- | aadé ksixát | ----- | it's connected there | ---.
P-(dé) ka-s-xáat~ (ø state)
for something to be connected, attached, tied (to) P
This verb requires a postpositional phrase which describes
where or what something is connected to. This is not a motion
verb however, and the conjugation prefix does not change when
different postpositions are used. In the Leer-Edwards theme, the
P-(dé) indicates that P (object of a postposition) is required, as is a
postposition, but it can be something other than -dé, as indicated
by the example sentences.
·Wé hít gukshitúdáy̓ kasixát wé kaxées'. The wire runs from the corner
of that house.
·Tláañ du eedé ksixát. The arrow is stuck in his body.
• k'idéin akawsixát | --- | k'idéin aksaxáty̓
s/he pulled it tight | --- | s/he pulls it tight (regularly).
O-ka-S-s-xaat'~ (ø event)
for S to tighten, pull on O (something fastened at the other end)
This verb can be used in a metaphorical sense: Du jeeyís
akawsixát. "S/he is pulling for him/her." This could be used in
reference to someone running for office, or a competitor in a race
of any kind.
2

XAAT

• --- | a yáy̓ kaaxát | ----- | it looks like it | ---.
N yáy̓ ka-ø-xaat~ (ø state)
for something to resemble N (esp. in shape)
This verb can also refer to one's behavior. For example: Tlél
a yáy̓ kooxát wéit'aa. "That one doesn't act normal, right."
·Chichuwaa cheech yáy̓ kaaxát. Dolphins look like porpoise.
·K'wát' yáy̓ kaaxát du çíl'ayi. His grindstone is shaped like an egg.

'

'

X

XAAT'
• aadáý

awsixáat' | aadáý yaa anasxát' | aadáý yoo
asixát'k
s/he dragged it away | s/he is dragging it away | s/he drags it away (regularly).
P-dáý O-S-s-xaat'~ (na motion)
for S to drag, pull O (esp. heavy object or limp object such as dead animal) away
from P; for S to haul, transport O (by non-motor power) away from P
·Aasgutúdáý gán yaa anasxát'. He is hauling firewood out of the woods.

• aadé awsixáat' | aadé yaa anasxát' | aadé yoo asixát'k
s/he dragged it there | s/he is dragging it there | s/he drags it there (regularly).
P-dé O-S-s-xaat'~ (na motion)
for S to drag, pull O (esp. heavy object or limp object such as dead animal)
toward P; for S to haul, transport O (by non-motor power) toward P
·Shayadihéini at óow wéide yaa ndusxát'. They are hauling lots of
someone's possessions over that way.
• awsixáat' | yaa anasxát' | yoo asixát'k
s/he drug it | s/he is dragging it along | s/he drags it (regularly).
O-S-s-xaat'~ (na motion)
for S to drag, pull O (esp. heavy object or limp object such as dead animal); for S
to haul, transport O (by non-motor power)
·Héen yaa anasxát'. He is hauling water.
·Hít kaságu yaa anasxát'. He is dragging rafters along.

xáatl

iceberg
·Xáatl kát uwañúý wé yaakw. That boat ran into an iceberg.

xáatl kaltsáçaa
xáatl'ákw

poles used to push aside ice (from a boat)

mouth ulcer; soreness of the mouth (as of a baby teething)

xáats'

clear sky, blue sky
·Xáats'de yaa ñunahéin. It is becoming twilight.

xáats'

sky blue

xákw

sandbar; gravel bar; sand beach; gravel beach
·Xákw ká ayaawadlaañ. He made it to the sand bar.

xákwl'i

soapberry
·Xákwl'i yak'éi yéi wdusneiyí. Soapberries are good when they're prepared.

a xákwti

its empty shell (of house); empty container
·Wé ñ'ateil xákwti aý jeet tán!. Hand me the empty pitcher!

xáshaa

saw
·Xáshaa yéi ndu.eich gán yéi daaduneiyí. A saw is used to work on wood.

at xáshdi téel

moccasins
et xáshdi téel (C)

,

Dictionary of Tlingit

·A kaaý sh tukdliçéi du tsaa doogú at xáshdi téel. She is proud of her
seal skin moccasins.
·At xáshdi téel sákw áwé kanágaa akaawach'ák'w aý jeeyís. He
carved a form for making moccasins for me.

at xáshdi x'óow
xát'aa

blanket sewn from scraps of hide

sled
xét'aa (C)

XEECH
• aawaxích | --- | axíchý
s/he exerted his/her full strength on it; s/he is exerting his/her full strength on it |
--- | s/he exerts his/her full strength on it (regularly).
O-S-ø-xeech~ (ø event)
for S to exert one's full strength on, strive for O; for S to concentrate on, put
effort into O
·Yeeytéen has du téiý' tóotý áyá toodé has yee uwaxích haa
ñu.éex'i. You all can see that our hosts thank you from their hearts.
XEEL'
• akaawaxíl' | yaa akanaxíl | akaxíl'ý
he/she/it bothered him/her; he/she/it is bothering him/her | he/she/it is starting to
bother him/her | he/she/it bothers him/her (regularly).
O-ka-S-ø-xéel'~ (ø event)
for S to bother, trouble, cause trouble or anxiety for O
·Du tl'óoçu áwé ash kaawaxíl'. Her liver is bothering her.

xéel'i

mossberry
·Xéel'i kútý a tukayátx'i yagéi. Mossberries have too many seeds.

xéen

housefly; bluebottle fly
·Xéen áwé woogéi yá ñutaan. There were a lot of blue bottle flies this
summer.

du xées' (C)

his/her shin
du xées'i
·Du xées' ñúnáý wudlix'ís'. His shin is really swelling.

a xées'i

its cutwater; the curved part of a bow or stern (of boat)
·A xées'i ágé tsú yéi duwasáakw a yaýak'áaw? Is the bow of a boat also called the yaýak'áaw?
·A xées'i s'é yánde .áýw! Tie the bow of the boat first!

xéesh

rash
·Xéesh áwé du lidíý' yéi yatee. He has a rash on his neck.

XEET
• akawshixít | akshaxeet | akshaxítý
s/he wrote it | s/he writes it; s/he is writing it | s/he writes it (regularly).
O-ka-S-sh-xeet~ (ø act)

,

,

X

for S to write, draw, or paint a picture of O; for S to print O by hand; for S to photograph, take pictures, X-rays of O
·S'igeidí ña yáay a káa kashaxít wé at doogú x'óow! Draw a Beaver and whale design on the leather blanket!
·Tsaa geení aankadushxit át teen akawshixít. She took a picture of the seal tail flippers with a camera.
• kawjixít | kashxeet | kashxítý
s/he wrote | s/he writes; s/he is writing | s/he writes (regularly).
ka-S-d-sh-xeet~ (ø act)
for S to write, draw,or paint; for S to take a photograph
·Lingít ý'éináý kashxeet áwé ashigóok. He knows how to write in the Tlingit language.
XEET'
• t'aa ká aawaxéet' | t'aa ká axít'kw | t'aa ká yei axéet'ch
s/he swept the floor | s/he is sweeping the floor | s/he sweeps the floor (regularly).
O-S-ø-xéet'~ (ça act)
for S to sweep O (esp. floor)
·Xít'aa een du neilí axít'gi nooch. He always sweeps his house with a broom.
• wudixéet' | daxít'kw | yei daxít'ch
s/he swept | s/he is sweeping | s/he sweeps (regularly).
S-d-xéet'~ (ça act)
for S to sweep
Tlél udaxít'k which literally translates as "s/he doesn't sweep" is an expression commonly used to insinuate that the person is slovenly, lazy.
XEEX
• aadé wjixeex | aadé yaa nashíx | aadé yoo jixíxk
he/she/it ran there | he/she/it is running there | he/she/it runs there (regularly).

P-dé S-j-xeex~ (na motion)
for (singular) S to run toward P
Note that the classifier sh- combined with the verb stem
-xeex becomes -sheex.
·Wé xóots awusnéex'i a yinaadé wjixeex haa keidlí. Our dog is running
toward the brown bear it smelled.
·Yóode wujixeexi dzísk'w a ítde woogoot aý éek'. My brother went after
the moose that ran off that way.
• anaý kaawaxeex | --- | anaý yei kaxíxch
it fell through it | --- | it falls through it (regularly).
P-náý ka-ø-xeex~ (ça motion)
for something (usually a round object) to fall, drop through P
·Du waañnáý kaawaxeex. He's staring at it. (Lit: It fell through his eye.)
• át kaawaxíx | --- | áý kaxeex
it fell into it | --- | it falls into it (regularly).

,

Dictionary of Tlingit

P-t~ ka-ø-xeex~ (ø motion)
for something (usually a round object) to fall, drop into P
·Kei kawduwaçix'i té du káak't kaawaxíx. The rock that was thrown hit
him on the forehead.
·Du kwéiyi ñínt kaawaxíx wé at katé. The bullet fell short of his mark.
• át uwaxíx | --- | áý xeex
it fell on it | --- | it falls on it (regularly).
P-t~ ø-xeex~ (ø motion)
for something to fall or drop on P; for a bullet to hit P; for a rumor, news to
spread, go around at P
·Óoxjaa héen ý'akát uwaxíx. Wind has hit the surface of the water.
·Kagán shaa kát uwaxíx. Light fell on the mountain.
• át wooxeex | --- | --it's falling around; it's wobbly | --- | ---.
P-t ø-xeex~ (na motion)
for something to fall around at P (esp. inside a container)
·Du wañltáaknáý át wooxeex. Something fell in her eye.
• át wujixeex | --- | át yoo jixíxk
he/she/it is running around; he/she/it ran around | --- | he/she/it runs around
(regularly).
P-t S-j-xeex~ (na motion)
for (singular) S to run around at P
Note that the classifier sh- combined with the verb stem
-xeex becomes -sheex.
·Ý'al'daayéeji éeñt wujixeex. The sandpiper is running around the beach.
·Ñ'asigóo kaltéelñ l'éiw kát át wusheex. It's fun running around barefoot
in the sand.
• át wujixíx | aadé nashíx | áý sheex
he/she/it ran to it | he/she/it is running to it | he/she/it runs to it (regularly).
P-t~ S-j-xeex~ (ø motion)
for (singular) S to run to P, arrive at P by running
Note that the classifier sh- combined with the verb stem
-xeex becomes -sheex.
·Wé aas seiyít wujixíx séew tóodáý. She ran to the shelter of the tree to get
out of the rain.
·Eesháank' kaltéelñ áwé haat wujixíx aý dachýánk'. Poor thing, my
grandchild ran over here shoeless.
• daak uwaxíx | --- | daak xíxch
it fell | --- | it falls (regularly).
daak ø-xeex~ (ø motion)
for the sun, moon to move through the sky into the open; for something (esp. a
small, compact object) to fall, drop
This verb can also be used in expressions such as: Déiý
yagiyee káx' áwé daak uxeexch "It falls on a Tuesday".
·Çagaan daak uwaxíx wé séew ítdáý. The sun came out after the rain.

,

,

• çunéi wjixíx | --- | çunéi shíxý
he/she/it started running | --- | he/she/it starts running (regularly).
çunéi S-j-xeex~ (ø motion)
for (singular) S to begin running
Note that the classifier sh- combined with the verb stem
-xeex becomes -sheex.
·Du gawdáani aadé woo.aadi yé, a niyaadé çunéi wjixíx. He started
running in the direction his horses went.
• du jeet shuwaxíx | du jeedé yaa shunaxíx | du jeeý

shuxeex
s/he ran out of it | s/he is running out of it | s/he runs out of it (regularly).
N jeet~ shu-ø-xeex~ (ø event)
for N to run out of something
• a káa wooxeex | --- | a káa yei xíxch
it fell on it | --- | it falls on it (regularly).
N káa ø-xeex~ (ça motion)
for an object (usually small, compact) to fall on N
• kei uwaxíx | kei naxíx | kei xíxch
it rose | it's rising | it rises (regularly).
kei ø-xeex~ (ø motion)
for the sun, moon to rise
This verb can also be used in expressions that don't pertain
to the sun or moon, as in: Neekw kei uwaxíx "News/gossip went
around".
• ñut wujixeex | --- | ñut kei shíxch
he/she/it ran away | --- | he/she/it runs away (regularly).
ñut S-j-xeex~ (ga motion)
for (singular) S to run away
Note that the classifier sh- combined with the verb stem
-xeex becomes -sheex.
·Du kooñénayi ñut wujixeex. His messenger ran away.
·Aý jináñ ñut wujixeex. He ran away from me.
• shuwaxeex | yaa shunaxíx | yoo shuyaxíxk
it came to an end | it's coming to an end | it comes to an end (quickly, regularly).
shu-ø-xeex~ (na event)
for something to end, come to an end, pass; for something to be used up (of
supplies, etc.)
• du tóot wooxeex | --- | du tóot yoo yaxíxk
s/he is worried about him/her/it | --- | s/he worries about him/her/it (regularly).
N tóot O-ø-xeex~ (na motion)
for O to worry N; for N to have O constantly on the mind
Note that literally translated, du tóot wooxeex means "it's
rolling around inside him/her".
• yaawaxeex | yaa yanaxíx | yoo yaxíxk
it happened | it's happening | it happens (regularly).

,

Dictionary of Tlingit

ya-ø-xeex~ (na event)
for something to take place, occur, happen
·çaaý shí teen áwé yaawaxeex wé ñu.éex'. A cry song took place at the
potlatch.
• yínde wooxeex | yínde yaa naxíx
it set | it is setting | it sets (regularly).
yínde ø-xeex~ (na motion)
for the sun, moon to set

| yínde yoo yaxíxk

xéidu

comb
shaxéidu
·Shaxéidu ýwaa.oo. I bought a comb.

xein

spawned-out salmon with white scabs, ready to die
·Xein nageich ñutaan eetíx'. After the summer there are a lot of
spawned-out salmon.

du xeitká

his/her thorax; flat upper surface of his/her chest

Xeitl

Thunderbird
·Xeitl naaý has sitee Shangukeidí. The Shangukeidí are Thunderbird.
·Xeitl a káa kawduwach'ák'w yá kées. A Thunderbird is carved on this
bracelet.

xeitl l'íkws'i (At)

lightning
xeitl l'úkýu, xeitl l'óokýu (T)

xeitl l'úkýu

lightning
xeitl l'óokýu (T), xeitl l'íkws'i (At)
·Xeitl l'úkýu yóo tliyaawú. The lightnting is way over there.

xeitl táax'aa

horsefly

·Xeitl táax'aa ýat wusitáax'. A horsefly bit me.

xén

plastic
·Yéi ýwaa.áý xén hél ushk'é wé microwave tóox' yéi du.oowú. I heard that it's not good to put plastic in the microwave.
·Tléix' ñ'ateil yáý áwé liyék wéi xén. That plastic container can hold one gallon.

xídlaa

herring rake
·Yaaw xídlaa yéi wdu.oowú, tlél uldzée nooch. Using a herring rake is not difficult.

xít'aa

broom; brush
·Xít'aa een du neilí axít'gi nooch. He always sweeps his house with a broom.

xíxch'

frog
·Xíxch' a yáax' kaýwaach'ák'w. I carved a frog on it's face.
·Xíxch' at óowu woosh jeedé duhéin nooch. The frog crest is claimed by more than one clan.

,

,

X

xi.áat

dusk; twilight
·Xi.átt ñuwaháa. It is dusk.

xoodzí

comet; falling star

xoodzí

burnt or charred wood

XOOK
• awsixúk | asxook | asxúký
s/he dried it | s/he is drying it | s/he dries it (regularly).
O-S-s-xook~ (ø act)

for S to dry O (by any method)
• uwaxúk | yaa naxúk | xúký
it dried | it's drying | it dries (regularly).
ø-xook~ (ø event)
for something to be dry, dried
·Wé ýáat a kajeiçí a kát uwaxúk. The scales of the fish dried on it.
·Yaa naxúk aý naa.ádi. My clothes are drying.

xóon

north wind
·Ýeil neech káa yéi nateech xóon wudunoogú. Foam is on the beach
when the north wind blows.
·Haa kát ayawashát wé xóon. The north wind hit us in gusts.

xóosht'

singed, burnt, or charred matter
·Xóosht' has du yáa yéi has ana.eich yaa (ha)s jinda.ádi. The dark
burnt ashes would be put on their faces when going to war.

xóots

grizzly bear
·Xóots tlein áwé aawaján wé ñáa. That man killed a big brown bear.
·Has du yáa daak uwagút wé xóots tlein kanat'á has a.éeni. While
they were picking blueberries, the brown bear came face to face with them.

xóow

memorial pile of rocks
·Xóow héen wátx' yéi wdudzinei. They put a memorial pile of rocks at the
mouth of the water.

Xudzidaa Ñwáan

people of Admiralty Island
·Xudzidaa Ñwáan áwé Aangóon ñu.oo. The people of Angoon are known
as Xudzidaa Ñwáan.

Xunaa

Hoonah
·Aý dlaak' tín Xunaadé ñugaýtootéen kanat'á ñuk'éet' yís. We are
going to travel to Hoonah to pick blueberries with my sister.
·Xunaa Ñáawu áwé ñúnáý has litseen. Hoonah people are very strong.

du xuýaawú

pubic hair

,

Dictionary of Tlingit

« Xw »
XWAACH
• awlixwách | alxwácht | alxwáchý
s/he scraped it | s/he's scraping it | s/he scrapes it (regularly).
O-S-l-xwaach~ (ø act)
for S to soften, make O flexible; for S to scrape O (hide) to soften it
·Wé watsíx doogú awlixwách. She scraped the caribou skin.
·Çooch doogú awlixwách. She softened a wolf hide.

xwaasdáa

canvas; tarp; tent
·Du gáni a kaháadi yís áwé xwaasdáa aawa.oo. He bought a tarp to
cover his firewood.
·Wé yées xwaasdáa çákw yáý yatee. The new tent is stiff.

du xwáayi
xwájaa
xweitl

his/her clan brother
skin scraper
fatigue

XWEITL
• ash wulixwétl | yaa ash nalxwétl | ash laxwétlý
he/she/it made him/her tired | he/she/it is making him/her tired | he/she/it makes
him/her tired (regularly).
O-S-l-xweitl~ (ø event)
for S to tire O, make O tired (either physically or emotionally)
·Ýat wulixwétl wé séew. I'm tired of the rain.
• kawlixwétl | yaa kanalxwétl | kalaxwétlý
it's itchy | it's starting to itch | it gets itchy (regularly).
ka-S-l-xweitl~ (ø event)
for S to itch, tickle
·Aý lú tukawlixwétl. My nose tickled (inside).
• wudixwétl | yaa ndaxwétl | daxwétlý
s/he's tired; s/he was tired | s/he's getting tired | s/he gets tired (regularly).
O-d-xweitl~ (ø event)
for O to be tired, weary
·Aatlein wudixwétl a ítdáý. She was really tired after that.

,

,

X'

« X' »
-x'

at (the scene of); at (the time of)
-ø
The postposition -x' has the alternate form -ø (unmarked)
when attaching to a noun ending in a long vowel.
·Atýá daakahídix' gishoo taayí ña k'wát' awdziçáaý. She ordered bacon
and eggs at the restaurant.
·Kawóot teen ñ'eikaxwéin a káa kañá! Embroider a flower on it with
beads!

x'aa

point (of land)
·X'aa daaý yaawañúý wé yaakw. The boat motored around the point.
·Wé x'aa çei xóon tléil aan utí. The North Wind does not bother the shelter
of the point.

X'AAK
• át uwax'ák | --- | áý x'aak
it swam underwater to it | --- | it swims underwater to it (regularly).
P-t~ S-ø-x'aak~ (ø motion)
for S to swim under water to P
·Héen wátt uwax'ák wé t'ási. The grayling swam to the mouth of the river.

a x'aakeidí

its seeds
·Tléiñw x'aakeidí áwé ts'ítskw gánde nagoodí tóox' yéi nateech.
Berry seeds are found in bird poop.
·Wé at x'aakeidí ín x'eesháa tóox' yéi na.oo! Put the seeds in a bottle!

X'AAÑW
• a kát seiwax'áñw | --- | a káý sax'aañw
s/he forgot | --- | s/he forgets (regularly).
N kát~ O-sa-ø-x'aañw~ (ø state)
for O to forget N
·Tlél a káý yiseix'aaçúñ wé yaakw kakúxaa! Don't you all forget the
bailer for the boat!
·A kát tsé iseix'áañw haa hít katíý'aayi! Don't forget our house key!

x'aa luká

on the ridge or elevated part of the point (of land)
·X'aa luká áwé áx' yéi nateech wé tsaa. The seal is always on the point.

x'aalx'éi

dwarf maple

a x'aan

its tip (of pointed object); top, tips of its branches (of
tree, bush)
·Tléi a x'aant áwé daañ wudiçwát' wé yadák'w. The young boy crawled

,

out the limb.
·K'idéin yax'át wé lítaa x'aan! Sharpen the tip of the knife good!

x'áan

anger
·X'áan át iwaýóot'i tlél ushk'é. Anger pulling you around is not good.

x'áan kanáayi

general; leader of war, battle

x'áan yinaa.át

war clothes (of moosehide)

X'AAS
• kawlix'áas | yaa kanalx'áas | --it's leaking | it's beginning to leak | ---.
ka-l-x'áas (ø event)
for something to drip, leak (at fairly fast rate)
·Awdagaaních áwé, dleit kaaý kalóoýjaa koolx'áasch hít kaadáý.
Because the sun is shining, the snow drips fast off the house.
·Awdagaaní yáa yagiyee, ldakát át kaadáý kaguýlax'áas. When it
sunshines today everything will be dripping off.

x'áas

waterfall
·X'áas tóot áwé át woohaan. She is standing around in the waterfall.

du x'aash

cheek of his/her buttocks

X'AAT
• ayaawax'át | ayax'áat | ayax'átý
s/he sharpened it | s/he's sharpening it | s/he sharpens it (regularly).
O-ya-S-ø-x'áat~ (ø act)
for S to sharpen O (an edge) with a file
·At ýéidi yax'aat a shóox' çanú! Sit down and do some arrow-head
sharpening!
·Kax'ás'aa yax'áat áwé ashigóok. He really knows how to sharpen the rip
saw.

x'áat'

island
·X'áat' káx' áwé yéi wootee Naatsilanéi. Naatsilanéi stayed on an island.

·K'wát' X'áadidé gaýtooñóoý kéidladi k'wádiçáa. We are going to Egg Island for seagull eggs.

x'áax'

apple; crabapple
·X'áax' yak'éi çuwakaan dleeyí een. Apple is good with deer meat.
·X'áax' tlaý ñúnáý si.áax'w. Crabapples are very sour.

x'áax' kahéeni

apple juice
·X'áax' kahéeni yéi wtusinei. We made apple juice.

x'ádaa

file
·X'ádaa yéi ndu.eich lítaa yís. A file is used to make a knife.

x'akaskéin

unfinished basket
·Wé x'akaskéin daax' áwé yéi jiné. She is working on the unfinished basket.

,

,

X'

x'átgu

dogfish; mudshark
·X'átgu áwé Shangukeidí has du at óowuý sitee. The dogfish is an artifact of the Thunderbiird people.

x'at'daayéejayi

black turnstone
·X'at'daayéejayi héenák'w át nagútch. The black turnstone walks around in shallow water.

x'éedadi

uprooted tree or stump (with roots protruding)
x'éededi (C)
·X'éedadi kaanáý yéi aý wudzigít at gutóox'. I fell over a stump in the woods.
·X'éedadi tóox' awdlisín. She hid in a tree stump.

x'ees

boil; inflammation and swelling
·Wé x'ees du kaanáý yatee. The boil is too much for him.

X'EES'
• wudix'ís' | yaa ndax'ís' | dax'ís'ý
it's swollen | it's beginning to swell | it swells (regularly).
d-x'ees'~ (ø event)
for something to swell, be swollen locally; for something to be matted, tangled in lumps
·Wudix'ís' du goosh. His thumb is swollen.
·Du káak' wudix'ís' ña kawdiyés'. His forehead is swollen and bruised.

du x'ées'i

lock of his/her hair; his/her matted hair
du shax'ées'i
·Du shax'ées'i kulijée. His matted hair is unattractive.

x'eesháa

bucket; pail
·X'eesháa yaa anatán. She is carrying a bucket.

x'éiçaa

truly, really; in truth, for sure
·X'éiçaa Lingít áwé wa.é. You are a true Lingít.

x'éiçaa át

truth
x'éiçaa ét (C)
·X'éiçaa átý sitee ñusaýán. Love is true.

x'éitaa

cutthroat trout
·X'éitaa nageich Jilñóotx'. There are a lot of cutthroat trout at Chilkoot.

a x'éix'u

its gill (of fish)
·A x'éix'u áwé yoo dudlik'útsk wé ýaat. One breaks the gills of the fish.
·Wé káast kaadéi lít wé a x'éix'u! Throw the gills in the barrel!

x'éiý

crab (king, spider)
·X'éiý ñaa ý'é yak'éi. King crab is a delight to the mouth.

x'içaañáa

brave, fearless man; temperamental, quick-tempered,
hot-headed or domineering man

,

X'

Dictionary of Tlingit

x'éeçaa ñáa (T)
·Ñúnáý x'içaañáa áwé wé ñáa. That man is a real warrior.
X'OO
• át akawsix'óo | aadé yaa akanasx'wéin | áý aksax'oo
s/he nailed it on it | s/he is nailing it on it | s/he nails it on it (regularly).
O-ka-S-s-x'oo~ (ø event)
for S to nail O
Note that the postpositional phrase át/aadé/áý "on it" is
not required with this verb, and therefore is not given in the
Leer-Edwards theme. It is given in the forms above however, to
show how the postposition changes with each mode. Without the
át, one could say: akawsix'óo "s/he drove nails in it".
·Tuháayi teen áwé át kawtusix'óo. We nailed it on it with a nail.
·Çayéis' du hídi kát akawsix'óo. He nailed tin on his roof.

x'óol'

whirlpool; boiling tide; chaos
·X'óol' áa litseen Aangóon yadá. The boiling tide is strong in Angoon.

x'oon sá

how many; some number (of)
·X'oon gaawx' sá? At what time?

x'óow

blanket; robe
·Yéil x'óow aawañáa du ýán aa jeeyís. She sewed a Raven blanket for her
husband.
·Yáat hán du x'óowu teen. Here he stands with his robe.

x'úkjaa

steam (visible, in the air); mist, fog (rising from a body of
standing water)
·X'úkjaa héen káa yéi wootee. Steam was on top of the water.

x'ús'

club
·X'ús' teen shawduwaýích. He was hit with a club.

x'úx'

paper; book, magazine, newspaper; letter, mail
·Yáa a daat x'úx' yáý áwé a daax' yéi jiýwaanei. I worked on it
according to the book.

·Aý éesh kak'dakwéiy s'aatíý sitee, x'úx' awuýáax'un. As a captain, my father used to haul mail.

x'úx' daakahídi

post office
·Tléix' dáanaa yéi ý'alitseen katíý'aa x'úx' daakahídix'. A key costs one dollar at the post office.

x'úx' daakax'úx'u

envelope

,

,

Xw

« Xw »
x'wán

boot(s)

x'wán

be sure to
This particle is used with the Imperative and Hortative verb modes.

X'WÁS'Ñ
• wulix'wás'ñ | yaa nax'wás'ñ | yoo lix'wás'ñk
it's numb | it's beginning to get numb | it gets numb (regularly).
l-x'wás'ñ (na event)
for something to be numb, have no feeling
-x'ús'ñ
·Aý k'í wulix'wás'ñ. My rump is numb.

,

Ý

Dictionary of Tlingit

« Ý »
-ý

(in prolonged contact) at; (repeatedly arriving) at; being, in the form
of
·Du gúk káý ayaawayeesh du sadaat'aayí. She pulled her scarf down
over her ears.
·Yeedát ñuyak'éi çaatáa yéi daané yís yá kaxwaan káý yaa nagúdi.
Today the weather is good for walking out on the frost to check the traps.

ýa-

I [subject]
·Ýáay een áwé ýwaliyéý wé kanéist. I built that cross out of yellow cedar.

ýá

you see
ýáa
This particle softens an assertion.
1

ÝAA

• aawaýáa | aýá | aýéiý
s/he ate it | s/he is eating it | s/he eats it (regularly).
O-S-ø-ýaa~ (ø act)
for S to eat O
·Atýa átch áwé uwaýáa aý kinaak.ádi. A moth ate my coat.
·Ch'áakw duýáa noojín wé kals'áak. They used to eat squirrels long ago.
• at uwaýáa | at ýá | at ýéiý
s/he ate | s/he eats; s/he is eating | s/he eats (regularly).
at S-ø-ýaa~ (ø act)
for S to eat
• yaý ayawsiýáa | yaý yaa ayanasýéin | yaý ayasaýéiý
s/he ate it all up | s/he is eating it all up | s/he eats it all up (regularly).
yaý O-ya-S-s-ýaa~ (ø event)
for S to eat up, finish, consume O (eating lots of pieces)
·Ñ'alkátsk yáxwch'ich yaý yawsiýáa haa aaní kaadáý. The sea otter
has devoured the yellowneck clams on our land.
2

ÝAA

• aawaýáa | aýáa | --s/he rowed | s/he is rowing | ---.
a-S-ø-ýáa (ø act)
for S to paddle, row
·Tláakw aýáa du aandaayaagú. He is rowing his rowboat quickly.

• át ayaawaýaa | --- | át yoo ayaýéik
s/he is transporting him/her/it around; s/he transported him/her/it around | --- |
s/he transports him/her/it around (regularly).
P-t O-ya-S-ø-ýaa~ (na motion)

,

,

Ý

for S to transport O around P by boat or car
·Káa tlein yíkt át yawduwaýaa wé aanñáawu. The rich person is being
driven around in a limosine.
• át ayaawaýáa | --- | áý ayaýaa
s/he transported him/her/it there | --- | s/he transports him/her/it there
(regularly).
P-t~ O-ya-S-ø-ýaa~ (ø motion)
for S to transport O by boat or car to P; for S to bring, take or fetch O by boat or
car to P
·Atýá tlein áýá ñu.éex'de yakñwaýáa. I am going to haul a lot of food to
the potlatch.
·Ñaanaawú tl'átgi kaadéi yakñwaýáa ñ'eikaxwéin. I will transport
flowers to the graveyard.
• ayaawaýáax'w | ayaýáax'w | --s/he hauled it | s/he is hauling it | ---.
O-ya-S-ø-ýáax'w (na act)
for S to regularly transport, haul O (mail, newspaper, e.g.) by boat or car
·Aý éesh kak'dakwéiy s'aatíý sitee, x'úx' awuýáax'un. As a captain,
my father used to haul mail.

ýáa

war party, attacking force of warriors or soldiers; army

ÝAACH
• aawaýaach | yaa anaýách | yoo ayaýáchk
s/he towed it | s/he is towing it | s/he tows it (regularly).
O-S-ø-ýaach~ (na motion)
for S to tow O (usually by boat)
·Daýáchx'i yaakw tlénx' át has anaýáchch.. Tugboats tow large vessels.

a ýaagú

its claw
·Nóosk ýaagú ñúnáý yalik'áts'. Wolverine claws are really sharp.

ýaaheiwú

black currant
·Ýaaheiwú tléiñwý sitee. Black currant is a fruit.

du ýaakw

his/her nail (of finger or toe)
·Du x̱aakw áx̱ ayawlix̱ásh. He cut his fingernails.

du x̱aakw eetí

his/her fingernail markings
·Du x̱aakw eetí áwé wé l'éiw káwu. His fingernail markings are in the sand.

x̱aanás'

rafter
x̱aanés' (C)
·X̱aanás' awliyéx̱ wé x̱áa. That man built rafters.

x̱aanás' éinaa

rack for drying fish

,

Ý

Dictionary of Tlingit

a ýaani

its prongs (of spear)
a ýaaní
·A ýaaní k'idéin yax'át! Sharpen its prongs well!

ýaat

root; especially spruce root
·Ýaat áyá gaýtulas'éil'. We're going to dig spruce roots.
·Wé ýaat kanat'á kahéeni káa yéi gaýtoo.oo. We will put the roots in the
blueberry juice.

ýáat

fish; salmon
·S'eiñ ýaat xáas'i áwé yak'éi çaltóot idateení latseen sákw at
eel'óoni. When you're out hunting a piece of smoked fish skin in your pocket is
good for energy.
·I léelk'u keekándei aneelçein - ýáat yéi adaané! Go check on your
grandpa - he's working on fish!

ýáat daakahídi

cannery
·Cháanwaanch áwé wuliyéý yá ýáat daakahídi. The Chinese built this
cannery.

ýáat çíjaa
ýáat héeni

fish pitchfork
salmon creek

ýáat k'áaý'i

bloodline inside fish, along the backbone

ýaat s'áaxw

woven root hat

ýáat yádi

whitefish; baby fish; tiny fish
·Ýáat yádi héen sháakdáý asçeiwú. She nets whitefish from the head of
the river.
·Ýáat yádi çíñs yís akaawaxaash. She cut the whitefish to barbeque over

the fire.

ýaatl'

algae found on rocks
·Ýaatl' áwé yagéi Jilñáatx'. There is a lot of algae in the Chilkat.

ÝAAW
• --- | daadziýáaw | kei isýáawch
--- | it's hairy | it gets hairy (regularly).
N daa-d-s-ýáaw (ga state)
for N to have a hairy body
Note that the posessive pronoun is used with this verb
when talking about a person. For example: du daadziýáaw "s/he
is hairy"; aý daadziýáaw "I am hairy".
·Gantutl'úk'ýu tléil daa.usýáaw. Woodworms are not furry.

ýáaw

log (fallen tree)
·Ýáaw yan ýút'! Pull the log to shore!
·Aý ñatlyát wujiýín wé ýáaw tlein. That big log fell on my side.

,

,

Ý

ýaawaaçéi

window
ýaawaaçí
·A tóonáý áwé at duwatéen wé ýaawaaçéi. You can see through the
window.

ýaawaaçéi kas'ísayi

window curtain
ýaawaaçí kas'ísaa (T), ýaawaaçí kes'íseyi (C)

ýaawaaçí

window
ýaawaaçéi

a ýaawú

its hair, fur; its quill(s) (of porcupine)
·Ñúnáý ý'alitseen a ýaawú. It's fur is very expensive.
·Wé ýalak'ách' ýaawú aý keidlí ý'éit yawdliçích. The porcupine quills
stuck in my dogs mouth.

du ýaawú

his/her body hair, fuzz

ýaay

steambath
·Ýaaydé naýtoo.aat. Let's go into the steambath.

ýáay

yellow cedar, Alaska cedar
·Kootéeyaa gaýdulyeiýí ýáay yéi ndu.eich. When a totem is made it is yellow cedar that is used.
·Ýáay kayeiýtáçu a takáx' yéi na.oo! Put yellow cedar shavings in the bottom of it!

ýalak'ách'

porcupine
ýalek'ách' (C)
·Ýalak'ách' katéiýi aý ý'é yak'éi. Porcupine soup is delightful to my mouth.
·Wé ýalak'ách' ýaawú aý keidlí ý'éit yawdliçích. The porcupine quills stuck in my dogs mouth.

ýaldleit

white fox
·Ýaldleit kinaa.át yéi aya.óo wé Çunanaa ñáa. That Athabaskan man is wearing a white fox overcoat.

ýalt'ooch' naaças'éi

black fox
·Ý'alitseen wé ýalt'ooch' naaças'éi doogú. The skin of a black fox is expensive.

du ýán

near him/her, by him/her
·Wé gáal' çeiýí aan nagú i léelk'w ýánde! Go with the clams to your grandparent!
·Du séek' du ýánt uwagút. Her daughter came to her.

ÝÁN
• awsiýán | asiýán | --s/he loved him/her/it | s/he loves him/her/it | ---.
O-S-s-ýán (ga state)
for S to love O

,

Ý

Dictionary of Tlingit

·Asiýán áwé du kéilk'. He loves his nephew.
·"Iýsiýán," yoo ayawsiñaa du yadák'u. She told her boyfriend, "I love
you."

du ýán aa

his/her mate, his "old lady"; her "old man"
·Yéil x'óow aawañáa du ýán aa jeeyís. She sewed a Raven blanket for her
husband.

ýat

me [object]
aý (An)
·Katíý'aa s'aatíý ýat guýsatée yá keijín yagiyeedáý. After Friday I will
be the jailer.
·Áx' ñaa ée at dultóow yé áa yéi ýat guçwatée seiçán. I will be in
school tomorrow.

ýát

I [independent]

ýát'aa

whip
·Ýát'aa yéi awsinei aý éesh. My father made a whip.

ÝEECH
• ashaawaýích | --- | ashaýíchý
s/he clubbed it | --- | s/he clubs it (regularly).
O-sha-S-ø-ýeech~ (ø event)
for S to club, hit O on the head
·X'ús' teen shawduwaýích. He was hit with a club.
• át akaawaýích | --- | áý akaýeech
s/he threw it to it | --- | s/he throws it to it (regularly).
P-t~ O-ka-S-ø-ýeech~ (ø motion)
for S to throw O (esp. liquid) to P
To give the meaning "throw out", use: yóo-t~ "over there".
For example: Yóot akaawaýích. "S/he threw it (liquid) out."
·Aý ý'éit aa kaýích tléiñw kahéeni! Give me some juice! (Lit: Throw some
juice at my mouth!)
• yaý akaawaýích | --- | yaý akaýíchý
s/he spilled it | --- | s/he spills it (regularly).
yaý O-ka-S-ø-ýeech~ (ø event)
for S to spill, upset O
·Yaa ntoo.ádi áwé, daak wudzigít yaý akaawaýích wutuwa.ini
kaneilts'ákw. When we were walking along, she fell down and spilled all the

swamp currants we picked.

du ýeek

his/her upper arm
du ýeik (C)
·Du ýeek áwé wool'éex'. His upper arm is broken.
·Wéi kashóok' gwéil aý ýeek káa yan satí! Set the heating pad on my upper arm!

ýeel

foam; whitecaps
ýeil

’

’

Ý

·Ýeil neech káa yéi nateech xóon wudunoogú. Foam is on the beach when the north wind blows.

ýéel

granite
·Ýéel yéi ndu.eich hítý dulyeiýí. Granite is used to build a house.

ýéel'

slime; thick mucus
·Wé ýéel' wuls'eexí lichán. When the slime rots it stinks.
·Wé ýéel' du jíndáý awliçoo. She wiped the slime off her hands.

ÝEEN
• a kát wujiýín | --- | a káý ishýeen
it fell on it | --- | it falls on it (regularly).
N-t~ j-ýeen~ (ø motion)
for a hard, solid object to fall, drop on N
·Aý ñatlyát wujiýín wé ýáaw tlein. That big log fell on my side.

ýéet'

giant clam
ýéit'
·Ýéet' a daat shkalneek ñudzitee. There is a story about a giant clam.

ýéeý

small owl
·Ýéeý wuduwa.áý. A small owl was heard.

ýéey

pack; backpack; pack sack

ÝEI
• (áa) uwaýéi | --- | (áa) ýeiý
s/he stayed overnight (there) | --- | s/he stays overnight (there) (regularly).
O-ø-ýei~ (ø event)
for O to stay overnight, spend the night, camp out overnight
-ýee~ (An)
·Áak'wx' uwaýéi wé shaawát. That woman camped at Auke Bay.
·Ñaa t'áak áwé áa uwaýée. She camped behind everyone.

at ýéidi

arrowhead
·Yei googénk'i at ýéidi teen áwé ýwaat'úk wé t'aawáñ. I shot the
Canada goose with a small arrow.
·At ýéidi yax'aat a shóox' çanú! Sit down and do some arrow-head
sharpening!

ÝEIK
• ash wusiýéñ | --- | ash saýéñý
he/she/it kept him/her awake | --- | he/she/it keeps him/her awake (regularly).
O-S-s-ýeiñ~ (ø event)
for S to keep O awake
-ýeeñ~ (An)
·Taat kanaý ýat wusiýéñ wé katl'úñjaa. All night I was kept awake by
that slow drip.

,

Ý

Dictionary of Tlingit

ýeil

foam
ýeel
·Ýeil yáý ý'ayatee. It's foaming at the mouth.
2

ÝEIT

• awsiýeit | kei anasýét | kei asýétch
s/he bred them | s/he is breeding them | s/he breeds them (regularly).
O-S-s-ýeit~ (ga event)
for S to breed O
-ýeet~ (An)
·Kanóox' áwé kéi anasýít. He is breeding turtles.
• has wudziýeit | kei (ha)s nasýét | kei (ha)s isýétch
they multiplied | they are multiplying | they multiply (regularly).
d-s-ýeit~ (ga event)
for something to multiply, increase in numbers; for animals to produce young,
breed
-ýeet~ (An)
ÝEITL
• wuliýéitl | liýéitl | kei laýéitlch
s/he got lucky | s/he's lucky | s/he gets lucky (regularly).
O-li-ýéitl (ga state)
for O to be blessed, be lucky
·Gu.aal kwshé iwulýéidliñ. Bless you. (Lit: I hope you get lucky.)
ÝEITL'
• áa akawdliýéitl' | áa akwdliýéitl' | --s/he was afraid of it | s/he is afraid of it | ---.
P-x' a-ka-u-S-d-l-ýéitl' (ga state)
for S to be afraid of, fear P
-ýéetl' (An)
·Náakw yís kayaaní ashigóok, áx' ñu.aa akwdliýéitl' ñaa ý'éiý aa
wuteeyí. He knows medicinal plants but he is afraid to give them to anyone.
·Áa akwdliýéitl' wé kaçít tú. He is afraid of the dark.
ÝÉITL'SHÁN
• kawliýéitl'shán | kuliýéitl'shán | kei klaýéitl'shánch
it was scary | it's scary | it gets to be scary (regularly).
O-ka-u-l-ýéitl'shán (ga state)
for O to be scary, dangerous
-ýéetl'shán (An)
·Héen yík héen kanadaayí wáa yateeyi yéix' kuliýéitl'shán nooch.
Sometimes currents in a river are dangerous.
·Tláakw naadaayi héen kuliýéitl'shán. A fast river is dangerous.
ÝEIX'W
• has wooýéix'w | has ýéx'w | has ýéx'wý
they slept | they're sleeping | they sleep (regularly).

,

,

Ý

S-ø-ýéix'w~ (na act)
for (plural) S to sleep, sleep in company with others, go to bed

a ýíji

its mane (esp. the hair on the neck hump of a moose)

ýík

puffin

du ýikshá

his/her shoulder
·Du ýikshá káý yaa anayéin wé jánwu. He is carrying the moutain goat
on his shoulder.

a ýoo

(in) the midst of it; among it
·Kanat'á a ýoo yéi nateech kaxwéiý. Blueberries are usually in the midst
of cranberries.
·Ldakát wooch ýoot has yawdiháa. Everybody came together.

a ýoo aa

some of them
·A ýoo aa ñu.oo woolnáý wooshñáñ has al'óon. Some people hunt the
wren.

du ýooní

his/her relative, friend; his/her tribesman
·Du naaý sitee áwé du ýooní. His tribesman are those of his clan.
·Haa ýooní Anóoshi aaní kaadé ñuwuteenín. Our friend had traveled to
Russia.

a ýooní

one that matches it; an amount that matches it; equivalent to it;
one like it
·A ýoonéet kaýwdiçíx'. I added to it.
·Wáa sá yaýwañaayí a ýoonéet kashaxít! Write what I am saying in
addition to it!
1

ÝOOT'

• aadé aawaýóot' | aadé yaa naýút' | aadé yoo ayaýút'k

he/she/it dragged him/her/it there | he/she/it is dragging him/her/it there |
he/she/it drags him/her/it there (regularly).

P-dé O-S-ø-ýoot'~ (na motion)

for S to drag, pull O (esp. light object or solid, stiff object) to P; for S to pull O in
quick movements to P

·Du çeiwú yaakwdé yaa anaýút'. He is pulling his seine in.

• aadé awsiýóot' | aadé yaa anasýút' | aadé yoo asiýút'k

s/he drug it there | s/he is dragging it there | s/he drags it there (regularly).

P-dé O-S-s-ýoot'~ (na motion)

for S to drag, pull O to P; for S to haul, transport O (by motor power) to P

·Ñu.éex'dei nasýóot' yá kañáshýi! Pack the steamed berries to the
potlatch!

• át aawaýóot' | --- | át yoo ayaýút'k

he/she/it is dragging him/her/it around; he/she/it dragged him/her/it around | --- |
s/he drags it around (regularly).

P-t O-S-ø-ýoot'~ (na motion)

for S to drag, pull O (esp. person) around at P; for S to pull O in quick movement

,

Dictionary of Tlingit

around at P
·X'áan át iwaýóot'i tlél ushk'é. Anger pulling you around is not good.
• shawdliýóot' | shalýóot' | yoo shadliýút'k
s/he sportfished | s/he's sportfishing | s/he sportfishes (regularly).
sha-S-d-l-ýóot' (na act)
for S to fish with rod, sportfish
·Ísh yíkde shalýóot'. She is casting into the deep water hole.
• yan aawaýút' | yánde yaa anaýút' | --s/he pulled it in | s/he is pulling it in | ---.
yan~ O-S-ø-ýoot'~ (ø motion)
for S to drag, pull O (esp. light object or solid, stiff object) in, to shore; for S to pull O in to shore in quick movement
·Ýáaw yan ýút'! Pull the log to shore!
2

ÝOOT'

• aawaýút' | aýút't | --s/he chopped it | s/he is chopping it | ---.
O-S-ø-ýóot'~ (ø act)
for S to chop O (wood); for S to chip O out (with adze)
·Yá kas'úwaa teen a yíkdáý ýút'! Chip the inside out with this chopper!
• akawliýóot' | aklaýút't | yei aklaýóot'ch
s/he chopped it up | s/he's chopping it up | s/he chops it up (regularly).
O-ka-S-l-ýóot' (ça act)
for S to chop up O; for S to split O (wood)
·Gán kañás'ti akawliýóot' wé ý'aan yís. He chopped kindling for the fire.
ÝOOÝ
• aawaýooý | aýooý | yei aýooých
s/he summoned him/her | s/he summons him/her; s/he is summoning him/her | s/he summons him/her (regularly).
O-S-ø-ýooý (ça act)
for S to call, summon O
·Tlék'çaanáý áwé has wuduwaýooý. They called them one by one.
·Çuwakaan ýaýooý nooch ñ'eikaxétl'k kayaaní teen. I always use a bunchberry leaf to call deer.
• shukawliýooý | --- | --s/he composed a song | --- | ---.
shu-ka-S-l-ýooý~ (na event)
for S to call forth a response (from opposite clan, by means of a song); for S to compose a song
·Shí áwé shukñwalaýóoý. I'm going to compose a song.

ýút'aa

adze

du ýúý

her husband
·Tóos' hítdáý áwé du ýúý. Her husband is from the Shark house.

·Ch'a tlákw áwé yéi nateech aý ýúý, ch'u atk'átsk'uý sateeyídáý.
My husband is like this often, and has been even since he was a child.

,

,

« Ýw »
(None.)

,

Ýw

Ý'

« Ý' »
a ý'áak

between them
When followed by the -t postposition (which is required by
positional verbs), the final -k optionally falls out, as in one of the
examples given here.
·Has du ý'áakt wuhaan du káak. His maternal uncle stood between them.
·Has du léelk'w du ý'áat .áa. Their grandmother is sitting between them.

ý'áakw

sockeye or coho salmon that has entered fresh water
·Ý'áakw ý'úýu haa ý'eis sa.í stoox kaanáý! Cook us red sockeye soup on
the stove!
·Ý'áakw hél a kajeiçí ñoostí. The freshwater sockeye doesn't have any
scales.

ý'áal'

skunk cabbage
·Ý'áal' tóox' wutusi.ée. We cooked it in skunk cabbage.

ý'aan

fire
·Ý'aan yeenayát'ch wé yées stoox tóox'. The fire lasts in the new stove.
·Ý'aan wusit'áaý'. The fire is burning hot.

ý'aan

red
·Ý'aan yáý wutuwanéegwál' a yá. We painted the side of it red.
·Ý'aan kakéin haat yéi ýwsiné kasné yís. I brought some red yarn for
knitting.

Ý'AAN
• at uwaý'án | at ý'áan | at ý'áný
s/he dried fish | s/he is drying fish | s/he dries fish (regularly).
at S-ø-ý'aan~ (ø act)
for S to dry (fish, meat) over fire, smoke lightly
·At tooý'aan áyá táakwni yís, kaldáanaañý haa nasteech. We are
smoking fish for the winter because we are usually without money.

ý'aan gook

fireside; by the fire, facing the fire
·Ý'aan gookx' áwé yéi añéech. Around the fire is where people sit.

ý'aan káý túlaa

fire drill, hand drill used to start fires by friction
·Ý'aan káý túlaa tín ý'aan yilayéý! Build a fire with the fire drill!

Ý'AAT'
• --- | kadliý'át' | ----- | they're green (unripe) | ---.
ka-d-l-ý'át' (state)
for berries to be unripe, green and hard
This verb only occurs in the imperfective. Here's an example

,

,

Ý'

sentence: Hél ushk'é duýaayí ch'a yeisú kalý'ádi - ikçwasdéek.
"It's not good to eat them when they're still green - you'll get
constipated."
·Yeisú kadliý'át' wé tléiñw. The berries are still green.

ý'áax'w

ling cod
·Ý'áax'w útlýi áwé yak'éi. Boiled ling cod is good.

du ý'adaa

his/her lips; area around his/her mouth

du ý'adaadzaayí

his/her whiskers
·Tlél ý'adaadzaayí du jee. He doesn't have whiskers.
·Sindi Claus yáý áwé dleit yáý yatee du ý'adaadzaayí. His whiskers
are white like Santa Clause.

a ý'adéex'i

cork, plug

ý'agáax'

prayer
·Ý'agáax' áwé litseen yéi yaawañaa aý léelk'w. My grandparent said that
prayer is powerful.
·Ý'agáax' has du çaneiýíý sitee. Prayer is their salvation.

ý'agáax' daakahídi

house of prayer; church
·Ýʼagáaxʼ daakahídixʼ ali.áých wé çíýʼjaa ñóok. He plays the organ at the
Church.
·Ýʼagáaxʼ daakahídixʼ áwé at kashéeýʼ shí áa dushí. Songs of praise
are sung in church.

ýʼaháat

door
·Wé ýʼaháatde nagú! Go to the door!
·Ýʼaháat kináak áwé át akawsixʼóo, du saayí. He nailed his name above
the door.

du ýʼahéeni

his/her saliva
·Du ýʼahéeni kaawadaa. His saliva is flowing.
·Ýʼahéeni du ýʼéit uwadáa. He is drooling.

ýʼakakeiýí

chain
·Ýʼakakeiýí aan wuduwa.áýw. He was bound with a chain.

ýʼakaséñʼwaa

lipstick
ýʼakaséiñʼu, ýʼadaaséiñʼu (T), ýʼakaséiñʼwaa
·Ýʼaan ýʼakaséñʼwaa yéi aya.óo. She is wearing red lipstick.

du ýʼakooká

in response, reply to him/her; answering him/her;
following his/her train of speech

ýʼalʼdaakeit

small covered box
·Ýʼalʼdaakeit awliyéý. She built a small covered box.

ýʼalʼdaayéeji

sandpiper (shore bird)
·Ýʼalʼdaayéeji éeñt wujixeex. The sandpiper is running around the beach.

ʼ

Ý'

Dictionary of Tlingit

a ý'anaa

in its way; keeping it away; protecting, shielding,
screening from it; blocking it
·A ý'anaa áwé át eehán. You are standing in its way.
·Haa ý'anaatý wuhán, yak'éiyi ñáa! Move out of our way, good man!

ý'aséikw

life; breath
·Du ý'aséigu yaa shunaxíx. He is running out of breath.

ý'astóoý

spit
·Shé a ýoodé ayatéen du ý'astóoýu. He sees blood in his sputum.

du ý'astus'aaçí
ý'asúnjaa

his/her jawbone; jaws

small bubbles (in water)

du ý'ás'

his/her lower jaw, mandible
·Du ý'ás' aawagwál wé ñáa. That man socked him on the jaw.
·Kaxées' teen wóoshdei kdudzixát du ý'ás'. His jaw is held together with
a wire.

du ý'as'guwéis'i

his/her tonsils
·Du ý'as'guwéis'i wuduwaxaash. His tonsils were taken out.

du ý'asheeyí

his/her song
·Anóoshi ý'asheeyí at shí ñóok tóode too.áýjin. We used to hear Russian
songs on the radio.

Ý'atas'aañ

Eskimo
·Yá Ý'atas'aañ ñúnáý ñusi.áat'i yéix' áwé yéi has yatee. Eskimos live
in a very cold place.

ý'atl'ooñ

cold sore
·Ý'atl'ooñ du jeewú. She has an ulcer inside her mouth.

ý'awool

doorway
·Wé ý'awool yinaat hán. She is standing in the doorway.

ý'awool kayáashi

porch; patio
·Ý'awool kayáashi ká áwé át .áa wé shaawát. The woman is sitting
around on the porch.

du ý'aýán

at hand (for him/her to eat or drink)
du ý'aýáni
·Du ý'aýáni yéi awsinei wé atýá. The food that was made for him was
placed close at hand.

a ý'aýéedli

its trim, trimming
·K'idéin aaý xásh wé t'áa at ý'aýéedli! Cut the trimming off the board
good!
·Wé çuwakaan dleeyí at ý'aýéedli k'idéin aaý xásh, téiý sákw! Cut
the trimming off the deer meat well for the broth!

'

'

Ý'

du ý'ayáý

according to his/her words, instructions
·Du ý'ayáý awliyéý wé kootéeyaa. He made the totem according to his
instructions.

du ý'ayee

ready, waiting for him/her to eat, drink; waiting for him/her to
speak or finish speaking
·Du ý'ayee yan yéi wdudzinéi. They set a place for him to eat.

ý'ayeit

food container; pot or pan; dish, large bowl

·Yak'éiyi ý'ayeit áwé du jeewú aý aat. My paternal aunt has nice dishes.

du ý'a.eetí

his/her food scraps, left-over food; crumbs of food left or
scattered where s/he has eaten

du ý'é

his/her mouth
·Çáý dleeyí gé i ý'é yak'éi? Does rabbit meat taste good to you?
·Yat'aayi héen du ñáawu ý'éit awsi.ín. She gave her husband's clan
brother coffee.

a ý'é

its mouth, opening
·A ý'éináý áwé kadul.eesh wé ñáas' kaadéi wé saak. Those hooligan
are strung through the mouth on the stick.

Ý'EEL'
• át wushiý'éel' | --- | át yoo shiý'íl'k
he/she/it is sliding around; he/she/it slid around | --- | he/she/it slides around
(regularly).
P-t O-sh-ý'éel'~ (na motion)
for O to slip, slide around at P
·Du keey shakanóox'u áwé tlei át nashý'íl'ch. His kneecap slides
around.
• át wushiý'íl' | aadé yaa nashý'íl' | --he/she/it slid there | he/she/it is sliding there | ---.
P-t~ O-sh-ý'éel'~ (ø motion)
for O to slip, slide to P
·Héent wushiý'íl'. He slipped into the water.
• kawshiý'íl'k | kashiý'íl'k | --it was slippery | it's slippery | ---.
ka-sh-ý'íl'k (state)
for something to be slippery (oil, ice, wet rocks, etc.)
·Tlél tlaý kooshý'íl'k yá kaxwaan. It's not very slippery with this frost.
• wushiý'éel' | yei nashý'íl' | yei ishý'éel'ch
s/he slipped | s/he is slipping | s/he slips (regularly).
O-sh-ý'éel' (ça event)
for O to slip, slide
Note a couple of common metaphorical uses of this verb.
Wushiý'éel' can be used to mean "S/he fell off the wagon" (as in
started drinking again). Another common expression is: Átk'

,

aheení wushiýéel' which means "s/he stopped believing, lost faith".

ý'éen

wall crest; wall screen

a ý'éeshi

its dried flesh, strips (of fish)
·L'ook at ý'éeshi áwé yak'éi. Coho salmon dryfish is good.
·Tsaa eeýí teen yak'éi at ý'éeshi. Seal oil is good with dryfish.

at ý'éeshi

dry fish

Ý'EEX'
• áý kawliý'éex' | --- | áý yoo kaliý'íx'k
he/she/it is stuck there | --- | he/she/it gets stuck there (regularly).
P-ý O-ka-l-ý'éex'~ (na motion)
for O to get stuck, be squeezed at P
Note that this verb gives a literal meaning only. It would be used to indicate that someone is stuck in a tight space, but not in the non-literal sense used in phrases such as "stuck at home" or "stuck there (due to weather)", etc.
·A ý'áakx' tsé ikanalý'éex'! Don't get stuck between it now!

ý'éex'w

wedge, shim

ý'éex'wál'

safety pin
ý'éigwál'

ý'éigwál'

safety pin
ý'éex'wál'

a ý'éináý

through its mouth
·Lingít ý'éináý kashxeet áwé ashigóok. He knows how to write in the Tlingit language.

ý'eint'áax'aa

labret, lip plug
·Ch'áakw ý'eint'áax'aa shaawát ý'é yéi ndu.eich. Long ago women would wear a labret.

du ý'eis

for him/her to eat or drink
·Dei káx' yéi jinéiyi ý'eis has at gawdzi.ée wé aantñeení. The townspeople cooked food for the people working on the road.
·Du kéilk' du ý'eis at wusi.ée. His niece cooked for him.

ý'eis'awáa

willow ptarmigan; pigeon
·Ý'eis'awáa l'eiýí kulitées'shan nooch. The dance of the ptarmigan is always a wonder to behold.

ý'éi shadagutýi lítaa

knife with fold-in blade
·Dleit ñáach áwé awliyéý wé ý'éi shadagutýi lítaa. The white man invented the pocket knife.

,

,

Ý'

ý'éishx'w

bluejay, Stellar's jay
ý'éishk'w (C)
·Ý'éishx'w áwé nageich ñutaan ítdáý. After the summer is over there are a lot of bluejays
·A kaséiñ'u ý'éishx'w kayaaý sitee. The color is in the likeness of a bluejay.

ý'éishx'w

dark blue

du ý'eitákw

his/her heel
·Du ý'eitákw yanéekw. His heel hurts.

Ý'EIÝ'
• awliý'éý' | --- | --he/she/it burned him/her/it | --- | ---.
O-S-l-ý'éiý'~ (ø event)

for S to burn O (flesh, skin); for S to scald O

-ý'éeý'~ (An)

·Du tl'eñshá áwé awliý'éý' wé stoox káx'. He burned his fingertip on the stove.

• wudiý'éý' | --- | daý'éý'ý

s/he got burned | --- | s/he gets burned (regularly).

O-d-ý'éiý'~ (ø event)

for O to be burned (of flesh, skin), become shriveled and brittle through burning

-ý'éeý'~ (An)

·Du jikóol wudiý'íý'. The back of his hand was burned.

·Du jiwán wudiý'íý'. The outside edge of her hand was burned.

ý'íx'

eggs (of eels, etc.)

du ý'óol'

his/her belly, paunch

·Du ý'óol' néekw nooch. His belly always hurts.

ý'oon

soft brown wood for tanning dye

·Ý'oon yéi ndu.eich wé at doogú kaséiñ'w yís. Soft brown wood is used for coloring the skin.

ý'óon

fur seal

du ý'oos

his/her foot, leg

·Çagaan át ý'oos uwatsóow. Sun rays are shining on it. (Lit: The sun is poking its feet out.)

·Wooshdakádin ý'oosdé awdiyiñ du téeli. He put his shoes on the wrong feet.

a ý'oosí

its leg

·A ý'oosí aaý aawaxásh wé shaawátch. The woman cut the legs off.

·A ý'oosí k'idéin át kalatéý'! Screw the leg on it good!

du ý'usgoosh

his/her big toe

·Du ý'usgoosh áwé wudlix'ís. His big toe is swollen.

'

Ý'

ý'uskeit

dancing leggings; leggings for climbing

du ý'ustáak
du ý'ust'ákl'i

sole of his/her foot
knob on outer side of his/her ankle

du ý'ustl'eeñ

his/her toe
du ý'ustl'eiñ

du ý'ustl'eiñ

his/her toe
du ý'ustl'eeñ

du ý'usyee

under his/her feet
·I yádi aý ý'usyeet wudiçwáat'. Your child is crawling around under my feet.

a ý'usyee

at the foot of it
·I téeli yee.át ý'usyeex' yéi na.oo! Put your shoes at the foot of the bed!

du ý'us.eetí

his/her footprint

a ý'us.eetí

its tracks
·Aasgutóot wugoodí, dzísk'w ý'us.eetí awsiteen. He saw moose tracks when he was walking in the woods.
·Xóots ý'us.eetí áwé awsiteen wé kík'i aa. The younger one saw the bear tracks.

a ý'úýu

its flesh (of fish)
·Ý'áakw ý'úýu haa ý'eis sa.í stoox kaanáý! Cook us red sockeye soup on the stove!

'

'

Ý'w

« Ý'w »
ý'wáal'
ý'waash

down (feathers)
sea urchin

ý'wáat'

Dolly Varden trout
·Ý'wáat' héen táakde has ayatéen. They see trout in the river.
·Ý'wáat tlénx' dust'eiý Çaat Héenidáý. People catch big trout at Garteeni.

ý'wéinaa

roasting stick (split so that the meat can be inserted; the end is

then bound)

'

« Y »
yá

this (right here)
yáa
·Ñúnáý woo.aat gis'óoñ yá xáanaa. The Northern Lights are really moving about this evening.
·Kaldaaçéináý yaa gaýtooñóoý, tlél çwadlaan yá éiý' yík. We will travel along slowly, it's not deep in this slough.

du yá

his/her face
When the postposition -x' is added to du yá, the vowel
becomes long and the -x' optionally falls out, producing: du yáa.
This accounts for the forms seen in the examples given here.
·Xóosht' has du yáa yéi has ana.eich yaa (ha)s jinda.ádi. The dark burnt ashes would be put on their faces when going to war.
·Ñaa yáý kei jisatánch wáadishgaa. The priest blesses people.

a yá

face, (vertical) side, (vertical) surface of it
·Ý'aan yáý wutuwanéegwál' a yá. We painted the side of it red.
·Çíl' yáý kei naltl'ét' wé yadák'w. The young boy is climbing the cliff face.

yaa

along; down
·Yaa ntoo.ádi áwé, daak wudzigít yaý akaawaýích wutuwa.ini kaneilts'ákw. When we were walking along, she fell down and spilled all the swamp currants we picked.
·Kaldaaçéináý yaa gaýtooñóoý, tlél çwadlaan yá éiý' yík. We will travel along slowly, it's not deep in this slough.

yaa

trout (sea)

1

YAA

• aadáý kawdiyaa | --- | --he/she/it disappeared from there | --- | ---.
P-dáý O-ka-di-yaa~ (na motion)
for O to disappear from P; for O to move (often almost imperceptably) from P;
for O to travel (indefinite as to method) from P
·Tle yeedát yáatý haa kaguýdayáa. We need to leave from here right now.

• --- | oowayáa | ----- | it looks like it | ---.
O-S-u-ø-yaa~ (ça state)
for S to resemble, look like O; for S to be almost identical with O
This verb can be a little confusing because of the thematic
prefix u-, which contracts with the object prefix a- (and the
classifier ya-), producing the prefix oowa- in the imperfective. Note
that this only happens when the subject and object are both third
person (and in this case, non-human). For third person

,

,

Y

human objects, the object pronoun ash is preferred. For example:
ash uwayáa "s/he looks like him/her." Since there's no object
prefix a- here
(which is used for non-human
objects), the prefix is uwa- in the
imperfective. Here's another example: Aý kéek' ýat uwayáa "My
little sister looks like me." Here's an example sentence with a first
person subject:
Aý tláa ýwaayáa "I look like my
mother." Note that the thematic
prefix u- contracts with the first
person subject prefix (and the
classifier ya-), producing ýwaa-. To say "they look like each other",
the pronoun wooch is used along with the d- classifier: wooch has
wudiyáa. In the negative, this verb can take on the meaning
"improper". For example: tlél oowaa "it's not right; it's not proper"
OR "it doesn't look like it."
·Tínx kaxwéiý oowayáa tl'átgi káx' ñu.aa ka.éiý. Bearberries look like
cranberries but they grow on the ground.
·Tléil oowaa wé aan káa ñududziteeyi yoo ý'atánk géide
ñudunoogú. It is wrong to act against the law of the land.
• yan kawdiyáa | --- | yaý kadayaa
it happened | --- | it happens (regularly).
yan~ ka-di-yaa~ (ø motion)
for an event to happen, take place
·Hú ñu.aa áyá ch'a çóot yéide yan kawdiyáa aý tláa, du éeshch
áyá du yát saa uwatí Shaaxeidi Tláa. But with my mother it happened
differently, because her father named her Shaaxeidi Tláa.
2

YAA

• aawayaa | yaa anayáan / yaa anayéin | kei ayeich
he/she/it carried it on his/her/its back | he/she/it is carrying in on his/her/its back
| he/she/it carries it on his/her/its back (regularly).
O-S-ø-yaa~ (ga event)
for S to carry O on back; for S to pack O

In the progressive aspect, there is dialect variation between
yaa anayáan and yaa anayéin and in the perfective habitual there
is dialect variation between agayáach and agayéich.
·Du ýikshá káý yaa anayéin wé jánwu. He is carrying the moutain goat
on his shoulder.
·Dáñde ñákw aawayaa i léelk'w. Your grandmother died. (Lit: Your
grandmother took her basket into the woods).
• ashawsiyaa | --- | yoo ashasiyéik
s/he anchored the boat | --- | s/he anchors the boat (regularly).
O-sha-S-s-yaa~ (na event)
for S to anchor O

,

Dictionary of Tlingit

• áý akaawayaa | áý yei akanayéin | áý yei akayéich
s/he spread it out | s/he's spreading it out | s/he spreads it out (regularly).
P-ý O-ka-S-ø-yaa~ (ça motion)
for S to spread out, unfold, lay out (singular) O along P
·Kinguchwáan x'óowu du káý kawduwayaa. He was covered with a
Hudson Bay blanket.
• shawdziyaa | --- | shasyéiý
s/he anchored | --- | s/he anchors (regularly).
sha-S-d-s-yaa~ (na event)
for S to anchor, lower anchor
·Déili áa has shawdziyaa. They anchored in a harbor.
• at wooyaa | yaa at nayáan / yaa at nayéin | kei at

yeich
he/she/it carried things on his/her/its back | he/she/it is carrying things on
his/her/its back | he/she/it carries things on his/her/its back (regularly).
at S-ø-yaa~ (ga event)
for S to carry things on back; for S to pack things
In the progressive aspect, there is dialect variation between
yaa at nayáan and yaa at nayéin. Both are correct.
·Yaa at nayáan wé gukkudayáat'. The donkey is packing things.

yaa at naskwéini
yáa at wooné

student; learner
respect

yaadachóon

straight ahead; directly ahead
yaadechóon (C)

yaak

mussel

yaakw

boat, canoe
·Wé yéi kuwooý'u yaakw yá yéil a káa gaýtoonéegwál'. We will paint a
raven on the widest side of the skiff.
·Yaý kei kçwadláaý'w wé yaakw. The boat will get stuck on the beach.

Yaakwdáat

Yakutat
·Sgóonwaan atyátx'i has shayadihéin Yaakwdáatx'. There are a lot of

school children in Yakutat.
·Tleidahéen áwé Yaakwdáatt aa wlihásh wé kanóox'. One time a turtle floated to Yakutat.

yaakw ýuká

deck of a boat
·Anóoshi aan kwéiyi áwé át wududziyíñ wé s'ísaa yaakw ýuká. They raised a Russian flag on the deck of that sailboat.

yaakw ýukahídi

cabin (of boat); pilot house

yaakw yasatáni

captain (of a boat)

yaakw yík

in the boat

,

,

yaakw yiks'ísayi

Y

sail

yaa ñudzigéiyi ts'ats'ée

pigeon
·Neek ash atláx'w yaa ñudzigéiyi ts'ats'ée. Pigeons carry messages.

yaan

hunger

du yaanaayí
ýáanadi

his/her enemy, adversary
backpack; pack sack

a yáanáý

beyond it, more than it; too much; excessively
·A yáanáý áwé kayliséñ'w yá néegwál'. You tinted this paint too much.
·A yáanáý yaawatáa. She slept in.

yaana.eit

wild celery
Warning: contains furanocoumarins which can cause rash
and edema

yaash ká

smokehouse shelf

YAAT'
• --- | dliyát'x' | ----- | they're long | ---.
d-l-yát'x' (ga state)
for (plural, general) objects to be long
·Dliyát'x' du waý'aýéiý'u. Her eyelashes are long.
• wooyáat' | yayát' | yát'ý
it became long | it is long | it becomes long (regularly).
ø-yáat'~ (na state)
for an object (usually stick-like) to be long
·Dagwatgiyáa lú yayát' ña yéi kwlisáa. A hummingbird's beak is long and
skinny.
• wuliyát' | liyát' | --it became long | it's long | ---.
l-yát' (na state)
for something to be long (of time or physical objects)
Speakers accept this verb with either a short, high stem
-yát' (as given here) or a long, high stem -yáat' throughout the
paradigm.
·S'eek l'eedí tléil ulyát'. A black bear's tail is short.
• yeeywooyáat' | yeeyayát' | yeeyát'ý
it was long (time) | it's long (time) | it's long (time) (regularly).
yee-ø-yáat'~ (na state)
for something to be long (of time)
·I tuwáx' yeewooyáat' yóo ñu.éex'. You thought the potlach was long.
·Ý'aan yeenayát'ch wé yées stoox tóox'. The fire lasts in the new stove.
• yéi kaawayáat' | yéi koowáat' | yéi kuwát'ý
it got that long | it is that long | it gets that long (regularly).

,

Dictionary of Tlingit

(yéi) ka-u-ø-yáat'~ (na state)
for an object (usually stick-like) to be (so) long
·Jinkaat ña gooshúñ ñaa ý'oos yéi koowáat' du yaagú. Her boat is
nineteen feet long.
• --- | yéi kwliyáat' | ----- | it's that long | ---.
(yéi) ka-u-l-yáat' (na state)
for a general object to be (so) long
·Tléix' ñaa ý'oos yéi kwliyáat' wé tíx'. That rope is one foot long.
·Tleidooshú ñaa ý'oos yéi kwliyáat' wé kaay. That measuring stick is six
feet long.

yaaw

herring
·Yaaw xídlaa yéi wdu.oowú, tlél uldzée nooch. Using a herring rake is
not difficult.

yaaý

into a boat, vehicle

yáay

whale
·S'igeidí ña yáay a káa kashaxít wé at doogú x'óow! Draw a Beaver
and whale design on the leather blanket!
·Wé yáay yaý woodláaý'w. The whale is stuck on the beach.

a yaayí

one of them (a pair)
·Hél gé a yaayí ñoostí? Is the matching pair missing?
·Du guk.ádi yaayí ñut akaawaçéex'. She lost one of her earrings.

yáay ý'axéni
yaa.aanuné

baleen; whalebone
oldsquaw duck

du yadák'u

his/her boyfriend
·"Iýsiýán," yoo ayawsiñaa du yadák'u. She told her boyfriend, "I love
you."

yadák'w

young man (not married)
·Tléi a x'aant áwé daañ wudiçwát' wé yadák'w. The young boy crawled
out the limb.
·Çíl' yáý kei naltl'ét' wé yadák'w. The young boy is climbing the cliff face.

yadak'wátsk'u

boy
·Wé yadak'wátsk'u chooneit tín áwé aawat'úk wé ts'ítskw. The young
boy shot the bird with a barbed arrow.

du yádi

his/her child
·I yádi aý ý'usyeet wudiçwáat'. Your child is crawling around under my
feet.
·Kast'áat' tlein áwé wóoshde añéis' aý yádi jeeyís. She is sewing
together a big quilt for my child.

yagee (T)

day, afternoon
yakyee (AtT), yagiyee

,

,

Y

·Du séek' yageeyí kayís áwé gáaxw awsi.ée. She cooked a duck for her
daughter's birthday.

yagiyee

day, afternoon
yakyee, yagee (T)
·Tleidooshú çuwakaan wutusiteen tléix' yagiyee. We saw six deer one
day.
·Daýadooshú yagiyee shunaaxéex aaçáa daak wusitani yé. It has
been raining for seven days.

yagootl

young deer

yagúnl'

growth on the face

du yahaayí

his/her soul (of departed person)
·Yéi sh kadulneek a yahaayí ñudzitee dáanaa. They say money has a spirit.

du yahaayí

his/her shadow; image
·Wé tóonáý ñaateen kaadé awsiteen du yahaayí. He saw his image in the mirror.
·Du eetí a kaýyeet akawlis'íx'w ñaa yahaayí wé shaatk'átsk'u. The young girl pasted a photo on the ceiling of her room.

yaka.óot'

button
yuka.óot', waka.óot'
·Gunýaa yaka.óot' aawa.oo. She bought abalone buttons.
·Gunýaa yaka.óot' du l.uljíni kát akaawañáa. She sewed the abalone buttons on her vest.

yaka.óot' x'óow

button blanket
yuka.óot' x'óow
·Yaka.óot' x'óow aawañáa du séek' jeeyís. She sewed a button blanket for her daughter.
·T'ooch' ña ý'aan yáý yatee wé yaka.óot' x'óow. That button blanket is black and red.

du yakçwahéiyagu
yakyee

his/her spirit

day, afternoon
yagiyee, yagee (T)

yakw daa.ideidí
yakwteiyí
yakwtlénx'

shell of a boat

tricks, sleight of hand; juggling
cruise ship; large ship

yakwyádi

skiff; small boat; flat-bottom canoe
·Yaakwdáatx' áwé yakwyádi kát át ñuyaawagoowún héen kát.
People used to travel around in flat-bottomed canoes in the rivers in Yakutat.

du yañáawu

his/her partner

,

Dictionary of Tlingit

yalooleit

cockle

yan~

ashore, onto ground; to rest
·Wé té tlein a kaháadi káa yan tán! Put that large rock on top of its cover!
·Ñaa ooý yéi daanéiyi yís sgóon yan ashawlihík She finished dentistry school.

yán

hemlock
·Yán aas daadáý kayeiý áwé átý gaçilayéiý s'agwáat kaséñ'ýu sákw. Shavings from a hemlock tree is what you will use for the brown dye.

yán

shore; land

a yanáa

over it, covering it (a container or something with an opening)
·Aý ñ'wádli yanáak aa tsé ñut gaytáan! Don't misplace my pot cover!
·Wé kóoñ kax'ás'ti a yanáa yan aawatán. He put plywood over the pit in the ground.

yanaý

underground
yaanaý

a yana.áat'ani

its lid, cover (of pot, etc.)
a yana.áat'i (T)
·Goosú á yana.áat'ani wé s'áaw a kát isa.eeyi ñ'wátl? Where is the cover for the pot you're cooking the crab in?
·Wé ñ'wátl yana.áat'ani ñut ýwaataan. I misplaced the lid for the pot.

yánde át

west wind; wind blowing ashore

yaneis'í (T)

face cream; cold cream

yaneis'

yanshuká

campsite; (out in) camp; (out in) the bush, wilderness
·Yanshukáx' áwé k'idéin wutuliyéý yá ñ'anáaýán. We built the fence
really well out here in the wilderness.

yanwáat

adult; elder

yanxoon

pile of driftwood, driftlogs; snag pile

Yanyeidí

Yanyeidí, locally known as "Bear"; a clan of the Eagle moiety
whose principal crest is the Brown Bear
·Çooch Yanyeidí ñaa at oohéini áwé. The Wolf crest is the property of the
Yanyeidí Clan.

YÁT
• ash kawdliyát | ash koolyát | yóo ash koodliyátk
s/he played | s/he is playing | s/he plays (regularly).
ash ka-u-S-d-l-yát (na act)
for S to play (esp. active games)
·Kooch'éit'aa áwé aan has ash koolyát wé atyátx'i. The children are

'

'

Y

playing with a ball.
·Tlél uýganñáas' teen ash kayeelyádiñ! Don't play with matches!

du yátx'i

his/her children

yat'aayi héen

coffee; hot water
·Yat'aayi héen a káa yéi nay.oo wéi a kát yadu.us'ku át! You all put
hot water in the wash basin!
·Yat'aayi héen du ñáawu ý'éit awsi.ín. She gave her husband's clan
brother coffee.

du yat'ákw

his/her temple; upper side of his/her face (from the
cheekbones to the top of the head)

du yat'éik

behind his/her back, where s/he can't see

du yat'éináý
yawéinaa

in secret (where nobody can see); away from people's view
face powder

yáxwch'

sea otter
yúxch' (C)
·Yáxwch'i doogú ý'alitseen. Sea otter fur is valuable.
·Ñ'alkátsk yáxwch'ich yaý yawsiýáa haa aaní kaadáý. The sea otter
has devoured the yellowneck clams on our land.

yáxwch'i yaakw

small canoe with high carved prow

yáxch' yaakw

yaý

to completion

a yáý

like it, in accordance with it, as much as it
·Yáa a daat x'úx' yáý áwé a daax' yéi jiýwaanei. I worked on it
according to the book.
·L át yáý ñoonook. He doesn't act normal.

yaýak'áaw

its crosspiece (of boat, snowshoe); thwart (of boat)
·Wéi yaakw yaýak'áaw kas'éet áa yéi du.oowú, k'idéin yéi
aguýlasháat. If a screw is put in the thwart of the boat, it will hold pretty well.

yaý at çwakú

saying, proverb; event that is so common it has become a
saying or proverb
yaý et çwakú (C)

yaýté
yayéinaa

Big Dipper; Ursa Major
whetstone

a yayík

sound, noise of it (something whose identity is unknown)
·A yayík gé iya.áých wé xóots héen yaaý dé. Do you hear the brown
bears by the water?
·Sagú yáý ñaa yayík du.aýji nooch héendei yaa ana.ádi. Men's voices
would always sound happy when they went to the sea.

,

getting ready for it; in anticipation of it

a ya.áak

room, space, place for it; time for it; chance, opportunity for it
·Haadéi at kagaýdujéil, a ya.áak x'wán yéi nasné! Make sure you make room, they will be bringing it all!
·Dáýnáý ñáa ya.áak áwé. It's wide enough for two people.

yé

place; way
This noun is unique in that it is very limited in its use and occurs mostly in attributive clauses.
·Kaçakl'eedí ldakát yéix' kanas.éich. Yarrow grows all over.
·A géide yoo ý'ayatánk wé aadé át kadu.aañw yé. He is speaking out against the proposed decision.

yee

your (plural) [possessive]
·Yá ñut'aayçáa gági ugootch yee éesh. During the warm season your father would come out.
·Ñúnáý wé yee woo.éex'i aa tsú yee ýoo yéi kçwatée toowú k'é teen.
Your hostess will welcome you all as well. (Lit: Your hostess will be among you all with good feelings.)

yee

you (plural) [object]
·Wooch teený yee nastí! Stay together!

yee-

you (plural) [subject]
yi·Yeeytéen has du téiý' tóotý áyá toodé has yee uwaxích haa ñu.éex'i. You all can see that our hosts thank you from their hearts.

a yee

inside it (a building)
·Ñuwduwa.éex' ANB hall yeedéi. People were invited to the ANB hall.
·Jikañáas' káý ashayaawatée wé çaat atx'aan hídi yeex'. She hung the sockeye salmon on the stick in the smokehouse.

YEECH

• anáñ

kawdliyeech | anáñ yaa kanalyích | anáñ yoo
kadliyíchk

they flew away from it | they are flying away from it | they fly away from it
(regularly).
P-náñ ka-d-l-yeech~ (na motion)
for creatures (that flap wings visibly) to fly away from P
·Dunáñ kawdliyeech wé káax'. The grouse flew away from him.
• át kawdliyeech | --- | at yoo kadliyíchk
they're flying around; they flew around | --- | they fly around (regularly).
P-t ka-d-l-yeech~ (na motion)
for creatures (that flap wings visibly) to fly around at P
·Ts'axweil át kawdliyeech. Crows are flying around.
·Gijook wéit kawdliyeech. Hawks are flying around there.

,

,

Y

• át kawdliyích | aadé yaa kanalyích | áý kalyeech
they flew there | they are flying there | they fly there (regularly).
P-t~ ka-d-l-yeech~ (ø motion)
for creatures (that flap wings visibly) to fly to P
·Gus'yadóoli taakw.eetíx' haaý kalyeech. Sandpipers fly here in the early
summer.
·Ñaashashýáaw taakw.eetíx' haaý kalyeech. The dragonflies come in
the summer time.

yeedát

now
yeedét (C)
·Çunayéide a daat sh tudinook yeedát. He feels differently about it now.
·Tle yeedát yáatý haa kaguýdayáa. We need to leave from here right now.

a yeeçáa

waiting for it
a yiçáa
·X'úx' wuýáax'u yeeçáa áyá tooñéen. We are waiting in anticipation of the
mail delivery.
·Gáanu hás, i yeeçáaý has sitee. They are outside waiting for you.

yeeñ

down to beach, shore
yeiñ, eeñ
1

YEEÑ

• át awsiyíñ | aadé yaa anasyíñ | áý asyeeñ
s/he pulled it up there | s/he is pulling it up there | s/he pulls it up there (regularly).
P-t~ O-S-s-yeeñ~ (ø motion)
for S to pull, hoist O up to P
·Anóoshi aan kwéiyi áwé át wududziyíñ wé s'ísaa yaakw ýuká. They raised a Russian flag on the deck of that sailboat.
• kei awsiyíñ | kei anasyíñ | kei asyíñch
s/he pulled it up | s/he is pulling it up | s/he pulls it up (regularly).
kei O-S-s-yeeñ~ (ø motion)
for S to pull, haul O (esp. of line) up; for S to hoist O up
• ý'oosdé awdiyíñ | ý'oosdé adayeeñ | ý'oosý adayíñý
s/he put them on | s/he's putting them on | s/he puts them on (regularly).
ý'oos-dé a-S-d-yeeñ~ (ø act)
for S to put on, pull on O (shoes, trousers)
Note that the postposition -dé changes to -ý in the imperative and repetitive imperfective forms.
·Tuñ'atáal ý'oosdé awdiyíñ. He put on his pants.
·Wooshdakádin ý'oosdé awdiyíñ du téeli. He put his shoes on the wrong feet.
2

YEEÑ

• aawayeeñ | --- | kei ayíñch
he/she/it bit him/her/it | --- | he/she/it bites him/her/it (regularly).

,

Y

Dictionary of Tlingit

O-S-ø-yeeñ~ (ga event)
for S to bite O; for S to carry O in mouth (of animal)
·Igayeiñ tsá wé keitl! Don't let the dog bite you!

a yeen
yees

(sometime) during it (period of time)
stone axe

yées

new; young; fresh
·Ý'aan yeenayát'ch wé yées stoox tóox'. The fire lasts in the new stove.
·Wé yées shaawát du shaatk'íý sitee. That young woman is his girlfriend.

yées ñu.oo
yées wáat

young adult(s); young people
young adult

yees'

scraper for hemlock bark

yées'

mussel (large mussel on stormy coast, used for scraping)

YEESH
• aaý kei aawayísh | --- | --s/he pulled it out of there | --- | ---.
P-dáý kei O-S-ø-yeesh~ (ø motion)
for S to pull O (a fairly light object) out of P
This verb would be used to talk about such things as
pulling out a sliver, opening a window (by pushing it up), pulling a
tooth, or pulling the sheets off a bed.
·Sheey kañáas'i du jíndáý kei aawayísh. She pulled a splinter out of her
hand.
• a káý aawayeesh | a káý yei anayísh | a káý yei

ayíshch
s/he pulled it over him/her/it | s/he is pulling it over him/her/it | s/he pulls it over
him/her/it (regularly).
N káý O-S-ø-yeesh~ (ça motion)
for S to pull O (fairly light object) over N; for S to cover N with O
Note that the verb in the example sentence below has the
ya- thematic prefix, meaning "face".

·Du gúk káy̓ ayaawayeesh du sadaat'aayí. She pulled her scarf down over her ears.

yéesh

leech; bloodsucker

du yéet

his/her son, cousin
·Du kíkt hán wé du yéet. His son is standing beside him.
·Kashxeedíy̓ sitee haa yéet. Our son is a scribe.

yeewháan

you (plural) [independent]

a yee.ádi

receptacle for it
·A yee.ádi gataan sháchgi tléiçu yís! Carry a container for swamp berries!

,

,

Y

yee.át

mattress; bedding
·I téeli yee.át y̓'usyeex' yéi na.oo! Put your shoes at the foot of the bed!
·I yee.ádi ká yís áyá yá x'óow. This blanket is to put on top of your bed.

yei

down; out of boat, vehicle
yéi

yéi

thus, specifically
yóo
·Ña y̓át tsú ay̓ toowú yak'éi yaa a káa yéi y̓at guçwateeyí yaa
Lingíty̓ y̓at sateeyí. And I too am thankful that I'm part of this being that I'm Lingít.
·Téil yéi aya.óo at doogú aklas'éñy̓i yís. She is using dry wood for smoking that hide.

a yeidí

its price, value; the money from the sale of it

·A ñín aý jee koogéi wé k'oodás' yeidí. I have less than the price of that shirt.

yéi jiné

work, job
·Çalsaayít áwé du yéi jineiyí a náñ woogoot. She went away from her work so that she could rest.
·Aý yéi jineiyí áwé kaxíl'aa k'idéin daané. My job is to clean erasers.

yéi jinéiyi

worker

2

YEIK

• --- | liyék | ----- | it holds more | ---.
l-yék (ga state)
for something to hold more, contain more; for something to hold a lot
This verb only occurs in the imperfective. To specify the
amount that something holds, state the amount followed by yáý,
as in: tléix' gúx'aa yáý liyék "it holds one cup". Two more examples
of this verb in context are: yáat'aa yáanáý liyék wéit'aa "this one
holds more than that one" and: wooch yáý liyék "they hold the
same amount".
·Tléix' ñ'ateil yáý áwé liyék wéi xén. That plastic container can hold one gallon.

yéik

Indian doctor's spirit

YEIL
• sh ñ'awdliyél | --- | sh ñ'alyélý
s/he lied | --- | s/he lies (regularly).
sh ñ'a-S-d-l-yéil~ (ø event)
for S to lie, decieve
To specify who one is lying to, use: N een "to N". For
example: Du een sh ñ'awdliyél "s/he lied to him/her".

,

Dictionary of Tlingit

yéil

raven
·Yaa uháan haa naaý sitee, Yéil áyá haa shukáý sitee. For our clan,
Raven is our main crest.
·Ýáat yís áwé has akawliník Yéilch, wé kéidladi ña kaçeet. Raven
talked the seagull and loon out of the salmon.

yéil kawóodi

petrified coral

yéil kooýétl'aa
yéil ts'áaxu

scarecrow
limpet

YEIL'
• kawduwayél' | yaa kanduyél' | kaduyél'ý
it's calm | it's calming down | it calms down (regularly).
ka-du-ø-yéil'~ (ø event)
for something (esp. bodies of water) to be calm, peaceful
·Áa Tlein káa kawduwayél'. It is calm on Atlin Lake.
• ñukawduwayél' | yaa ñukanduyél' | ñukaduyél'ý
the weather is calm | the weather is calming down | the weather calms down
(regularly).
ñu-ka-du-yéil'~ (ø event)
for the weather to be calm, peaceful, without storm
·Ñukawduwayél' áyá - naakéede naýtooñooý. It's calm out - let's go up
the bay.
·Ñukawduyéil'i áwé Galyéýdei çunayéi uñooých wéi yaakw tlein.
The big boat would start traveling to the Kahliyet River when the weather was
calm.

yéil'

elderberry

YEIN
• ashakawliyén | --- | ashaklayéný
s/he's waving it | --- | s/he waves it (regularly).
O-sha-ka-S-l-yéin~ (ø event)
for S to wag O (tail); for S to wave O (hand, etc.); for S to twirl, spin O around
above one's head
·Aan kwéiyi shakawdudliyén. Someone is waving a flag.
·Du tl'eeñ áwé aý yáa ash akaawliyén. He's shaking his finger at me.

yéin

sea cucumber

yeis

fall; autumn
·Kalaçéi nooch aasgutú yeist ñuwuhaayí. The forest is brilliant when fall comes.

yeisú

just now; just then; still; yet
·Ý'éidei kakçilatiý' yé ch'a yeisú lingít áwu. There are still people in the place you are locking.
·Yeisú kadliý'át' wé tléiñw. The berries are still green.

'

'

Y

YEIS'
• kawdiyés' | --- | kadayés'ý
he/she/it is bruised | --- | he/she/it buises easily.
O-ka-d-yéis'~ (ø event)
for O to be colored, discolored, bruised
·Ý'aan yáý kawdiyés' wé çáach. The rug is colored red.
·Du káak' wudix'ís' ña kawdiyés'. His forehead is swollen and bruised.
1

YEIÝ

• akaawayéý | akayéiý | akayéýý
s/he whittled it | s/he is whittling it | s/he whittles it (regularly).
O-ka-S-ø-yeiý~ (ø act)
for S to whittle, plane O; for S to make O (kindling)
·Aankayéýaa tín akaawayéý. He planed it with a plane.
·Du tséegi a lú akaawayéý. He sharpened the point of his barbecue stick.
• átý awliyéý | átý alyéiý | átý alyéýý
s/he used it for it | s/he is using it for it | s/he uses it for it (regularly).
P-ý O-S-l-yeiý~ (ø act)
for S to use O for P; for S to make O into P
·Ýéel yéi ndu.eich hítý dulyeiýí. Granite is used to build a house.
·Kaçakl'eedí náakwý dulyéiý. Yarrow is used for medicine.
• awliyéý | alyéiý | --s/he built it | s/he is building it | ---.
O-S-l-yeiý~ (ø act)
for S to build O; for S to make, construct O
-yeeý~
·Aý léelk'u hás jeeyís áwé wududliyéý wé atx'aan hídi tlein. That big smoke house was built for my grandparents.

·Tle a tuwán áwé atýá daakahídi áa wdudliyéý. They built a restaurant next to it.

yéiý

deadfall trap for large animals

yetý

starting off taking off
yedaý

yéts' shál

black horn spoon

a yiçáa

waiting for it
a yeeçáa
·Wé bus yiçáa ýa.áa. I am sitting waiting for the bus.

a yík

inside it (a river, road, boat, or other shallow concave landform or object)
·Káa tlein yíkt át yawduwaýaa wé aanñáawu. The rich person is being driven around in a limosine.
·Kaldaaçéináý yaa gaýtooñóoý, tlél çwadlaan yá éiý' yík. We will travel along slowly, it's not deep in this slough.

,

Y

Dictionary of Tlingit

a yik.ádi

its internal organs, viscera; its guts
a yik.édi (C)
·Naaliyéidei kanasxá wé ýáat yik.ádi! Dump the fish guts far away!
·Yak'éi k'ínk' ýoox' ýáat yik.ádi. The fish guts are good in fermenting stink heads.

yíñdlaa

spark

a yinaa

in its way; blocking its way; acting as a shield for it
·Wé ý'awool yinaat hán. She is standing in the doorway.

a yinaadé

in the direction or general area of it; (headed) toward it
a yinaadéi, a niyaadé, a niyaadéi
·Áa agaýtool'oon yé yinaadé yaa gagú! Walk toward the place we will hunt!
·Wé xóots awusnéex'i a yinaadé wjixeex haa keidlí. Our dog is running toward the brown bear it smelled.

yinaaháat

body armor, breastplate

du yinaanáý

his/her family line of descent, side
·Yaa aý léelk'w aý tláa yinaanáý Ñéin yóo dusáagun yaa Xutsnoowúdáý. My grandmother on my mother's side was called Ñéin, from Angoon.
·John Soboleff yóo duwasáa - yaa aý éesh yinaanáý, aý éesh du éesh. John Soboleff was his name - on my father's side, my father's father.

a yís

for it; to that end
·Yan eewanéi gé a yís? Are you ready for it?
·Du ée yan at wududlitóow ñaa ooý yéi daanéiyi yís. She completed dentistry school.

yoo

back and forth; to and fro; up and down

yoo aan ka.á

earthquake
yoo aan ke.á (C)

yoo at koojeek

curiosity

yoo katan lítaa
yooñ

curved carving knife

cormorant

yóot~

away, off (to someplace indefinite)
·Çítçaa ayaýsaháa yóode woogoot. She went over there to gather spruce needles.

yoo tutánk
du yoowá

consciousness, thought process, thinking
his/her abdomen; surface of his/her belly; front of his/her body

du yoowú

his/her stomach; gizzard (of bird)
·Sh tóoçáa wditee aý yoowú. My stomach was satisfied.

'

'

Y

yoo ý'ala.átk

conversation, dialog; talk, discourse (between more than
one person)
yoo ý'ale.étk (C)

yoo ý'atánk

speech, talk; language; word, phrase, sentence, or

discourse

yoo ý'aténk (C)
·I yoo ý'atángi káa yan hán! Stand on your words!
·Wáançaneensx' yanaý kei shak'íý'ch aý yoo ý'atángi. Sometimes my words get hung up.

yú

that (distant), yonder
yóo
·Yóo diyáanaý.aadáý áwé haat yaýwaaýáa wéi kax'ás'ti haa hídi sákw. I hauled the lumber from across the other side for our house.
·Yóo tliyaa aasdéi ksaxát wéi kaxées' aý at shí ñóok gúgu yís! Attach the wire to that tree over there for my radio antenna!

yuka.óot'

button
yaka.óot', waka.óot'
·Dleit yáý kaatee wé yuka.óot'. The button is white.

yuka.óot' x'óow

button blanket
yaka.óot' x'óow

yúxch' (C)

sea otter
yáxwch'

yuý

outside

'

'

« . »
.AA1
• --- | át as.áa | ----- | s/he has him/her seated there | ---.
P-t O-S-s-.aa~ (position)
for S to have O (live creature) seated at P
This verb only occurs in the imperfective.
·T'ook kát as.áa du yádi. He has his child seated on the papoose board.
• --- | át la.áa | ----- | it's situated there | ---.
P-t l-.áa (position)
for a building to be situated at P
This verb only occurs in the imperfective.
·Yaa Aangóont áyá la.áa haa hídi Aanx'aagi Hít yóo duwasáakw.
Our clan house standing in Angoon is called Aanx'aagi Hít.
·Héen t'iká át la.áa du hídi. His house sits beside the river.

• --- | .áa | ----- | s/he sits; s/he is sitting | ---.
S-ø-.aa~ (position)
for (singlular) S to be seated
This verb only occurs in the imperfective. Note that a noun
phrase with (-t) postposition is used to indicate where one is
sitting, but this noun phrase is not required by the verb. For
example, one could say: .áa "s/he is sitting", or: át .áa "s/he is
sitting there".
·Ch'a tlákw .áa áwé yanéekw du k'í. His rump hurts from sitting all the
time.
·Has du léelk'w du ý'áat .áa. Their grandmother is sitting between them.

.AA2
• aý ý'éit yawdzi.áa | aý ý'éide yaa yanas.éin | aý ý'éiý
yas.aa
s/he kissed me | s/he is kissing me | s/he kisses me (regularly).
N ý'éit~ ya-S-d-s-.aa~ (ø motion)
for S to kiss N
• a daa yawdzi.aa | a daa yas.éiý | a daa yas.éiý
s/he examined it | s/he is examining it | s/he examines it (regularly).
N daa ya-S-d-s-.aa~ (na act)
for S to examine, inspect, look into, judge, assess N
The form: a daa yas.éiý gives both a basic imperfective
meaning "s/he is examining it" and a repetitive imperfective
meaning "s/he examines it (reguarly)".

,

,

.

·Du kalóox'sháni néegooch áwé du daa yawdudzi.aa. He is being
examined because of his bladder pain.

.AA3
• akawsi.aa | aksa.éiý | yoo aksi.éik
s/he grew it | s/he grows it; s/he's growing it | s/he grows it (regularly).
O-ka-S-s-.aa~ (na act)
for S to cause O (plant) to grow; for S to turn on O (hose), cause O to flow
The form: aksa.éiý gives both a basic imperfective meaning
"s/he grows it; s/he is growing it" and a repetitive imperfective
meaning "s/he grows it (regularly)".
• kaawa.aa | ka.éiý | yoo kaya.éik
it grew | it grows; it's growing | it grows (regularly).
ka-ø-.aa~ (na act)
for a plant to grow; for a stream of water to flow, pour forth
·Aas tlénx' áa kaawa.aa. Big trees grew there.
·Tlél kalchaneit áa koo.éiý Yaakwdáat. Mountain ash doesn't grow in
Yakutat.
• kawsi.aa | kasa.éiý | yoo ksi.éik
it grew | it grows; it's growing | it grows (regularly).

ka-s-.aa~ (na act)
for a plant to grow
In classical Tlingit, this verb meant specifically for a plant
with a long stalk to grow (the length of the plant indicated by the
s- classifier), however this meaning has been lost for most current
speakers, and now just means for a plant in general to grow.
·Kaçakl'eedí ldakát yéix' kanas.éich. Yarrow grows all over.

.AAK1
• shóot awdi.ák | --- | shóoý ada.aak
s/he built a fire | --- | s/he builds a fire (regularly).
shóot~ a-S-d-.aak~ (ø event)
for S to build a fire (using wood)
·Wé gán aan nagú wé ñáa shaan du shóot açida.aagít! Go with the
wood to build a fire for the elderly man!
·Aan áwé shóot aýwdi.ák wé kayeiýtáçu. I built a fire with the wood
shavings.

.AAÑW
• át akaawa.aañw | --- | át yoo akaya.áñwk
s/he gave him/her orders | --- | s/he gives him/her orders (regularly).
át O-ka-S-ø-.aañw~ (na event)
for S to give orders to, command, instruct O
·A géide yoo ý'ayatánk wé aadé át kadu.aañw yé. He is speaking out
against the proposed decision.
• yan akaawa.áñw | yánde yaa akana.áñw
s/he made a decision | s/he's making a decision | ---.

,

| ---

,

yan~ O-ka-S-ø-.aañw~ (ø motion)
for S to make a decision about O; for S to finish planning O

.AAN1
• --- | tuli.aan | ----- | s/he is kind | ---.
O-tu-l-.aan (ga state)
for O to be kind, gentle
·Haa ñoon sh kalneegí áwé ñúnáý tuli.aan. Our preacher is very kind.

.AAT1
• aadé has woo.aat | aadé yaa (ha)s na.át | aadé yoo
(ha)s ya.átk
they walked there | they are walking there | they walk there (regularly).
P-dé S-ø-.aat~ (na motion)
for (plural) S to walk, go (by walking or as a general term) to P
·Gáande yaa nay.ádi wooch yáý x'wán anayl'eiý! Be sure to all dance
alike when you walk out!
·Dleeyçáa áwé aadéi aawa.aat. People went there for meat.

• aaçáa

has woo.aat | aaçáa yaa (ha)s na.át | aaçáa yoo

ya.átk
they went to get it | they are going to get it | they go get it (regularly).
P-çaa S-ø-.aat~ (na motion)
for (plural) S to go after P, go seeking P (on foot)
Note that -çaa takes the opposite tone of the final syllable of
the noun that it attaches to. Hence: kanat'áçaa "(going) after
blueberries", but shaawçáa "(going) after gumboots".
·Ñuk'éet' áwé gaýtoo.áat kalchaneit tléiçuçáa. We are going to pick
mountain ash berries.
• áa

kei (ha)s uwa.át | áa kei (ha)s na.át | áa kei (ha)s
.átch

they walked up there | they are walking up there | they walk up there (regularly).
kei S-ø-.aat~ (ø motion)
for (plural) S to walk up, go up (by walking or as a general term)
• anaý

has yaawa.át | anaý yaa (ha)s wuna.át | anaý
yaa (ha)s .átch

they walked through it | they are walking through it | they walk through it
(regularly).
P-náý ya-u-S-ø-.aat~ (ø motion)
for (plural) S to walk, go (by walking or as a general term) through, by way of P
·Nás'k yagiyee a kaanáý has yaawa.át. They walked for three days.
• át has uwa.át | aadé yaa (ha)s na.át | áý has .aat
they walked there | they are walking there | they walk there (regularly).
P-t~ S-ø-.aat~ (ø motion)
for (plural) S to walk, go (by walking or as a general term) to P

'

'

.

·Ana.óot ñu.oo haa ýánt has uwa.át. Aleut people came to see us.
·Wéis' du shaktóot uwa.át. She got lice in her hair.
• át has woo.aat | --- | át yoo (ha)s ya.átk
they are walking around; they walked around | --- | they walk around (regularly).
P-t S-ø-.aat~ (na motion)
for (plural) S to walk, go (by walking or as a general term) around at P
·Dei át has woo.aat wéi yées kéidladi. The young seagulls are already
walking around.
·A daat aawa.aat. People are walking around on it.
• áý has woo.aat | áý yei (ha)s na.át | áý yei (ha)s .átch

they walked down along it | they are walking down along it | they walk down along it (regularly).

P-ý S-ø-.aat~ (ça motion)

for (plural) S to walk, go (by walking or as a general term) down along P

·Gántiyaakw Séedix' yaakw tlein yíý aawa.aat. People boarded the big boat at Petersburg.

• --- | áý yaa (ha)s na.át | ----- | they are walking along there | ---.

P-ý yaa S-ø-.aat~ (ga motion)

for (plural) S to be walking, going (by foot or as general term) along P

This is an example of a progressive epiaspectual paradigm (Leer, 91), which basically means that all forms are based on the progressive aspect. The progressive epiaspect is characterized by: 1)having the yaa preverb in all forms, 2)having no perfective form, and 3)denotes semantically a continuous transition from one location or state to another.

·Wé kaçít tóoý yaa ntoo.ádi awdlidées. As we walked along in the darkness, the moon shined bright.

·Wé dzísk'u tlein ítý yaa na.át wé çooch. The wolves are following behind the big moose.

• gági (ha)s uwa.át | gági yaa (ha)s na.át | gági (ha)s

.átý

they emerged | they are emerging | they emerge (regularly).

gági S-ø-.aat~ (ø motion)

for (plural) S to emerge, walk out into the open

• has

ashoowa.aat | yaa (ha)s ashuna.át | kei (ha)s ashu.átch

s/he led them | s/he is leading them | s/he leads them (regularly).

yaa O-shu-S-ø-.aat~ (ga event)

for S to lead (plural) O (especially by walking ahead)

Note that yaa occurs in every form except the perfective.

This verb has a plural stem, meaning that multiple people or animals are being led. In the paradigm given here, the plural object pronoun has "them" is used. One could also use ñaa "people", as in: ñaa shoowa.aat "s/he led people". Another option is the object prefix ñu- "people", as in: ñushoowa.aat "s/he led

,

,

people". For both of these, note that the third person object pronoun a- on the verb is dropped. If you want to indicate that animals are being led, omit the has/ñaa/ñu- and use: ashoowa.aat "s/he led them (animals)".

·K'idéin yaa ñaa shuna.át wé ñaa sháade háni. The leader is leading the people well.

• has ayawdi.át | yaa (ha)s ayanda.át | has ayada.átý

they turned back | they are turning back | they turn back (regularly).

a-ya-u-S-d-.aat~ (ø motion)

for (plural) S to turn back, go back (by walking or as general term)
• has woo.aat | yaa (ha)s na.át | yoo (ha)s ya.átk
they walked | they are walking | they walk (regularly).
S-ø-.aat~ (na motion)
for (plural) S to walk, go (by walking or as a general term)
·Ñaa daakeidí een yaa ana.át. People are walking along with a casket.
·Yan yéi jiwtooneiyí a ítnáý tsá gaýtoo.áat. After we have finished work,
then we will go.
• héide has yaawa.át | héide yaa (ha)s wuna.át | héide

yaa (ha)s .átch
they moved over that way | they are moving over that way | they move over that
way (regularly).
héide ya-u-S-ø-.aat~ (ø motion)
for (plural) S to move over (away from speaker)
• ñaa éet has jiwdi.át | --- | ñaa ée yoo has jidi.átk
they attacked someone | --- | they attack people (regularly).
ji-S-d-.aat~ (ø event)
for (plural) S to attack, assault, fall upon
To indicate who is being attacked, use: N éet~ "they
attacked N". For example: Haa éet has jiwdi.át. "They attacked
us". It is also acceptable to use this verb without specifying who
was attacked. For example: Has jiwdi.át "They attacked".
Therefore, the N éet~ is not required and is not given in the
Leer-Edwards theme.
·Xóosht' has du yáa yéi has ana.eich yaa (ha)s jinda.ádi. The dark
burnt ashes would be put on their faces when going to war.
• ñut has woo.aat | ñut kei (ha)s na.át | ñut kei (ha)s

.átch
they got lost | they are getting lost | they get lost (regularly).
ñut S-ø-.aat~ (ga motion)
for (plural) S to get lost (on foot)
• woosh

kaanáý has wudi.aat | woosh kaanáý kei (ha)s
nada.át | woosh kaanáý kei (ha)s da.átch

they gathered together | they are beginning to gather together | they gather
together (regularly).
woosh kaanáý S-d-.aat~ (ga motion)
for (plural) S to assemble, congregate, gather together (for meetings)

,

,

.

·Wé naa sháadi náñx'i áwé woosh kaanáý has wudi.aat. The clan
leaders gathered there.
• woosh

ýoot has wudi.át | woosh ýoodé yaa (ha)s
nada.át | woosh ýooý has da.aat
they gathered together | they are gathering together | they gather together
(regularly).
woosh ýoot~ S-d-.aat~ (ø motion)
for (plural) S to assemble, congregate, gather together (for meetings)
Woosh and wooch seem to be interchangeable here.
·Wé aanñáax'u wéix' woosh ýoot has wudi.át. The chiefs gathered
there.
·Wooch ýoot wuduwa.át. People came together.

.AAT2
• aadé awli.aat | aadé yaa anal.át | aadé yoo ali.átk
s/he carried them there | s/he is carrying them there | s/he carries them there
(regularly).
P-dé O-S-l-.aat~ (na motion)
for S to carry, take (plural) O (esp. baggage and personal belongings) to P
·Haaw héende awli.aat çáax'w káý. She put branches in the water for
herring eggs.
• --- | át akla.át | ----- | s/he has them lying there | ---.
P-t O-ka-S-l-.át (position)
for S to have O (small, round or hoop-like objects) lying at P
This verb only occurs in the imperfective. Note that in the
example sentence below, the classifier in the verb: waañt akal.át is
l- and NOT la- . For some common nouns such as waañ "eye", it
is possible to leave off the overt possessor du "his/her". The Delement of the classifier (in this
case l-) replaces the overt
possessor. Therefore, in the sentence below there is no overt
possessor of waañ, and the verb has the D- component of the
classifier (l-), producing the phrase: waañt akal.át.
·Wañdáanaa waañt akal.át. She has eyeglasses on. (Lit: She has glasses
lying on her eyes.)
• --- | át kala.át | ----- | they are lying there | ---.
P-t ka-l-.át (position)
for small, round or hoop-like objects to lie at P
This verb only occurs in the imperfective.
• --- | át la.át | ----- | they're lying there | ---.
P-t l-.át (position)
for several things to lie at P; for several persons or animals to lie dead,
unconscious, or incapacitated at P
This verb only occurs in the imperfective.
·Dei kát la.ádi çéechadi aaý yéi awsinei. He removed the windfall lying

,

,

in the road.
·Téil dei yaaýt la.át. Scraps of pitchwood are lying along the road.
•a

daa yoo (ha)s tuwli.át | a daa yoo (ha)s tuli.átk | a
daa yoo (ha)s tuli.átk

they thought about it | they think about it; they are thinking about it | they think
about it (regularly).
N daa yoo tu-S-l-.aat~ (ø act)
or (plural) S to think over, consider, make up
one's mind about N
• du jeet akawli.át | --- | du jeeý akla.aat
s/he gave them to him/her | --- | s/he gives them to him/her (regularly); s/he is
trying to give them to him/her.
N jeet~ O-ka-S-l-.aat~ (ø motion)
for S to give, take, hand O (small, round or hoop-like objects) to N
·Guk.át aý jeet kawdudli.át. I was given earrings.
• du jeet awli.át | --- | du jeeý al.aat
s/he gave them to him/her | --- | s/he gives them to him/her (regularly); s/he is
trying to give them to him/her.
N jeet~ O-S-l-.aat~ (ø motion)
for S to give, take, hand (plural) O (esp. baggage and personal belongings) to N
• kei ayawli.át | --- | kei ayala.átch
s/he turned the boat | --- | s/he turns the boat (regularly); s/he is trying to turn the
boat.
kei O-ya-S-l-.aat~ (ø event)
for S to turn O (boat)
·X'aa çeiyí niyaadé kei ayawli.át. He steered (his boat) toward the inside
of the point.
• yan awli.át | --- | yaý al.aat
s/he put them down | --- | s/he puts them down (regularly).
yan~ O-S-l-.aat~ (ø motion)
for S to put down, lay down, leave (plural) O (esp. baggage and personal
belongings)
·Ch'a áa yan awli.át wé gán láý'i. He just left the wet outer part of
firewood there.
·Du jiyeex' yan awli.át du dañéis'i. She placed her sewing nearby for her.
• yoo (ha)s ý'awli.át | yoo (ha)s ý'ali.átk | yoo (ha)s

ý'ali.átk
they conversed | they are conversing | they converse (regularly).
yoo ý'a-S-l-.aat~ (ø act)
for (plural) S to speak, talk, converse
The form: yoo (ha)s ý'ali.átk gives both a basic imperfective
meaning "they are conversing" and a repetitive imperfective
meaning "they coverse (regularly)".
·Wé naakéedáý lingít çunayáade yóo has ý'ali.átk. The people from
the north speak differently.

,

,

.

·Wé hoon s'aatí een yóo ý'ali.átk aý aat. My paternal aunt is talking with the storekeeper.

.AAT'
• awsi.át' | as.áat' | as.át'ý
s/he chilled it | s/he is chilling it | s/he chills it (regularly).
O-S-s-.áat'~ (ø act)
for S to make O cold, cool
The form: as.át'ý has both a basic imperfective meaning
"s/he is chilling it" and a repetitive imperfective meaning "s/he chills it (regularly)".
• ñuwsi.áat' | ñusi.áat' | kei ñusa.áat'ch
the weather was cold | the weather is cold | the weather gets cold (regularly).
ñu-s-.áat' (ga state)
for the weather to be cold
·Yá Ý'atas'aañ ñúnáý ñusi.áat'i yéix' áwé yéi has yatee. Eskimos live in a very cold place.
·Ñusi.áat' gáan - kakéin k'oodás' yéi na.oo! It's cold out - wear a sweater!

.AAX'W1
• wusi.áax'w | si.áax'w | kei sa.áax'wch
it was sour | it's sour | it gets sour (regularly).
O-s-.áax'w (ga state)
for O to be bitter, sour (of taste); for O to be spicy hot
·X'áax' tlaý ñúnáý si.áax'w. Crabapples are very sour.
·Wusi.áax'w du yoo ý'atángi, ch'a aan áwé du ý'éide ñuwdudzi.aaý. His words were biting, yet people listened to him.

.AAÝ1
• aawa.áý | --- | --s/he heard it | --- | ---.
O-S-ø-.aaý~ (ø event)
for S to hear O
·Yéi ýwaa.áý xén hél ushk'é wé microwave tóox' yéi du.oowú. I heard that it's not good to put plastic in the microwave.
·Yaa ñaa lunagúçu a kayéik has aawa.áý. They heard the sound of people running.
• --- | ali.áých | ali.áých
--- | s/he is playing it | s/he plays it (regularly).
O-S-l-.áých (ga state)
for S to play O (musical instrument)
The form: ali.áých gives both a basic imperfective meaning
"s/he is playing it" and a repetitive imperfective meaning "s/he plays it (regularly)".
• --- | asaya.áých | ----- | s/he hears a voice | ---.

'

'

O-sa-S-ø-.áých (ga state)
for S to hear O (voice)

·Gus'yadóoli wéide saýaa.áých. I hear the sandpiper over there.
• aseiwa.áý | --- | --s/he heard a voice | --- | ---.
O-sa-S-ø-.aaý~ (ø event)
for S to hear O (a voice, esp. singing)
·Tusconx' áwé aa saýwaa.áý gus'yé kindachooneidí. I heard some
doves in Tuscon.
• át wusi.áý | --- | áý sa.aaý
s/he's listening to it; s/he listened to it | --- | s/he listens to it (regularly).
P-t~ S-s-.aaý~ (ø motion)
for S to listen to P
• awli.áý | --- | ali.áých
s/he played it | --- | s/he plays it (regularly).
O-S-l-.áaý~ (ø event)
for S to play O (musical instrument)
·Ý'agáax' daakahídix' ali.áých wé çíý'jaa ñóok. He plays the organ at
the Church.
·Sh tóo awdlitóow çíý'jaa ñóok al.áýji. He taught himself to play the
piano.
• --- | aý'aya.áých | ----- | s/he understands him/her | ---.
O-ý'a-S-ø-.áých (ga state)
for S to hear O with understanding; for S to understand, comprehend O
·Tlél k'idéin iý'eiýa.áých. I don't understand you well.
• aý'eiwa.áý | --- | --s/he understood him/her | --- | ---.
O-ý'a-S-ø-.aaý~ (ø event)
for S to hear O with understanding; for S to understand, comprehend O
• --- | aya.áých | ----- | s/he can hear it | ---.
O-S-ø-.áých (ga state)
for S to be able to hear O
·Yéi ýa.áýjin yáa chíl xook Jilñáatx' áwé yéi daadunéiyin. I used to
hear of smoked salmon being prepared on the Chilkat.
·Çunayéide at ýaa.áých. I'm hearing strange sounds.
• a kayéikçaa ñoowdzi.aaý | --- | a kayéikçaa yoo

ñudzi.áýk
s/he listened for the sound of it | --- | s/he listens for the sound of it (regularly).
P-çaa ñu-S-d-s-.aaý~ (na motion)
for S to listen for P
·A kayéikçaa áwé ñuntoos.áých shtéen káa haadé yaa nañúýu. We
always listen for the sound of the steam engine when it's coming.

,

,

.

• du ý'éide ñuwdzi.aaý | --- | du ý'éide yoo ñudzi.áýk
s/he listened to him/her | --- | s/he listens to him/her (regularly).
N ý'éide ñu-S-d-s-.aaý~ (na motion)
for S to listen to N
·Wusi.áax'w du yoo ý'atángi, ch'a aan áwé du ý'éide ñuwdudzi.aaý.
His words were biting, yet people listened to him.

• du ý'éit wusi.áý | --- | du ý'éiý sa.aaý

s/he's listening to him/her; s/he listens to him/her | --- | s/he listens to him/her (regularly).

N ý'éit~ S-s-.aaý~ (ø motion)

for S to listen to, obey, give heed to N

·Gunalchéesh aý ý'éit yeeysa.aaýí. Thank you all for listening to me.

.AAÝ2

• át aawa.aaý | --- | át yoo aya.áýk

s/he is carrying it around; s/he carried it around | --- | s/he carries it around (regularly).

P-t O-S-ø-.aaý~ (na motion)

for S to carry, take O (textile-like object) around at P

• --- | át .áý | ----- | it's lying there | ---.

P-t ø-.áý (position)

for a textile-like object to lie at P

This verb only occurs in the imperfective.

·Wéit .aý kinaak.át a káx' áwé ýwsiteen i gwéili. On top of that coat
lying there is where I saw your bag.

• du jeet aawa.áý | du jeedé yaa ana.áý | du jeeý a.aaý

s/he gave it to him/her | s/he is giving it to him/her | s/he gives it to him/her (regularly).

N jeet~ O-S-ø-.aaý~ (ø motion)

for S to give, take, hand O (textile-like object) to N

·Ñóok yígu aý kast'áat'i - aý jeet .áý. My quilt is in the box - give it to me.

.AAÝW

• adaawsi.áýw | adaasa.áaýw | adaasa.áýwý

s/he wrapped it up | s/he's wrapping it up | s/he wraps it up (regularly).

O-daa-S-s-.aaýw~ (ø act)

for S to tie O together in a bundle; for S to wrap O up

·Ñaa yat'éináý x'wán daasa.áýw wé ñóok! Wrap that box when no one is
looking now!

• yánde aawa.áýw | yánde a.aaýw

s/he tied it up | s/he's tying it up | ---.

yánde O-S-ø-.aaýw~ (ø act)

for S to tie up, secure O (esp. a boat to shore)

,

| ---

,

.EE

• awsi.ée | as.ée | as.éeý

s/he cooked it | s/he cooks it; s/he is cooking it | s/he cooks it (regularly).

O-S-s-.ee~ (ø act)

for S to cook O

·Ý'áakw ý'úýu haa ý'eis sa.í stoox kaanáý! Cook us red sockeye soup on
the stove!

·Wé ñáa dzísk'u shaayí gangooknáý as.eeyín. He used to cook moose

head next to the campfire.
• at wusi.ée | at sa.ée | at is.éeý
s/he cooked | s/he is cooking | s/he cooks (regularly).
at S-s-.ee~ (ø act)
for S to cook
·Du léelk'w du ý'eis at wusi.ée. Her grandmother cooked for her.
·Du kéilk' du ý'eis at wusi.ée. His niece cooked for him.
• yan uwa.ée | yánde yaa na.éen | yaý .ee
it's cooked | it's cooking | it cooks (regularly, quickly).
yan~ ø-.ee~ (ø motion)
for food to be cooked, done cooking
·Wé sakwnéin éewu yan ça.eet eeçáa áwé ýa.áa. I am sitting, waiting
for the bread to finish cooking.

.EEN1
• aawa.ín | a.éen | a.íný
s/he picked them | s/he's picking them | s/he picks them (regularly).
O-S-ø-.een~ (ø act)
for S to pick O (esp. berries) into a container
·Aatlein dáxw aawa.ín. She picked lots of lowbush cranberries.
·Shaaý a.éen haa hídi daatý kanéegwál' sákw. She is picking gray
currants from around our house for a berry and salmon egg dish.
• át awsi.ín | --- | áý as.een
s/he carried it there | --- | s/he carries it there (regularly).
P-t~ O-S-s-.een~ (ø motion)
for S to carry O (container full of liquid or small objects) to P
·Yaawat'aayi káaxwei ín x'eesháa tóot haat awsi.ín. She brought hot
coffee in a bottle.
·Yat'aayi héen du ñáawu ý'éit awsi.ín. She gave her husband's clan
brother coffee.
• du jeet awsi.ín | --- | du jeeý as.een
s/he gave it to him/her | --- | s/he gives it to him/her (regularly).
N jeet~ O-S-s-.een~ (ø motion)
for S to give, take, hand O (container full of liquid or small objects) to N
·Wé shaatk' gúx'aa kát cháayoo aý jeet awsi.ín. The young girl gave
me tea in a cup.
• neil awsi.ín | --- | neilý as.een
s/he brought it inside | --- | s/he brings it inside (regularly).

,

,

.

neil O-S-s-.een~ (ø motion)
for S to bring O (container full of liquid or small objects) inside
·Gán kañás'ti ñóok tóox' neil awsi.ín. He brought the kindling inside in a
box.
• yan awsi.ín | --- | yaý as.een
s/he put it down | --- | s/he puts it down (regularly).
yan~ O-S-s-.een~ (ø motion)

for S to put down, lay down, leave, place O (a container full of liquid or small objects)
·Wé shaawát du çushkáa yan awsi.ín du s'íx'i. The woman put her plate on her lap.
·Stoox káa yan sa.ín wé at téiýi! Set the broth on top of the stove!

.EESH
• akawli.ísh | akla.eesh | akla.íshý
s/he strung them together | s/he is stringing them together | s/he strings them together (regularly).
O-ka-S-l-.eesh~ (ø act)
for S to thread, string together O (esp. beads)
·A ý'éináý áwé kadul.eesh wé ñáas' kaadéi wé saak. Those hooligan are strung through the mouth on the stick.

.EEX'
• aawa.éex' | --- | yei a.éex'ch
s/he invited him/her | --- | s/he invites him/her (regularly).
O-S-ø-.éex' (ça event)
for S to invite O, ask O to a party
·Haa k'ínk' yan wuneeyí a yís áyá ñooýwaa.éex'. I invited everyone for when our stink heads are done.
·Ñúnáý wé yee woo.éex'i aa tsú yee ýoo yéi kçwatée toowú k'é teen. Your hostess will welcome you all as well. (Lit: Your hostess will be among you all with good feelings.)
• aawa.éex' | --- | yoo aya.éex'k
s/he called out to him/her | --- | s/he calls out to him/her (regularly).
O-S-ø-.éex' (na event)
for S to call out to, shout to, holler at O

.ÍT'CH
• kawdli.ít'ch | kadli.ít'ch | yoo kadli.ít'ch
it's sparkling; it sparkled | it's sparkling; it sparkles | it sparkles (regularly).
ka-d-l-ít'ch (na state)
for something to sparkle, reflect light
·Dís ý'usyee kawdli.ít'ch wé dleit káý. Moonbeams are sparkling on the snow.
·Kadli.ít'ch éedaa xáanax'. The phosphoresence glows at night.

,

,
1

.OO
• áa ñoowa.oo | áa ñuya.óo / áa ñuwa.óo | --s/he lived there | s/he lives there | ---.
ñu-S-ø-.oo~ (na act)
for S to live, live at, dwell permanently
To specify where one lives, use: P-x' "at P". For example:
Sheet'káx' ñuya.óo. "S/he lives in Sitka". Note that áa and áx' are synonymous, both meaning "there". Often when occuring directly before the verb, the preferred form is áa.

·Shayadihéin Áankichx' ñuwa.oowu Lingít. There are a lot of Tlingit
people living in Anchorage.
·Du káak ýáni ñuya.óo. He is living with his maternal uncle.
• áa yéi aawa.oo | --- | áa yéi a.úýx'
s/he put them there | --- | s/he puts them there (regularly).
P-x' yéi O-S-ø-.oo (na event)
for S to put, leave (plural) O at P
·Wé at x'aakeidí ín x'eesháa tóox' yéi na.oo! Put the seeds in a bottle!
·Wéi yaakw yaýak'áaw kas'éet áa yéi du.oowú, k'idéin yéi
aguýlasháat. If a screw is put in the thwart of the boat, it will hold pretty well.
• yéi aawa.oo | yéi aya.óo | --s/he wore it | s/he's wearing it | ---.
yéi O-S-ø-.oo~ (na state)
for S to wear, put on, dress in O; for S to use O
·Ch'áakw ý'eint'áax'aa shaawát ý'é yéi ndu.eich. Long ago women
would wear a labret.
·Téil yéi aya.óo at doogú aklas'éñýi yís. She is using dry wood for
smoking that hide.

.OO2
• aawa.oo | --- | yoo aya.eik
s/he bought it | --- | s/he buys it (regularly).
O-S-ø-.oo (na event)
for S to buy O
·Aanñáawuch áwé woo.oo, wé tlagu hít tlein. A rich person bought the
big old house.
·Hoon daakahídidáý çánch has aawa.oo. They bought tobacco from the
store.
• akaawa.oo | --- | yoo akaya.eik
s/he bought it | --- | s/he buys it (regularly).
O-ka-S-ø-.oo (na event)
for S to buy O (usually round, spherical object)
While the ka- prefix once referred specifically to something
round or spherical in shape, this distinction may be falling out of
use, as some modern speakers consider akaawa.oo and aawa.oo to
mean exactly the same thing.
·Aý léelk'w jeeyís áyá kaýwaa.oo yá kanéist guk.át. I bought these
cross earrings for my grandmother.

,

,

.

.OOK
• awli.úk | --- | al.úký
s/he boiled it | --- | s/he boils it (regularly).
O-S-l-.ook~ (ø event)
for S to boil O (esp. water)
• wudli.úk | yaa nal.úk | il.úký
it's boiling; it boiled | it's starting to boil | it comes to a boil (regularly).
d-l-.óok~ (ø event)

for something to boil
·Wudli.úk gé wé yat'aayi héen? Did the coffee boil?

.OON
• aawa.ún | --- | --s/he shot it | --- | ---.
O-S-ø-.óon~ (ø event)
for S to shoot O (with firearms)
·Cháash a kaadéi kawtuwachák wé wutuwa.uni dzísk'w. We packed branches on the moose that we shot.
·A kageidéex' áwé ýwaa.ún wé çuwakaan tlein. I shot the big deer in its side
• --- | a.únt | ----- | s/he is shooting at it | ---.
O-S-ø-.únt (na act)
for S to shoot at O (with firearms)

.OOS
• wuli.oos | li.oos | --s/he was noisy | s/he's being noisy | ---.
O-l-.oos (ga state)
for O to be crazy, lively, noisy, never still
·Yá atk'átsk'u li.oos ch'ak'yéis' yáý. This child is as playful as a young eagle.

.OOS'
• aawa.óos' | a.ús'k | yoo aya.ús'k
s/he washed it | s/he is washing it | s/he washes it (regularly).
O-S-ø-.óos'~ (na act)
for S to wash O
·Wé i wañdlóoçu aaý na.óos'! Clean the sleep from your eyes!
·Aawa.óos'i jiçwéinaa gáaný ashayaawatée. She hung the towel that she washed outside.
• akaawa.óos' | aka.ús'k | yoo akaa.ús'k
s/he washed it | s/he's washing it | s/he washes it (regularly).
O-ka-S-ø-.óos'~ (na act)
for S to wash O (usually surface of pot, table, etc.)
·S'íx' kawtoo.óos'i ítnáý agaýtoolñáa. After we have washed the dishes we will play cards.

,

,

.OOW
• aawa.óow | a.óow | --s/he bought them | s/he buys them | ---.
O-S-ø-.óow
for S to buy lots of O
This verb only seems to occur in the perfective and imperfective. More research is needed.
·Yak'éiyi naa.át aaý du.óow wé hoon daakahídi. Good clothing can be bought from that store.
·Costcodáý aawa.óow atýá. He bought food from Costco.

~

English to Tlingit

,

English-to-Tlingit Lexicon

English to Tlingit
abalone
abalone: gunýaa.

abdomen
his/her abdomen; surface of his/her belly; front of his/her body: du yoowá.

aboard
s/he carried it aboard; s/he took it aboard (container or hollow object): TAAN yaaý aawataan. s/he went aboard: GOOT1 yaaý woogoot.

about
around it; about it; concerning it: a daa. (resting) at; coming to, arriving at; moving about: -t. (telling) about it: a daat.

above
above it: a kináak. top of it (something with a rounded top, as a mountain); above it; (elevated) over it: a shakée.

acceptably
enough, acceptably: çaa.

accident
accident; unfortunate mistake or mishap: ñaañýwdaagané (A). s/he had an accident; s/he got hurt; something bad happened to him/her: NEI ñáakwt uwanéi.

accidentally
accidentally, wrongly: ñáakwt~.

accomplish
s/he won it; s/he got it; s/he accomplished it; s/he defeated him/her: DLAAÑ ayaawadlaañ.

according to
according to his/her words, instructions: du ý'ayáý. according to the way s/he does it: du jiyáý.

accustomed to
s/he got used to it; s/he became accustomed to it (the flavor, pronunciation of something): DAA2 du ý'éiý woodaa.

acknowledge

s/he said that; s/he confessed that; s/he acknowledged that: ÑAA1 yéi yaawañaa.

across
area across, on the other side (especially of body of water): diýáanaý.á.

actually
actually; in fact; contrary to what was thought: ñachoo.

,

English-to-Tlingit Lexicon

add
s/he contributed to it; s/he donated to it; s/he added to it: ÇEEX' át kawdiçíx'.

adequate
(big) enough for him/her to have or use; adequate for him/her: du jeeçáa.
enough; adequate: tl'açáa.

Admiralty Island
people of Admiralty Island: Xudzidaa Ñwáan.

adult
adult; elder: yanwáat. young adult: yées wáat.

advise
s/he instructed him/her; s/he advised him/her: JAA ashukaawajáa.

adze
adze: ýút'aa. stone adze: s'oow ýút'aa.

afraid
s/he was afraid of it: ÝEITL' áa akawdliýéitl'.

African-American
Black (man or person); African-American: t'ooch' ñáa.

after
after it: a ít. (distributed) in the area of; (going) after, (waiting) for; about the
time of: -çaa. then, around, after, for: aaçáa.

afterlife
afterlife, "happy hunting ground": daçanñú.

afternoon
day, afternoon: yakyee, yagiyee, yagee (T).

again
again; still; some more: tsu.

against
against it; wrongly, improperly: a géit~. against it, wrong (so as to foul up
what s/he had done): du jiyagéiý.

age
his/her age: du katáagu. it aged; it spoiled: S'EEX wulis'íx. s/he is old:
SHAAN wudishán.

aground
aground, into shallow water: kux.

ahead

front of it; ahead of it: a shuká. straight ahead; directly ahead:
yaadachóon.

Ahtna
Ahtna, Copper River Athabascan: Iñkaa.

,

Alaska
Alaska: Anáaski.

alcohol
liquor; booze; alcoholic beverage: kasiyaayi héen.

alcoholic
alcoholic: náaw éesh.

alder
alnus alder (beach or mountain alder): keishísh. red alder: shéiý'w.

Aleut
Aleut: Ana.óot, Giyañw.

algae
algae found on rocks: ýaatl'. ocean algae: káas'.

all
all; every: ldakát.

along
along; down: yaa. along, via; including the time of: -náý.

alongside
alongside it; catching up with it: a kík.

already
already, (by) now: de.

also
also, too, as well: tsú.

although
although, even though, however, nonetheless, yet: ch'a aan.

aluminum
aluminum: géxtl'.

always
always, all the time, constantly: tlákw, ch'a tlákw. always; [auxiliary]:
nooch.

American
American: Waashdan Ñwáan.

American Indian
American Indian: T'aawyáat.

among

(in) the midst of it; among it: a ýoo.

ancestor
ancestor(s) of his/her clan or nation; his/her background, heredity: du
shagóon. in front of him/her; his/her geneology, history; his/her ancestors:
du shuká.

,

English-to-Tlingit Lexicon

anchor

anchor: shayéinaa. s/he anchored: YAA2 shawdziyaa. s/he anchored the boat: YAA2 ashawsiyaa.

Anchorage
Anchorage: Áankich.

and
and: ña.

anemic
he/she/it was weak; s/he is anemic; it is mild (of weather): TSEEN tlél wultseen.

angel
messenger; angel: kooñénaa.

anger
anger: x'áan.

Angoon
Angoon: Aangóon.

angry

s/he's angry: NOOK2 x'áant uwanúk.

ankle
knob on outer side of his/her ankle: du ý'ust'ákl'i. outer side of his/her foot up to the anklebone: du shutóoý'.

answer
in response, reply to him/her; answering him/her; following his/her train of speech: du ý'akooká.

ant
ant: wanatóox, wanatíx.

antenna
its antenna (of radio): a gúgu.

anticipate
getting ready for it; in anticipation of it: a yayís. s/he anticipated it; s/he foresaw it; s/he expected him/her/it: TEE2 ashoowsitee.

anus
his/her anus: du tuñ.woolí.

anxiety

anxiety; wracked nerves; preoccupation; something weighing on one's mind: tux'andaxeech.

anybody
anyone, anybody; whoever: ch'a aadóo sá, ch'a aa sá.

anything
anything; whatever: ch'a daa sá.

,

English-to-Tlingit Lexicon

any time
any time (in the future); whenever (in the future): ch'a gwátgeen sá.

anywhere
anywhere, anyplace; wherever: ch'a goot'á sá.

apparent

he/she/it appeared before him/her; it was apparent to him/her: TEE1 du wañshiyeex' yéi wootee.

appealing

it was fun; it was enjoyable; it was appealing: GOO1 ñ'awsigóo.

appear

he/she/it appeared before him/her; it was apparent to him/her: TEE1 du wañshiyeex' yéi wootee.

apple
apple; crabapple: x'áax'. apple juice: x'áax' kahéeni. crabapple: lingít x'áax'i.

approve
s/he praised him/her; s/he approved it: SHEIÝ' akaawashéý'.

area
the foot of it; below it (raised place); flat area at the end of it (lake); down from the crest of it (slope); the end of it (dock): a shuyee.

aristocrat
high class person, aristocrat: aanyádi.

arm
crook of his/her arm; in his/her embrace: du jiçei. his/her upper arm: du ýeek.

armor
armor made of tough hide or wooden rods: sankeit. body armor, breastplate: niyaháat, yinaaháat.

armpit
his/her armpit: du éenee. his/her armpit hair: du éenee ýaawú.

armspan
armspan; fathom: waat.

army
war party, attacking force of warriors or soldiers; army: ýáa.

arnica
large-leaved avens (Geum macrophyllum) or possibly arnica species-- Arnica
species, especially A. amplexicaulus, A. latifolia, A. gracilis: aankanáagu.

around
around it; about it; concerning it: a daa. around it (bypassing it, avoiding it);
around the end of it: a shuwadaa. around the outside surface of it: a
daaká. (in) the area of it or around it, (in) its vicinity: a déin.

,

English-to-Tlingit Lexicon

arrest
s/he caught it; s/he grabbed him/her/it; s/he arrested him/her; s/he trapped him/her/it: SHAAT aawasháat.

arrive

he/she/it arrived there; he/she/it went there: GOOT1 át uwagút. they walked there; they arrived there; they went there: .AAT1 át has uwa.át.

arrow
arrow: chooneit. arrowhead: at ýéidi. blunt arrow for stunning: gútl. sharp arrow for killing: tláañ.

arthritis
arthritis: daa.ittunéekw.

artifact
his/her handiwork, artifact: du ji.eetí.

ash
ash; ashes: kél't'. ashes: gan eetí.

ashore
ashore, onto ground; to rest: yan~.

ask
s/he asked for it; s/he cried for it: ÇAAÝ awdziçáaý. s/he asked him/her: WOOS'1 aý'eiwawóos'. s/he told him/her that; s/he said that to him/her; s/he asked him/her to do that: ÑAA1 yoo ayawsiñaa.

asleep
s/he fell on his/her face; s/he fell asleep while sitting up: GAAS' yan yaawagás'.

assault
s/he beat him/her up; s/he assaulted him/her; s/he violently attacked him/her:
1
JAAÑW aawajáañw.

assist

he/she/it is helping me; s/he helped me: SHEE1 aý éet wudishée.

as soon as
(along) with, by means of; as soon as: een, teen.

astray
astray, getting lost: ñut.

at

at (the scene of); at (the time of): -x'. (in prolonged contact) at; (repeatedly arriving) at; being, in the form of: -ý. is/are at: -u. (resting) at; coming to, arriving at; moving about: -t.

Athabaskan
Athabaskan (Indian): Çunanaa.

at least
at least, once in a while: ch'a k'ikát.

,

English-to-Tlingit Lexicon

Atlin
Atlin: Áa Tlein. people of Atlin: Áa Tlein Ñwáan.

attack
s/he beat him/her up; s/he assaulted him/her; s/he violently attacked him/her:
1
1
JAAÑW aawajáañw. they attacked someone: .AAT ñaa éet has jiwdi.át.

attic
upstairs; attic: hít shantú.

Auke Bay
Auke Bay: Áak'w. people of Auke Bay, southern Lynn Canal, Juneau area, and northern Admiralty Island: Áak'w Ñwáan.

auklet
auklet or murrelet: ch'eet, kéel. Was'eeneidí; a clan of the Eagle moiety whose principal crests are the Wolf and Auklet: Was'eeneidí.

aunt
his/her maternal aunt: du tláak'w. his/her paternal aunt: du aat.

aurora borealis
northern lights; aurora borealis: gis'óoñ.

autumn
fall; autumn: yeis.

avalanche
snowslide; snow avalanche: dleit ñaadí.

aven
large-leaved avens (Geum macrophyllum) or possibly arnica species-- Arnica species, especially A. amplexicaulus, A. latifolia, A. gracilis: aankanáagu.

awake
he/she/it kept him/her awake: ÝEIK ash wusiýéñ.

away
away from it, leaving it behind (taking something away from him/her): du jináñ. away, off (to someplace indefinite): yóot~. beside it; out past it; out away from it; (on) the outskirts of it (town): a t'iká. (going, taking something) away from it: a náñ. in its way; keeping it away; protecting, shielding, screening from it; blocking it: a niyaa, a ý'anaa. in secret (where nobody can see); away from people's view: ñaa yat'éináý, du yat'éináý.

awful

it looked terrible; it looked awful; it was eerie; it was unattractive: JEE2 kawlijée.

awl
awl; chopping block: s'úwaa.

axe
axe: shanaýwáayi, shunaýwáayi. stone axe: tayees, yees.

'

English-to-Tlingit Lexicon

babiche
babiche, string, leather thonging: dzaas.

baby
baby: t'ukanéiyi.

babysitter
babysitter: atyátx'i latíni.

back
at his/her back; right behind him/her: du dzúk. behind him/her; back of
him/her; at his/her back: du t'áak. behind his/her back, where s/he can't see:
du yat'éik. his/her back: du díý'. near the base of it; at the foot of it; the
back, rear or it (house); behind it (house); under the shelter of it (a standing
object or structure): a k'iyee. (on) the back of it (fish); on the crest, ridge,
backbone of it (hill, ridge, point): a litká.

back and forth
back and forth; to and fro; up and down: yoo.

back end
its back end; stern (of boat): a k'óol'.

backpack
backpack; pack sack: yáanadi. pack; backpack; pack sack: ýéey.

backwards
backwards: ñuý dak'óol'een.

bacon
bacon: gishoo taayí.

bad
he/she/it was bad; he/she/it was evil: K'EI tlél wushk'é.

bag
bag; sack: gwéil.

baggage
baggage, luggage; things, stuff packed up for carrying: at la.át.

baggy
its wrinkled, baggy skin, hide: a daaleilí.

bailer
bailer: kakúxaa. wooden bailer (for boat): sheen.

bait hooks

s/he baited hooks: NAAÑW1 yawdináñw.

bald
bald spot; bald head: shaý'wáas' (T).

baleen
baleen; whalebone: yáay ý'axéni.

,

English-to-Tlingit Lexicon

ball
ball: kooch'éit'aa.

balloon
balloon: kadu.uxýu át.

bandage
s/he bandaged it; s/he bound it up; s/he wrapped it: S'EET akaawas'ít.

bangs
his/her bangs: du kak'ýaawú.

banister
banister; railing: a daaý yaa dulsheech át.

baptize

s/he baptized him/her: TEE2 héent ayaawatée.

barbecue
s/he barbecued it: TSEEK awlitsík.

bare
bare; naked: kaldaaçákw.

barefoot
barefoot; shoeless: kaltéelñ.

bark
dry woody outer bark: loon. flaky surface of the outer bark of conifers, especially hemlock: s'agwáat. its bark: a daayí. yellow cedar bark (for weaving): teey woodí.

barnacle
barnacle: s'ook.

barrel
barrel: káast.

base
its base (of tree or other plant); the lower part of its trunk or stem: a k'eeyí. near the base of it; at the foot of it; the back, rear or it (house); behind it (house); under the shelter of it (a standing object or structure): a k'iyee. the base or foot of it (a standing object): a k'í.

basket
basket: ñákw. basket of woven red cedar bark: néil'. basket or pan used to collect berries by knocking them off the bush: kadádzaa yeit. basket with a rattle in the lid: tudaxákw. basket with rattle in the lid: tuñdaadaxákw. berrying basket: kaltásk. berrying basket or can hung around the neck,

resting on the chest: seiçatáanaa. birch bark basket: at daayí ñákw. flat open basket woven from wide strips of bark (for carrying fish, etc.); large platter: táal. long, flat loosely woven basket for pressing out herring oil: kaat. roots or vines used in basket decoration: léet'. round basket made of split red cedar branches: ts'anéi. unfinished basket: x'akaskéin.

,

English-to-Tlingit Lexicon

bastard
fatherless child; bastard: neechkayádi.

bathe
s/he bathed: SHOOCH wudishúch.

bay
bay: çeey, çeiy (TC), eey. head of the bay: çeey tá.

be

he/she/it was that way: TEE1 yéi wootee. it existed; s/he was born: TEE1
ñoowdzitee. it's situated there: .AA1 át la.áa. s/he became a (noun): TEE1
(noun)-ý wusitee. s/he was with him/her; s/he stayed with him/her; s/he
lived with him/her: TEE1 du ýánx' yéi wootee. the building was situated
there (suddenly as if overnight): NOOK1 áa wdinook. the weather was that
way: TEE1 yéi ñoowatee.

beach
beach; waterside; down on the beach, shore: éeñ. down to beach, shore:
yeeñ. from the woods onto the beach, shore: éeçi. out of the water onto the
beach, shore: dáaçi. shoreline; beach: neech. the beach, shore below it (a
town): a eeçayáak.

beached
it got stuck on the beach: DLAAÝ'W yaý woodláaý'w.

bead
bead: kawóot. light bluish-gray trade bead(s): s'eeñ kawóot.

beak
dark yellow; eagle's beak: ch'áak' loowú. its beak: a loowú.

bear
Chookaneidí; a clan of the Eagle moiety whose principal crests are the Porpoise
and Brown Bear: Chookaneidí. grizzly bear: xóots. Teikweidí, locally
called "Brown Bear"; a clan of the Eagle moiety whose principal crest is the
Brown Bear: Teiñweidí. Yanyeidí, locally known as "Bear"; a clan of the
Eagle moiety whose principal crest is the Brown Bear: Yanyeidí.

bearberry
alpine bearberry, kinnikinnick: tínx.

beard
its whiskers, beard (of fish): a ñ'anooýú.

bear root
bear root, Indian potato: tsáats.

beat

s/he beat it; s/he rang it; s/he stabbed it: GWAAL aawagwaal.

beat up
s/he beat him/her up; s/he assaulted him/her; s/he violently attacked him/her:
1
JAAÑW aawajáañw.

,

beaver
beaver: s'igeidí. beaver dam: s'igeidí áayi. beaver's den: s'igeidí ýaayí. Deisheetaan, locally called "Beaver"; a clan of the Raven moiety whose principal crest is the Beaver: Deisheetaan.

because
because of; by means of: -ch. because of it; due to it; by virtue of it; on the strength of it; encouraged by it: a tuwáadáý.

become

s/he became a (noun): TEE1 (noun)-ý wusitee.

bed
bed: káa ýeýx'u yeit. mattress; bedding: yee.át.

bee
bee's nest: gandaas'aají kúdi. bee; wasp: gandaas'aají.

beer
beer: géewaa.

beetle
beetle: k'ul'kaskéxkw.

before
before his/her eyes; where he/she can see (it): du wañshiyee.

begin
beginning: çunayéi. start, begin: çunéi.

behave

s/he did it; s/he behaved that way: NOOK2 yéi ñoowanook.

behind
at his/her back; right behind him/her: du dzúk. behind him/her; back of him/her; at his/her back: du t'áak. behind his/her back, where s/he can't see: du yat'éik. behind it: a t'éik. behind it; back inland from it; on the landward side of it (something on the water): a t'áak. near the base of it; at the foot of it; the back, rear or it (house); behind it (house); under the shelter of it (a standing object or structure): a k'iyee.

believe

s/he believed him/her; s/he trusted him/her: HEEN1 du éek' aawaheen.

believer
believer: átk' aheení.

bell
bell: gaaw.

belly
his/her abdomen; surface of his/her belly; front of his/her body: du yoowá.
his/her belly, paunch: du ý'óol'. his/her flank, side of his/her belly: du
ñaatl.

,

English-to-Tlingit Lexicon

bellybutton
his/her navel, bellybutton: du kool.

below
the foot of it; below it (raised place); flat area at the end of it (lake); down from
the crest of it (slope); the end of it (dock): a shuyee, a shuwee. underneath
it; beneath it; below it: a tayee.

belt
belt: séek.

bend
s/he bent it: TAAN akaawataan.

bent
it's bent: TAAN yóo katán.

berries
half-dried, compressed food, esp. berries or seaweed: kat'ákýi. swamp
berries: sháchgi tléiçu. various odd looking, tasteless, or otherwise
undesirable berries, some poisonous; meaning varies locally, incl. twistedstalk
(Streptopus species), snowberry (Symphoricarpos albus), fool's huckleberry
(Menziesia ferruginea), etc.: s'içeeñáawu tléiçu.

berry
berry, berries: tléiñw. berry juice: tléiñw kahéeni. dish made with
berries and salmon eggs: kanéegwál'. green, unripe berry: kaý'át'.
mashed berries: kaçútlýi. s/he picked berries: K'EET' ñoowak'ít'.
steamed berries: kanálýi. steamed berries put up in soft grease: kañáshýi.

berry bush
berry bush: tléiñw wás'i.

beside
beside, alongside, next to him/her: du t'añká. beside, alongside, next to it: a
t'añká. beside it, at its side: a t'aañ. beside it, next to it: a tuwán.
beside it; out past it; out away from it; (on) the outskirts of it (town): a t'iká.

between
between them: a ý'áak. enclosed within (the folds of) it, between the folds,
covers, walls of it: a çei.

beyond
beyond it, more than it; too much; excessively: a yáanáý.

bicycle
bicycle: a kát sh kadultseýt át.

big

big: tlein. he/she/it is big, tall (live creature or building): GEI1 ligéi. it got this big; there were this many: GEI1 yéi kaawagéi. it's big (round, spherical object): GEI1 kayagéi. it's that big around: TLAA yéi kwditláa. it was big; there were many; there was plenty: GEI1 woogéi. they're big: GEI1 digéix', GEI1 kadigéix'. they're that big: GEI1 yéi kwdigéi.

,

English-to-Tlingit Lexicon

Big Dipper
Big Dipper; Ursa Major: yaýté.

bight
cove; bight: kunaçeey.

bile
his/her bile: du teiyí.

bind
s/he bandaged it; s/he bound it up; s/he wrapped it: S'EET akaawas'ít.

birch
birch: at daayí. birch bark basket: at daayí ñákw.

bird
green bird (sparrow or finch): asx'aan sháach'i. grey singing bird
(sparrow or finch): tlagu ts'ats'éeyee. robin-like bird: shooý'. songbird;
bird: ts'ats'ée, ts'ítskw.

bison
bison, buffalo; ox, muskox; cow; horse: xaas.

bite

he/she/it bit him/her/it: YEEÑ2 aawayeeñ. it bit him/her/it: TAAX' ash
wusitáax'. it pierced it; it bit him/her/it: ÇEECH át yawdiçích, ÇEECH
aadé yawdiçeech.

bitter

it was sour; it was bitter; it was spicy: .AAX'W1 wusi.áax'w.

black
black: t'ooch'. Black (man or person); African-American: t'ooch' ñáa.
black with dirt, filth, stain: ts'áñl.

black bass
black bass: lit.isdúk.

black bear
black bear: s'eek.

blackboard
blackboard, chalkboard: kadushxit t'aa yá.

black cod
black cod: ishñeen.

black currant

black currant: ýaaheiwú.

blacksmith
blacksmith: çayéis' layeiýí, çayéis' t'éiý'i.

bladder
his/her bladder: du kalóox'shani.

,

blame

s/he brought it onto him/her (esp. shame, blame, joy): TEE2 du kát ashuwatée.

blanket
blanket; robe: x'óow. blanket sewn from scraps of hide: at xáshdi x'óow. cotton; cotton blanket, quilt: kast'áat'. Hudson Bay blanket: kinguchwáan x'óowu. quilt; cotton blanket: kast'áat' x'óow. wool blanket (used as potlatch gift or for dancing): l'ée.

blessed
s/he got lucky; s/he was blessed: ÝEITL wuliýéitl.

blind
blind person: l ñooshtéeni. s/he is blind: TEEN tlél ñooshtéen.

blindfold
blindfold: wañkadóox'.

block
in its way; keeping it away; protecting, shielding, screening from it; blocking it: a niyaa.

blond
grayish; blond (hair): l'áaý'.

blood
blood: shé. bloodline inside fish, along the backbone: ýáat k'áaý'i.

bloodsucker
leech; bloodsucker: yéesh.

blossom
flower; blossom: ñ'eikaxwéin.

blow

it blew; it's blowing: NOOK2 wuduwanúk. it's blowing around; it blew around; s/he is sailing around; s/he sailed around: S'EES át wulis'ees. it's blowing in the wind there: S'EES aadé kawdlis'ées. spray of air exhaled through its blowhole (of sea mammal): a óoxu.

blowfish
moonfish, suckerfish, blowfish: tl'éitl'.

blubber
fat; blubber: taay.

blue

dark blue: ý'éishx'w. green, light blue: s'oow. sky blue: xáats'.

blueberry
alpine blueberry: ts'éekáýk'w. blueberry; huckleberry: kanat'á.
blueberry juice; purple: kanat'á kahéeni. huckleberry; blueberry:
naanyaa kanat'aayí. swamp blueberry: láý' loowú.

,

bluejay
bluejay, Stellar's jay: ý'éishx'w.

blunt
it's dull; it's blunt: ÇEEL yaawdiçíl.

board
board: t'áa.

boat
boat, canoe: yaakw. gas-powered boat: s'eenáa yaakw. in the boat:
yaakw yík. old, worn-out boat: l'áañw. shell of a boat: yakw
daa.ideidí. skiff; small boat; flat-bottom canoe: yakwyádi. steamboat;
riverboat: gántiyaakw. stern (of a boat): a géek.

body
his/her body parts: du daashagóon. his/her/its body: du daa.it.

boil1
it's boiling; it boiled: .OOK wudli.úk. s/he boiled it: .OOK awli.úk. s/he
steamed it; s/he boiled it: TAA3 awsitáa.

boil2
boil; inflammation and swelling: x'ees.

boiled
boiled food; broth: téiý, a téiýi.

bone
bone: s'aañ. his/her bone marrow: s'añtu.eeýí. his/her skeleton, bare
bones: du xaagú.

book
paper; book, magazine, newspaper; letter, mail: x'úx'.

boot
boot(s): x'wán.

boredom
loneliness; boredom: tuteesh.

born

it existed; s/he was born: TEE1 ñoowdzitee.

borrow
s/he borrowed it: HEES' aawahées'. s/he borrowed it (round, spherical
object): HEES' akaawahées'.

boss

boss: ñaa s'aatí. his/her boss, master: du s'aatí.

both
both: ch'u déiý.

bother
he/she/it bothered him/her; he/she/it is bothering him/her: XEEL' akaawaxíl'.

,

English-to-Tlingit Lexicon

bottle
bottle; jug: t'ooch'ineit, ín x'eesháa.

bottom
(around) the bottom of it: a tuñdaa. the bottom of it (a cavity): a táak. the
inside surface of its bottom (of container, vessel): a taká.

bough
bough, branch with needles on it, especially of hemlock: haaw. bough, branch
with needles on it, especially of spruce: cháash.

boulder
underwater reef; large rock or boulder lying under the water: hintu.eejí.

bow1
its cutwater; the curved part of a bow or stern (of boat): a xées'i.

bow2
bow (ribbon tied into a bow): laçwán.

bow and arrow
bow: sáñs. close quarter bow and arrow: sheixw, sheexw.

bowl
food container; pot or pan; dish, large bowl: ý'ayeit.

bowstay
its bowstay: a lukatíx'i.

box
bentwood box: láñt. box: ñóok. large box for storing grease, oil: daneit.
small covered box: ý'al'daakeit.

boy
boy: yadak'wátsk'u. boys, young men: k'isáani.

boyfriend
his/her boyfriend: du yadák'u. his/her husband's clan brother; his/her man,
boyfriend, husband: du ñáawu.

bracelet
bracelet: kées.

brailer bag
dipper, scoop, ladle; brailer bag: kaxwénaa.

brain
his/her brain: du tlaçeiyí.

branch

bough, branch with needles on it, especially of hemlock: haaw. bough, branch
with needles on it, especially of spruce: cháash. its secondary branch: a
t'áni. limb, primary branch; limb knot: sheey. old, dead branch: tl'áxch'.

brant
brant (small goose): ñín.

,

English-to-Tlingit Lexicon

brass
brass: iññáach'.

brave
brave, fearless man; temperamental, quick-tempered, hot-headed or domineering man: x'içaañáa.

bread
bread crumbs: sakwnéin kaý'eiltí. Easter bread; communion bread: léikwaa. flour; bread: sakwnéin. (loaf of) bread: sakwnéin éewu.

break
it broke (general, solid object): L'EEX' wool'éex'. it broke (long object): L'EEX' wulil'éex'. s/he broke it (general, solid object): L'EEX' aawal'éex'. s/he broke it (long object): L'EEX' awlil'éex'. s/he broke it (rope-like object): K'OOTS awlik'oots. s/he did something wrong; s/he broke the law: GEET2 at géit wudzigít.

breast
his/her breast: du l'aa.

breastplate
body armor, breastplate: niyaháat.

breath
life; breath: ý'aséikw, daséikw.

breed

s/he bred them: ÝEIT2 awsiýeit. they multiplied; they bred: ÝEIT2 has wudziýeit.

bright

it's bright; it's shining: GAAN1 kawdigán.

bring
hand it here, bring it here: haandé. s/he brought it onto him/her (esp. shame, blame, joy): TEE2 du kát ashuwatée. s/he brought it out; s/he picked it up (general, often compact object): TEE2 kei aawatée. s/he brought it out; s/he picked it up (long, complex object): TAAN kei awsitán.

British
Canadian, British: Ginjoochwáan, Ginjichwáan.

broke
broke; penniless; without money: kaldáanaañ.

broom
broom; brush: xít'aa.

broth
boiled food; broth: téiý, a téiýi. soup broth; soup: taýhéeni.

,

English-to-Tlingit Lexicon

brother
her brother, cousin: du éek'. her younger sister; his younger brother; cousin:
du kéek'. his/her clan brother: du xwáayi. his/her clan brother or sister,
distant relative, comrade: du t'aaçí. his older brother, cousin: du húnýw.

brother-in-law
his/her brother-in-law, sister-in-law: du káani.

brown
brown: s'agwáat.

brown bear
solid-ribbed brown bear: s'uñkasdúk.

bruise
s/he injured it; s/he wounded it; s/he bruised it: CHOON awlichún.

bruised
he/she/it is bruised; it's colored; it's discolored: YEIS' kawdiyés'. he/she/it is
injured; he/she/it is wounded; he/she/it is bruised; s/he is hurting (emotionally):
CHOON wudichún.

brush1
broom; brush: xít'aa. clothes brush: naa.át kaxít'aa. pencil; pen; brush:
kooxéedaa.

brush2
windfall; dead tree(s) or brush that has fallen: çéejadi. woods; bush; brush,
underbrush: at gutú.

bubble
bubbles, esp. from whale: kúñdlaa. fast drip with bubbles: kúñjaa. small
bubbles (in water): ý'asúnjaa.

bucket
bucket; pail: x'eesháa.

buckshot
buckshot; moccasin lining: at tuý'wáns'i.

buffalo
bison, buffalo; ox, muskox; cow; horse: xaas.

build

s/he built it; s/he made it; s/he constructed it: YEIÝ1 awliyéý.

building
house; building: hít.

bullet
bullet: at katé.

bullhead
bullhead: éetkatlóoýu. bullhead, sculpin: wéiý'. little bullhead (found
under beach rocks): té tayee tlóoýu. mud bullhead: tlóoý.

,

English-to-Tlingit Lexicon

bump
bump, lump, hump, mound: gootl.

bunchberry
bunchberry: ñ'eikaxétl'k.

buoy
fixed buoy: eech kakwéiyi. floating buoy: eech kwéiyi.

burden
under the burden, weight of it; belabored or suffering from it (a burden, hardship): a jiyeet.

burl
growth on the trunk of a tree, burl: gúnl'.

burn
he/she/it burned him/her/it; s/he scalded him/her/it: Ý'EIÝ' awliý'éý'. it's on (light); it's burning (fire): GAAN1 át akaawagán. s/he burned it up: GAAN1 kei awsigán.

burned
s/he got burned: Ý'EIÝ' wudiý'éý'.

burnt
burnt or charred wood: xoodzí. singed, burnt, or charred matter: xóosht'.

bush
bush: wás'. false azalea (fruitless bush): k'éets'an. wilderness; the bush: katñaañú, çalçaañu. woods; bush; brush, underbrush: at gutú.

buttock
cheek of his/her buttocks: du x'aash. crack of his/her buttocks; his/her butt crack: du tuý'ax'aayí. his/her buttocks, butt: du tóoñ. his/her buttocks, thighs: du çáts.

button
button: ñaayaku.óot'i (At), yuka.óot', yaka.óot'.

button blanket
button blanket: ñaayuka.óot'i x'óow (T), yaka.óot' x'óow, yuka.óot' x'óow.

buy

s/he bought it: .OO2 aawa.oo. s/he bought it (round, spherical object): .OO2 akaawa.oo. s/he bought them (lots of something): .OOW aawa.óow.

by
near him/her, by him/her: du ýán. near him/her, by him/her (at hand, for

him/her to work with): du jiýán.

cabin
cabin (of boat); pilot house: yaakw ýukahídi.

cable
cable: çayéis' tíx'.

,

English-to-Tlingit Lexicon

cache
platform cache; house cache; shed: chál.

cairn
cairn; rock pile: té xóow.

calendar
calendar: dís wooýéiyi.

call

s/he called him/her/it that (name): SAA2 yéi aawasáakw. s/he called
him/her on the phone: TAAN du jeet ý'awditán, TAAN du jeedé
ý'awditaan. s/he called out to him/her; s/he shouted to him/her: .EEX'
aawa.éex'. s/he composed a song; s/he called forth a response (from opposite
clan by means of a song): ÝOOÝ shukawliýooý. s/he summoned him/her;
s/he called him/her: ÝOOÝ aawaýooý.

calm
it's calm; it's peaceful: YEIL' kawduwayél'. peace, calm: kayéil'. the
weather is calm: YEIL' ñukawduwayél'.

cambium
cambium, sap scraped from inner bark: sáx'.

camera
camera: aankadushxit át.

camp
campsite; (out in) camp; (out in) the bush, wilderness: yanshuká. s/he
stayed overnight; s/he camped out: ÝEI uwaýéi.

can
berrying basket or can hung around the neck, resting on the chest:
seiçatáanaa. cup; can: gúx'aa.

Canadian
Canadian, British: Ginjoochwáan, Ginjichwáan.

canary
goldfinch, canary: s'áas'.

cancer
rotting sore; gangrene; cancer: tl'ooñ.

candle
candle: toow s'eenáa.

candlefish
eulachon; candlefish; hooligan: saak.

cane
cane; walking stick; staff: wootsaaçáa.

cannery
cannery: ýáat daakahídi.

,

English-to-Tlingit Lexicon

cannibal
tribe of cannibals, man-eaters: ñusaýañwáan.

cannister
large cannister: naasa.áa.

canoe
boat, canoe: yaakw. canoe made of cottonwood: dúñ. canoe of caribou
skins: jaañúý. canoe under construction: dáaý. dug-out canoe designed to
go through shallow waters: seet. sea otter hunting canoe with an angular
prow for breaking the waves: ch'iyáash. skiff; small boat; flat-bottom canoe:
yakwyádi. small canoe with high carved prow: yáxwch'i yaakw.

canvas
canvas; tarp; tent: xwaasdáa.

canyon
draw, gully, box canyon: séet.

cape
shawl; cape; poncho: teiñ.

Cape Fox
people of Cape Fox, Saxman: Sanyaa Ñwáan.

captain
captain (in the navy): kak'kakwéiy s'aatí (At). captain (of a boat): yaakw
yasatáni. captain; person in charge: kak'dakwéiy s'aatí.

captive
captive: çalsháatadi.

capture
s/he held it; s/he captured it: SHAAT awlisháat.

car
car, automobile: káa.

caribou
caribou: watsíx.

carpenter
carpenter: at layeiý s'aatí.

carrot
carrot: s'ín.

carry
he/she/it carried it on his/her/its back; he/she/it packed it on his/her/its back:
2

YAA aawayaa. he/she/it carried things on his/her/its back; he/she/it packed things on his/her/its back: YAA2 at wooyaa. s/he carried him/her/it (live creature): NOOK1 awsinook. s/he carried it aboard; s/he took it aboard (container or hollow object): TAAN yaaý aawataan. s/he carried it all there; s/he took it all there: JEIL aadé akaawajeil. s/he carried it inside; s/he took it inside (container full of liquid or small objects): .EEN1 neil

,

awsi.ín. s/he carried it inside; s/he took it inside (general, compact object): 2
TEE neil aawatée. s/he carried it; s/he took it (container or hollow object): 2
TAAN aawataan. s/he carried it (solid, complex object): TEE awsitee. s/he carried it there; s/he took it there (container full of liquid or small objects): .EEN1 át awsi.ín. s/he carried it there; s/he took it there (container or hollow object): TAAN át aawatán. s/he carried it there; s/he took it there (general, compact object): TEE2 aadé aawatee. s/he carried it there; s/he took it there (solid, often complex object): TEE2 aadé awsitee. s/he carried stuff there; s/he took stuff there: JEIL aadé at kaawajeil. s/he carried them there; s/he took them there (esp. baggage or personal belongings): .AAT2 aadé awli.aat. s/he is carrying him/her/it around; s/he carried him/her/it around (live creature): NOOK1 át awsinook. s/he is carrying it around; s/he carried it around (container or hollow object): TAAN át aawataan. s/he is carrying it around; s/he carried it aroundj (textile-like object): .AAÝ2 át aawa.aaý.

cartilage
cartilage, gristle: a túñl'i. cartilage, gristle at the end of its bones: a s'añshutúñl'i. cartilage, gristle between its bones: a s'añý'áak túñl'i.

carve
s/he carved it: CH'AAK'W akaawach'ák'w. s/he cut it up; s/he carved it; s/he sliced it: XAASH akaawaxaash.

carver
carver: at kach'áak'u.

casket
coffin; casket: ñaa daakeidí.

cast

s/he sportfished; s/he casted: ÝOOT'1 shawdliýóot'.

cat
cat: dóosh.

cataract
cataract: gáal'.

catch
s/he caught it; s/he grabbed him/her/it; s/he arrested him/her; s/he trapped him/her/it: SHAAT aawasháat.

caterpillar
worm; larva; grub; caterpillar; snake: tl'úk'ý.

Caucasian
White, European, Caucasian (man or person): Gus'k'iyee ñwáan, dleit

ñáa.

cave
cave: tatóok, katóok.

cedar
red cedar: laaý. yellow cedar, Alaska cedar: ýáay.

,

ceiling
its ceiling: a kaýyee.

cellar
pit; hole dug in the ground; cellar: kóoñ.

centipede
centipede: atxaayí.

chain
chain: wóoshnáý ý'akakéiýi, ý'akakeiýí.

chainsaw
chainsaw: sh daxash washéen.

chair
chair: káayaçijeit.

chalkboard
blackboard, chalkboard: kadushxit t'aa yá.

chance
room, space, place for it; time for it; chance, opportunity for it: a ya.áak.

chaos
whirlpool; boiling tide; chaos: x'óol'.

charcoal
charcoal: t'ooch'.

charm
sympathetic magic, charm: héiýwaa.

charred
singed, burnt, or charred matter: xóosht'.

chase

he/she/it chased it into the open: KEIL'1 daak awlikél'.

cheek
his/her cheek: du wásh. inside of his/her cheek: du washtú. (outside of) his/her cheek: du washká.

chest
chest pain; tuberculosis: wuwtunéekw. his/her chest: du wóow. his/her thorax; flat upper surface of his/her chest: du xeitká. (on) his/her chest: du woowká.

chickadee

chickadee: ñaatoowú.

chicken
spruce grouse, spruce hen; chicken: káax'.

chief
rich man; man of wealth; chief: aanñáawu.

,

English-to-Tlingit Lexicon

child
child: atk'átsk'u. fatherless child; bastard: neechkayádi. his/her child:
du yádi.

children
children: atyátx'i, adátx'i. his/her children: du yátx'i.

Chilkat blanket
Chilkat blanket: naaxein.

chill
s/he chilled it: .AAT' awsi.át'.

chin
his/her chin: du téey.

Chinese
Chinese: Cháanwaan.

chinook salmon
king salmon; chinook salmon; spring salmon: t'á.

chip

s/he chopped it (wood); s/he chipped it out (with adze): ÝOOT'2 aawaýút'.

chisel
chisel: tíyaa. rounded carving chisel: kach'ák'waa.

chiton
gumboots; chiton: shaaw.

choir
singers, choir: at shéex'i.

Chookaneidí
Chookaneidí; a clan of the Eagle moiety whose principal crests are the Porpoise
and Brown Bear: Chookaneidí.

chop
s/he chopped it (esp. tree, branch): S'OOW aawas'úw. s/he chopped it up;
s/he split it (wood): ÝOOT'2 akawliýóot'. s/he chopped it (wood); s/he
chipped it out (with adze): ÝOOT'2 aawaýút'.

chopper
chopper: kas'úwaa.

chopping block
awl; chopping block: s'úwaa.

Chugach
Chugach Eskimo: Gutéiý'.

chum salmon
dog salmon; chum salmon: téel'.

church
house of prayer; church: ý'agáax' daakahídi.

,

circle

s/he drove around it; s/he went around it; s/he circled it (by boat, car): ÑOOÝ1 a daaý yaawañúý.

claim
possession; that which is claimed: ñaa at oohéini. s/he claimed it; s/he owns it: HEIN aawahéin.

clam
baby clams: dzéex'w. clam: gáal'. giant clam: ýéet'. its edible part (of clam): a çeiyí. littleneck clams: tl'ildaaskeit. razor clam: ñ'alkátsk. slime (inside clamshell): átl'áni. tiny clams (too small to eat): dzóox'.

clan
nation; moiety; clan; band of people: naa.

clan house
head of a clan house; master of the house: hít s'aatí.

claw
its claw: a ýaagú.

clay
clay; alluvial silt: s'é.

clerk
salesman; clerk; storekeeper: dahooní.

cliff
cliff: çíl'.

climb
he/she/it climbed the face of it: TL'EIT' a yáý wudlitl'éit'. he/she/it climbed up it: TL'EIT' a daaý kei wdlitl'ét'.

clock
clock: gaaw.

cloth
cheesecloth, loose-woven cloth; netting, screen: kaçádaa. cloth; sailcloth: s'ísaa.

clothes
clothes, clothing; garment: naa.át. under or inside his/her clothes; next to his/her skin: du doonyaa.

cloud
cloud cover; sky, cloudy sky: góos'. cloud(s): ñugóos'.

cloudberry
yellow cloudberry: néý'w.

cloudy
it was cloudy: GÓOS' ñoowligóos'.

,

club
club: x'ús'. s/he clubbed it; s/he hit it on the head: ÝEECH ashaawaýích.

coal
coal: t'ooch' té.

coal oil
kerosene; coal oil: uýganhéen.

coat
coat, overcoat: kinaa.át, kinaak.át.

cobbler
shoemaker, cobbler: téel layeiýí.

cockle
cockle: yalooleit.

cod
ling cod: s'áaý'. tomcod: chudéi.

coffee
coffee: káaxwei. coffee; hot water: yat'aayi héen.

coffin
coffin; casket: ñaa daakeidí.

coho
L'uknax.ádi, locally called "Coho"; a clan of the Raven moiety whose principal
crest is the Coho: L'uknaý.ádi.

coho salmon
coho salmon; silver salmon: l'ook. sockeye or coho salmon that has entered
fresh water: ý'áakw.

coin
money, coin, dollar: dáanaa.

cold
chest cold: ñusa.áat' néekw. cold weather: ñusa.áat'. the weather was
cold: .AAT' ñuwsi.áat'.

cold sore
cold sore: ý'atl'ooñ.

cold water
cold water: si.áat'i héen.

color
its color: a kaséiñ'u.

colored
he/she/it is bruised; it's colored; it's discolored: YEIS' kawdiyés'.

colt
colt: gawdáan yádi.

,

comb
comb: xéidu, ñaa shaksayéigu.

come out
it fell (small, compact object); it came out (sun, moon): XEEX daak uwaxíx.

comet
comet; falling star: xoodzí.

comfort
comfort: ñaa toowú lat'aa. he/she/it comforted him/her: T'AA du toowú awlit'áa.

commander
director, planner; commander: át ñukawu.aaçú.

community
people; community: ñu.oo.

complete
s/he finished it; s/he completed it: NEI yan awsinéi, HEEK yan ashawlihík.
to completion: yaý.

complexion
his/her skin, complexion: du dook.

component
its what it is (to be) made of; its parts, components, materials: a shagóon.

compose
s/he composed a song; s/he called forth a response (from opposite clan by means of a song): ÝOOÝ shukawliýooý.

comrade
his/her clan brother or sister, distant relative, comrade: du t'aaçí.

conceited
s/he is proud; s/he is conceited; s/he is particular; s/he is picky: ÇEI sh tukdliçéi.

concentrate
s/he exerted his/her full strength on it; s/he concentrated on it; s/he strove for it: XEECH aawaxích.

confess

s/he said that; s/he confessed that; s/he acknowledged that: ÑAA1 yéi yaawañaa.

conflict

trouble; conflict: kaxéel'.

connect

s/he connected it there: XAAT1 aadé akawsixát.

connected

it's connected there; it's tied there: XAAT1 aadé ksixát.

,

English-to-Tlingit Lexicon

conscious
consciousness, thought process, thinking: yoo tutánk.

consider
s/he thought about it; s/he considered it; s/he made up his/her mind about it: TAAN a daa yoo toowatán. they thought about it; they considered it; they made up their minds about it: .AAT2 a daa yoo (ha)s tuwli.át.

conspicuous
he/she/it was fancy; he/she/it was conspicuous; he/she/it was prominent: ÇEI kawliçéi.

construct

s/he built it; s/he made it; s/he constructed it: YEIÝ1 awliyéý.

container
container for it: daakeit. container for traveling provisions; lunch basket, lunch container: wóow daakeit.

contribute
s/he contributed; s/he donated: ÇEEX' kawdiçéex'. s/he contributed to it; s/he donated to it; s/he added to it: ÇEEX' át kawdiçíx'.

control
out of control; blindly: uý kei.

conversation
conversation, dialog; talk, discourse (between more than one person): yoo ý'ala.átk.

converse

they conversed; they spoke; they talked: .AAT2 yoo (ha)s ý'awli.át.

cook
s/he cooked: .EE at wusi.ée. s/he cooked it: .EE awsi.ée.

cooked
it's cooked: .EE yan uwa.ée.

copper
copper: eeñ.

copper shield
copper shield: tináa.

coral
coral: hintakx'úxi, hintaak x'óosi. petrified coral: yéil kawóodi.

cord
cord (of wood): at kaayí.

cork
cork, plug: a ý'adéex'i.

cork up
s/he corked it up; s/he covered his/her mouth: DEEX' aý'eiwadíx'.

,

cormorant
cormorant: yooñ.

corner
corner: gúkshi. (in) the corner of it: a gukshatú, a gukshitú (An).
(in) the corner, (on or along) the edge, end of it: a shutú.

correctional facility
correctional facility: áa ñuyadujee yé.

corset
corset: kasanka.át.

cotton
cotton; cotton blanket, quilt: kast'áat'. cottongrass, Alaska cotton, swamp
cotton: sháchk kaý'wáal'i.

cottonwood
cottonwood: dúñ.

country
earth; land, country; soil: tl'átk.

courage
strength of mind or heart; courage; resolve: toowú latseen.

cousin
her brother, cousin: du éek'. her fraternal niece, nephew, cousin: du
káalk'w. her older sister, cousin: du shátý. her younger sister; his
younger brother; cousin: du kéek'. his/her daughter, cousin: du sée.
his/her paternal uncle, cousin: du sáni. his/her son, cousin: du yéet.

cove
cove; bight: kunaçeey. in a fort, shelter, cove: noow çei.

cover
(draped) over it, covering it: a náa. its covering; cover (over a large opening
or something without an opening): a kaháadi. its lid, cover (of pot, etc.): a
yana.áat'ani. over it, covering it (a container or something with an
opening): a yanáa. s/he corked it up; s/he covered his/her mouth: DEEX'
aý'eiwadíx'. s/he covered it: TAAN a yanáaý at wootaan. s/he pulled it
over him/her/it; s/he covered him/her/it with it: YEESH a káý aawayeesh.
smokehole cover: gaan ý'aháadi.

cow
bison, buffalo; ox, muskox; cow; horse: xaas. cow: wasóos.

coward
coward: ñ'atýáan.

crab
crab (king, spider): x'éiý. dungeness crab: s'áaw.

cradleboard
cradleboard; papoose carrier: t'ook.

,

cramp
it cramped; it's cramping; he/she/it got shocked (by electricity): SHOOK' kawdlishúk'.

cranberry
bog cranberry; low bush cranberry: ñ'eishkaháagu. high bush cranberry: kaxwéiý. lowbush cranberry, bog cranberry: dáxw.

crane
heron; Canada crane: láý'. sandhill crane: dóol.

cranky
crankiness; irritation; petulance: ñukahín.

crawl
he/she/it crawled there on his/her/its belly; he/she/it crept there on his/her/its belly: TLOOX' aadé wootlóox'. he/she/it is crawling around on his/her/its belly; he/she/it crawled around on his/her/its belly; he/she/it is creeping around on his/her/its belly; he/she/it crept around on his/her/its belly; he/she/it is squirming around; he/she/it squirmed around: TLOOX' át wootlóox'. s/he crawled away (from the open): ÇWAAT'1 daañ wudiçwát'. s/he is crawling around there; s/he crawled around there: ÇWAAT'1 át wudiçwáat'.

crazy
crazy; insane; disturbed; mentally unbalanced: sh kahaadí. person who acts crazy or possesssed: lookanáa. s/he was noisy; s/he was crazy; s/he was lively: .OOS wuli.oos.

cream
face cream; cold cream: yaneis'í (T).

creek
creek; small stream: héenák'w. fishing hole; hole in stream, river, creek: ísh. mouth of it (a river, creek): a wát. river, stream, creek: héen. river; stream; creek: kanaadaayi héen, naadaayi héen. salmon creek: ýáat héeni.

creep
he/she/it crawled there on his/her/its belly; he/she/it crept there on his/her/its belly: TLOOX' aadé wootlóox'. he/she/it is crawling around on his/her/its belly; he/she/it crawled around on his/her/its belly; he/she/it is creeping around on his/her/its belly; he/she/it crept around on his/her/its belly; he/she/it is squirming around; he/she/it squirmed around: TLOOX' át wootlóox'.

crest
(on) the back of it (fish); on the crest, ridge, backbone of it (hill, ridge, point): a litká. wall crest; wall screen: ý'éen.

crevice
rock crevice; fissure in rock: té ñáas'.

crew
worker; crew: ganaswáan.

,

crochet
knitting, crocheting: kasné. s/he knitted; s/he crocheted; s/he wove: NEI
kawdzinéi. s/he made it (by weaving, knitting, crocheting); s/he mended it
(net): NEI akawsinei.

crooked
it's crooked; s/he is crooked, wicked: TEEÝ' kawdzitíý'.

cross
cross: kanéist.

crosspiece
its crosspiece (of boat, snowshoe); thwart (of boat): yaýak'áaw.

crotch
his/her crotch; between his/her legs: du çatsý'áak.

crow
crow: ts'axweil.

crowbar
pry; stick or tool for prying; crowbar: kít'aa.

crowd
they crowded the place; they all went there: HAA át has yawdiháa.
townspeople; crowd or large group of people: aantñeení.

cry
crying, weeping: çaaý. he/she/it cried out: ÇAAÝ kawdiçaaý. person who
cries easily: ánk'w. s/he asked for it; s/he cried for it: ÇAAÝ awdziçáaý.
s/he cried: ÇAAÝ wooçaaý.

cup
cup; can: gúx'aa.

cure
s/he saved him/her/it; s/he healed him/her/it; s/he cured him/her/it: NEIÝ
awsineiý. s/he was saved; s/he was healed; s/he was cured; s/he recovered;
s/he was satisfied: NEIÝ wooneiý.

curious
curiosity: yoo at koojeek.

curlew
curlew: ayaheeyáa.

curly
his/her curly hair: du shakakóoch'i.

currant

black currants or swamp currants: kaneilts'íkw (At). gray currant, stink
currant: shaaý.

currants
black currants or swamp currants: kaneilts'ákw. currants: kadooheiý.aa.

,

English-to-Tlingit Lexicon

current
current; tidal action: héen kanadaayí. current, tide: haat.

curtain
window curtain: ýaawaaçéi kas'ísayi.

cut
cut; knife wound: ñ'éiñ'w. s/he cut him/her/it (accidentally); s/he wounded him/her/it: Ñ'EIK'W1 aawañ'ék'w. s/he cut himself/herself; s/he wounded himself/herself (with a sharp instrument): Ñ'EIK'W1 sh wudiñ'ék'w. s/he cut it off; s/he sawed it off: XAASH aaý aawaxásh. s/he cut it (rope-like object): XAASH awlixaash. s/he cut it up; s/he carved it; s/he sliced it: XAASH akaawaxaash. s/he cut it (with a knife); s/he sawed it: XAASH aawaxaash. s/he cut; s/he did some cutting: XAASH wudixaash.

cute
Cute!: Óos'k'!. she is pretty; it is cute: ÇEI shakliçéi.

daddy long legs
daddy long legs; mosquito eater: táax'aa ý'uskudayáat'.

dagger
dagger; machete, long knife: gwálaa. double-ended dagger: shak'áts'.

Dakl'aweidí
Dakl'aweidí, locally called "Killer Whale"; a clan of the Eagle moiety whose principal crest is the Killer Whale: Dañl'aweidí.

dam
beaver dam: s'igeidí áayi.

dance
dance: al'eiý. neck cord worn for dance: kaséiñ'w. s/he danced: L'EIÝ aawal'eiý. s/he danced out: L'EIÝ daak aawal'éý. s/he started dancing: L'EIÝ çunéi aawal'éý.

dandruff
dandruff: shakéil'.

dangerous
it was scary; it was dangerous: ÝÉITL'SHÁN kawliýéitl'shán.

dark
it's dark: ÇEET ñukawjiçít.

darkness
darkness: kaçít.

daughter
his/her daughter, cousin: du sée.

Printed in Great Britain
by Amazon

21771591R00289